주한미군지위협정(SOFA)

서명 및 발효 4

주한미군지위협정(SOFA)

서명 및 발효 4

한국학술정보

| 머리말

미국은 오래전부터 우리나라 외교에 있어서 가장 긴밀하고 실질적인 우호 · 협력관계를 맺어 온 나라다. 6 · 25전쟁 정전 협정이 체결된 후 북한의 재침을 막기 위한 대책으로서 1953년 11월 한미 상호방위조약이 체결되었다. 이는 미군이 한국에 주둔하는 법적 근거였고, 그렇게 주둔하게 된 미군의 시설, 구역, 사업, 용역, 출입국, 통관과 관세, 재판권 등 포괄적인 법적 지위를 규정하는 것이 바로 주한미군지위협정(SOFA)이다. 그러나 이와 관련한 협상은 계속된 난항을 겪으며 한미 상호방위조약이 체결로부터 10년이 훌쩍 넘은 1967년이 돼서야 정식 발효에 이를 수 있었다. 그럼에도 당시 미군 범죄에 대한 한국의 재판권은 심한 제약을 받았으며, 1980년대 후반 민주화 운동과 함께 미군 범죄 문제가 사회적 이슈로 떠오르자 협정을 개정해야 한다는 목소리가 커지게 되었다. 이에 1991년 2월 주한미군지위협정 1차 개정이 진행되었고, 이후에도 여러 사건이 발생하며 2001년 4월 2차 개정이 진행되어 현재에 이르고 있다.

본 총서는 외교부에서 작성하여 최근 공개한 주한미군지위협정(SOFA) 관련 자료를 담고 있다. 1953년 한미 상호방위조약 체결 이후부터 1967년 발효가 이뤄지기까지의 자료와 더불어, 이후 한미 합동위원회를 비롯해 민 · 형사재판권, 시설, 노무, 교통 등 각 분과위원회의 회의록과 운영 자료, 한국인 고용인 문제와 관련한 자료, 기타 관련 분쟁 자료 등을 포함해 총 42권으로 구성되었다. 전체 분량은 약 2만 2천여 쪽에 이른다.

2024년 3월

한국학술정보(주)

| 일러두기

· 본 총서에 실린 자료는 2022년 4월과 2023년 4월에 각각 공개한 외교문서 4,827권, 76만 여 쪽 가운데 일부를 발췌한 것이다.

· 각 권의 제목과 순서는 공개된 원본을 최대한 반영하였으나, 주제에 따라 일부는 적절히 변경하였다.

· 원본 자료는 A4 판형에 맞게 축소하거나 원본 비율을 유지한 채 A4 페이지 안에 삽입하였다. 또한 현재 시점에선 공개되지 않아 '공란'이란 표기만 있는 페이지 역시 그대로 실었다.

· 외교부가 공개한 문서 각 권의 첫 페이지에는 '정리 보존 문서 목록'이란 이름으로 기록물 종류, 일자, 명칭, 간단한 내용 등의 정보가 수록되어 있으며, 이를 기준으로 0001번부터 번호가 매겨져 있다. 이는 삭제하지 않고 총서에 그대로 수록하였다.

· 보고서 내용에 관한 더 자세한 정보가 필요하다면, 외교부가 온라인상에 제공하는 『대한민국 외교사료요약집』 1991년과 1992년 자료를 참조할 수 있다.

| 차례

정/리/보/존/문/서/목/록

기록물종류	문서-일반공문서철	등록번호	912 9585	등록일자	2006-07-27
분류번호	741.12	국가코드	US	주제	
문서철명	한.미국 간의 상호방위조약 제4조에 의한 시설과 구역 및 한국에서의 미국군대의 지위에 관한 협정 (SOFA) 전59권. 1966.7.9 서울에서 서명 : 1967.2.9 발효 (조약 232호) *원본				
생산과	미주과/조약과	생산년도	1952 - 1967	보존기간	영구
담당과(그룹)	조약	조약	서가번호	--	
참조분류					
권차명	V.14 실무교섭회의, 제1-4차, 1962.9-10월				
내용목차	1. 교섭재개 합의, 9.6 (p.2~18) 2. 대표단 구성 (p.19~33) 3. 사전 준비 (p.34~50) 4. 제1차 회의, 9.20 (p.51~98) 5. 제2차 회의, 9.28 (p.99~137) 6. 제3차 회의, 10.10 (p.138~201) 7. 제4차 회의, 10.19 (p.202~259) * 서울에서 개최 * 일지 : 1953.8.7 이승만 대통령-Dulles 미국 국무장관 공동성명 - 상호방위조약 발효 후 군대지위협정 교섭 약속 1954.12.2 정부, 주한 UN군의 관세업무협정 체결 제의 1955.1월, 5월 미국, 제의 거절 1955.4.28 정부, 군대지위협정 제의 (한국측 초안 제시) 1957.9.10 Hurter 미국 국무차관 방한 시 각서 수교 (한국측 제의 수락 요구) 1957.11.13, 26 정부, 개별 협정의 단계적 체결 제의 1958.9.18 Dawling 주한미국대사, 형사재판관할권 협정 제외 조건으로 행정협정 체결 의사 전달 1960.3.10 정부, 토지, 시설협정의 우선적 체결 강력 요구 1961.4.10 장면 국무총리-McConaughy 주한미국대사 공동성명으로 교섭 개시 합의 1961.4.15, 4.25 제1, 2차 한.미국 교섭회의 (서울) 1962.3.12 정부, 교섭 재개 촉구 공한 송부 1962.5.14 Burger 주한미국대사, 최규하 장관 면담 시 형사재판관할권 문제 제기 않는 조건으로 교섭 재개 통고 1962.9.6 한.미국 간 공동성명 발표 (9월 중 교섭 재개 합의) 1962.9.20~ 1965.6.7 제1-81차 실무 교섭회의 (서울) 1966.7.8 제82차 실무 교섭회의 (서울) 1966.7.9 서명 1967.2.9 발효 (조약 232호)					

마/이/크/로/필/름/사/항

촬영연도	*롤 번호	화일 번호	후레임 번호	보관함 번호
2006-11-22	I-06-0067	09	1-259	

0001

1. 교섭 재개 합의, 9. 6

0002

2

장관과 "버-거" 대사 간의 회담요지

1. 시 일 : 1962. 9. 3. 1500부터 1530까지
2. 장 소 : 장관 회의실
3. 참석자 : 외무부장관, 정무국장
   "버-거" 대사
4. 회담경위 : 장관의 초치에 의함
5. 회담요지 :

가. 주둔군 지위협정에 관한 교섭재개를 위하여 장관은 별첨과 같은 Aide Memoire 를 "버-거" 대사에게 수교하고 서울과 워싱톤에서 각각 동시에 별첨과 같은 공동성명서를 서울시간 9월 6일 (목요일) 0900시 (워싱톤 시간 9월 5일 1930시)에 발표하기로 합의하였음.

나. "버-거" 대사는 "하비브" 참사관을 미측 실무교섭단 수석대표로 임명할 것이라고 말하였음. 여기에대하여 장관은 한국측 실무교섭단 구성에 관하여 명확한 언명을 하지않고 다만 실무교섭에 관한 구체적인 사항은 정무국장과 "하비브" 참사관 사이에 협의케 하자고 말하였음.

다. "버-거" 대사는 공동성명서의 국문 번역문을 얻고저 원하면 대사관 직원을 9월 5일 외무부로 보내겠다고 말하였음.

62-4-31

미주과	안 고 재 월 일	담 당	과 장	국 장	특별보좌관	차 관	장 관

보통문서로 재분류(1966.12.31)

1969년 9월 30일 미주과장 직권으로 파기 비밀로 재분류

0003

62-4-11 (13)

0004

Dispatched Copy

3

AIDE-MEMOIRE

With reference to the Foreign Minister's note of March 12, 1962, requesting the United States Government to reopen negotiations for an agreement covering the Status of the United States Armed Forces in Korea and subsequent discussions on this subject, the Foreign Minister informed the American Ambassador that the Government of the Republic of Korea is prepared to reopen negotiations as soon as mutually convenient.

In this connection, the Foreign Minister shared with the American Ambassador the view that any status of forces agreement involves complex matters and it is likely that negotiations will require a considerable period of time. The Foreign Minister stated that, under such circumstances, it is possible to discuss less complex subjects first, and more complex subjects later as negotiations make progress.

With regard to judicial standards comparable to those of the United States, the Foreign Minister noted that the United States has been able to work out status of forces agreements with countries which have judicial processes

0005

62-4-1

0002

0006

and procedures differing from those of the United States.

The Foreign Minister expressed his sincere desire that the both Governments do their utmost toward bringing about agreements covering relevant subjects within a reasonable period of time.

Ministry of Foreign Affairs

Seoul, September 3, 1962

62-4-11 비3본 79-3(가)

0008

JOINT ROK - US PRESS STATEMENT

Resumption of Negotiations of Status of Forces Agreement

The American Ambassador has informed the Minister of Foreign Affairs that the United States Government is prepared to reopen negotiations for an agreement covering the status of the United States Armed Forces in the Republic of Korea. The Foreign Minister welcomed this development on behalf of his government.

Both sides agreed that negotiations would resume at the working level sometime in September. It is recognized that any status of forces agreement involves complex matters and it is expected that negotiations will require a considerable period of time. Accordingly, it is (~~recognized~~) understood that in view of the forthcoming constitutional changes in Korea, the conclusion of a Status of Forces Agreement will await the restoration of civil government.

미주과	담 당	과 장	국 장	특별보좌관	차 관	장 관

0009

0010

With regard to judicial standards comparable to those of the U.S., the Foreign Minister noted that the U.S. has been able to work out status of forces agreements with countries which have judicial processes and procedures differing from those of the U.S.

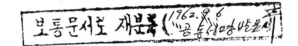

보통문서로 재분류 (1962.9.6 공동성명발표시)

1962, 9, 6, 에 예고문에 의거 일반문서로 재분류됨

0011

① Surplus payments — interests —
(Rename
in terms of public relations. ③ Change
② U.N. — not work out.

0012

대한민국 외무부

번 호: WD-0913
일 시: 061100

발신전보

1급비밀
종 별

수신인: 주미대사

~~한미 행정협정 체결교섭 재개 미합의~~

1. "버-거" 대사는 귀임하여 공동성명서 최종안에서 "normal judicial procedures"라는 귀절을 삭제하는데 동의하였음.

2. 따라서 양측은 9월중에 교섭을 개시할것에 합의하고 한국 서울에서는 9. 6. (목요일) 09:00 시, 와싱톤 시간 9. 5. (수요일) 19:30 시에 각각 동시 발표하기로 하였음.

3. 공동성명 발표에 관한 미국측의 (특히 국회, 국방성 및 언론계) 반응에 대하여 예의 관찰하시고 보고하시압.

4. 기타 상세한것은 다음 파우치편으로 송부위계임. (정.미) 끝.

앙고재 9월 4일	담 당	과 장	국 장	특별보좌관	차 관	장 관
						후결

1962년 9월 6일 직권으로 일반문서로 재분류

접수 1962 9 5 외무부

송신시간:

통제관		자체 통제		기안처	미주과 이원호
결 재					

타자 . 판치	검 인	주무자	과 장

필 요 ☐ 보안불필요 ☐

0013

메 모

9월 4일 정무국장과 다비브 참사관은 전화로 제 1 차 주둔군 지위협정 실무자 교섭회의를 9월 20일 오후 2 시에 개최하기로 합의하였음. 끝

미주과	양고재	담당	과장	국장	특별보좌관	차관	장관

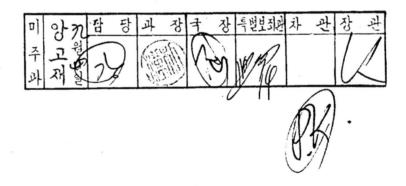

0014

1

정무국장과 "하비브" 참사관 간의 회담

1. 시 일 : 1962. 9. 4. 하오 3시부터 4시까지

2. 장소 : 정무국장실

3. 참석자 : 정무국장, 미주과장

   "하비브" 참사관, "후렉" 1등서기관

4. 회담경위 : "하비브" 참사관의 요청에 의함

5. 회담내용 : 1). 대표단 구성문제

"하비브" 참사관은 주둔군지위 협정에 관한 교섭을위하여 미국측 교섭대표단은 "하비브" 참사관을 수석으로 하여 "후렉" 1등서기관, "포드" 1등서기관, "루이스" 영사 그리고 미제 8군 참모차장 "코나" 대령, 8군 법무감 "솔프" 대령 및 유엔군 민사처대표 등으로 상임대표단을 구성할 예정이며 그외에 특정한 사항에 관한 전문가의 지식이 필요할적에는 그때 그때 그러한 전문가를 참석시키도록 할 예정이라고 말하면서 우리측의 대표단 구성을 문의하여 왔음.

여기에대하여 정무국장은 우리측에서는 현재 외무차관을 한국측 교섭단의 수석대표로하고 정무국장, 미주과장, 조약과장 및 2,3 명의 보좌관과 재무부, 국방부, 법무부의 각 국장급 실무자로서 대표단을 구성할 생각을하고 있으며 미측과 마찬가지로 ~~역시~~ 전문가는 수시로 필요에따라 참석시키도록 할것을 고려하고 있다고 하였음.

"하비브" 참사관은 한국측 수석대표가 차관급이면 미국측은 "하비브" 참사관이 수석으로 그대로 임명될수 있는지 "버-거" 대사에게 문의하여 보아야 하겠다고 말하면서 재차 차관급을 수석대표로 하는 문제에 대해서 한국측은 확정적이냐고 다짐하였음

정무국장은 현재 그렇게 생각하고 있는중이라고 말하면서 다른 부처 국장급이 대표로 참석하는 관계로하여 우리측은 차관급 수석대표가 더 적절할것이라고 말하였음.

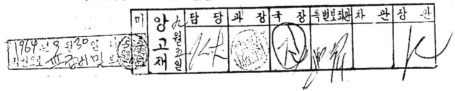

미	앙고재 9월 5일	담당	과장	국장	특별보좌관	차관	장관

1964년 9월 30일 ... 지침으로 ... 로

79-1(3)

0016

"하비브" 참사관은 그렇게되면 미측에서도 "메지스트 매티" 부대사를 수석대표로 임명할것인지 자기로서는 말하기 곤란하다고 말하면서 대사에게 보고하여 대사가 결정토록 할것이라고 말하였음.

2) 회담 개최일자

회담 개최일자에 관하여 "하비브" 참사관은 외무부장관께서 9월 20일경에 제 1 차 회담을 개최하기를 희망한다는 말씀이 있은것으로 알고 있다고 말하면서 일자 문제는 솔직히 말하여 장면 씨에 대한 언도일자를 잘 참작하여 미국본국 여론의 자극을 회피하기 위하여 언도일자 직전이나 직후는 적당하지 못할것이라 하면서 만일에 9월 27일에 언도가 있게된다는 것이 사실이라면 1 주일앞둔 9월 20일이나 21 일경에 제1 차 회의를 개최할수는 있을것이나 만일에 그이전에 언도가 나는경우에는 외무부장관이 원하는대로 20일경에 회담을 개최하기가 어려우며 그보다며 앞당겨 개최하기에는 준비관계상 곤란함으로 부득불 연기하지 않을수 없은것이라고 말하면서, 정무국장에게 장면 씨에 대한 언도일자를 확인하여 달라고 부탁하였음.

정무국장은 곧 알아서 알려주겠다고 말하였음.

3) 제 1 차 회담 진행방식

"하비브" 참사관은 제 1 차 회담에서 먼저 쌍방이 공개적으로 개회식을 한다음 비공개회의로 들어가서 필요한 기타 문제를 토의하고 우선 신문보도, 기록 등등의 문제에 관한 사무수행절차를 결정하고 특히 끝나기전에 항상 다음회합의 토의 의제를 정함으로써 쌍방이 충분한 준비를 사전에 하여와서 교섭진행을 신속화하여야 할것이라고 말하였음.

이와관련하여 정무국장은 공개적 개회식만은 장관과 대사가 직접 함으로서 더효과 가 클것이라고 생각한다고 말하고 그가능성에 관하여 문의하였음.

"하비브" 참사관은 돌아가서 대사와 의논하여 보겠다고 말하고 우리측에서 준비하여 수교한 한미공동성명서 국문 텍스트를 확인하여 그결과를 알려주겠다고 말함.

0017

→

미관 112-1

0018

4) 한일간 해저전선 문제

정무국장은 이어서 문제의 한일간 해저전선 건은 해결할수 있는 방도가 없느냐고 문의하면서 평화조약 조문에 의거하여 동해저 전선의 분할문제는 미국측 전문가의 입장에서 볼적에는 극히 단순하고 간단한 문제라고 생각되며, 평화조약의 초안자 및 체결에 참여한 미국측 관계자는 여기에대한 간단한 의견이 있을것이라고 말하였음.

여기에 대하여 "하비브" 참사관은 동석한 "후렉" 1등서기관에게 이문제를 와싱톤 당국에 다시 조회하여 보라고말하면서 특히 평화조약 초안시에 무슨 양해가 있었는지 좀더 자세히 알아보라고 말하였음.

정무국장은 이문제는 현재의 한일회담에서 분리하여 해결하여야 할 문제라고 말하고 미국측이 적절한 조치만 취하여 주면 간단히 해결될 문제라고 말하였음.

5) "멕화든" 회사 문제

정무국장은 "멕화든" 회사건에 관하여 그후에 대사관에서 다시 또 하나의 각서를 받았다고 말하면서 안보내기로 양해가 된것으로 아는데 또 보내온것은 무슨 까닭이냐고 말하였음.

"하비브" 참사관은 매우 놀래면서 자기는 거기에대하여 전혀 모르는 사실이라고 하면서 유감의 뜻을 표하였음. 이어서 동참사관은 미측의 두각서에 대한 회답은 필요없다고 말하고 그동안 구두로 정무국장이 설명하여 준것으로서 충족하다고 말하고 돌아갔음.

6) "하비브" 참사관의 재차 방문

"하비브" 참사관은 약 20분후에 재차 정무국장을 방문하고 개회식문제와 수석대표 문제에 관하여 버거대사와 의논한결과 개회사는 외무부장관과 버거대사가 참석하여 직접행함으로서 더많은 효과를 올리도록 하는데 대사가 동의하였다고 말하면서 다만 수석대표 문제에 관하여는 "하비브" 참사관을 임명하는것을 원한다고 말하였음.

공동성명서 국문 텍스트는 정확하며 그대로 완전히 수락한다고 말하였음.

0010

0020

공동성명 발표에 관한 메모

1962. 9. 6. 18:30시 정무국장과 하비브 참사관은 전화로 동일 오전 9시에 서울에서 발표된 공동성명서에 관하여 장관과 버거 대사사이에 합의사항에 의하면 워싱톤에서도 동시에 (현지시간 9월 5일 19:30시) 발표토록 되어있었는데 불구하고 주미대사의 보고에 의하면 국무성은 동성명을 발표하지 않고 다만 서울에서 발표한 사실에대한 보도가 외신을 통하여 들어오면 미국내 기자들이 거기에대하여 질의를 할적에 "코멘트" 할 예정으로 있다는 사실을 알려왔는바 이는 경솔한 장관과 버거 대사간의 합의에 배치된 일이라고 지적하고 항의를 제기하였음.

하비브 참사관은 그 사실은 자기도 잘모르는 바라고 말하면서 알아보겠다고 하고 그러나 서울에서 발표된것이 한미 공동성명서로서 양국이 공동으로 발표한것이니 만큼 실제에효과에 있어서는 마찬가지라고 말하였음.

정무국장은 그렇지만 전기 사실은 장관과 버거대사간의 합의에 배치되는 일이라고 재차 지적하였음. 끝

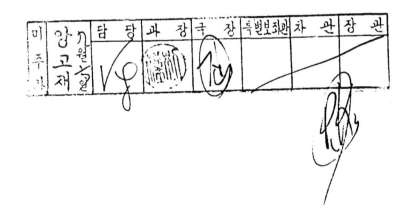

미주과	안 고재 7월 일	담당	과장	국장	특별보좌관	차관	장관

1-1

0021

1962년 9月 6日 午前 9時
以前 發表를 禁함.

韓美共同聲明書

1 美駐屯軍 地位協定 交涉再開

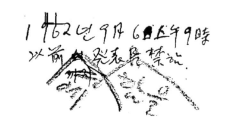

駐韓美國大使는 外務部長官에게 美國政府가 駐韓美軍地位協定에 關한 交涉을 再開할 用意가 있음을 通報하였다. 外務部長官은 韓國政府를 代表하여 이 提議를 歡迎하였다.

兩國政府는 九月中에 實務交涉을 再開할 것에 合意하였다. 어떠한 駐屯軍地位協定도 複雜한 問題를 內包하고 있는 故로 交涉은 相當한 時日을 要할 것을 認定하는 바입니다. 따라서 韓國에 不遠間 있을 憲法改正에 鑑하여 駐屯軍地位協定의 締結은 民政移讓을 기다려 이루어지게 될 것으로 豫期하는 바입니다.

0022

대 한 민 국 외 무 부

번 호: YM-0902
일 시: 081305

발신전보

종 별

수 신 인: 주 재외 공관장

미 주둔군 지위 협정

1. 1962. 9. 6 오전 9 시 서울에서 미 주둔군 지위협정 체결 교섭재개에 관한 한미 양국간의 공동 성명서를 발표 하였다.

2. 동 성명서 내용은 다음 파우치편에 송부할것임. (정미) 끝

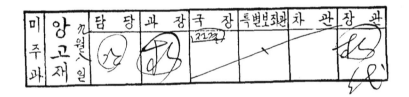

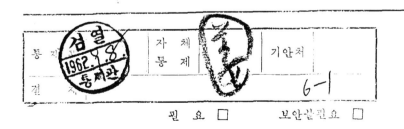

장 관

미주과	양고재	9월 7일	담 당	과 장	국 장	특별보좌관	차 관	장 관

통 제	1962. 9. 8. 검열 통제관	자체 통제		기안처
결 재				6-1

필 요 ☐ 보안불필요 ☐

수신시간:

타자.관치	검 인	주무자	과 장

0023

기 안 용 지

자체 통제		기안처	미주과 강석재	전화번호 / 근거서류접수일자

과장	국장	차관보.의관	차관	장관

관계관 서명						
기안 년월일	1962. 9. 8	시행 년월일	1962. 9. 8	보존 년한		정서기장
분류 기호	의정무 8575	전통	9.10	종결		
경유 수신 참조	배부처 참조			발신	장관	

제목: 미주둔군지위 협정체결을 위한 교섭 재개 공동 성명서 발표

정부는 미주둔군지위 협정을 체결하기 위한 교섭을 재개하고저 그동안 미국측과 꾸준한 외교교섭을 하여 왔던바 이제 양국이 조속한 시일내에 동 협정체결을 위한 교섭을 재개할것에 합의를 보아 9월 6일 오전 9시 서울에서 별첨과 같은 공동 성명서를 발표하였음으로 ~~알려드리오니 후지하시기 바랍니다~~. 이을 통보합니다

별첨: 한미간 주둔군지위협정 체결 공동 서명서, 한문 및 영문 각 1통

배부처: E (1—16) M (1— 3) C (1— 8) 끝

승인양식 1—1—3 (1112—040—016—018) (190mm×260mm16절지)

5-1

0024

1962年9月6日上午9時
以前에 發表함을 禁함

韓美共同聲明書

美駐屯軍 地位協定 交涉再開

駐韓美國大使는 外務部長官에게 美國政府가 駐韓美軍地位協定에 關한交涉을 再開할 用意가있음을 通報하였다.
外務部長官은 韓國政府를 代表하여 이提議를 歡迎하였다.

兩國政府는 9月中에 實務交涉을 再開할것에 合意하였다. 이러한 駐屯軍地位協定도 複雜한問題를 內包하고 있는故로 交涉은 相當한時日을 要할것을 認定하는 바이다. 따라서 韓國에 不遠間있을 憲法改正에 依하여 駐屯軍地位協定의 締結은 民政移讓을 기다려 이루어지게 될것으로 理解하는 바이다.

0025

5-2

Strictly not to be
released before 9 a.m.
on September 6, 1962

JOINT ROK-US PRESS STATEMENT

Resumption of Negotiations of Status of Forces Agreement

The American Ambassador has informed the Minister of Foreign Affairs that the United States Government is prepared to reopen negotiations for an agreement covering the status of the United States Armed Forces in the Republic of Korea. The Foreign Minister welcomed this development on behalf of his government.

Both sides agreed that negotiations would resume at the working level sometime in September. It is recognized that any status of forces agreement invovles complex matters and it is expected that negotiations will require a considerable period of time. Accordingly, it is understood that in view of the forthcoming constitutional changes in Korea, the conclusion of a Status of Forces Agreement will await the restoration of civil government.

0026

5-3

2. 대표단 구성

0027

기 안 용 지

자체통제	(서명)	기안처	미주과 강석재	전화번호 ⑧3052	근거서류접수일자

과장	국장	차관보직관	차관	장관	내각수반	의장
(인)	(서명)	(서명)	(서명)	(서명)	(서명) 9/7	(서명)

관계관 서명	

기안 년월일	1962. 9. 6	시행 년월일	1962. 9. 6	보존 년한	갑	정서 기장
분류 기호	외정무 846	전체 통제	검열 1962. 9. 7	종결		
경유 수신 참조	내각수반 대통령권한 대행 국가재건최고회의 의장			발신	장관	
제목	미주둔군 지위협정 교섭재개와 대표단 구성					

미주둔군 지위협정 교섭재개에 관하여

1. 9월 6일 오전 9시(서울시간)(5일 오후 7:30분)에 서울과 와싱톤에서 각각 교섭재개에 관한 공동 성명서를 발표하였으며

2. 제 1차 회담은 9월 20일 오후에 개최키로 미대사관측과 합의를 보았으며

3. 대표단 구성문제에 관하여 우리측은 한국측 수석대표로서 외무차관을, 미국측은 수석대표로서 "매지스트레티" 부대사를 각각 임명하도록 희망하였던바 미국측은 대사관 형편과 사정에 의하여 "매지스트레티" 부대사의 수석대표 임명은 불가능하며 대신 "하비브" 참사관을 결정적으로 임명하고져 한다고 말하였으며

4. 제 1차 교섭회의의 개최는 성대한 효과를 기하기 위하여 외무부 장관과 주한 미대사가 각각 양측을 대표하여 개회사를 하는데 동의하였는데

내각수반비서실 접수 1962. 9월 7일 9시

(1112—040—016—018) (190mm×260mm16절지)

4-1

0028

5. 미측은 그들의 대표단을 대령 "하비브" 참사관을 수석으로 하여 1 등서기관 2 명 영사 1 명 그리고 8군 참모부장 (대령), 법무감(대령) 및 유엔군 민사처 대표 1 명등의 실무자로서 구성할 것이라는 비공식 통보를 하여왔으며

6. 금주말 (9월 7일) 까지는 양측의 대표단 명단을 상호 교환하기로 되어있는 제반 실정에 감하여

우리측 대표단을 다음과 같이 구성하기를 건의하나이다.

- 다 음 -

수석대표	외무부 정무국장	진 필 식
대표	외무부	미주과장
		조약과장
		2 등서기관 이경훈 (기록)
		" 신정섭 (")
		사무관 이창범 (")
		외무서기관 지성구 (공보)
	국방부	관계요원
	재무부	세관국장
	법무부	법무국장

(기타 부처 소관사항이 토의될시는 해당부처 관계 국장도 포함시킨다) 끝

0020

승인양식 1-1-2 (1112-040-016-017) (190mm×260mm 16절지)

4-2

SOFA

Republic of Korea Negotiating Team

Status of Forces Agreement

Chief Negotiator: CHIN, ~~Phil~~ PIL Shik
Director
Bureau of Political Affairs
Ministry of Foreign Affairs

Negotiators:

Ministry of Foreign Affairs

PAK, Kun
Chief, America Section

LHO, Shin Yung
Chief, Treaty Section

LEE, Kyung Hoon (Record)
2nd Secretary

SHIN, Chung Sup (Record)
2nd Secretary

LEE, Chang Bum (Record)
Secretary

CHI, Sung Koo (Press)
Press Officer

Ministry of Finance

SHIN, Kwan Sup
Director
Bureau of Customs

Ministry of Justice

LEE, Kyung Ho
Director
Bureau of Legal Affairs

Ministry of National Defense

Representative

2

0030

SOFA

미주과장과 "후렌" 1등서기관과의 회담요지

1. 시 일 : 1962. 9. 7. 1600 부터 1630까지
2. 참석자: 미 주 과 장
   "후렌" 1등서기관
3. 장 소 : 미주과장실
4. 회담경위: "후렌" 1등서기관의 요청에 의함.
5. 회담 요지:

(1) 미 주둔군 지위협정에 관한 미측 교섭단

"후렌" 1등서기관은 동 협정의 교섭 재개에 대비하여 미측 교섭단의 구성을 완료하였으며 그명단을 미주과장에게 수교하였음 (별첨)

미주과장은 한국측 명단은 아직 고위층의 결재를 받고 있는 중임으로 결정적인 것은 수교할수 없다고 말하고 금명간 재가가 나면 작성하여 대사관측에 제시하여 주겠다고 말하였음.

(2) 한일회담 제5차 예비교섭에 관한 정보교환

"후렌" 1등서기관은 6일 하오에 있은 제5차 예비교섭에 관한 정보를 요구하여 왔으므로 미주과장은 별첨 주일대표부로 부터의 보고 내용을 동 1등서기관에게 설명하여 주었음.

"후렌" 1등서기관은 제 4차와 제5차 예비교섭 경과에 대하여 실망적인 태도를 보였음.

별첨:

1. 미주둔군지위협정에 관한 미측 교섭단 명단
2. 한일 제5차 예비회담에 관한 주일대표부로 부터의 보고. 끝

미주과	강 원 / 교 / 재 원	담 당	과 장	국 장	특별보좌관	차 관	장 관

3-1

0031

STATUS OF FORCES NEGOTIATIONS

United States Negotiating Team

American Embassy:

Philip C. Habib, Counselor of Embassy for Political Affairs

William J. Ford, First Secretary (Economic)

Benjamin A. Fleck, First Secretary (Political)

Robert A. Lewis, Second Secretary and Consul

United States Forces, Korea:

Brigadier General J. D. Lawlor, Deputy Chief of Staff, 8th USA

Colonel G. G. O'Connor, USA, Deputy Chief of Staff

Colonel W. A. Solf, USA, Staff Judge Advocate

Alternate: Lt. Colonel R. E. Miller, USA, Staff Officer JAJ

Captain R. M. Brownlie, USN, ACofS, J-5

Alternate: Lt. Colonel G. T. Sudermann, USAF, Staff Officer, J-5

0032

기 안 용 지

자체 통제		기안처	미주과 황영재	전화번호	근거서류접수일자
과 장	국 장	차관보좌관	차 관	장 관	
관계관 서명					
기안 년월일	1962. 9. 12.	시행 년월일	1962. 9. 12.	보존 년한	영
분류 기호	외정무 1383	전체 통제		종결	
경유 수신 참조	국방부장관			발신	장 관
정서		기장			

검열 1962. 9. 14 통제관

제 목 미주둔군 지위협정체결 교섭대표 임명 및 회의소집

미주둔군 지위협정체결 교섭을 위한 한국측 대표단 임명에 관하여 앞서 전화로 귀하의 양해를 얻은 바와 같이 귀부 군무과장 이남구 대령을 한국측 대표단의 일원으로 임명하였음을 통보하오며 아울러 다음과 같이 회의를 소집코저 하오니 필히 ~~동 대령을~~ 귀부교섭대표를 참석시켜 주시기 바랍니다.

- 아 래 -

1. 회의목적 : 미주둔군 지위협정체결 교섭을위한 준비회담
2. 회의일시 : 1962. 9. 14. 오전 10 시
3. 회의장소 : 외무부 정무국장실 끝

승인양식 1-1-3 (1112-040-013-018) (190mm×260mm16절지)

7-1

0033

외 무 부

외정무 1962. 9. 14.

수 신 국방부장관

제 목 미주둔군 지위협정체결 교섭대표 임명 및 회의소집

미주둔군 지위협정체결 교섭을위한 한국측 대표단 임명에 관하여 앞서 전화로 귀하의 양해를 얻은바와 같이 귀부 군무과장 이남구 대령을 한국측 대표단의 인원으로 임명하였음을 통보하오며 아울러 다음과같이 회의 소집코저 하오니 필히 귀부 소속대표를 참석시켜 주시기 바랍니다.

- 아 래 -

1. 회의목적 : 미주둔군 지위협정체결 교섭을위한 준비회담
2. 회의일시 : 1962. 9. 19. 오전 10 시
3. 회의장소 : 외무부 정무국장실 끝

외무부장관 최 덕 신

0034

기 안 용 지

자 체 통 제		기안처	미주과 강석재	전화번호	근거서류접수일자

과장	국장	차관보좌관	차관	장관		

관계관 서명					
기안 년월일	1962. 9. 12	시행 년월일	1962. 9. 12	보존 년한	영
분류 기호	외정무1384	전 통 제	통제관	종결	
경유 수신 참조	재무부 장관		발신	장관	
제목	미주둔군 지위협정 체결 교섭대표 임명 및 회의 소집				

정서 기장

미주둔군 지위협정체결 교섭을 위한 한국측 대표단 임명에 관하여 전화로 귀하의 양해를 얻은바와 같이 귀부 세관국장을 한국측 대표단의 일원으로 임명하였음을 통보하오며 아울러 다음과 같이 준비회의를 소집코저 하오니 필히 외무부측대표로 참석시켜 주시기 바랍니다.

— 아 래 —

1. 회의 목적: 미주둔군 지위협정체결 교섭을 위한 준비회합
2. 회의 일시: 1962. 9. 19 오전 10시
3. 회의 장소: 외무부 정무국장실 끝

1962

보통문서로 재분류(교섭재개시)

승인양식 1—1—3 (1112—040—016—018) (190mm×260mm16절지)

8-1

0035

외 무 부

의정무 1962. 9. 14.

수 신 재무부장관

제 목 미주둔군 지위협정 체결 교섭대표 임명 및 회의소집

미 주둔군지위 협정체결을 위한 한국측 대표단 임명에 관하여 앞서 전화로 귀하의 양해를 얻은바와 같이 귀부 세관국장을 한국측 대표단의 일원으로 임명하였음을 통보하오며 아울러 다음과 같이 준비 회의를 소집코저 하오니 필히 귀부소속대표를 참석시키어 주시기 바랍니다.

- 아 래 -

1. 회의목적 : 미주둔군 지위협정체결 교섭을위한 준비회합
2. 회의일시 : 1962. 9. 19. 오전 10시
3. 회의장소 : 외무부 정무국장실 끝

외 무 부 장 관 최 덕 신

0036

8-2

기 안 용 지

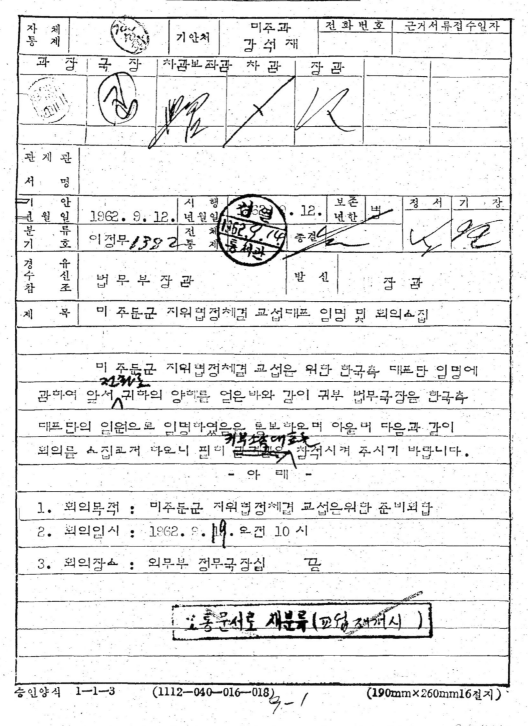

자 체 통 제		기안처	미주과 강석재	전화번호	근거서류접수일자
과 장	국 장	차관보좌관	차 관	장 관	
관계관 서 명					
기 안 년월일	1962. 9. 12.	시 행 년월일	1962. 9. 12.	보존 년한	정서 기장
분 류 기 호	이정무 1382	전 체 통 제	1962.9.14 통제관	종결	
경 유 수 신 참 조	법무부장관		발 신	장관	
제 목	미 주둔군 지위협정체결 교섭대표 임명 및 회의소집				

미 주둔군 지위협정체결 교섭을 위한 한국측 대표단 임명에 관하여 앞서 전화로 귀하의 양해를 얻은 바와 같이 귀부 법무국장을 한국측 대표단의 일원으로 임명하였음을 통보하오며 아울러 다음과 같이 회의를 소집코저 하오니 필히 귀측대표로 참석시켜 주시기 바랍니다.

\- 아 래 -

1. 회의목적 : 미주둔군 지위협정체결 교섭을위한 준비회합
2. 회의일시 : 1962. 9. 19. 오전 10 시
3. 회의장소 : 외무부 정무국장실 끝

보통문서로 재분류(1966. 12. 31. 예고문에 의거)

승인양식 1-1-3 (1112-040-016-018) (190mm×260mm16절지)

9-1

0087

외 무 부

외정무 1962. 9. 14.

수 신 법무부장관

제 목 미주둔군 지위협정체결 교섭대표 임명 및 회의소집

미주둔군 지위협정체결 교섭을위한 한국측 대표단 임명에관하여 앞서 전화로 귀하의 양해를 얻은바와 같이 귀부 법무국장은 한국측 대표단의 일원으로 임명되었음을 통보하오며 아울러 다음과같이 회의를 소집코저 하오니 필히 귀부 소속대표를 참석시켜 주시기 바랍니다.

- 아 래 -

1. 회의목적 : 미주둔군 지위협정체결 교섭을위한 준비회합
2. 회의일시 : 1962. 9. 19. 오전 10 시
3. 회의장소 : 외무부 정무국장실 끝

외무부장관 최 덕 신

0038

9-2

미주과장과 "후렛" 1등서기관과의 회담요지

시 일 : 1962. 9. 14. 상오 11시부터 11시 10분 까지

장 소 : 미주과장실

참석자 : 미주과장

"후렛" 1등서기관

회담경위 : "후렛" 1등서기관의 요청에 의함

회담요지 :

"후렛" 1등서기관은 주둔군지위 협정 실무자교섭을 위한 미측 교섭단 명단에 별첨 미 제 8군 참모부장 "로우메" 준장이 추가되었다고 말하고 그러나 미측수석은 여전히 "하비브" 참사관임에는 변동이 없다고 말하였음.

미주과장관 우리측 명단은 동일 하오에 전달하여 주도록 조치하겠다고 말하였음.

끝

0039

기 안 용 지

자체 통제		기안처	미주과 강석재	전화번호	근거서류접수일자
과장	국장	외무차관보	차관	장관	내각 수반
		전결			
관계관 서명					
기안 년월일	1962. 9. 17	시행 년월일	1962. 9. 18	보존 년한	정서 / 기장
분류 기호	외정무 8197	전체 통제		종결	
경유 수신 참조	국방부장관		발신	장관	
제목	미주둔군 지위협정 교섭대표 임명				

1962. 9. 12.자 외정무 1383으로 미주둔군 지위협정 실무자 교섭을위한 대표임명과 한국 대표단의 사전준비를 위한 회의소집을 통고한바 있거니와 이번 미국측으로부터 미국대표단에 미제 8군 참모부장 "로우머" 준장을 추가하였다는 연락이있어 이를 알리오니 참고하시기 바라나이다. 끝.

승인양식 1-1-1 (1112-040-016-016) (190mm×260mm16절지)

0040

외 무 부

외정무 1962. 9. 18.

수 신 국방부장관

제 목 미주둔군 지위협정 교섭대표 임명

1962. 9. 12.자 외정무 1383 으로 미주둔군 지위협정 실무자 교섭을위한 대표임명과 한국대표단의 사전준비를 위한 회의 소집을 통고한바 있거니와 이번 미국측으로부터 미측대표단에 미제 8 군 참모부장 "로우더" 준장을 추가하였다는 연락이 있어 이를 알리오니 참고하시기 바라나이다. 끝

1962.9.18 외무부

외 무 부 장관 최 덕 신

0041

1

3. 사전준비

0042

기 안 용 지

자체 통제		기안처	미주과 강석재	전화번호	근거서류접수일자

과 장	국 장	차관보 좌관	차 관		장 관	내각 수반

관계관 서명	기획조정관					
기안 년월일	1962. 9. 18.	시행 년월일		보존 년한		정서 기장
분류 기호	의정무	전체 통제		종결		
경유 수신 참조	건의			발신		
제 목	미주둔군 지위협정 제1차 한미실무자 회의 개최					

1962. 9. 20. 하오 3시부터 개최될 예정인 미주둔군 지위협정 체결을위한 제 1 차 회의를 별첨 안(1)의 진행절차에 따라 진행토록하며 아울러 동회의에서 장관이 행할 개회식사를 별첨 안(2)와 여히 건의하오니 이를 채택하여 주시기 바라나이다.

별첨 : 1. 회의진행 절차

2. 장관 개회 식사 끝

0043

승인양식 1-1-1 (1112-040-016-016) (190mm×260mm16절지)

11-1

안 (1)

주둔군 지위협정 체결을 위한
제 1 차 한미실무자 회의
진행절차 (안)

1. 일 시 : 1962. 9. 20. 오후 3시

2. 장 소 : 외무부 회의실

3. 진행절차 :

1) Opening Speech: (공개)

한국측 ... 외무부장관

미국측 ... Berger 대사

2) 대표단 소개 : (공개)

한국측 ... 외무부장관

미국측 ... 미국대사

3) 회의진행방법 토의 : (비공개)

가. 회의 회수	주 1 회
나. 장소	외무부 회의실
다. 용어	한국어와 영어를 공용토록 함.
라. 공동회의 오록 작성	양측이 교대교대로 작성하여 쌍방 관계관이 공동으로 검토하여 합의서명을 한다음 차기회의에서 양측 수석대표에 의해 확인받도록 함.

0044

11-2

마. 보도문제 양측이 Press Officer 를 지명하여 회의종료시 마다 양측이 공표하기로 합의한 내용을 발표한다.

4) 의제문제 토의 :

가. 형사재판관할권 문제와 토지, 시설 사용문제를 포함한 주둔군 지위협정에서 규제하여야 할 전반적인 문제를 의제에 포함시킨다는 원칙적 합의를 본다.

나. 이러한 원칙적 합의하에 비교적 합의가용이한 문제부터 토의를 선행한다.

다. 의제는 다음사항을 포함한다

(가) 본협정의 규율대상이 되는 개체의 정의

(나) 출입국 관리

(다) 관세 업무

(라) 조세문제

(마) 주둔군이 사용하는 토지 시설문제

(바) 주둔군의 구매업무 및 후생문제

형사재판 관할권 및 청구권 문제

노무조달 문제

협정의 효력, 개정문제

본 협정과 저촉되는 기존협정의 처리문제

0045

11-3

다. 상기의제는 합의가능이한 문제부터 그정도에 따라

대체로 3 개부류로 제분하면 대략 아래와 같다.

(1) 가장 용이하다고 생각되는 문제

(가) 정의

(나) 전시 특례조항

(다) 운전면허, 제복 기타

(라) 무기 휴대

(마) 군사우편

(바) 주둔군 및 재산의 안전

(사) 합동위원회 설치

(아) 분쟁해결 조항

(자) 세출외 자금기관 문제

(2) 비교적 용이하다고 생각되는 문제

(가) 출입국 관리

(나) 선박 항공기의 출입

(다) 관세문제

(라) 조세 및 기타 내국세 문제

(마) 항해 기상업무의 통제문제

(바) 물자 및 노무의 조달문제

0046

11-4

(사) 통화 및 외환관계 문제

(아) 미국인 계약자

(3) 비교적 곤란하다고 생각되는 문제

(가) 형사재판 관할권 문제

(나) 민사재판권 문제

(다) 일반청구권 문제

(라) 토지 및 시설의 사용과 동보상 문제

5) 차기회의 개최:

가. 차기회의는 차주 목요일로 한다

나. 의제는 그날회의에서 합의를보지 못한 문제를 계속 토의하고 협정에서 규정할 실질적인 문제의 토의에 들어간다.

6) Press Release:

가. 공표내용의 대강은 Press Officer 에게 위임하여 상호 합의하에 공표토록한다.

7) 폐회

0047

11-5

정무국장과 "하비브" 참사관과의 회담요지

1. 시 일 : 1962. 9. 14. 1700 - 1800
2. 장 소 : 정무국장실
3. 참석자 : 정무국장, 미주과장

   "하비브" 참사관, "후멜" 1 등서기관
4. 회담경위 : "하비브" 참사관의 요청에 의함.
5. 회담요지 :

   가. 영국선박의 북한괴뢰기 게양사건

   "하비브" 참사관은 영국선박에 의한 북한괴뢰기 게양사건에 관한 우리측 각서를 받았다고 하면서 이사건은 영국선박이 저질은 사건이며 미국으로서는 직접적으로 하등 관련이 없으며 따라서 우리측 각서에대하여 참고로만 삼고 회답을 직접 하지 않아도 좋을듯이 생각되는데 한국측의 의견은 어떤지 문의하였음.

   정무국장은 같은 각서를 영국 대사관에도 수교하였다고 말하고 다만 미국이 이사건의 발생경위에 관한 참고될수 있는 정보를 얻으면 제공하여 달라고 말하였음.

   여기에대해서 동참사관은 적절한 계통을통하여 발생경위에 관한 정보를 수집하여 줄것을 의뢰하였으니 얻는데로 한국측에 알려주겠다고 말하였음.

   나. 한.일회담

   한일회담에 관하여 정무국장은 제 6 차 예비회담까지의 경과와 내용을 설명하고 특히 제 5 차후의 일주일간의 기한을 두어 일본측의 새제안을 제시할수 있는 준비를 위하여 기다렸으나 제 6 차 회의에서는 제안을 제시하여 오지않았으며 따라서 제 3 차 회의 이후의 회담은 소위 말하는 "후리 토킹" 식의 비공식 의견교환으로 끝나고 별무 진전이 없었으며

1-0-1

0048

일본측은 "오히라" 외상이 "이께다" 수상을 설복시키는데 현재로서는 실패한것 같다고 말하였음.

하비브 참사관은 자기도 그와 비슷한 보고를 받았다고 말하면서 한국측이 우선 어업 및 법적지위 등에관한 실무교섭을 진행하면서 인내성을 가지고 회담을 계속하여 주기를 희망하였음.

다. 미주둔군 지위협정 실무 교섭재개

하비브 참사관은 주둔군 지위협정에 관한 실무교섭을 20일 하오 2시에 재개토록 예정되어 있던것을 버거 대사의 개인 사정으로 부득이 동일 하오 3시로 연기하여 재개토록 하는데 한국측에서 어떤 불편이 없는지 문의하였음.

정무국장은 미국사정이 그렇다면 우리측으로서 한시간 연기하는데는 의의가 없다고 말하고 이어 별첨과 같은 우리측 교섭대표의 명단을 수교하였음.

하비브 참사관은 19일 하오쯤 다시 정식실무 교섭의 재개에 앞서 사전 사무적협의를 하면 좋겠다고 말하였으며 여기에 대하여 정무국장은 동의하였음.

라. 라오스 문제

라오스 문제에 대하여 정무국장은 상주대사 파견을 위한 우리측의 그동안의 방침과 노력을 설명하고 특히 만일에 라오스 정부의 아그레망이 지연되는 경우 우선 잠정적 조치로서 대리대사를 파견하는것이 어떠할지 미국측의 의견을 문의하였음.

여기에대하여 하비브 참사관은 현지 주재 미국대사에게 문의하여 그의 의견을 타진하여 알려주겠다고 약속하였음.

미주과	양고재 九월 일	담당	과장	국장	차관보	차관	장관
		가					

0049

10-2

1962. 9. 19

제 목: 미 주둔군 지위교섭재개 제1차회의에서의 주한 미대사 식사

1962. 9. 19 하오 3시에 "하비브" 참사관과 "후렉" 1등 서기관은 정무국장을 방문하고 별첨과 같은 미국대사의 개회 인사문(안)을 제시하였으며 우리측은 별첨과 같은 장관 인사문을 수교하였음을 보고하나이다.

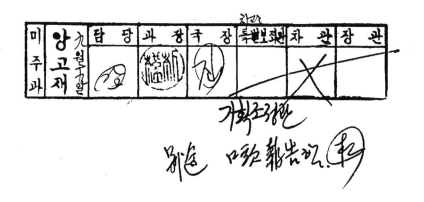

미주과	기안	담당	과장	국장	특별보좌관	차관	장관
	양고재 九월구일	(서명)	(인)	(서명)		X	

기획조정관

別添 口頭報告했음. (인)

0050

12-1

OPENING SESSION, SOFA NEGOTIATIONS

REMARKS BY AMBASSADOR BERGER

Mr. Minister, Friends and Colleagues -

1. As we begin negotiations today it is important that we have a clear view of our common objective. That objective is to strengthen further the already close ties existing between Korea and the United States. Our joint task is to conclude an agreement which will contribute to this objective in a manner satisfactory to both sides. The United States Government is entering these negotiations with the earnest intent to conclude an agreement which will meet this objective.

2. My country is aware of the great interest of the Korean people in these negotiations. There is the same intense interest, I can assure you, among the people of the United States and my government.

3. A Status of Forces Agreement covers many kinds of activities. It encompasses extensive, complex and varied administrative arrangements. The areas to be discussed include postal facilities, port and airplane facilities, servicing of ships and aircraft, customs regulations, tax regulations, the use of facilities for the defense of Korea, and matters of jurisdiction over personnel. These are intricate and complicated matters. They posed complex problems between the United States and other countries. Complicated problems are a challenge to the skills of the negotiators, but they are not necessarily barriers to agreement. The wide range of questions which will arise and will need to be resolved in the course of these negotiations will provide the fabric to fashion a mutually satisfactory agreement.

4. Difficult and complex though the problems may be, we expect to draw up a Status of Forces Agreement which will further those amicable associations between the United States and Korea that have historically provided the power and the will to resist threats to freedom. This task calls for unity of purpose, mutual respect and a real effort to understand each other's problems. On this our common security depends. It is in this spirit and with this purpose, that the United States enters these negotiations for a Status of Forces Agreement with the Republic of Korea.

0051

12-2

1962. 9. 20. 하오 3시
이전에 발표함을 금함.

1962년 9월 20일 한미간 주둔군지위 협정 교섭 회의개최에 즈음한 외무부장관 식사

버거 대사, 여러내빈 그리고 교섭대표 여러분,

본인은 공동방위를 위하여 대한민국에 주둔하고 있는 미합중국 군대지위에 관한 협정체결 교섭을 재개함에 즈음하여 12년전 미국을 위시한 자유국가의 연합군이 한국군과 긴밀한 협조하에 공산침략자와 싸웠다는 사실을 자랑스럽게 상기하고저 하는 바입니다.

본인은 또한 오늘의 이교섭재개가 직접적이고 긴급한 공산침략의 위협에 직면한 가운데서 자유세계가 보여주는 또하나의 고귀한 협조의 실예임을 기쁨으로 주목코저 하는 바입니다.

특히 이회담은 전통적 한미관계의 오랜특징인 가장 화목한 우의와 협조의 정신 그리고 부동한 상호 신뢰의 웅변적 상징인 것입니다.

본인으로서는 [이번회담에 있어서] 우리양국 국민간에 발생하는 개개사건의 방지나 또는 일국의 타국에대한 주권의 주장이 ~~이번회담에 있어서~~ 본질적문제가 되는것이 아니라고 생각하며 오히려 이번 기회의 참된 의의와 주둔군 지위협정 교섭의 중대한 사명을 다루는 엄숙한 목적은 자유국가간의 관계는 평등과 상호 존중의 명예로운 원칙위에 서야하고 또한 실제로 서있다는 사실, 그리고 그러한 원칙위에 기반을둔 여사한 관계야말로 참으로 위대하며 영구히 평화속에 지속된다는 사실을 만방에 시위하려는 우리의 공동결심에 있는 것입니다.

본인은 오늘의 회담재개가 구체적 행동과 결과로서 한 자유의 선봉국가와 현세기의 가장 위대한 국가간의 관계가 바로 그러하다는 것을 증명하게 될것으로 확신하는 바입니다.

0052

11-6

협정체결이 실현되기까지에는 허다한 난관을 극복해야 하며 복잡한 많은문제를 해결해야 할것입니다. 그러나 우리들은 우리들의 목적, 단결과 인내에 있어서 결코 실패하지 않을것입니다.

본인은 이자리에 계신 여러 교섭대표들의 노력이 조속히 협정을 성공적인 체결로 이끌어 한미간의 우호관계의 역사에 또하나의 이정표를 마련할것을 충심으로 원하는 바입니다.

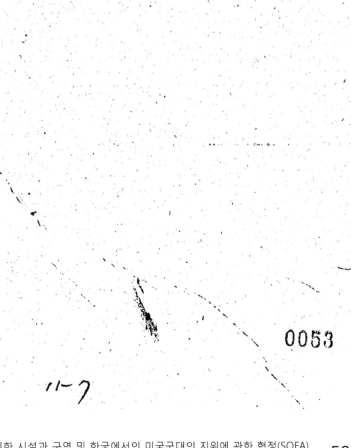

0053

11-7

Strictly not to be released before 3 p.m. on Sept. 20, 1962

STATEMENT BY FOREIGN MINISTER CHOI DUK SHIN AT THE OPENING OF STATUS OF FORCES NEGOTIATION BETWEEN THE GOVERNMENTS OF THE REPUBLIC OF KOREA AND THE UNITED STATES, SEOUL, KOREA

SEPTEMBER 20, 1962

Mr. Ambassador, guests and negotiators,

On this occasion of the resumption of negotiations for an agreement covering the status of United States Forces that are stationed in the Republic of Korea for the purpose of common defense, I wish to note with pride that it was barely a dozen year ago when the united forces of the United States and other free nations, shoulder to shoulder with their Korean ally, fought back the Communist aggressors. I wish further to note with pleasure that today's resumption of negotiations represents another of many noble examples of Free World cooperation in the face of direct and immediate threat of Communist aggression.

In particular, this gathering eloquently symbolizes the most amicable spirit of friendship and cooperation as well as the unshakable mutual confidence that have long been characteristic of traditional relations between the Republic of Korea and the United States.

It is, to me, not so much the prevention of this or that incident involving nationals of our two countries nor the assertion of one's sovereignty over that of another that is at stake in this coming negotiations. Rather, the true significance of this occasion and the solemn purpose with which we are to engage in the exacting task of the status of forces negotiations lie

0054

11-8

in our joint resolve to demonstrate to the world that the relations of free nations shall be, and in fact are, based on an honorable principle of equality and mutual respect, and that only such relations founded on such principle are truly great and lasting in peace.

I am confident that today's reopening of negotiations will prove, through concrete action and results, that such is the case of relations between a frontier state of freedom and the greatest nation of the century.

Many difficulties will have to be overcome; and many a complex problem must be solved, before an agreement can be effected. But, in our purpose, unity and patience, we cannot fail.

I sincerely hope that the efforts of these negotiators present here will soon lead to the successful conclusion of an agreement, which will lay another milestone in the annals of the friendly relations between the Republic of Korea and the United States.

0055

11-7

UNITED STATES INFORMATION SERVICE
駐韓美國公報院
SEOUL KOREA

PRESS RELEASE
時事通報

第六二一四四九號

(西紀一九六二年九月十八日)

行政協定 協商開幕席上에 行한
버거美國大使의 人事

(다음은 「사뮤엘·D·버거」駐韓美國大使가 九月二十日 韓美行政協定 協商開幕席上에서 行한 人事全文이다)

外務部長官, 議員및 同僚여러분—

오늘 協商을 시작함에 있어서 우리가 우리의 共同目標에關하여 明白한見解를가진 다는것은 重要합니다 韓美兩國間에 이미 存在하는 緊密한 紐帶를 더욱 强化하는 것입니다 우리의 共同課業은 雙方에 다같이 滿足스러운 方法으로 이 目標에 寄與하게될 協定을 締結하는데 있읍니다 美國政府는 이 目標를 達成하게될 協定을 締結하려는 眞摯한 意圖를 가지고 協商을 시작하려는 것입니다

美國은 이번 協商에 對해서 韓國民이 至大한 關心을 가지고 있다는것을 잘 알고있읍니다 美國民과 나의 本國政府도 똑같이 큰 關心을 가지고있다는 것을 나는 이 자리에서 分明히 말할수 있읍니다

行政協定은 여러가지 活動에 關한 것입니다 同協定은 廣汎하고 複雜한 各種의 行政措置를 다루는 것입니다 討議될 分野에는 郵遞施設, 港灣및 航空施設, 船舶및 航空機修理, 關稅規定, 課稅規定, 韓國防衛施設使用및 人員에對한 司法管轄權가 包含되어 있읍니다

0056

이 問題들은 複雜微妙합니다 이들은 美國과 他國間에 複雜한 問題들을 提起하였읍니다 複雜한 問題들은 協商하는 사람들에게 技術을 要하게끔 하는것일지언정 이들이 반드시 合意에 이르는것을 妨害하는 것은 아닙니다 이 協商을 通하여 提起되고 또 解決되어야만 하는 實質的인 問題들은 相互 滿足할만한 合意를 이룩할 기틀이 될 것입니다

이 問題들이 비록 困難하고 複雜한것이기는 하나 歷史的으로 自由에 對한 威脅에 對抗키 爲하여 힘과 意志를 북돋아준 韓美間의 緊密한 交分이 더욱 鞏固해지도록 軍人身分協定의 妥結을 우리는 期待하는 바입니다 이 諸條은 目的의 一致, 相互尊重및 各自의 問題를 理解하고자 하는 眞正한 努力을 要求하고 있읍니다 우리의 共通된 安全保障은 여기에 달려있읍니다

美國이 韓國과 더불어 軍人身分協定 協商에 들어가는 것은 이같은 精神과 趣旨에서인 것입니다

(끝)

0057

UNITED STATES INFORMATION SERVICE
駐 韓 美 國 公 報 院
SEOUL KOREA

PRESS RELEASE
時 事 通 報

62-449
Sept. 20, 1962

AMBASSADOR BERGER'S REMARKS AT OPENING OF SOFA NEGOTIATIONS

Ambassador Samuel D. Berger made the following statement today at the opening of the Status of Forces Agreement negotiations between the Republic of Korea and United States Governments:

"Mr. Minister, Friends and Colleagues -

"As we begin negotiations today it is important that we have a clear view of our common objective. That objective is to strengthen further the already close ties existing between Korea and the United States. Our joint task is to conclude an agreement which will contribute to this objective in a manner satisfactory to both sides. The United States Government is entering these negotiations with the earnest intent to conclude an agreement which will meet this objective.

"My country is aware of the great interest of the Korean people in these negotiations. There is the same intense interest, I can assure you, among the people of the United States and my government.

"A Status of Forces Agreement covers many kinds of activities. It encompasses extensive, complex, and varied administrative arrangements. The areas to be discussed include postal facilities, port and airplane facilities, servicing of ships and aircraft, customs regulations, tax regulations, the use of facilities for the defense of Korea, and matters of jurisdiction over personnel. These are intricate and complicated matters. They posed complex problems between the United States and other countries. Complicated problems are a challenge to the skills of the negotiators, but they are not necessarily barriers to agreement. The wide range of questions which will arise and will need to be resolved in the course of these negotiations will provide the fabric to fashion a mutually satisfactory agreement.

"Difficult and complex though the problems may be, we expect to draw up a Status of Forces Agreement which will further those amicable associations between the United States and Korea that have historically provided the power and the will to resist threats to freedom. This task calls for unity of purpose, mutual respect and a real effort to understand each other's problems. On this our common security depends. It is in this spirit and with this purpose, that the United States enters these negotiations for a Status of Forces Agreement with the Republic of Korea."

*** *** ***

0053

Kang file

4. 제1차 회의, 9.20

0059

대한민국 외무부

번 호: WD-0911
일 시: 221540

발신전보

수신인:

연 WD — 0913

1. 미 주둔군 지위협정 체결 실무 교섭회의는 예정대로 9월 20일 오후 3시에 개최하였음.

2. 회의는 양측을 대표하여 외무장관 및 버— 거대사의 식사 (추후 송부할 위계임) 대표단의 소개가 있은후 실무교섭 회의로 들어가서 절차 문제를 론의하였음. 제2차 회의는 9월 28일 개최키로 합의를 봄.

3. 귀하는 미주둔군 지위협정 교섭에 관련한 미국의 입법부, 행정부 의 반응, 동태, 및 일반여론을 앞으로 계속 동찰하여 수시 보고하시기 바람. (정미) 끝

장 관

미주과	앙고재 9월 21일	담당	과장	국장	특별보좌관	차관	장관

보통문서로 재분류 (1966. 12. 31.)

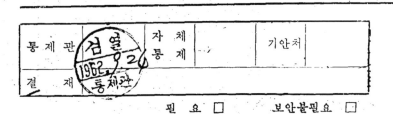

1966. 12. 31에 예고문에 의거 일반문서로 재분류됨

송신시간:

통제관	검열 1962. 9. 26 통제관	자체 통제		기안처	
결재					

타자	1966년 9월 30일 주 미주과 직권으로 보통문서로 재분류			장

필요 ☐ 보안불필요 ☐

0060

1962. 9. 20. 하오 3시
이전에 발표함을 금함.

1962년 9월 20일 한미간 주둔군지위 협정 교섭 회의개최에 즈음한 외무부장관 식사

버거 대사, 여러내빈 그리고 교섭대표 여러분,

본인은 공동방위를 위하여 대한민국에 주둔하고 있는 미합중국군대지위에 관한 협정체결 교섭을 재개함에 즈음하여 12 년전 미국을 위시한 자유국가의 연합군이 한국군과 긴밀한 협조하에 공산침략자와 싸웠다는 사실을 자랑스럽게 상기하고저 하는 바입니다.

본인은 또한 오늘의 이교섭재개가 직접적이고 긴급한 공산침략의 위협에 직면한 가운데서 자유세계가 보여주는 또 하나의 고귀한 협조의 실예임을 기쁨으로 주목코저 하는 바입니다.

특히 이회담은 전통적 한미관계의 오랜특징인 가장 화목한 우의와 협조의 정신 그리고 부동한 상호 신뢰의 웅변적 상징인 것입니다.

본인으로서는 우리양국 국민간에 발생하는 개개사건의 방치 또는 일국의 타국에대한 주권의 주장이 이번회담에 있어서 본질적문제가 되는것이 아니라고 생각하며 오히려 이번 기회의 참된 의의와 주둔군 지위협정 교섭의 중대한 사명을 다루는 엄숙한 목적은 자유국가간의 관계는 평등과 상호 존중의 명예로운 원칙위에 서야하고 또한 실제로 서있다는 사실, 그리고 그러한 원칙위에 기반을둔 여사한 관계야말로 참으로 위대하며 영구히 평화속에 지속된다는 사실을 만방에 시위하려는 우리의 공동결심에 있는 것입니다.

본인은 오늘의 회담재개가 구체적 행동과 결과로서 한 자유의 선봉국가와 현세기의 가장 위대한 국가간의 관계가 바로 그러하다는 것을 증명하게 될것으로 확신하는 바입니다.

frequency
frequently
as frequently as possible
as frequently as possible
as frequently as possible

We will be prepared to favorably consider such proposal : but I don't like to agree on the principle of unilateral call of meeting

0061

협정체결이 실현되기까지에는 허다한 난관을 극복해야 하며 복잡한 많은문제를 해결해야 할것입니다. 그러나 우리들은 우리들의 목적, 단결과 인내에 있어서 결코 실패하지 않을것입니다.

본인은 이자리에 계신 여러 교섭대표들의 노력이 조속히 협정을 성공적인 체결로 이끌어 한미간의 우호관계의 역사에 또하나의 이정표를 마련할것을 충심으로 원하는 바입니다.

possible

possible

frequently

as possible

등 as frequently as possible

as possible

0062

Strictly not to be
released before 3 p.m.
on Sept. 20, 1962

STATEMENT BY FOREIGN MINISTER CHOI DUK SHIN AT THE OPENING OF STATUS OF FORCES NEGOTIATION BETWEEN THE GOVERNMENTS OF THE REPUBLIC OF KOREA AND THE UNITED STATES, SEOUL, KOREA

SEPTEMBER 20, 1962

Mr. Ambassador, guests and negotiators,

On this occasion of the resumption of negotiations for an agreement covering the status of United States Forces that are stationed in the Republic of Korea for the purpose of common defense, I wish to note with pride that it was barely a dozen year ago when the united forces of the United States and other free nations, shoulder to shoulder with their Korean ally, fought back the Communist aggressors. I wish further to note with pleasure that today's resumption of negotiations represents another of many noble examples of Free World cooperation in the face of direct and immediate threat of Communist aggression.

In particular, this gathering eloquently symbolizes the most amicable spirit of friendship and cooperation as well as the unshakable mutual confidence that have long been characteristic of traditional relations between the Republic of Korea and the United States.

It is, to me, not so much the prevention of this or that incident involving nationals of our two countries nor the assertion of one's sovereignty over that of another that is at stake in this coming negotiations. Rather, the true significance of this occasion and the solemn purpose with which we are to engage in the exacting task of the status of forces negotiations lie

0063

in our joint resolve to demonstrate to the world that the relations of free nations shall be, and in fact are, based on an honorable principle of equality and mutual respect, and that only such relations founded on such principle are truly great and lasting in peace.

I am confident that today's reopening of negotiations will prove, through concrete action and results, that such is the case of relations between a frontier state of freedom and the greatest nation of the century.

Many difficulties will have to be overcome; and many a complex problem must be solved, before an agreement can be effected. But, in our purpose, unity and patience, we cannot fail.

I sincerely hope that the efforts of these negotiators present here will soon lead to the successful conclusion of an agreement, which will lay another milestone in the annals of the friendly relations between the Republic of Korea and the United States.

0064

駐屯軍 地位協定의
重要項目 및
問題点

1. 土地 및 施設의 使用

(1) 美國政府의 補償問題

(2) 美國政府의 維持費負担問題 (all expenditure incident to the maintenance of F and A)

(3) 美軍使用土地施設의 臨時使用权 (interim use)

(4) 返還時의 原状復旧問題 (Restoration)

(5) 返還時 尤甚한 被害를 입은 私有財産에 対한 美國의 補償義務 (Restoration or compensation to the ROK Gov't in case of private property which is extremely demolished)

2. 船舶 航空機의 出入

(1) 入港料 및 着陸料免除船舶 및 航空機의 範囲 (category of vessel to which exemption of landing fee be granted)

(2) 出入時 美軍의 韓國当局에 対한 通告義務 (notification to Korean authority of the entry and exit of U.S. Forces)

(3) 航空交通管理 및 通信体系의 統合問題 (Control of air navigation and coordination of communication system)

3. 刑事裁判管轄权

(1) 一般的 管轄权問題 (general jurisdiction)

(2) 専属的 管轄权問題 (Exclusive jurisdiction)

(3) 裁判权競合問題 (Concurrence of Jurisdiction)

(4) 公務執行中與否의 決定問題

(5) 裁判权의 抛棄

0065

(6) 搜査 및 訴訟節次上의 相互協助問題

(7) 韓國法院에 起訴된 美軍의 裁判上의 權利

4. 民事裁判權 및 請求權.

(1) 韓國法院의 民事裁判權.

(2) 軍用財産의 損害에 對한 相互間의 請求權抛棄.

(3) 其他 損害에 對한 仲裁人의 責任問題決定權 및 報償額 査定權.

(4) 軍隊構成員의 公務中人的損害에 對한 相互間의 請求權抛棄

(5) 一定額未滿의 損害額에 對한 請求權 抛棄

(6) 韓國政府以外 第三者에 加한 損害에 對한 請求權 ~~抛棄~~

(7) 請求權에 對한 賠償額 分担問題

(8) 非公務執行中에 發生한 損害에 對한 報償金 問題

(9) 美軍使用土地 및 施設內에 있는 强制執行對象物

(10) 公務執行中 發生한 損害인지 與否에 對한 決定權.

(11) 調達契約으로부터 發生한 紛爭 處理方法.

0066

5. 関稅問題

(1) 韓國稅関当局이 執行하는 法令에 対한 服從義務.

(2) 美軍이 搬入하는 物資의 免稅範囲 및 要件.

(3) 稅関検査免除範囲.

(4) 免稅로 輸入한 物資의 國内에서의 処分問題

(5) 特权濫用防止問題

6. 租稅其他 内國稅課徵問題

(1) 免稅対象 및 範囲.

7. 歲出外 資金機関

(1) 歲出外資金機関의 設置 및 免除問題

(2) 同機関의 販売物品에 対한 免稅 및 國内에서의 処分問題

8. 物資等 現地購買問題

(1) 購買方式에 関한 韓國法律의 適用問題

(2) 労務者 雇傭 및 解雇節次

0067

9. 美國人契約者.

(1) 美國人契約者에 對한 韓國法令의 適用問題
(2) 特權과 免除의 性質과 範圍.
(3) 關稅, 租稅 其他 內國稅로 부터의 免除範圍.
(4) 契約者에 對한 刑事裁判管轄權 問題

10. 外換管理.

(1) 韓國에서 取得한 外換의 外國으로의 移轉問題
(2) 特權濫用 防止問題.

11. 軍票.

(1) 美國이 認定한 者에 對한 一定地域內에서의 軍票使用許可.
(2) 非認可者가 使用하는 軍票의 回收問題
(3) 軍用銀行施設의 設置.

12. 軍事郵便

(1) 軍事郵便局의 設置 및 그 業務
(2) 特權濫用防止를 爲한 措置.

13. 戰時特例條項

(1) 敵對行為 發生時의 協定適用問題 協議.

14. 合同委員會 設置.

(1) 委員會의 機能.
(2) 委員會의 構成
(3) 委員會가 問題를 解決할수 없는 경우의 措置.

0068

15. 最終條項

(1) 協定의 發效.

(2) 協定의 終結.

(3) 協定의 改正

(4) 既存協定의 廢棄問題

0060

A COMPARATIVE TABLE OF AGREEMENTS CONCERNING STATUS OF FORCES

ITEM \ AGREEMENT	US-JAPAN 1952	UN-JAPAN 1954	US-JAPAN 1960	NATO 1951	US-ICELAND 1951	US-PHILIP. 1947	US-LIBYA 1954	US-ETHIOPIA. 1953,	ROK-UN 1955(Draft)	ROK-US 1952(Draft)
1. Definitions	1	1	1	1	1	-	24	24	1	1
2. Facilities and Areas	2,3,4	5	2,3,4	-	-	1,3,17,19,21,22, 23,26, Annex A&B	1,2,4,6 7,10,11	1,2,3,4 7,10	3	4,5,6,7, 8,9
3. Access by Vessels and Aircraft	5	4	5	-	-	4	3,8,9	-	-	10
4. Control of Navigations & Meteorological Services	6,8	-	6,8	-	-	-	-	-	-	11
5. Use of Public Utilities and Services	7	6	7	-	-	7	5	6	-	-
6. Entry and Exit	9	3	9	3	[illegible]	11	16	14	2	3
7. Driving Permits, Number Plate and Uniforms	10	7	10	4,5	3,4	-	21	15	11,12	22
8. Carrying of Arms	-	-	-	6	5	-	22	21	13	23
9. Customs Duties	11	13	11	11,12,13	8,9	5	25	18	8	14
10. Procurement of Materials, Services and Labour	12	14	12	9	6	-	13,23	16,22,23	6	17
11. Taxation	13	12	13	10	7	12	24	-	7	15
12. US Contractors	14	-	14	-	-	-	-	-	-	18
13. Non-appropriated Fund Organizations	15	9	15	-	-	18	17	13	9	16
14. Respect of Receiving State's Law & Criminal Jurisdiction	16,17	2,16	16,17	2,7	2	13,14,20	20,27	17	4,14	2,12
15. Civil Jurisdiction and Claims	18	18	18	8	12	23	19	19	5	13
16. Foreign Exchange Control	19	10	19	14	10	-	-	-	-	19
17. Currency	20	11	20	-	-	-	26	20	-	20
18. Military Post Office	21	8	21	-	-	16	15	12	10	21
19. Training in Reserve Organization	22	-	22	-	-	28	-	-	-	24
20. Mutual Cooperation	-	-	-	-	-	2	-	-	-	-
21. Security of Forces and Properties	23	17	23	-	-	15	-	-	-	-
22. Maneuvering Areas	-	-	-	-	-	6	-	11	-	-
23. Health and Sanitation	-	-	-	-	-	8	18	5	-	-
24. Surveys	-	-	-	-	-	9	14	8,9	-	-
25. Cemetries, Historical Sites, and Mineral Resources	-	-	-	-	-	10,24	-	-	-	-

0070

3. Access by Vessels and [redacted]craft	5	4	5	-	-	4	3,8,9	-	-	10
4. Control of Navigations & Meteorological Services	6,8	-	6,8	-	-	-	-	-	-	11
5. Use of Public Utilities and Services	7	6	7	-	-	7	5	6	-	-
6. Entry and Exit	9	3	9	3	-	11	15	14	2	3
7. Driving Permits, Number Plate and Uniforms	10	7	10	4,5	3,4	-	21	13	11,12	22
8. Carrying of Arms	-	-	-	6	5	-	22	21	13	23
9. Customs Duties	11	13	11	11,12,13	8,9	5	25	18	8	14
10. Procurement of Materials, Services and Labour	12	14	12	9	6	-	13,23	16,22,23	6	17
11. Taxation	13	12	13	10	7	12	24	-	7	15
12. US Contractors	14	-	14	-	-	-	-	-	-	18
13. Non-appropriated Fund Organizations	15	9	15	-	-	18	17	13	9	16
14. Respect of Receiving State's Law & Criminal Jurisdiction	16,17	2,16	16,17	2,7	2	13,14,20	20,27	17	4,14	2,12
15. Civil Jurisdiction and Claims	18	18	18	8	12	23	19	19	5	13
16. Foreign Exchange Control	19	10	19	14	10	-	-	-	-	19
17. Currency	20	11	20	-	-	-	26	20	-	20
18. Military Post Office	21	8	21	-	-	16	15	12	10	21
19. Training in Reserve Organization	22	-	22	-	-	28	-	-	-	24
20. Mutual Cooperation	-	-	-	-	-	2	-	-	-	-
21. Security of Forces and Properties	23	17	23	-	-	15	-	-	-	-
22. Maneuvering Areas	-	-	-	-	-	6	-	11	-	-
23. Health and Sanitation	-	-	-	-	-	8	18	5	-	-
24. Surveys	-	-	-	-	-	9	14	8,9	-	-
25. Cemetries, Historical Sites, and Mineral Resources	-	-	-	-	-	10,24	-	-	-	-
26. Voluntary Enrollment	-	-	-	-	-	27	-	-	-	-
27. Expenditures and Accounting	25	15	24	-	-	-	-	-	-	-
28. Consultation for Joint Defense	24	-	-	-	-	-	-	-	-	-
29. Adjustment in the Event of Hostilities	-	-	-	15	-	-	-	-	15	25
30. Joint Committee and Settlement Disputes	26	20	25	16	-	-	29	-	16	26
31. Privileges for NATO Forces	-	-	-	11	11	-	-	-	-	-
32. Other Obligations	-	-	-	-	-	-	32	-	-	-
33. Final Clauses	27,28,29	19,21,22, 23,24,25	26,27,28	17,18, 19,20	-	29	30	25	17,18,19	27,28,29

0070

0071

STATUS OF FORCES NEGOTIATIONS

September 20, 1962

AGENDA FOR FIRST MEETING

1. Opening Remarks

Foreign Minister Choi

Ambassador Berger

2. Introduction of Negotiators

Foreign Minister will introduce Korean negotiators.

American Ambassador will introduce U.S. negotiators.

(* Hereafter, the Minister and the Ambassador will leave the meeting room and the meeting will enter closed session)

3. Discussion on Procedural Matters

a. Language and the use of interpreters

b. Records (Joint summary record, designation of rapporteurs) Agreed minutes

c. Frequency of meeting

d. Press relations

e. Other business

4. Agenda for Next Meeting

5. Date of Next Meeting

0072

13-16

Strictly not to be
released before 3 p.m.
on Sept. 20, 1962

OPENING SESSION, SOFA NEGOTIATIONS

REMARKS BY AMBASSADOR BERGER

Mr. Minister, Friends and Colleagues -

1. As we begin negotiations today it is important that we have a clear view of our common objective. That objective is to strengthen further the already close ties existing between Korea and the United States. Our joint task is to conclude an agreement which will contribute to this objective in a manner satisfactory to both sides. The United States Government is entering these negotiations with the earnest intent to conclude an agreement which will meet this objective.

2. My country is aware of the great interest of the Korean people in these negotiations. There is the same intense interest, I can assure you, among the people of the United States and my government.

3. A Status of Forces Agreement covers many kinds of activities. It encompasses extensive, complex and varied administrative arrangements. The areas to be discussed include postal facilities, port and airplane facilities, servicing of ships and aircraft, customs regulations, tax regulations, the use of facilities for the defense of Korea, and matters of jurisdiction over personnel. These are intricate and complicated matters. They posed complex problems between the United States and other countries. Complicated problems are a challenge to the skills of the negotiators, but they are not necessarily barriers to agreement. The wide

0073

range of questions which will arise and will need to be resolved in the course of these negotiations will provide the fabric to fashion a mutually satisfactory agreement.

4. Difficult and complex though the problems may be, we expect to draw up a Status of Forces Agreement which will further those amicable associations between the United States and Korea that have historically provided the power and the will to resist threats to freedom. This task calls for unity of purpose, mutual respect and a real effort to understand each other's problem. On this our common security depends. It is in this spirit and with this purpose, that the United States enters these negotiations for a Status of Forces Agreement with the Republic of Korea.

0074

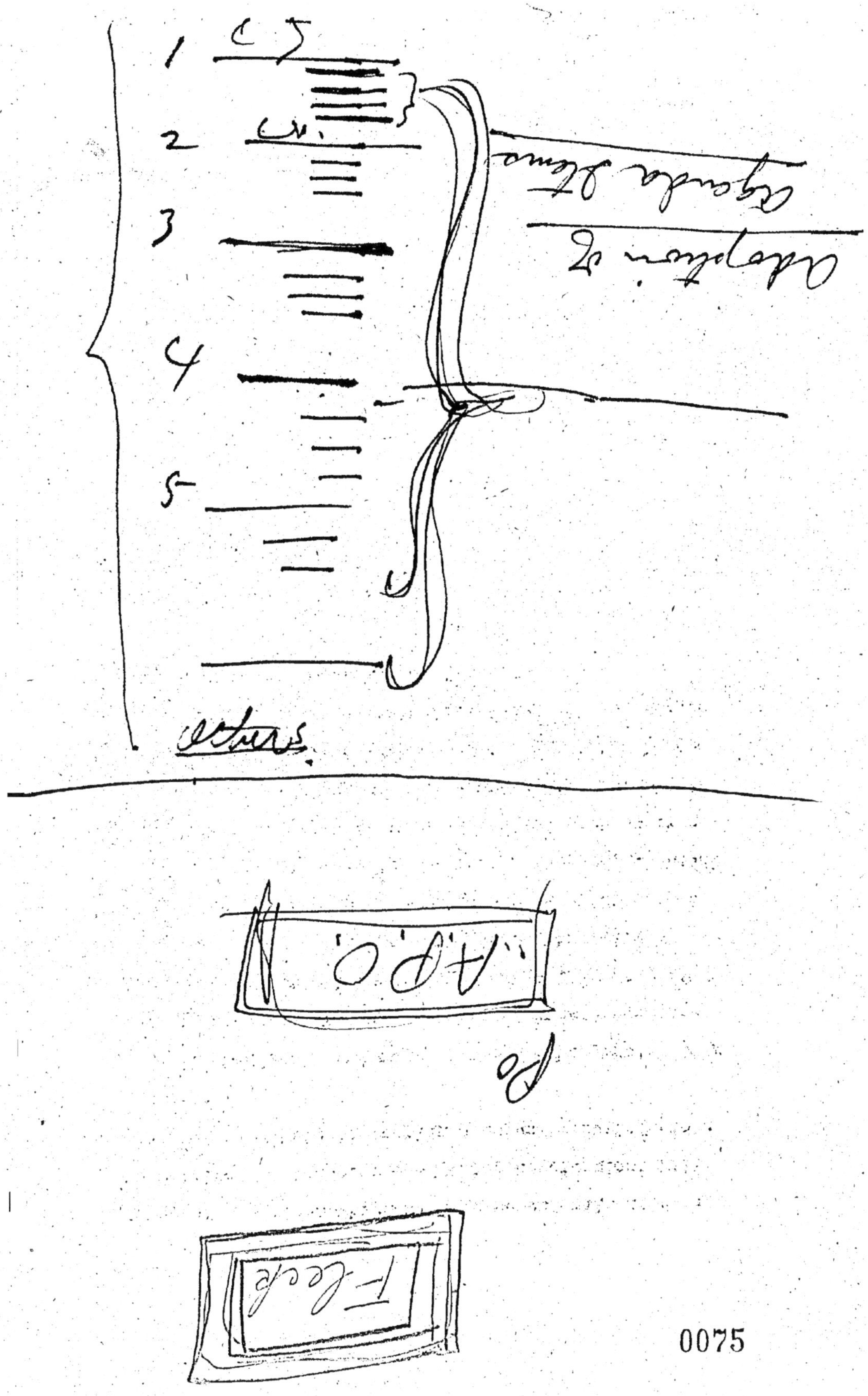

0075

한미 주둔군 지위협정 교섭회의

제 1 차 회의 한미 공동성명

오늘 회의에서 대한민국측을 대표한 외무부 최덕신 장관과 미국측을 대표한 사무엘 디 버거대사는 한미간 주둔군 지위협정에 관한 교섭회의의 재개를 환영하였다.

양측의 식사에 이어 외무부장관과 버거대사는 한국측과 미국측의 실무자들을 소개하였다.

최초회의에서는 교섭회의 절차사항과 여러가지 기타 예비적인 행정사항을 토의하였다. 금번 토의에서는 차후 교섭의 신속한 진행을위한 기초를 닦아놓았다. 이번회의에서는 교섭의 진전상황을 일반국민에게 주지시키기 위하여 수시로 공동발표를 하는데 양측이 합의하였다.

다음 회의는 9월 28 일에 개최하기로 합의하였다.

~~0075~~

0076

13-15

(부록3)

NEGOTIATION OF STATUS OF FORCES AGREEMENT RESUMED

At today's meeting the Minister of Foreign Affairs, Choi Duk Shin, speaking for the Republic of Korea, and Ambassador Samuel D. Berger, speaking for the United States, welcomed the resumption of negotiations for Korea and the United States of America. Following these opенning remarks, the Foreign Minister and Ambassador Berger introduced the members of the Korean and American negotiating teams.

The initial discussions dealt with the procedures to be followed and various other preliminary administrative matter. These discussion laid the groundwork for the expeditiuus conduct of subsequeut negotiations. It was agreed that joint press statements would be issued from time of time in crder to keep the public informed of the progress of negotiations.

By common agreement, the next meeting was scheduled for Sept. 28.

0077

13-13

담 당	과 장	국 장	차 관	장 관	9월 24일	조약과

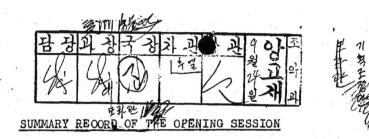

SUMMARY RECORD OF THE OPENING SESSION

September 20, 1962

1. Time and Place: 3:00 to 4:40 p.m. on September 20, 1962 at Converence Room of the Ministry of Foreign Affairs

2. Present:

ROK Side:

H.E. Choi, Duk-Shin	Minister of Foreign Affairs
Mr. Chin, Pil Shik	Director Bureau of Political Affairs Ministry of Foreign Affairs
Mr. Shin, Kwan Sup	Director Bureau of Customs Ministry of Finance
Mr. Lee, Kyung Ho	Director Bureau of Legal Affairs Ministry of Justice
Mr. Pak, Kun	Chief, America Section Ministry of Foreign Affairs
Col. Lee, Nam Koo	Chief, Military Affairs Section Ministry of National Defense
Mr. Chi, Sung Koo (Press Officer)	Press Officer Ministry of Foreign Affairs
Mr. Shin, Chung Sup (Rapporteur)	2nd Secretary Ministry of Foreign Affairs
Mr. Lee, Chang Bum	3rd Secretary Ministry of Foreign Affairs
Mr. Kang, Suk Ja (Interpreter)	3rd Secretary Ministry of Foreign Affairs

0078

1-2

미분 88-14

0079

US Side:

H.E. Samuel D. Berger	Ambassador of the United States
Mr. Philip C. Habib	Counselor of the Embassy for Political Affairs
Brig. Gen. J.D. Lawlor	Deputy Chief of Staff 8th Army
Col. G.G. O'Connor	Deputy Chief of Staff 8th Army
Col. W.A. Solf	Staff Judge Advocate 8th Army
Capt. R.M. Bownlie	Assistant Chief of Staff USN/K
Mr. William J. Ford	First Secretary of the Embassy
Mr. Benjamin A. Fleck (Rapporteur and Press Officer)	First Secretary of the Embassy
Lt. Col. R.E. Miller	Staff Officer, JAG 8th Army
Lt. Col. G.T. Suderman	Staff Officer, J-5 USAF/K
Mr. Robert A. Lewis	Second Secretary and Consul of the Embassy

3. Opening Addresses:

Foreign Minister Choi and Ambassador Berger addressed the opening session. (See Annex No. 1 & 2)

4. Introduction:

Minister Choi introduced the negotiators of the ROK side; Ambassador Berger introduced the U.S. negotiators; and then they withdrew from the conference site. 0080

1-3

미번 88-14

0081

5. Gist of Talks:

a. Exchange of Greetings

The chief delegate of the Korean side, Mr. Chin, extended heartfelt greetings to the American delegation and expressed the hope that the negotiations would soon lead to the successful conclusion of an agreement which would contribute to the promotion of friendly ties between the two countries. On behalf of the American delegation, Mr. Habib thanked Mr. Chin and concurred in the latter's hope for a successful conclusion of an agreement.

b. Official Languages and Use of Interpreters

It was agreed that both Korean and English would be used as official languages and that each side would provide its own interpreter.

c. Records

Mr. Habib suggested that no verbatim records of the negotiating sessions be kept. He suggested that a rapporteur be appointed by each side and that the two rapporteurs in consultation with each other prepare a summary record of each meeting. He further proposed that whenever agreement was reached on a substantive question an agreed minute be made and referred to the following meeting for confirmation. Mr. Chin agreed in principle to these proposals. He then designated Mr. Shin Chung Sup as rapporteur for the Korean side and Mr. Habib designated Mr. Fleck for the American side.

d. Frequency of Meetings

Both sides stated their desire to schedule meetings as frequently as possible. Mr. Chin proposed that it be agreed in principle to have meetings at least once every week. Mr. Habib objected to the establishment of any fixed interval between meetings and suggested that at each meeting the date

0082

14

미분 88-14

0083

of the subsequent meeting be fixed. Mr. Chin responded with a suggestion that from time to time either side might wish to call a meeting, for instance, for the purpose of explaining its views on a specific subject. He suggested agreement that either side might call a meeting at any time on its initiative. Mr. Habib replied that the US side would willingly consider any such proposal but could not agree in principle that either side could call meeting without the agreement of the other side.

Points of Agreement:

1) Meetings will be held as frequently as possible.
2) At each meeting the date of the subsequent meeting will be fixed.
3) No fixed interval between meetings will be established.
4) When one side wishes to call a meeting, the other side will willingly consider the request.

e. Press Relations

Mr. Habib proposed that statements to the press be prepared jointly and issued from time to time in order to keep the public informed. He pointed out the undesirability of individual members of either delegation discussing negotiations with the press. He proposed that one member of each delegation be designated as press officer to draft such joint statements as the negotiators might wish to issue. Mr. Chin agreed to these proposals but pointed out that the reporters will be waiting for news at the end of each session. He proposed, therefore, that a statement be issued to the press at the end of each meeting. Mr. Habib replied that the US side did not believe it desirable to create on the part of the press

0084

1-5

미문 88-14

0085

and the public a sense of urgent expectation of hot headlines. Inasmuch as some meetings may be purely explanatory in nature there would not necessarily be anything to report to the press. Therefore, the American side did not believe it desirable to issue a statement following every meeting. A policy of flexibility was desirable since there might be at some point occasion to issue a statement without even holding a meeting. The negotiators should lead the press and should not let the press lead them. Mr. Chin replied that if no statement were issued the press would indulge in undesirable speculation. Mr.Habib then agreed to the issuance of a statement after each meeting, for the time being, but reserved the right to reopen this question at a later date. Mr. Chi and Mr. Fleck were appointed press officers for their respective delegations.

Points of Agreement:

1) Both sides agreed on the undesirability of individual negotiators discussing the negotiations with the press.
2) For the time being a statement prepared by the two press officers will be issued after each meeting. The US side reserves the right to reopen this question at a later date.

f. Other Items

Mr. Habib proposed that each side be free to introduce additional experts on specific matters as required, with the names and fields of expertise to be notified to the other side in advance. Mr. Chin agreed.

Mr. Chin announced that Mr. Cho Shin Yong and Mr. Lee Kyung Hoon, members of the Korean delegation, were absent from the country on official business but would join the delegation upon their return.

0086

1-6

비문 88-14

0087

g. Agenda for Next Meeting

Mr. Habib proposed that the agenda for the next meeting consist of a general review of the scope and content of a status of forces agreement, with the understanding that such a review would not be definitive. Subject matter could be discussed under general headings and specific sub-titles, but additional matters could be raised at subsequent meetings. Mr. Chin agreed. Mr. Habib then stated that he would like to make one point clear. He pointed out that the present negotiations are concerned solely with an agreement between Korea and the United States and that the negotiators afe not bound by the provisions of other status of forces agreements, although either side may introduce whatever material it believes relevant. Mr. Chin stated that it should be the purpose and intent of the negotiators to work out the best possible SOFA, which would be comprehensive and all-inclusive.

h. Date of Next Meeting

It was agreed to hold the next meeting on September 28 at 2:00 p.m.

i. Joint Press Release

The joint press release prepared by Mr. Chi and Mr. Fleck was read by Mr. Chi and was approved by the negotiators.

보통문서로 재분류(1966.12.31)

1966.12.31 에 예고문에 의거 일반문서로 재분류됨

0088

1-7

비분 88-14

0080

of the subsequent meeting be fixed. Mr. Chin responded with a suggestion that from time to time either side might wish to call a meeting, for instance, for the purpose of explaining its views on a specific subject. He suggested agreement that either side might call a meeting at any time on its initiative. Mr. Habib replied that the US side would willingly consider any such proposal but could not agree in principle that either side could call meeting without the agreement of the other side.

Points of Agreement:

1) Meetings will be held as frequently as possible.
2) At each meeting the date of the subsequent meeting will be fixed.
3) No fixed interval between meetings will be established.
4) When one side wishes to call a meeting, the other side will willingly consider the request.

e. Press Relations

Mr. Habib proposed that statements to the press prepared jointly and issued from time to time in order to keep the public informed. He pointed out the undesirability of individual members of either delegation discussing negotiations with the press. He proposed that one member of each delegation be designated as press officer to draft such joint statements as the negotiators might wish to issue.
Mr. Chin agreed to these proposals but pointed out that the reporters will be waiting for news at the end of each session. He proposed, therefore, that a statement be issued to the press at the end of each meeting. Mr. Habib replied that the US side did not believe it desirable to create on the part of the press and the public a sense of urgent expectation of hot headlines. Inasmuch as some meetings may be purely

0030

174

0091

...meeting be fixed. ... in accordance with

...rom time to time to ... consider with the

, for instance, for the purpose of ...

...cific subject. It was agreed that

...call a meeting at any time on its initiative

...that the other side would willingly consider

...but would not force an impasse in that either

...meeting without the agreement of the other sid

[illegible]:

...ings will be held ... as possible.

...week ... the date of the ... meeting

...be fixed.

...ings internal ... meetings will be

...blished.

...one side wishes to call a meeting, the

...other side will willingly consider the request.

...ity:

...that ... statements to the press

... and ... in order to

...informed. He pointed out the ... ility

...there ... selection ... necessity ...

...ease. He proposed that the number of ...

...anced ... the ... to ... joint

...the ... might wish to issue.

...others ... that the

... for ... at the end of each ...

...before, ... to the

...of each ... the

... in the ... of

... of

[illegible]

(부록 III)

NEGOTIATION OF STATUS OF FORCES AGREEMENT RESUMED

At today's meeting the Minister of Foreign Affairs, Choi Duk Shin, speaking for the Republic of Korea, and Ambassador Samuel D. Berger, speaking for the United States, welcomed the resumption of negotiations for Korea and the United States of America. Following these openning remarks, the Foreign Minister and Ambassador Berger introduced the members of the Korean and American negotiating teams.

The initial discussions dealt with the procedures to be followed and various other preliminary administrative matter. These discussion laid the groundwork for the expeditious conduct of subsequeut negotiations. It was agreed that joint press statements would be issued from time of time in order to keep the public informed of the progress of negotiations.

By common ggreement, the next meeting was scheduled for Sept. 28.

0092

1-16

사 진

0093

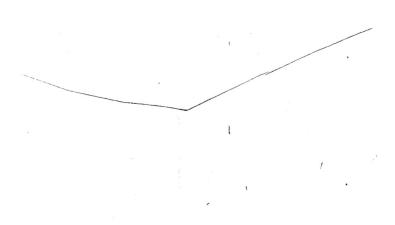

009

0095

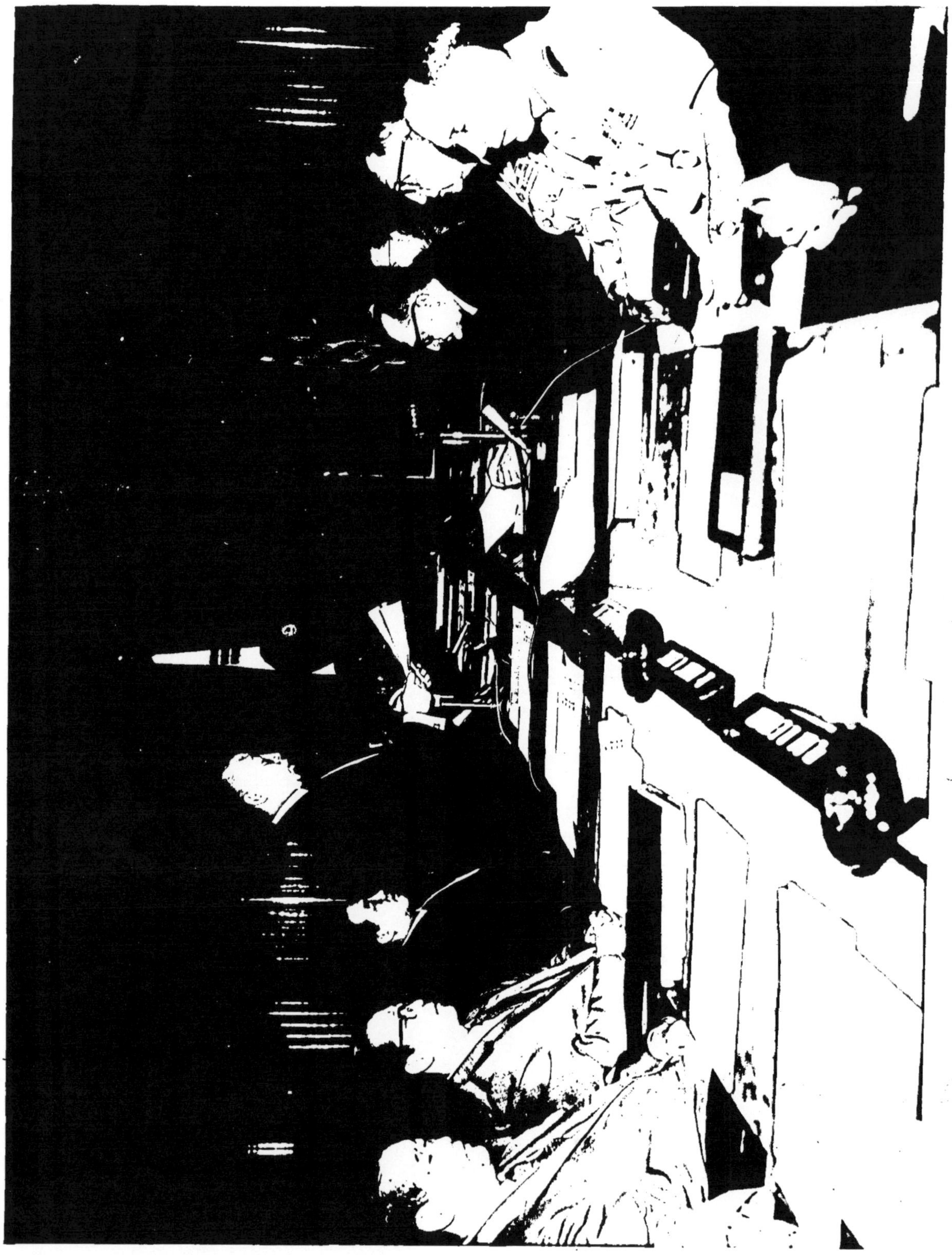

0097

0097

0098

외무부 문서보존실

외 무 부

년 월 일

내무부:

12조, 16조, 20조(담배 암매),

22조(운전 면허), 23조, 2조.

조 약 과 장

외 무 부

년 월 일

재무부:

14조, 15조, 16조, 18조, 19조,

20조, 21조 2항, 26조, 유틸리티

문제.

조 약 과 장

0099

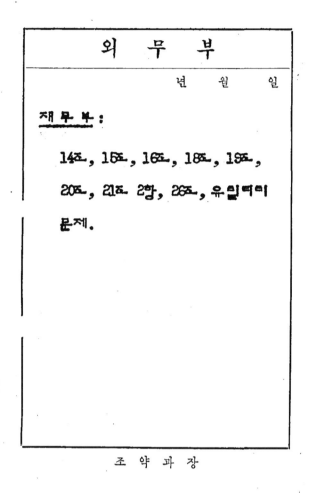

외 무 부

년 월 일

법무부:

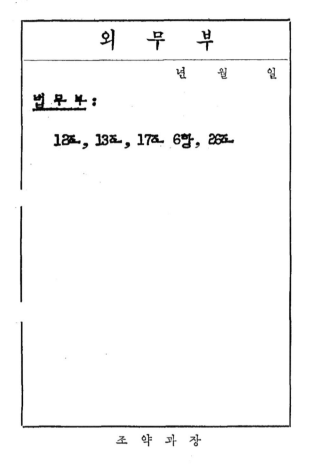

12조, 13조, 17조 6항, 26조

조 약 과 장

외 무 부

년 월 일

국방부:

4조, 5조, 6조, 7조, 8조, 9조,

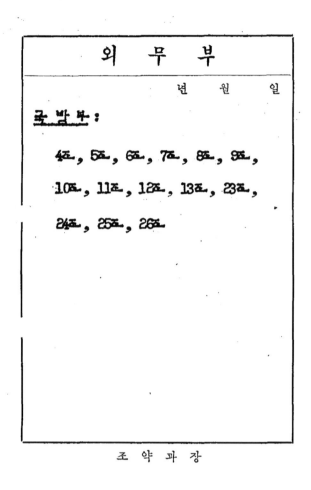

10조, 11조, 12조, 13조, 23조,

24조, 25조, 26조

조 약 과 장

0100

외 무 부

년 월 일

건설부

~~부흥부~~:

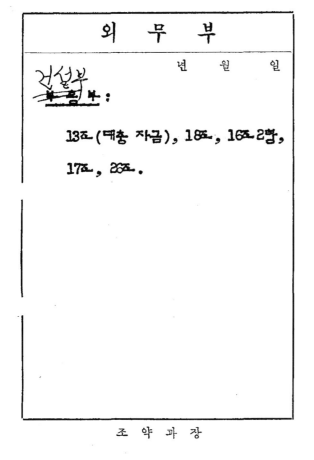

13조(대충 자금), 18조, 16조 2항,

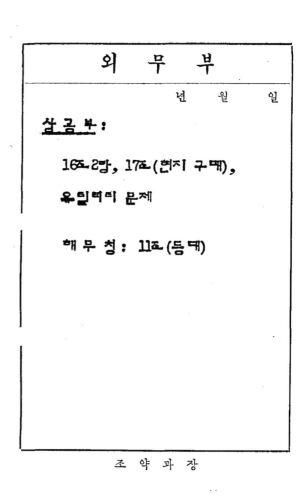

17조, 26조.

조 약 과 장

외 무 부

년 월 일

상공부:

16조 2항, 17조(현지 구매),

유틸리티 문제

해무청: 11조(등대)

조 약 과 장

0101

외 무 부

년 월 일

보건 사회부 :

17조.

조 약 과 장

외 무 부

년 월 일

교 통 부 :

10조, 11조 1 및 2항, 22조(운전).

조 약 과 장

0102

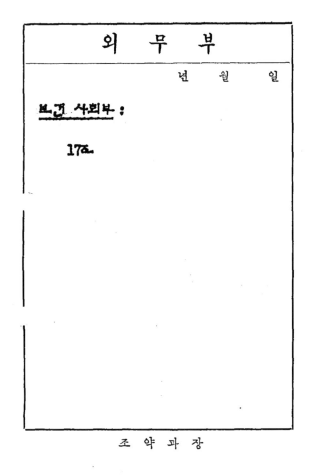

외 무 부

년 월 일

여권과장:

3조, 18조 (계약자 출입)

조 약 과 장

0103

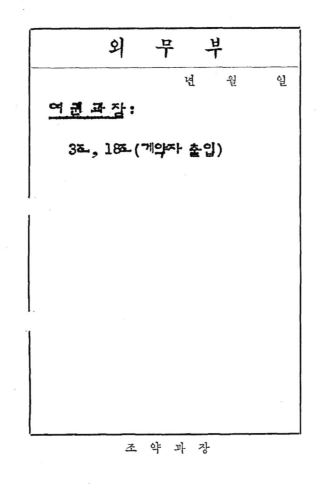

기 안 용 지

0102

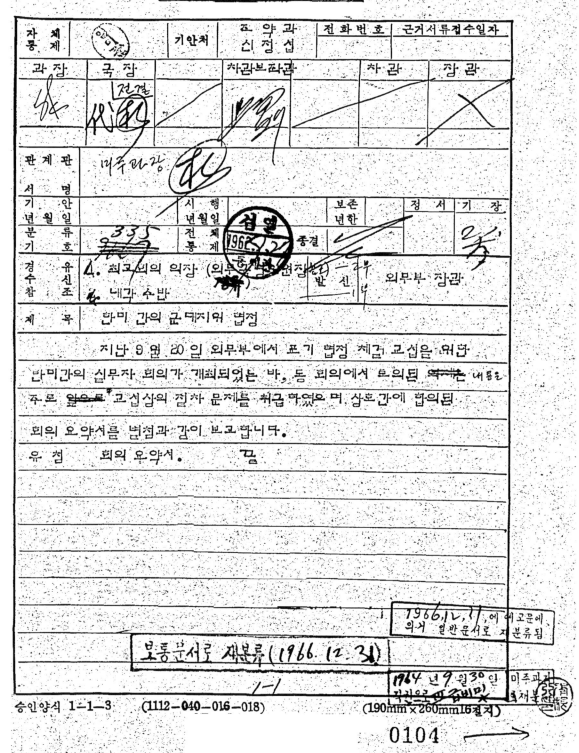

자체 통제		기안처	조약과 신정섭	전화번호	근거서류접수일자

과장	국장		차관보좌관	차관	장관
	전결				

관계관 서명	미주과장

기안 년월일		시행 년월일		보존 년한		정서	기장
분류 기호	335	전체 통제	1966.12.27	종결			

경수참 유신조	1. 최고회의 의장 (외무국방위원장) 2. 내각 수반	발신	외무부 장관

제목	한미 간의 군대지위 협정

지난 9월 20일 외무부에서 표기 협정 체결 교섭을 위한 한미간의 실무자 회의가 개최되었는 바, 동 회의에서 토의된 ~~약~~내용은 주로 ~~앞으로~~ 교섭상의 절차 문제를 취급하였으며 상호간에 합의된 회의 요약서를 별첨과 같이 보고합니다.

유첨 회의 요약서. 끝

1966.12.31.에 예고문에 의거 일반문서로 재분류됨

보통문서로 재분류(1966. 12. 31)

1-1

1964년 9월 30일 미주과 ... 재분류

승인양식 1-1-3 (1112-040-016-018) (190mm×260mm16절지)

0104

0105

주둔군 지위협정교섭 제1차회의 요약기록

1962. 9. 20.

1. 시일 및 장소 : 1962. 9. 20. 하오 3시부터 4시 40분까지

   외무부 회의실

2. 참석자 :

   한국측

최 덕 신	외무부장관
진 필 식	외무부 정무국장
신 관섭	재무부 세관국장
이 경 호	법무부 법무국장
박 근	외무부 미주과장
이 남 구 대령	국방부 군무과장
지 성 구 (공보관)	외무부 공보관
신 정 섭 (기록자)	외무부 2등서기관
이 창 범	외무부 3등서기관
강 석 재 (통역)	외무부 3등서기관

   미국측 :

사뮤엘 디. 버-거	주한미국대사
필립 시. 하비브	주한미대사관 참사관
제이. 디. 로텍 준장	주한미8군 참모차장
윌리암 제이. 호드	주한미대사관 1등서기관
지.지. 오코나대령	주한미8군 참모차장
알.엠. 부룬티대령	주한미해군참모부장
다불.에이. 솔프대령	주한미8군법무참모

0106

벤자민 에이. 후텔	주한미대사관 1등서기관
로버트. 에이. 루이스	주한미대사관 2등서기관겸 영사
지. 티. 소머멘중령	주한미군 미사참모
알. 이. 밀러중령	주한미8군 법무장교

3. 개회식사:

최 외무장관 및 버-거 주한미대사는 개회식사를 행하였다.

4. 소 개:

최 외무장관은 한국측 교섭자들을 소개하였고 버-거 주한미국 대사는 미국측 교섭자를 소개한후 회의장에서 퇴장하였다.

5. 회담 요지:

가. <u>인사교환</u>

한국측 수석대표 "진" 씨는 미국대표단에 진심으로의 인사를 표하였으며 교섭이 양국간의 우호적 유대를 증진하는데 기여하게될 협정의 성공적인 체결에 조속히 도달하게되기를 원한다는 희망을 표명하였다. 미국대표단을 대신하여 "하비브" 씨는 "진"씨에 감사를 표하였으며 협정의 성공적인 체결을위한 후자의 희망에 동의하였다.

나. <u>공식언어 및 통역관 이용</u>

공식언어로서 한국어 및 영어를 모두 사용하며 또한 각측이 자신의 통역관을 제공하도록 합의하였다.

다. <u>기 록</u>

"하비브" 씨는 교섭회의 축어기록은 작성하지 말자고 제의하였다. 그는 1명의 기록자를 각측이 임명하여 2명의 기록자가 상호 협의하여 매회의의 요약 기록서를 작성할것을 제의하였다. 그는 또 언제든지 실질적 문제에 관하여

0107

합의가 이루어지면 합의의사록을 작성하여 차기회의에서 확인을 받도록 할것을 제의하였다. "진"씨는 이들제의에 대하여 원측적으로 동의하였다. 그는 한국측 기록자로서 "신정섭"씨를 지명하였고 "하비브"씨는 미국측을 위하여 "후텔" 씨를 지명하였다.

다. 회의 빈도

양측은 가능한 한 회의를 자주 가지도록 하자는 희망을 진술하였다. "진"씨는 최소 매주 1회식 회의를 가지는 것을 원측으로 하는데 동의할것을 제의하였다. "하비브" 씨는 회의간에 어떠한 고정된 간격을두는것에 반대하였으며 매회의시에 다 음 회의의 일자를 정할것을 제의하였다. "진"씨는 때때로 어느측에서 예를들면 특정문제에 관한 그의 견해를 설명할 목적으로 회의를 소집하고자 원할지 모른다고 제의함으로서 대답하였다. 그는 어느측이나 자진하여 언제든지 회의를 소집할수 있음에 합의토록 제의하였다. "하비브"씨는 미국측은 그러한 제안을 기꺼히 고려할것이나 어느측이먼지 타방의 합의없이 회의를 소집할수 있다는 원측에 동의할수 없다고 응답하였다.

합의사항

1) 회의는 가능한 한 자주 개최할것임.
2) 매회의시에차기회의 일자를 결정할것임.
3) 회의간에 고정된 간격을 두지않을것임.
4) 어느 한쪽이 회의소집을 원할 경우에 타방은 그요청을 기꺼히 고려할것임.

마. 보도관계

"하비브"씨는 신문 발표문을 대중에 알리기 위하여 공동으로 작성하고 수시로 발표할것을 제안하였다. 그는 대표단의 각 대표들이 교섭내용을 기자들과 토의하지 말것을 지적 하였다. 그는 교섭자들이 발표하기를 원하는 그러한 공동 발표문을 작성하도록 각대표단에서 1명의 대표를 공보관으로 임명할것을 제안하였다. "진"씨는 이들 제안에 동의 하였으나 기자들은 매회의 말에 "뉴스"를 위하여 대기하고 있을것이라고 지적하였다. 그는 따라서 매회의가 끝나면 발표문을 기자에 발표토록 제안하였다. "하비브" 씨는 미국측은 신문이나 대중들에게 자극적인 표제를 성급히 기대하는 감을 일으키는 것은 바람직스러운 일이 아니라고 믿는다고 응답하였다. 어떠한 회의든 성질상 순수히 설명적인 것인만큼 신문에 발표할것이 반드시 있는 것이 아니다. 따라서 미국측은 매회의후에 발표문을 발표 할것이 요망되는것이 아니라고 믿는다. 어떤점에 관해서는 회의를 개최함이 없이 발표문을 발표할 경우가있을것임으로 융통성있는 정책이 요망된다. 교섭자들이 신문을 인도 해야하며 신문으로 하여금 이끌려서는 아니된다. "진"씨는 만약 아무런 발표문을 발하지 않는다면 신문은 공연한 억측을 하게될것이라고 응답하였다. 그러자 "하비브"씨는 당분간 매회의후에 발표문을 발표할것에 동의하였으나 후일 이문제를 제기할 권한을 보류하였다. "지"씨와 "후렌" 씨는 각기 대표단을 위한 공보관으로 임명되었다.

합의사항

1) 양측은 개개 교섭자가 교섭내용을 기자들과 토의하는 것은 요망스러운 일이 아니라는데 합의하였다.

2) 당분간 2명의 공보관이 작성한 발표문을 매회의이후에 발표할것이다. 미국측은 후일 이문제를 제기할권한을 보류한다.

0109

바. 기타 사항

"하비브"씨는 각축은 사건에 타방에 이름과 전문분야를 통보하여 특수문제에 관한 필요한 추가적인 전문가들을 회의에 참석케할수 있을것을 제안하였다. "진"씨는 이에 동의하였다. "진"씨는 한국대표단원인 "로신영" 씨 및 "이경훈"씨는 공무로 해외출장 중이며 귀국하면 대표단에 참가할것이라고 발표하였다.

사. 차기회의 의제

"하비브" 씨는 차기회의의 의제는 그러한 검토가 확정적이 아니라는 양해하에 주둔군 지위협정의 범위와 내용에대한 일반적인 검토로 할것을 제안하였다. 제목사항은 일반적인 표제나 특수한 부제하에서 토의될수 있으며 추가적인 사항은 다음회의에서 제기될수 있다. "진"씨는 동의하였다.
다음 "하비브"씨는 한가지점을 명백히 해두고저 한다고 말하였다. 그는 현재의 교섭은 순전히 한미간의 협정에 관계한것이며 교섭자들은 비록 어느측이나 관계된다고 생각하는 문제는 무엇이든지 제기할수 있으나 다른 주둔군 지위협정 조항에 의하여 구애받지 아니한다는 점을 지적하였다.
"진"씨는 포괄적이며 모든것을 포함하는 가능한 최선의 주둔군지위 협정을 만드는일이 교섭자들의 목적이며 의도이어야 한다고 말하였다.

아. 차기회의 일자

차기회의는 9월 28일 하오 2시에 개최하도록 합의되었다.

자. 공동신문 발표

"지"씨 및 "후텔" 씨가 작성한 공동신문 발표문이 "진" 씨에 의하여 낭독되었으며 교섭자들에 의하여 승인되었다.

1966, 12, 31,에 예고문에 의거 일반문서로 재분류됨

0110

SUMMARY RECORD OF THE OPENING SESSION
STATUS FORCES NEGOTIATIONS

21/25

September 20, 1962

美北課

1. Time and Place: 3:00 to 4:40 p.m. on September 20, 1962 at Conference Room of the Ministry of Foreign Affairs

2. Present:

ROK Side:

H.E. Choi, Duk-Shin	Minister of Foreign Affairs
Mr. Chin, Pil Shik	Director Bureau of Political Affairs Ministry of Foreign Affairs
Mr. Shin, Kwan Sup	Director Bureau of Customs Ministry of Finance
Mr. Yi, Kyung Ho	Director Bureau of Legal Affairs Ministry of Justice
Mr. Pak, Kun	Chief, America Section Ministry of Foreign Affairs
Col. Lee, Nam Koo	Chief, Military Affairs Section Ministry of National Defense
Mr. Chi, Sung Koo (Press Officer)	Press Officer Ministry of Foreign Affairs
Mr. Shin, Chung Sup (Rapporteur)	2nd Secretary Ministry of Foreign Affairs
Mr. Lee, Chang Bum	3rd Secretary Ministry of Foreign Affairs
Mr. Kang, Suk Jae (Interpreter)	3rd Secretary Ministry of Foreign Affairs

0111

2-22

. US Side:

H.E. Samuel D. Berger	Ambassador of the United States
Mr. Philip C. Habib	Counselor of the Embassy for Political Affairs
Brig. Gen. J.D. Lawlor	Deputy Chief of Staff 8th Army
Mr. William J. Ford	First Secretary of the Embassy
Col. G.G. O'Connor	Deputy Chief of Staff 8th Army
Capt. R.M. Brownlie	Assistant Chief of Staff USN/K
Col. W.A. Solf	Staff Judge Advocate 8th Army
Mr. Benjamin A. Fleck (Rapporteur and Press Officer)	First Secretary of the Embassy
Mr. Robert A. Lewis	Second Secretary and Consul of the Embassy
Lt. Col. G.T. Suderman	Staff Officer, J-5 USAF/K
Lt. Col. R.E. Miller	Staff Officer, JAG 8th Army

3. Opening Addresses:

Foreign Minister Choi and Ambassador Berger addressed the opening session.

4. Introduction:

Minister Choi introduced the negotiators of the ROK side; Ambassador Berger introduced the

0112

2-23

U.S. negotiators; and then they withdrew from the conference site.

5. Gist of Talks:

a. Exchange of Greetings

The Chief delegate of the Korean side, Mr. Chin, extended heartfelt greetings to the American delegation and expressed the hope that the negotiations would soon lead to the successful conclusion of an agreement which would contribute to the promotion of friendly ties between the two countries. On behalf of the American delegation, Mr. Habib thanked Mr. Chin and concurred in the latter's hope for a successful conclusion of an agreement.

b. Official Languages and Use of Interpreters

It was agreed that both Korean and English would be used as official languages and that each side would provide its own interpreter.

c. Records

Mr. Habib suggested that no verbatim records of the negotiating sessions be kept. He suggested that a rapporteur be appointed by each side and that the two rapporteurs in consultation with each other prepare a summary record of each meeting. He further proposed that whenever agreement was reached on a substantive question that an agreed minute be made and referred to the following meeting for confirmation. Mr. Chin agreed in principle to these proposals. He then designated Mr. Shin Chung Sup as rapporteur for the Korean side and Mr. Habib designated Mr. Fleck for the American side.

0113

2-24

d. Frequency of Meetings

Both sides stated their desire to schedule meetings as frequently as possible. Mr. Chin proposed it be agreed in principle to have meetings at least once every week. Mr. Habib objected to the establishment of any fixed interval between meetings and suggested that at each meeting the date of the subsequent meeting be fixed. Mr. Chin responded with a suggestion that from time to time either side might wish to call a meeting, for instance, for the purpose of explaining its views on a specific subject. He suggested agreement that either side might call a meeting at any time on its initiative. Mr. Habib replied that the US side would willingly consider any such proposal but could not agree in principle that either side could call meeting without the agreement of the other side.

Points of Agreement:

1) Meetings will be held as frequently as possible.
2) At each meeting the date of the subsequent meeting will be fixed.
3) No fixed interval between meeting will be established.
4) When one side wishes to call a meeting, the other side will willingly consider the request.

e. Press Relations

Mr. Habib proposed that statements to the press prepared jointly and issued from time to time in order to keep the public informed. He pointed out the undesirability of individual members of either delegation discussing negotiations with the press. He proposed that one member ~~of each delegation~~ be designated as

0114

2-25

press officer to draft such joint statements as the negotiators might wish to issue.

Mr. Chin agreed to these proposals but pointed out that the reporters will be waiting for news at the end of each session. He proposed, therefore, that a statement be issued to the press at the end of each meeting. Mr. Habib replied that the US side did not believe it desirable to create on the part of the press and the public a sense of urgent expectation of hot headlines. Inasmuch as some meetings may be purely explanatory in nature there would not necessarily be anything to report to the press. Therefore, the American side did not believe it desirable to issue a statement following every meeting. A policy of flexibility was desirable since there might be at some point occasion to issue a statement without even holding a meeting. The negotiators should lead the press and should not let the press lead them. Mr. Chin replied that if no statement were issued the press would indulge in undesirable speculation. Mr. Habib then agreed to the issuance of a statement after each meeting, for the time being, but reserved the right to reopen this question at a later date. Mr. Chi and Mr. Fleck were appointed press officers for their respective delegations.

<u>Points of Agreement</u>:

1) Both sides agreed on the undesirability of individual negotiators discussing the negotiations with the press.

2) For the time being a statement prepared by the two ~~press officers~~ be issued after

each meeting. The US side reserves the right to reopen this question at a later date.

f. Other Items

Mr. Habib proposed that each side be free to introduce additional experts on specific matters, as required, with the names and fields of expertise to be notified to the other side in advance. Mr. Chin agreed.

Mr. Chin announced that Mr. Lho Shin Yong and Mr. Lee Kyung Hoon, members of the Korean delegation, were absent from the country on official business but would joint the delegation upon their return.

g. Agenda for Next Meeting

Mr. Habib proposed that the agenda for the next meeting consist of a general review of the scope and content of a status of forces agreement, with the understanding that such a review would not be definitive. Subject matter could be discussed under general headings and specific sub-titles, but additional matters could be raised at subsequent meetings. Mr. Chin agreed. Mr. Habib then stated that he would like to make one point clear. He pointed out that the present negotiations are concerned solely with an agreement between Korea and the United States and that the negotiators are not bound by the provisions of other status of forces agreements, although either side may introduce whatever material it believes relevant. Mr. Chin stated that it should be the purpose and intent of the negotiators to work out the best possible SOFA, which would be comprehensive and all-inclusive.

0116

2-27

h. Date of Next Meeting

It was agreed to hold the next meeting on September 28 at 2:00 p.m.

i. Joint Press Release

The joint press release prepared by Mr. Chi and Mr. Fleck was read by Mr. Chi and was approved by the negotiators.

0117

2-28

5. 제2차 회의, 9.28

0118

THE FOREIGN SERVICE
OF THE
UNITED STATES OF AMERICA

0110

American Embassy,
Seoul, Korea,
September 25, 1962.

Mr. Pak, Kun,
Chief, America Section,
Ministry of Foreign Affairs.

Dear Mr. Pak:

In reference to our conversation concerning contract employees of the United States Forces Korea I have received information from Japan that contract employees entering Japan under the provision of article XIV of the SOFA with Japan are in fact exempt from Japanese laws, and regulations on the registration and control of aliens as provided for in article IX.

I trust that the above confirms the information received from the Korean Mission in Japan.

Very truly yours,

For the Ambassador:

Robert A. Lewis
American Consul

SOFA 참고자료
Kang file

34-1

SOFA NEGOTIATION

Agenda for 2nd Session

14:00 Sept. 28, 1962

1. The Scope and Contents of Negotiations

2. Other Business

3. Agenda and Date of Next Meeting

4. Press Release

0120

1627

Principal Items and Questions of SOFA

1. Entry (1) Exemption (2) Requirements, (3) Change of status + removal

2. Use of Facilities and Areas
(土地 및 施設의 使用)

(1) Compensation
(補償問題)

(2) Expenditures incident to the Maintenance of Facilities and Areas
(土地. 施設의 維持費 問題)

(3) Interim Use of Facilities and Areas
(土地. 施設의 臨時使用权)

(4) Restoration Problems when US returns Facilities and Areas
(返還時의 原狀復旧問題)

(5) Restoration or Compensation for the Damage to Private Property which is extremely demolished during the US use.
(返還時 尤甚한 被害를 입은 私有財產에 対한 補償問題)

3. Accession of Vessels and Aircraft
(船舶. 航空機의 出入)

(1) Extents of Vessels and Aircrafts to which Tolls or Landing Fees are exempted.
(入港料 또는 着陸料 免除船舶의 範囲)

(2) Notification to Korean Authorities of entry of US Vessels and Aircraft.
(出入에 関한 韓國当局에 対한 通告義務)

(3) Control of Navigation and Coordination of Communication Systems.
(航空交通管理 및 通信体系의 統合問題)

4. Criminal Jurisdiction
(刑事裁判管轄权)

(1) General Jurisdiction
(一般的管轄权)

(2) Exclusive Jurisdiction
(専屬的管轄权)

(3) Concurrence of Jurisdiction
(管轄权의 競合問題)

(4) Determination of Duty-on or Duty-off.
(公務執行中 與否의 決定問題)

(5) Waiver of Right to exercise Jurisdiction
(管轄权의 抛棄)

(6) Mutual Assistance in Carrying out of Investigations and in Collection and Production of Evidence.
(搜查 및 証據蒐集上의 相互協助問題)

0121

18-28

(7) Rights of US forces and Other Personnel prosecuted under ROK Jurisdiction.
(韓國法院에 起訴된 者의 裁判上의 权利)

5. Civil Jurisdiction and Claims
(民事裁判权 및 請求权)

(1) Civil Jurisdiction over US Personnel
(韓國法院의 民事裁判权)

(2) Waiver of Claims for Damage to Property owned or Used by Armed Forces.
(軍用財産의 損害에 対한 請求权의 抛棄)

(3) Determination of Liability and Assessment of Claims in case of the other Property.
(其他 財産에 対한 責任問題의 決定과 請求权의 査定)

(4) Mutual Waiver of Claims for Damage arising out in the Performance of Official Duty.
(公務中에 発生한 損害에 対한 請求权의 抛棄)

(5) Selection of Arbitrator who shall determine the Liability on Damage.
(責任問題를 決定할 仲裁人의 選定問題)

✓ (6) Waiver of Claims for Injury or Death suffered in the Performance of Official Duty.
(公務中 人的損害에 対한 相互間의 請求权 抛棄)

✓ (7) Waiver of Claims for the Damage less than certain Amohnt.
(一定額 未満의 損害額에 対한 請求权 抛棄)

(8) Claims for the Damage causing to the third Party.
(韓國政府 以外 第三者에 加한 損害에 対한 請求权)

(9) Distribution of Cost incurred in satisfying Claims
(損害賠償額 分担問題)

(10) Claims arising out of tortious acts or omissions not done in performance of official duty.
(非公務中에 発生한 損害에 対한 請求权)

(11) Determination whether the Damage was ocurred during the performance of official duty or not.
(公務執行中에 発生한 損害인지 與否에 対한 決定权)

(12) Settlement of Dispute arising out of Contracts.
(調達契約으로 부터 発生한 紛争의 解決)

6. Custom Duties
(関税問題)

(1) Application of Korean Laws and Regulations
(韓國税関当局이 執行하는 法令에 対한 服從問題)

(2) Extents and Requirements of Exemption to Goods imported by US Forces.
(美軍이 搬入하는 物資에 対한 免税範囲 및 要件)

0122

(16-29)

(3) Exemption of Custom Clearance
(稅關檢査의 免除範圍)

(4) Internal Disposition of Goods imported free.
(免稅로 輸入한 物資의 國內에서의 处分問題)

(5) Prevention of Abuse of Privileges.
(特权濫用防止問題)

7. Taxation and Other Internal Charges
(租稅 其他 內國稅問題)

(1) Extent of Exemption
(免稅範圍 및 対象)

8. Non-appropriated Fund Organization
(歲出外 資金 機関)

(1) Establishment of Organization
(機関의 設置)

(2) Tax Exemption on Sales of Merchandise and Services by the Organization and Internal Disposition of such Merchandise and Services.
(同機関의 販賣物品에 対한 免稅 및 國內에서의 处分問題)

9. Local Procurement of Goods etc..
(物資等의 現地購買問題)

(1) Application of Korean Law to the Purchase of Goods etc..
(購買方式 等에 関한 韓國法律의 適用問題)

(2) Employment and Dismiss of Korean Labours
(勞動者의 雇傭 및 解雇問題)

10. US Contractors
(美國人 契約者)

(1) Application of Korean Law to the US Contractors
(契約者에 対한 韓國法律의 適用問題)

(2) Extent of Privileges and Immunities be granted.
(特权과 免除의 賦與範圍)

(3) Criminal Jurisdiction over Contractors.
(契約者에 対한 刑事管轄权問題)

11. Foreign Exchange Control
(外換管理)

(1) Transmission into or outside of Korea of US dollars realized in Korea
(韓國에서 取得한 外換의 移転問題)

(2) Prevention of Abuse of Privileges
(特权濫用防止問題)

0123

16-30

12. Military Payment Certificate(MPC)
(軍票)

(1) Use of MPC by Authorized Persons in certain Area.
(一定地域内에서의 軍票使用許可 問題)

(2) Control of Use of MPC by Unauthorized Persons.
(非認可者가 使用하는 軍票의 団束問題)

(3) Establishment of Military Bank Facilities.
(軍用銀行施設의 設置)

13. Military Post Office
(軍事郵便)

(1) Establishment of MPO and its Functions
(軍事郵便局의 設置 및 그 業務)

(2) Necessary Measures preventing Abuse of Privileges
(特权濫用防止를 為한 措置)

14. Exceptional Clause in case of Hostilities
(戦時 特例規定)

(1) Consultation for Modification on the Application of Agreement in case of Hostilities
(敵対行為 発生時의 協定適用問題 協議)

15. Joint Committee
(合同委員会)

(1) Function of Committee
(機能)

(2) Composition of Committee
(構成)

16. Miscellaneous Items
(其他 條項)

(1) Driving License
(運転免許)

(2) Carrying Arms
(武器携帯)

(3) Training in Reserve Organization
(予備役機関에서의 訓練)

17. Final Clause
(最終條項)

(1) Entry into force of Agreement
(発効)

(2) Expiry of Agreement
(終了)

(3)Revision of Agreement
(改正)

(4) Abrogation of Existing Agreement incompatible with the Agreement.
(既存協定의 廃棄問題)

1K-31

0124

미 주둔군 지위협정 실무교섭

제 2 차 회의 의제

1962. 9. 18. 오후 2 시

협정의 범위 및 내용 (06)

1. 전문 및 용어의 정의

   가. 목적과 이유

   나. 용어의 정의

      (ㄱ) 미군대 구성원

      (ㄴ) 군속

      (ㄷ) 가족

2. 출입국 관리문제

   가. 면제

   나. 요건

   다. 신분의 변경 및 퇴거

3. 시설 및 토지문제

   가. 사용허가

   나. 보상 (~~사용료 혹은 임대료~~) 문제

   다. 유지비 문제

   라. 시설 및 토지의 반환문제

   마. 임시 사용권

   바. 시설, 운영, 안전 및 통제조치 문제

   사. 원상회복 및 개선에 관한 문제

4. 선박 항고기의 출입과 교통 통제및 통신체계 문제

   가. 선박 항공기의 출입, 통과권 및 이용료 면제, 출입에관한 통고

   나. 통제 및 통신체계에 관한 조정과 협조

14-31 0125

다. 기상정보

5. 형사재판 관할권 문제

가. 일반적 관할권의 원칙

나. 전속적 관할권

다. 경합적 관할권

(ㄱ) 미국의 제 1 차 적 관할권

(ㄴ) 한국의 제 1 차 적 관할권

(ㄷ) 공무와 비공무 집행중 여부의 결정

라. 관할권의 포기

마. 체포 수사 증거 수집상의 상호협조

바. 구금

사. 형집행 문제

아. 2 중처벌 방지문제

자. 한국법원에 기소된자의 재판상의 권리

차. 헌병의 사용문제

6. 민사재판 및 청구권 문제

가. 한국법원의 민사재판권 및 판결집행의 면제 범위

나. 양국 군용재산 손해에 대한 청구권

다. 양국 비군용재산 손해에 대한 청구권 및 중재인사용 문제

라. 제 3 자에 가한 손해에 대한 청구권

마. 공무집행중 입은 인적손해에 대한 청구권의 포기

바. 미군대 구성원 혹은 고용자의 불법적 작위 혹은 불작위로 인한 손해청구권

사. 차량의 불법사용으로 인한 손해청구권

아. 강제집행을 행할 사유동산의 인도

14-32

0126

자. 공무 혹은 비공무집행중 여부의 결정에관한 증거수집에 있어서의 협조

차. 중재인을 통한 분쟁의 중재

타. 계약상의 분쟁 해결문제

7. 관세문제

가. 관세통제의 일반적 원칙

나. 통관세의 면제범위

다. 세관검사의 면제범위

라. 무세통관 물품의 국내에서의 처분문제

마. 특권 남용방지

8. 조세문제

가. 군용재산에 대한 면제

나. 소득에 대한 면제범위

다. 특정 부동산에 대한 면제문제

9. 세출외 자금기관

가. 일반적 허가

나. 면세범위

다. 세출외 자금기관 물자의 처분에대한 제한

라. 수입량에 대한 제한

마. 한국 관헌에대한 정보제공

10. 물자구입, 용역 및 노무 문제

가. 구매업무 등에관한 한국법률의 적용문제

나. 의무적 조정문제

다. 사적 목적을위한 구매에대한 세금의 불면제

라. 일반적 노무 기준

마. 제 3국 국민의 고용금지

바. 한국 노무자의 고용 및 해고문제

0127

K-33

11. 미군대 계약자 문제

가. 한국법률의 적용에관한 일반적 규정

나. 계약자 지정에대한 제한

다. 특권과 면제 범위

라. 계약자에 대한 형사재판 관할권 문제

12. 외환관리

가. 일반적 원칙

나. 한국내에 있어서 혹은 한국외로의 외환이전에 대한 허가문제

다. 특권남용 방지문제

라. 일정지역내에서의 군표사용 허가문제

마. 비인가자의 군표사용 단속문제

바. 군용은행 시설의 설치

13. 합동위원회

가. 기능

나. 구성

14. 군사우편

가. 군사우편국의 설치 및 업무

나. 특권남용 방지를위한 조치

15. 기타조항

가. 전시특례 조항

(ㄱ) 전시에 있어서의 협정적용에 관한 수정을위한 협의

나. 운전면허

다. 무기 휴대

라. 예비역 훈련

16. 최종조항

가. 발효 나. 만기

다. 개정 라. 본협정과 양립하지 않는 기존협정의 폐기문제

0128

14-34

기 안 용 지

자체 통제		기안처	조약과 신정섭
전화번호		근거서류접수일자	
과장	국장	차관보 직관	차관 / 장관
관계관 서명	미주과장	기획조정관	
기안 년월일	62.9.30	시행 년월일	
분류 기호	외방조 343 협정일반 (2)	전체 통제	검열 1962.10 종결
보존 년한		정서	기장
경유 수신 참조	최고회의 의장 (외무국방위원장 참조) 내각 수반	발신	외무부 장관
제목	한미 군대 지위 협정		

지난 9월 28일 외무부에서 표기 협정 체결 교섭을 위한 제2차 한미간의 실무자 회의가 개최되었으며 그 토의 내용을 별첨과 같이 보고합니다.

유첨. 군대지위협정 체결교섭 제2차 한미실무자회의 토의내용

1966.12.31. 에 의거 일반문서로 재분류됨

보통문서로 재분류(1966.12.31)

승인양식 1-1-3 (1112-010-016-018) (190mm×260mm16절지)

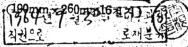

1964년 9월 30일 예고문에 의거 직권으로 로재분류

군대 지위 협정 체결 교섭 제 2 차 한미 실무자회의

토의 내용

1. 시간 및 장소

가. 시간: 1962 년 9 월 28 일 오후 2 시 부터 4 시 15 분까지

나. 장소: 외무부 회의실

2. 참석자

한국측:	진 필식(수석 대표)	외무부 정무국장
	신 관섭	재무부 세관국장
	이 경호	법무부 법무국장
	박 근	외무부 미주과장
	이 남구 대령	국방부 군무과장
	지 성구	외무부 공보관
	신 정섭	외무부 2 등서기관
	이 창범	외무부 3 등서기관
	강 석재	" "
미국측:	필립 시. 하비브(수석대표)	미대사관 정치담당참사관
	제이. 디. 로타 준장	미 8 군 참모차장
	지.지. 오코나 대령	미 8 군 참모차장
	알, 엠. 브라운리 대령	주한 미 해군 참모차장
	윌리암 제이. 포드	미대사관 1 등서기관
	벤자민 에이. 프텍	" "
	알. 이. 밀터 중령	미 8 군 법무관
	지. 티. 스드만 중령	주한 미 공군 민사처장
	로버트 에이. 루이스	미 대사관 2 등서기관 겸 영사

0130

2-2

미국문 8813(5)

0131

4 3. 토의 의제

가. 협정 교섭의 범위와 내용

나. 기타 사항

다. 차기회의의 의제와 기일

라. 공동 발표

5 4. 토의 내용

가. 미국측은 8군 법무장교 밀러 중령을 통하여 군대 지위 협정 교섭의 내용과 범위에 관하여 별첨 (1)과 같은 미리 준비된 설명서를 낭독하였으며 그 주요 골자는 아래와 같음.

(1) 교섭의 일반적 목적과 방침은 어디까지나 주둔군의 임무수행을 촉진하고 원활히 하는데 있음.

(2) 협정의 범위와 대상

(가) 토지 및 시설

(나) 공익물 및 용역

(다) 관세 및 세금

(라) 노동

(마) 지방 구매

(바) 민사 청구권

(사) 협정에 규정할 인적 대상

(아) 출입국 관리

(자) 파견국의 용역 및 시설 사용

(차) 형사 관할권

(카) 형법의 행정적 운용 문제

(타) 기타 사항

(3) 현재 한미간에는 군대지위에 관하여 공식 또는 비공식의 여러가지 개별적인 협정 또는 합의사항이 있으므로 이들을 ~~종합하면~~ 군대지위 협정에 (에 삽입하여야) 할것으로 생각함.

0132

2-3

마문 88-13

0133

이상의 설명에 이어 하비브 미측 수석 대표는 이에 대한 보충설명을 하고 다음과 같이 말함:

(가) 회의 진행에 있어 상기 문제에 대한 원칙적인 합의 사항은 본국 정부의 승인을 득하여 한건식 개별적으로 조문화 하여 처리함.

(나) 협정의 체결은 민정복귀 후에 할것을 재확인 함.

(다) 토지 및 시설에 대하여 미국정부는 보상을 할수 없으며 한국 정부가 이를 부담할 것.

(라) 형사관할권 문제는 미국회의 의견 및 정부의 기본 방침에 따라 미국의 제도의 표준에 빗등해야 할 것.

나. 미국측의 상기 발언에 대하여 아국측의 수석대표 진 외무부 정무국장은 미국측의 협정 교섭에 관한 범위와 내용 설명이 매우 포괄적인 것인데 대하여 환영의 뜻을 표명하고 이는 앞으로의 교섭에 많이 참고가 될 것으로 생각한다고 전제하고 아래와 같은 요지의 발언 (별첨 (2) 참조)을 한후 박 외무부 미주과장을 통하여 우리측이 구상하는 협정의 범위와 내용을 별첨 (3)과 같이 설명케 함.

(1) 우리측의 협정 교섭의 기본 목적과 정신은 주둔군의 임무수행을 위한 각종 편의제공과 접수국의 권익 보호와 법률 및 질서의 존중에 있으므로 앞으로 상기 양 문제의 조화와 균형을 모색함으로서 주둔군의 사명 완수를 돕고 나아가서 양국의 유대강화를 도모코저 하는데 있음.

(2) 아국측의 생각하는 군대지위 협정의 범위와 내용 (박 미주과장이 설명)

(가) 전문과 정의

(나) 출입국 관리

(다) 토지와 시설

(라) 선박 및 항공기의 출입국관리 및 통신 제도

(마) 형사 관할권

0134

2-4

미문 88-13

0135

(바) 민사 관할권

(사) 관세

(아) 조세

(자) 자금외 세출기관

(차) 물품, 용역 및 노동의 구매

(카) 군대 계약자

(타) 외환관리와 군표사용

(파) 합동위원회

(하) 군사 우편

(ㄱ) 기타

(ㄴ) 최종 조항

(3) 진 수석 대표는 미측 수석 대표의 보충설명에 대하여:

(가) 회의 진행에 있어 회의에서 원칙적으로 합의된 것을 본국 정부의 승인을 득한 후 최종적으로 결정한다는데 대하여 미측 안에 동의함.

(나) 토지 및 시설의 보상문제 및 형사 관할권에 관한 미국측의 발언에 대하여는 금일의 토의 의제가 이들 문제를 상세히 토의하도록 되어 있지 않으므로 보상문제와 형사관할권의 표준 문제를 여기서 토의함은 부적당 하다고 생각하며 이 문제들은 차후 구체적으로 토의할 것을 요망하며 다만 한가지 밝혀둘 것은 이양문제에 대하여 우리 정부측에서 과거 여러 차례에 걸쳐 문서상으로 또 구두로 ~~이들 문제에 관하여~~ 우리의 기본 태도를 천명한 바 있음을 재확인하며 양국측의 기본 태도의 차이점은 앞으로 교섭에서 상호 절충함의 하는것이 본 회의 목적이며 사명이라 생각한다고 함.

다. 기타 사항

하비브 미측 수석 대표는 본인의 결석시는 토마 준장이 미측 수석 대표를 담당할것을 말하였으며 우리측은 이런 경우 이경호 법무국장이 수석이 될것이라고 진 수석 대표가 발언함.

0136

2-5

기문 88-13

0137

라. 차기회의의 의제 및 기일

(1) 차기회의의 의제는 금일 양측이 제의한 협정의 범위와 내용에 관하여 연구하고 가능하면 개별적으로 토의할 것을 합의함.

(2) 기일은 10 월 10 일 하오 2 시로 합의됨.

마. 공동 발표

별첨 (4) 과 같은 공동 발표문을 채택함.

보통문서로 재분류(1966. 12. 31.)

1966. 12. 31. 에 예고문에 의거 일반문서로 재분류됨

0138

26

외정 88-13(5)

0138-1

별첨(1)

10/30

SCOPE AND CONTENT OF STATUS OF FORCES AGREEMENT

Mr. Chin; Mr. Habib; General Lawlor; Gentlemen.

Today I shall discuss these matters:

(1) The general purposes and objectives of Status of Forces Agreements.

(2) Comments, mostly in the form of problem questions, on major subject areas usually included in Agreements.

(3) A few concluding remarks concerning our negotiations.

May I, at the same time, mention several things which I shall not do:

(1) I shall not present a United States position on any Article or provision of any particular Status of Forces Agreement.

(2) I shall not base my comments on any specific agreement, past, present, or proposed.

(3) I do not mean, in any way, to suggest that everything I mention must be the subject of negotiation, or, on the other hand, that there are not many other important subjects to be considered.

GENERAL PURPOSES AND OBJECTIVE OF SOF

I would like to begin by asking you to consider the general purposes AND objectives of Status of Forces agreements.

FIRST:

WHY DO WE HAVE STATUS OF FORCES AGREEMENTS?

The peace we fought for so desperately during World War II was threatened by new aggressions even as it was being established. The free nations of the world soon found it necessary to band together in various mutual security and defensive alliances.

The United States was a leader in the creation of some of these alliences. It did, and still does, devote vast amounts of its national income and production, and large numbers of its armed forces, to the maintenance of these alliences.

One consequence of this course of action is that for many years our armed forces, essential civilians, and in many cases dependents, have been sent to and

0130

stationed in friendly foreign countries, at the express invitations of those countries. Our forces have gone to, and remain in, these nations as quests, friends, and allies.

The United States, as a sending state, needed assurances that facilities and areas, utilities and services, labor, access to supplies, training areas, freedom of movement, certain rights, privileges and immunities for its personnel, and some form of security of person and property, would be given by the receving states.

The nations of the free world, having respect for the rule of law, entered into government to government agreements which are now commonly referred to as Status of Forces Agreements. These agreements are the charter, the body of rules, which set out the concessions and guarantees each government makes to the other with respect to visiting armed forces. They contain statements of the obligations and duties, of the privileges, rights and immunities of the governments and personnel concerned.

SECOND:

WHO ARE INCLUDED IN STATUS OF FORCES AGREEMENTS?

Normally these agreements contain provisions concerning:

(1) the military members of the armed forces of the visiting country,

(2) the civilian employees and other civilians accompanying the armed forces,

(3) dependents of the foregoing personnel, and

(4) certain other civilians, such as invited contractors and their employees and depenaents.

THIRD:

WHEN ARE STATUS OF FORCES AGREEMENTS APPLICABLE?

and:

FOURTH:

WHERE ARE THEY APPLICABLE?

The short answer is that they apply at those times and in those places upon which the parties agree.

They were developed in peacetime, and they are designed to be effective in peacetime. Some have provisions for total or partial revocation in the event of hostilities. The situation in Korea is unique in that we are in a condition of suspended hostilities pursuant to an Armistice Agreement; an Armistice Commission holds frequent meetings; we are facing an armed enemy to the north which makes frequent incursions into and takes hostile action toward the Republic of Korea. Part of the Soverign territory of the Republic of Korea is still in enemy hands.

0140

2-8

The areas in which they apply may vary. For example, the NATO agreements were drawn in contemplation of the probability that most parties would be both sending and receiving states and the agreements would be equally applicable in both countries. Bilateral agreements, like the US - Japan Agreement, are between a sending and a receiving state, and they apply in the receiving state.

The parties may agree that the agreement is applicable only in the metropolitan area of a country, or they may include colonies.

There are many variations on the WHEN and WHERE. I repeat that peculiar circumstances and the particular requirements of the parties should determine the course of negotiations and the content and scope of any SOF agreement.

FIFTH:

WHAT IS INCLUDED IN A STATUS OF FORCES AGREEMENT?

Gentlemen: You have all seen and studied various examples of these agreements. I can't contribute many new ideas, but a brief review of key topics should serve to emphasize the scope of our task. In this section of my remarks I shall raise and ask many more questions than I shall answer.

There are some items which I consider to be fundamental from the view point of a sending state:

(1) It is essential that the agreement facilitate in every way possible the successful accomplishment of the sending state's mission. If this cannot be accomplished, the agreement is more of a hindrance than a help.

(2) It must provide some assurances of protection and security for the sending state's property, and the persons and property of its personnel.

(3) There must be some provision for an acceptable system of law and order.

(4) The Agreement should give substantial assurance that the sending state's requirements can and will be met. I refer, for example, to those matters which affect the strategic and tactical position of our forces, those touching upon our logistical situation and needs; some understanding with respect to essential but non-tactical support, and some understanding with respect to support which contributes to the morale, welfa[illegible] and well-being of the members of our forces.

That concludes my general observations. Let us turn now to an examination of particular subjects for negotiati[illegible] and consider a few of the questions which may arise.

0141

2-9

1. STATUS OF OUR FORCES AND PROPERTY AS A WHOLE(ENTITY).

a. Facilities and areas.

Visiting forces require space and facilities, and certainly they cannot just take them. They must rely on the host country to provide them. Special areas and facilities are the geographic tools we need for the accomplishment of our mission. There are requirements for such things as

Command facilities and areas
Troop housing and ancillary facilities and areas
Recreational, training, and maneuver areas
Ranges
Aerial and water ports and docks
Supply bases
Maintenence facilities

These are essentials, and there must be adequate access to and transportation nets between these areas and facilities. How shall these be provided for in the Agreement?

Some orderly process of requests for and return of properties, for exchange of, and maintenance of facilities is desirable.

b. Utilities and Services.

A closely related topic is that of utilities and services. Will they be provided in sufficient quantity to permit full utilization of areas and facilities and to support other essential functions? And under what terms will they be provided? In time of emergency or shortage, there may be an especially urgent need for utilities and services. Will there be any guarantee of equitable distribution? Will the forces by assured of adequate utilities and services to accomplish the mission?

c. Customs, Duties, and Taxes

Exemptions from customs, duties, and taxes are important to visiting forces as an agency. Our forces are stationed in foreign countries to accomplish mutually desired objectives. The amount we can contribute is related directly to the dollars we have available. Every dollar diverted from its intended purpose detracts just that much from our effectiveness and from our mission. Every dollar paid out in local taxes and customs in such a diversion.

Consequently, visiting forces are usually granted extensive exemptions from host country national and local taxes and customs on imports, utilities and services, local procurements, sales and purchases, official vehicles, and non-appropriated fund activities, to mention a few....

0142

2-10

d. Labor.

Visiting forces employ large numbers of local skilled and unskilled labor. Should there be some guarantee that, in the event of an emergency, a fair share of labor will be provided on an equitable basis? On the other hand, the visiting force must give due consideration to the impact its labor requirements and wages have on the host country's economy. Methods of personnel recruitment, status of personnel, protection from strikes, grievance, and hiring and severance procedures are a few of the aspects of local labor requirements.

e. Local Procurement (Off-Shore Procurement).

Local procurement of equipment and supplies also has a significant economic impact on the host country. What assurances can the visiting forces have that competitive bidding and responsible contractors will be available? What exemptions from taxes, customs, other fees, and other restrictions will be granted to the local contractors who are needed to fill some of the official requirements of the visiting forces?

f. Claims.

It is inevitable that death, injury, and damage to property will be suffered by individuals and property of both nations and by third parties. Should government to government claims be waived? On the other hand, should both governments undertake to pay innocent third parties? Shall there be different legal or agreed liabilities depending upon whether acts or omissions causing damage were in performance of duty or outside the scope of duty? Someone must pass upon claims. Someone must pay them. Who and how? Will visiting forces personnel have a right to make claims against the host government? Whose tort and negligence laws shall apply? Will visiting forces personnel be exempt from civil judgments for acts done in the performance of duty? Various methods of settling claims have been adopted, and doubtless this will be another matter which we shall have to resolve in our future meetings.

I have touched upon many of the questions and problems pertaining to visiting forces and their property as a whole. There also may be a requirement for many and detailed provisions which directly affect individual members of the visiting forces.

2. Persons included

Before the status, obligations and duties, the rights, privileges and immunities of these individuals can be considered intelligently, a determination must be made as to what persons, other than nationals of the receiving state, are actually to be covered by the Agreement.

First, of course, are the military members - the soldiers, sailors, airmen, and marines - who are sent to the host country.

0143

2-11

Also included are members of the civilian component, those civilian employees who accompany the armed forces because they are essential to the accomplishment of the mission. In this group, for example, are such divergent categories as Red Cross, technical representatives, non-appropriated fund activity, and educational (University of Maryland) personnel.

The more fortunate members of the forces are accompanied by, or they are joined by their dependents, and the dependents are included within the terms of these agreements.

Then there are members of our armed forces who come into the host country on temporary duty, or leave, or who merely pass through for personal or official reasons. There are official visitors. In many instances they are given recognition in these agreements.

There is another category of persons: invited contractors, their employees and their dependents. These people (or in some instances corporations) are private contractors, but they do business solely for the visiting forces, and they are considered necessary, for any of several reasons, for the accomplishment of our forces' missions.

3. STATUS OF INCLUDED PERSONS

Once the categories of included persons have been defined, their status, as individuals, must be spelled out in some detail. This brings into consideration questions of their rights, privileges, and immunities; their duties and obligations, the extent to which they are subject to or exempt from local laws. I shall mention a few of them:

a. Exit and Entry.

The visiting forces must somehow come into the country, and at some time they must leave. What documentation will they be required to furnish? What exemptions will they have from alien registration laws? What reports, if any, on exit and entry will be required? What obligation do the respective governments assume, and what guarantees will they give, with respect to exit and entry? And, what rights of movement and travel within the host country will be granted?

b. Use of Sending State Services and Facilities.

The United States goes to great expense to provide certain facilities and services for its personnel. Who shall have the right to use our APO's patronize our Post Exchanges and commissaries, to use military payment Certificates, and to avail themselves of many other benefits we provide for the morale and welfare of the persons we deem to be essential to the success of our mission? Will these rights and privileges vary according to categories of personnel?

0144

2-12

c. Customs, Duties and Taxes.

What exemptions shall visiting force personnel have from the duties, customs, and tax laws? Please note that the RIGHT of the receiving state to tax and collect customs from individuals is NOT here in question. It is conceded that the host country has this right.

As a general rule host countries have in large measure foregone these rithts. For example, this is true of income taxes on income earned as members of visiting forces; it is extended to the importation of household goods and other items intended for personal use or as gifts to persons similarly authorized to import them duty free. What about items imported to be given to local charitable institutions?

And, may automobiles be imported for personal use free of customs, free of local road or use taxed, and exempt from local licensing procedures?

Deaths, trnasfers of property, sales to local nationals, income earned on the local economy, and a myriad of other special situations may require resolution. Should this be left to subsequent subsidiary agreements, or Agreed Minutes, or WHAT?

d. Criminal Jurisdiction.

The exercise of criminal jurisdiction is perhaps the most emotionally charged and most discussed subject of any Agreement. I am sure you are well sware of various formulas which have been adopted, with the way in which they have worked, and with the 1953 Senate Resolution on Status of Forces. Consequently, I shall not elaborate on criminal jurisdiction as such as this time.

e. Criminal Law Administration.

There are many other aspects of criminal law which become obscured by the issue of criminal jurisdiction. For example: who may issue warrants of arrest or search and seizure, and who may execute them in what places? There are questions of arrest, apprehension, and pretrial and post-trial confinement.

There may be times when the visiting state forces may want to apprehend local nationals for good cause. May they? Under what conditions? How far can visiting state forces go in the protection of their persons and property?

What special rules will apply within areas and facilities occupied by the visiting forces?

Obviously, the sending state does not have jurisdiction over nations of the receiving state. What actions will the receiving state undertake with respect to offenses committed against the sending state and its

0145

personnel and property when the offender is a local national or otherwise under the jurisdiction of the receiving state? What protections and security will the host country provide?

Who shall have the right to custody of sending state offenders? What confinement facilities will be provided, and health, sanitary, and subsistence standards? What right of inspection? Should there be provision for transfer of custody back to the sending state?

I have mentioned just a few of the many aspects of criminal administration. I suggest a few others: Rules of evidence; availability of counsel; process for witnesses; substantive rithts of accused persons; provisions for pretrial investigation; and provision of logistic support for confined persons.

4. ADMINISTRATIVE PROVISIONS:

It takes many people to administer, interpret, and apply a SOFA when large areas and large groups of personnel are involved. How will differences be resolved and who will take care of the day to day problems and decisions?

CONCLUDING REMARKS:

So far, most of my remarks have been devoted to visiting forces, individually and collectively.

In a very real sense many other persons are directly or indirectly affected by, or otherwise concerned with these agreements and the forces to which they pertain.

For Example:
(1) Officials of both governments who have responsibilities prescribed in the agreements.

(2) The legislators of the sending state's people. These elected representatives of the people are interested in the welfare of our military forces and their accompanying civilians who are stationed in foreign countries.

(3) The legislators of host countries who, by the agreement, may be obligated to undertake necessary legislative action with respect to provisions of the Agreement which require legislative action for their execution.

(4) Local nationals and contractors who seek employment and contracts with the visiting forces.

(5) Local inhabitants who associate with and feel the economic impact and benefits which come with our forces.

(6) Parties who suffer death, injury, or damage to property.

0146

2-14

(7) Farmers, orphans, and many others who receive assistance and care as a result of official or personal gratuitous contributions of time, money and materials.

In his opening remarks Ambassador Berger mentioned that a Status of Forces Agreement covers many kinds of activities. Viewed as a whole it comprehends extensive, complex and varied administrative arrangements.

We, the US forces and the Republic of Korea, already have formal and informal agreements and understandings which both sides recognize and observe. In a very real sense they are a form of Status of Forces Agreement.

Such arrangements have evolved and grown in the Republic of Korea during the many years in which our forces and your people have stood together in common defense. Should not many of the broad principles reflected in these satisfactory arrangements be incorporated in any SOFA we negotiate?

보통문서로 재분류(1966.12.31)

1966.12.31에 예고문에 의거 일반문서로 재분류됨

0147

2-15

별첨(2)

12/25

SOFA NEGOTIATION

Proposed Scope and Contents of the Status of Forces Negotiations

The present status of forces negotiations are based on our common conviction that the existing friendly and close feelings between the peoples of Korea and the United States will be further strengthened by an agreement defining the status of the U.S. armed forces stationed in the Republic of Korea on a more normal and regular basis, and that such an agreement will contribute greatly to the successful fulfillment of the basic objectives under the Mutual Defense Treaty.

For this purpose, we have before us the difficult task of reconciling two basic requisites i.e. the necessity to grant privileges and immunities to the United States Armed Forces stationed in the Republic of Korea to the extent commensurate with their special status on the one hand, and that of upholding the laws and regulations of the receiving state on the other. Neither one should preclude the other; Nor should one be satisfied at the expense of the other. We have to discover an optimum equilibrium between the above two basic requisites with a view toward working out a best framework of coordination and cooperation in our joint struggle against the Communist threat.

In view of such a nature of our task, it is suggested that negotiations cover the following items:

0148

2-16

별첨 (3)

1. Preamble and definition of terms

   a. Purpose and justification

   b. Definition of terms

      (1) Member of the United States Forces

      (2) Civilian component

      (3) Dependent

2. Entry and Exit

   a. Exemption

   b. Requirements

   c. Change of status and removal

3. Facilities and areas

   a. Authorization of use

   b. Compensation

   c. Maintenance

   d. Return of facilities and areas

   e. Interim use

   f. Establishment, operation, safety and control measures

   g. Restoration and improvement

4. Access of vessels, aircraft, and traffic control and communication systems

   a. Access of vessels and aircraft, regulation, exemption of fees, notification of entry.

   b. Coordination and cooperation in traffic control communication systems, etc.

   c. meteorological service

5. Criminal jurisdiction

   a. Principle of general jurisdiction

0140

2-17

b. Exclusive jurisdiction

c. Concurrent jurisdiction

(1) Primary jurisdiction of the United States

(2) Primary jurisdiction of the Republic of Korea

(3) Determination of on-duty and off-duty offenses

d. Waiver of jurisdiction

e. Mutual assistance in arrest, investigation, collection and production of evidences

f. Custody

g. Implementation of sentence

h. Double jeopardy

i. Rights of U.S. forces and other personnel accused of crimes under ROK jurisdiction

j. Use of military police

6. Civil jurisdiction and Claims

a. Civil jurisdiction over U.S. personnel and extent of immunity from the enforcement of judgement in civil proceedings

b. Claims for damages to military properties of both Governments

c. Claims for damages to non-military properties of both Governments and use of arbitrator

d. Claims for damages to third party

e. Waiver of claims for injury or death suffered while on duty

f. Claims against member or employees of the United States Forces for tortious acts or omission

g. Claims arising out of unauthorized use of vehicles

h. Turn-over of private movable property under compulsory execution

i. Cooperation in the procurement of evidence concerning the determination of on- or off-duty

0150

2-18

j. Submission of disputes to arbitrator

k. Settlement of disputes arising out of contractors

7. Customs

a. General principle of customs regulation

b. Extent of exemption from customs duties

c. Extent of exemption from customs examination

d. Internal disposition of duty-free goods

e. Prevention of abuse of privileges

8. Taxation

a. Exemption on military properties

b. Exemption on income

c. Exemption on certain movable properties

9. Non-appropriated fund organization

a. General authorization

b. Extent of tax exemption

c. Restriction of disposal of NAFO goods

d. Restriction of the amount of importation

e. Furnishing of information to the Korean authorities

10. Purchase of goods, services and labour

a. Application of Korean Law to the purchase of goods etc.

b. Obligatory coordination with the Korean Government

c. No tax exemption for personal purchase.

d. General labour standard

e. Prohibition of employment of a third state subject

f. Employment and dismissal of Korean labours

11. Armed forces contractors

a. General rule of application of Korean law

b. Restriction in the designation of contractors

c. Extent of privileges and immunities

d. Criminal jurisdiction over contractors

0151

278

12. Foreign Exchange Control and use of MPC

a. General principle of control

b. Authorization of transmission of U.S. dollars into or outside of Korea

c. Prevention of the abuse of privileges

d. Use of MPC by authorized persons in certain area

e. Control of use of MPC by unauthorized persons

f. Establishment of Military Bank facilities

13. Joint Committee

a. Function

b. Composition

14. Military post office

a. Establishment of APO and its functions

b. Necessary measures preventing abuse of privileges

15. Miscellaneous items

a. Exceptional clause in case of hostilities

(1) Consultation for modification on the application of agreement in case of hostilities

b. Driving license

c. Carrying of arms

d. Training in Reserve organization

16. Final clause

a. Entry into force

b. Expiration

c. Revision

d. Abrogation of existing agreements incompatible with the agreement

보통문서로 재분류(1966.12.31)

1966,12,31,에 예고문에 의거 일반문서로 재분류됨

0152

2-20

별첨(4)

대한민국 외무부와 주한미국대사관의 공동발표

오늘의 회담에서는 지위협정의 범위와 내용에 관해서 일반적인 토의와 의견교환이 있었다. 토의된 문제들에는 통상지위 협정의 규정에 포함되는 인적범위와 어떠한 형태의 활동이 포함될것인가 하는 문제들이 토의되었다.

[redacted]

[redacted] 토지와 시설, 공익 사업문과 용역, 세관절차 노무자 획득, 장비와 보급품의 구매, 소송절차, 형사재판 관할권, 기타 관련된 사항에 관한 규정을 포함시키는 문제를 토의하였다.

다음회담은 10월10일 오후 2시로 작정하였다.

0153

2-21

담당	계장	국장	차관	장관	10월 4일	조약과
					공람재	

미주과 보좌관 기획조정관

SUMMARY RECORD OF THE SEDOND SESSION
STATUS FORCES NEGOTIATIONS

September 28, 1962

I. Time and Place: 2:00 to 4:15 p.m. on September 28, 1962 at Conference Room of the Ministry of Foreign Affairs

II. Attendants:

ROK Side:

Mr. Chin, Pil Shik	Director Bureau of Political Affairs Ministry of Foreign Affairs
Mr. Shin, Kwan Sup	Director Bureau of Customs Ministry of Finance
Mr. ~~Lee~~ Yi, Kyung Ho	Director Bureau of Legal Affairs Ministry of Justice
Mr. Pak, Kun	Chief, America Section Ministry of Foreign Affairs
Col. Lee, Nam Koo	Chief, Military Affairs Section Ministry of National Defense
Mr. Chi, Sung Koo	Press Officer Ministry of Foreign Affairs
Mr. Shin, Chung Sup (Rapporteur)	2nd Secretary Ministry of Foreign Affairs
Mr. Lee, Chang Bum	3rd Secretary Ministry of Foreign Affairs
Mr. Kang, Suk Jae (Interpreter)	3rd Secretary Ministry of Foreign Affairs

3-1

0154

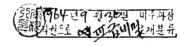

US Side:

Mr. Philip C. Habib	Counselor of the Embassy for Political Affairs
Brig. Gen. J.D. Lawlor	Deputy Chief of Staff 8th Army
Col. G.G. O'Connor	Deputy Chief of Staff 8th Army
Capt. R.M. Bownlie	Assistant Chief of Staff USN/K
Mr. William J. Ford	First Secretary of the Embassy
Mr. Benjamin A. Fleck (Rapporteur and Press Officer)	First Secretary of the Embassy
Lt. Col. R.E. Miller	Staff Officer, JAG 8th Army
Lt. Col. G.T. Suderman	Staff Officer, J-5 USAF/K
Mr. Robert A. Lewis	Second Secretary and Consul of the Embassy

III. Gist of Talks:

a. U.S. Presentation of Views on Scope and Content

1. Substantive discussion began with the presentation by Lt. Colonel Miller, of the views of the U.S. side regarding the scope and content of a Status of Forces Agreement. At the beginning of his remarks Miller emphasized that his comments did not include a statement of the U.S. position in regard to any article or any particular agreement and that his remarks were not intended to be definitive nor to

0155

3-2

exclude consideration at a later date of additional subjects for inclusion in an agreement.

2. Miller then reviewed the general purposes and objectives of a SOFA in broad terms, following this with reference to specific topics, including facilities and areas; utilities and services; customs duties; and taxes; labor; local procurement; claims; categories of persons to be included; use of sending state services and facilities; and criminal jurisdiction. (Copies of the U.S. and Korean presentations on scope and content were made available to the rapporteurs at the end of the meeting.)

b. U.S. Statement on Payment for Facilities and Criminal Jurisdiction

3. Following Miller's presentation, Mr. Habib stated that whenever the two sides reached agreement on the text of specific articles, the U.S. side would submit the agreed language to Washington for approval before constructing the final text of the agreement. He presumed the Korean side would also proceed ad referendum.

4. Mr. Habib stated he also wished to reaffirm the understanding expressed in the joint press statement of September 6, 1962, that the conclusion of a SOFA will await the restoration of civilian government in the Republic of Korea.

5. Mr. Habib then referred to the position of the U.S. Government regarding payment for the use of facilities, as set forth prior to and at the time of negotiations held in April 1961, in the Aide Memoire submitted to the Foreign Minister on June 15, 1962, and in the various conversations between the American Ambassador and the Foreign Minister before the latter

0156

3-3

date. Habib stated that the ROKG was aware thereby that the U.S. Government is not willing to pay compensation for the facilities used by U.S. Forces in Korea and shall continue to insist that the ROKG be responsible for all and any such claims, public or private. He added that the U.S. Government will, of course, cooperate to the maximum in releasing such facilities as may no longer be needed and in accepting satisfactory alternative facilities offered by the ROKG.

6. Turning to the subject of criminal jurisdiction, Habib stated that while detailed consideration of this subject would occur later in the negotiations, the U.S. side wished to make one basic observation at this time. In any agreement covering Status of Forces, he said, the U.S. Government is obligated to insist upon arrangements which will ensure that U.S. personnel will be guaranteed trials comparable to U.S. standards. He pointed out that this is a basic principle of particular concern to the U.S. Congress and is fundamental to the negotiation of all status of forces agreements.

c. <u>Korean Presentation of Views on Scope and Content</u>

7. Mr. Chin, the chief delegate of the Korean side, appreciated Col. Miller's presentation and said that the material would be of a great help in the course of their negotiations, for it was very comprehensive and all inclusive. Referring to the scope and content of SOFA as conceived by the Korean side, he said that the purpose of negotiations is to reconcile the need to grant facilities and privileges to the armed forces of the sending state with the necessity to uphold the law and rights of the receiving state.

0157

3-4

Thus, he continued, "we have the difficult tasks of reconciling the two basic requisites." Mr. Chin further said "we have to discover an optimum equilibrium between the above two basic requisites with a view toward working out a best framework of coordination and cooperation in our joint struggle against the Communist threat."

8. Dr. Pak, on behalf of the Korean side, presented the views of the Republic of Korea on the scope and content of SOFA in the form of an outline, which contained the following principal subjects:

(1) Preamble and definition of terms

(2) Entry and exit

(3) Facilities and areas

(4) Access of vessels, aircraft, and traffic control and communication systems

(5) Criminal jurisdiction

(6) Civil jurisdiction and claims

(7) Customs

(8) Taxation

(9) Non-appropriated fund organization

(10) Purchase of goods, services and labour

(11) Armed forces contractors

(12) Foreign exchange control and use of MPC

(13) Joint Committee

(14) Military post office

(15) Miscellaneous items

(16) Final clause

(The complete outline, including sub-items, was made available to the rapporteur of the U.S. side.)

0158

3-5

d. <u>Korean Response to the U.S. statement on Payment for Facilities and Criminal Jurisdiction</u>

9. In response to Mr. Habib's supplementary explanation with respect to:

(1) procedural aspect of negotiations, Mr. Chin agreed to proceed <u>ad referendum</u> as proposed by Mr. Habib;

(2) the conclusion time of the agreement after the restoration of civil government, Mr. Chin stated that negotiations would require a considerable period of time, and therefore, both sides should do their utmost with a view to completing negotiations on most subjects before next summer and be ready for the conclusion of the agreement as soon as possible after civil government is restored;

(3) the U.S. position on compensation for facilities and areas and the judicial standard comparable to that of the United States, Mr. Chin reminded Mr. Habib of the fact that the Korean government had also expressed on many past occasions its views to the United States government in written or oral form. Mr. Chin stressed that there are differences of views ~~on these~~ Even though ~~Mr. Chin was aware of the existing matters, Mr. Chin~~ of which both sides were ~~differences of their views, he stressed that it is~~ aware, it is the very task of the gathering to solve such differences through negotiations. He also told Mr. Habib that it was not quite relevant to discuss the specific position of each government on those subjects at that time, when they were only considering the overall scope and content of the proposed SOFA. Mr. Habib agreed that these matters would be discussed at the appropriate stage of negotiations.

0159

3-6

e. <u>Other Business</u>

10. Mr. Habib announced that in his absence, Brig. General Lawlor would lead the U.S. negotiating team. Mr. Chin stated that in his absence Mr. ~~Yi~~ Lee Kyung-ho would lead the Korean team.

f. <u>Agenda and Date of Next Meeting</u>

11. It was agreed that the next meeting begin with an exchange of views concerning the presentations just made on scope and content and that following such an exchange, the negotiators would proceed to consider the sequence in which the various subjects would be negotiated.

The next meeting was scheduled for October 10 at 2:00 p.m.

보통문서로 재분류(1966.12.31.)

196 , , ,에 예고문에 의거 일반문서로 재분류됨

0160

3-7

6. 제3차 회의, 10. 10

0161

기 안 용 지

자체 통제		기안처	조약과 이창범	전화번호	근거서류접수일자
수석대표		차관보 좌관		차관	장관
				후결	
관계관 서명	대표 : 미주과장 조약과장				
기안 년월일	1962. 10. 1.	시행 년월일		보존 년한	정서 기장
분류 기호	외정미 722 3454	전체 통제	검열 1962. 통제관	종결	
경유 수신 참조	배부처 참조			발신	외무부장관
제목	한미간의 주둔군 지위협정 교섭 문제				

1962. 9. 28. 표기협정 체결을 위한 제 2 차 실무자회의에서 미국측이 제시한 협정의 범위와 내용을 별첨과 같이 송부하니 이를 검토하고 특히 아래 문제에 관하여 귀부의 의견을 10 월 8 일 까지 회시하여 주기 바랍니다.

아 래

1. 미국측이 제시한 협정의 범위 및 내용 중 귀부소관사항에 대한 구체적인 의견 제시
2. 미국측 안의 결론(Concluding Remarks, PP 8--9) 에서 언급된 한미간에 현존하는 공식 또는 비공식적인 주둔군 지위에 관한 협정, 약정, 양해사항,등을 완전 파악하여 동 목록 및 내용에 관한 일람표 작성. 끝

유 첨: 미국측이 제시한 협정의 범위 및 내용 1 부.

배부처: 재무부, 법무부, 국방부

예고문 : 일반문서로 재분류(1966. 6. 30.)

보통문서로 재분류(별첨과 분리 시)

승인양식 1-1-3 (1112-040-016-018) (190mm×260mm16절지)

0162

12/30

SCOPE AND CONTENT OF STATUS OF FORCES AGREEMENT

Mr. Chin; Mr. Habib; General Lawlor; Gentlemen.

Today I shall discuss these matters:

(1) The general purposes and objectives of Status of Forces Agreements.

(2) Comments, mostly in the form of problem questions, on major subject areas usually included in Agreements.

(3) A few concluding remarks concerning our negotiations.

May I, at the same time, mention several things which I shall not do:

(1) I shall not present a United States position on any Article or provision of any particular Status of Forces Agreement.

(2) I shall not base my comments on any specific agreement, past, present, or proposed.

(3) I do not mean, in any way, to suggest that everything I mention must be the subject of negotiation, or, on the other hand, that there are not many other important subjects to be considered.

GENERAL PURPOSES AND OBJECTIVE OF SOF

I would like to begin by asking you to consider the general purposes AND objectives of Status of Forces agreements.

FIRST:

WHY DO WE HAVE STATUS OF FORCES AGREEMENTS?

The peace we fought for so desperately during World War II was threatened by new aggressions even as it was being established. The free nations of the world soon found it necessary to band together in various mutual security and defensive alliances.

The United States was a leader in the creation of some of these alliences. It did, and still does, devote vast amounts of its national income and production, and large numbers of its armed forces, to the maintenance of these alliences.

One consequence of this course of action is that for many years our armed forces, essential civilians, and in many cases dependents, have been sent to and

파기하라(별도통고서)

0163

stationed in friendly foreign countries, at the express invitations of those countries. Our forces have gone to, and remain in, these nations as quests, friends, and allies.

The United States, as a sending state, needed assurances that facilities and areas, utilities and services, labor, access to supplies, training areas, freedom of movement, certain rights, privileges and immunities for its personnel, and some form of security of person and property, would be given by the receving states.

The nations of the free world, having respect for the rule of law, entered into government to government agreements which are now commonly referred to as Status of Forces Agreements. These agreements are the charter, the body of rules, which set out the concessions and guarantees each government makes to the other with respect to visiting armed forces. They contain statements of the obligations and duties, of the privileges, rights and immunities of the governments and personnel concerned.

SECOND:

WHO ARE INCLUDED IN STATUS OF FORCES AGREEMENTS?

Normally these agreements contain provisions concerning:

(1) the military members of the armed forces of the visiting country,

(2) the civilian employees and other civilians accompanying the armed forces,

(3) dependents of the foregoing personnel, and

(4) certain other civilians, such as invited contractors and their employees and depenaents.

THIRD:

WHEN ARE STATUS OF FORCES AGREEMENTS APPLICABLE?

and:

FOURTH:

WHERE ARE THEY APPLICABLE?

The short answer is that they apply at those times and in those places upon which the parties agree.

They were developed in peacetime, and they are designed to be effective in peacetime. Some have provisions for total or partial revocation in the event of hostilities. The situation in Korea is unique in that we are in a condition of suspended hostilities, pursuant to an Armistice Agreement; an Armistice Commission holds frequent meetings; we are facing an armed enemy to the north which makes frequent incursions into and takes hostile action toward the Republic of Korea. Part of the Soverign territory of the Republic of Korea is still in enemy hands.

0164

The areas in which they apply may vary. For example, the NATO agreements were drawn in contemplation of the probability that most parties would be both sending and receiving states and the agreements would be equally applicable in both countries. Bilateral agreements, like the US - Japan Agreement, are between a sending and a receiving state, and they apply in the receiving state.

The parties may agree that the agreement is applicable only in the metropolitan area of a country, or they may include colonies.

There are many variations on the WHEN and WHERE. I repeat that peculiar circumstances and the particular requirements of the parties should determine the course of negotiations and the content and scope of any SOF agreement.

FIFTH:

WHAT IS INCLUDED IN A STATUS OF FORCES AGREEMENT?

Gentlemen: You have all seen and studied various examples of these agreements. I can't contribute many new ideas, but a brief review of key topics should serve to emphasize the scope of our task. In this section of my remarks I shall raise and ask many more questions than I shall answer.

There are some items which I consider to be fundamental from the view point of a sending state:

(1) It is essential that the agreement facilitate in every way possible the successful accomplishment of the sending state's mission. If this cannot be accomplished, the agreement is more of a hindrance than a help.

(2) It must provide some assurances of protection and security for the sending state's property, and the persons and property of its personnel.

(3) There must be some provision for an acceptable system of law and order.

(4) The Agreement should give substantial assurance that the sending state's requirements can and will be met. I refer, for example, to those matters which affect the strategic and tactical position of our forces, those touching upon our logistical situation and needs; some understanding with respect to essential but non-tactical support, and some understanding with respect to support which contributes to the morale, welfare and well-being of the members of our forces.

That concludes my general observations. Let us turn now to an examination of particular subjects for negotiation and consider a few of the questions which may arise.

0165

1. STATUS OF OUR FORCES AND PROPERTY AS A WHOLE(ENTITY).

a. Facilities and areas.

Visiting forces require space and facilities, and certainly they cannot just take them. They must rely on the host country to provide them. Special areas and facilities are the geographic tools we need for the accomplishment of our mission. There are requirements for such things as

Command facilities and areas
Troop housing and ancillary facilities and areas
Recreational, training, and maneuver areas
Ranges
Aerial and water ports and docks
Supply bases
Maintenence facilities

These are essentials, and there must be adequate access to and transportation nets between these areas and facilities. How shall these be provided for in the Agreement?

Some orderly process of requests for and return of properties, for exchange of, and maintenance of facilities is desirable.

b. Utilities and Services.

A closely related topic is that of utilities and services. Will they be provided in sufficient quantity to permit full utilization of areas and facilities and to support other essential functions? And under what terms will they be provided? In time of emergency or shortage, there may be an especially urgent need for utilities and services. Will there be any guarantee of equitable distribution? Will the forces by assured of adequate utilities and services to accomplish the mission?

c. Customs, Duties, and Taxes

Exemptions from customs, duties, and taxes are important to visiting forces as an agency. Our forces are stationed in foreign countries to accomplish mutually desired objectives. The amount we can contribute is related directly to the dollars we have available. Every dollar diverted from its intended purpose detracts just that much from our effectiveness and from our mission. Every dollar paid out in local taxes and customs in such a diversion.

Consequently, visiting forces are usually granted extensive exemptions from host country national and local taxes and customs on imports, utilities and services, local procurements, sales and purchases, official vehicles, and non-appropriated fund activities, to mention a few.

0100

d. Labor.

Visiting forces employ large numbers of local skilled and unskilled labor. Should there be some guarantee that, in the event of an emergency, a fair share of labor will be provided on an equitable basis? On the other hand, the visiting force must give due consideration to the impact its labor requirements and wages have on the host country's economy. Methods of personnel recruitment, status of personnel, protection from strikes, grievance, and hiring and severance procedures are a few of the aspects of local labor requirements.

e. Local Procurement (Off-Shore Procurement).

Local procurement of equipment and supplies also has a significant economic impact on the host country. What assurances can the visiting forces have that competitive bidding and responsible contractors will be available? What exemptions from taxes, customs, other fees, and other restrictions will be granted to the local contractors who are needed to fill some of the official requirements of the visiting forces?

f. Claims.

It is inevitable that death, injury, and damage to property will be suffered by individuals and property of both nations and by third parties. Should government to government claims be waived? On the other hand, should both governments undertake to pay innocent third parties? Shall there be different legal or agreed liabilities depending upon whether acts or omissions causing damage were in performance of duty or outside the scope of duty? Someone must pass upon claims. Someone must pay them. Who and how? Will visiting forces personnel have a right to make claims against the host government? Whose tort and negligence laws shall apply? Will visiting forces personnel be exempt from civil judgments for acts done in the performance of duty? Various methods of settling claims have been adopted, and doubtless this will be another matter which we shall have to resolve in our future meetings.

I have touched upon many of the questions and problems pertaining to visiting forces and their property as a whole. There also may be a requirement for many and detailed provisions which directly affect individual members of the visiting forces.

2. Persons included

Before the status, obligations and duties, the rights, privileges and immunities of these individuals can be considered intelligently, a determination must be made as to what persons, other than nationals of the receiving state, are actually to be covered by the Agreement.

First, of course, are the military members - the soldiers, sailors, airmen, and marines - who are sent to the host country.

0167

Also included are members of the civilian component, those civilian employees who accompany the armed forces because they are essential to the accomplishment of the mission. In this group, for example, are such divergent categories as Red Cross, technical representatives, non-appropriated fund activity, and educational (University of Maryland) personnel.

The more fortunate members of the forces are accompanied by, or they are joined by their dependents, and the dependents are included within the terms of these agreements.

Then there are members of our armed forces who come into the host country on temporary duty, or leave, or who merely pass through for personal or official reasons. There are official visitors. In many instances they are given recognition in these agreements.

There is another category of persons: invited contractors, their employees and their dependents. These people (or in some instances corporations) are private contractors, but they do business solely for the visiting forces, and they are considered necessary, for any of several reasons, for the accomplishment of our forces' missions.

3. STATUS OF INCLUDED PERSONS

Once the categories of included persons have been defined, their status, as individuals, must be spelled out in some detail. This brings into consideration questions of their rights, privileges, and immunities; their duties and obligations, the extent to which they are subject to or exempt from local laws. I shall mention a few of them:

a. Exit and Entry.

The visiting forces must somehow come into the country, and at some time they must leave. What documentation will they be required to furnish? What exemptions will they have from alien registration laws? What reports, if any, on exit and entry will be required? What obligation do the respective governments assume, and what guarantees will they give, with respect to exit and entry? And, what rights of movement and travel within the host country will be granted?

b. Use of Sending State Services and Facilities.

The United States goes to great expense to provide certain facilities and services for its personnel. Who shall have the right to use our APO's patronize our Post Exchanges and commissaries, to use military payment certificates, and to avail themselves of many other benefits we provide for the morale and welfare of the persons we deem to be essential to the success of our mission? Will these rights and privileges vary according to categories of personnel?

0168

c. Customs, Duties and Taxes.

What exemptions shall visiting force personnel have from the duties, customs, and tax laws? ~~Please note that the RIGHT of the receiving state to tax and collect customs from individuals is NOT here in question. It is conceded that the host country has this right.~~

As a general rule host countries have in large measure foregone these rithts. For example, this is true of income taxes on income earned as members of visiting forces; it is extended to the importation of household goods and other items intended for personal use or as gifts to persons similarly authorized to import them duty free. What about items imported to be given to local charitable institutions?

And, may automobiles be imported for personal use free of customs, free of local road or use taxed, and exempt from local licensing procedures?

Deaths, trnasfers of property, sales to local nationals, income earned on the local economy, and a myriad of other special situations may require resolution. Should this be left to subsequent subsidiary agreements, or Agreed Minutes, or WHAT?

d. Criminal Jurisdiction.

The exercise of criminal jurisdiction is perhaps the most emotionally charged and most discussed subject of any Agreement. I am sure you are well sware of various formulas which have been adopted, with the way in which they have worked, and with the 1953 Senate Resolution on Status of Forces. Consequently, I shall not elaborate on criminal jurisdiction as such as this time.

e. Criminal Law Administration.

There are many other aspects of criminal law which become obscured by the issue of criminal jurisdiction. For example: who may issue warrants of arrest or search and seizure, and who may execute them in what places? There are questions of arrest, apprehension, and pretrial and post-trial confinement.

There may be times when the visiting state forces may want to apprehend local nationals for good cause. May they? Under what conditions? How far can visiting state forces go in the protection of their persons and property?

What special rules will apply within areas and facilities occupied by the visiting forces?

Obviously, the sending state does not have jurisdiction over nations of the receiving state. What actions will the receiving state undertake with respect to offenses committed against the sending state and its

0169

personnel and property when the offender is a local national or otherwise under the jurisdiction of the receiving state? What protections and security will the host country provide?

Who shall have the right to custody of sending state offenders? What confinement facilities will be provided, and health, sanitary, and subsistence standards? What right of inspection? Should there be provision for transfer of custody back to the sending state?

I have mentioned just a few of the many aspects of criminal administration. I suggest a few others: Rules of evidence; availability of counsel; process for witnesses; substantive rithts of accused persons; provisions for pretrial investigation; and provision of logistic support for confined persons.

4. ADMINISTRATIVE PROVISIONS:

It takes many people to administer, interpret, and apply a SOFA when large areas and large groups of personnel are involved. How will differences be resolved and who will take care of the day to day problems and decisions?

CONCLUDING REMARKS:

So far, most of my remarks have been devoted to visiting forces, individually and collectively.

In a very real sense many other persons are directly or indirectly affected by, or otherwise concerned with these agreements and the forces to which they pertain.

For Example:

(1) Officials of both governments who have responsibilities prescribed in the agreements.

(2) The legislators of the sending state's people. These elected representatives of the people are interested in the welfare of our military forces and their accompanying civilians who are stationed in foreign countries.

(3) The legislators of host countries who, by the agreement, may be obligated to undertake necessary legislative action with respect to provisions of the Agreement which require legislative action for their execution.

(4) Local nationals and contractors who seek employment and contracts with the visiting forces.

(5) Local inhabitants who associate with and feel the economic impact and benefits which come with our forces.

(6) Parties who suffer death, injury, or damage to property.

0170

(7) Farmers, orphans, and many others who receive assistance and care as a result of official or personal gratuitous contributions of time, money and materials.

In his opening remarks Ambassador Berger mentioned that a Status of Forces Agreement covers many kinds of activities. Viewed as a whole it comprehends extensive, complex and varied administrative arrangements.

We, the US forces and the Republic of Korea, already have formal and informal agreements and understandings which both sides recognize and observe. In a very real sense they are a form of Status of Forces Agreement.

Such arrangements have evolved and grown in the Republic of Korea during the many years in which our forces and your people have stood together in common defense. Should not many of the broad principles reflected in these satisfactory arrangements be incorporated in any SOFA we negotiate?

0171

이, 참

국 방 부

국군무 2082 관리번호 83 1962. 10. 5

수신 외무부 장관 귀하

제목 한미간의 주둔군 지위협정 교섭 문제

검토필(196.4.12-30.)

1. 귀부 외방교 344호 (62. 10. 1) 에 대한 응신입니다.

2. 당부 소관 사항인 시설 및 구역에 대한 제 2 차 실무자 회의에서 미국측이 제시한 협정의 범위에 대하여 추가할 사항은 아래와 같읍니다.

가. 토지 및 시설의 사용에 대한 보상 청구

나. 미군이 사용한 토지 및 시설을 한국 정부에 반환시 원상복구 및 원상복구에 소요되는 보상청구

다. 토지 및 시설의 일시적인 사용 끝.

장 관 박 병

0172

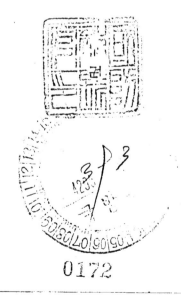

법 무 부 이, 창.

관리 번호 101

법무법 2655 1962. 10. 10.

수신 외무부장관

제목 한미간의 주둔군지위협정 고섭문제

외방고 344(62.10.1)에 대하여 별지와 같이 응신합니다

유첨 의견서 1부. 끝

검토필(1962.12.30.)

법무부장관 조 병

보통문서로 재분류(1966.12.31.)

발송 No. 1962.10.10 법무부

0173

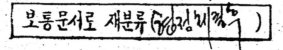

意 見 書

1. 美國側이 提示한 協定의 範圍와 內容中 当部所管事項

가. 出入國管理

美軍構成員, 軍屬및그 直系家族의 出入國은 韓國法令에서 除外하되 旅券또는 身分證을 所持하여야하고 身分의 変更이 있으면 韓國法令의 適用을 받도록하고 前示美軍構成員等이라도 犯法行為等으로 韓國政府의 追放要求가 있으면 追放하도록 規定할것

나. 刑事裁判权

美軍法被適用者는 美軍法에 依한 裁判权을 가지며 美軍法被適用者와 그家族이 韓國內에서 犯한 罪로서 韓國法令에 依하여 処罰할수있는것은 韓國이 裁判权을 갖는다 一國의 法律에 依하여 罪가되는 境遇에는 그國家의 法律에 依한 專屬的裁判权을 갖는다.

裁判权이 競合할 境遇 美國의 財產과 安全그리고 美軍構成員等에 対한 犯罪와 軍務執行中의 犯罪는 美國側이 第一次的인 裁判权을 가지며 그以外의 境遇는 韓國側이 第一次的인 裁判权을 갖는다 그리고 第一次的 裁判权은 友好的인 考慮에 依하여 他方当事國에 移讓할수 있도록 한다.

0174

2-1

그以外 搜査其他節次에 관하여도 相互通告 協助하도록한다.

다. 民事請求权

韓國國民保護上 美軍의 軍務執行으로 因한 損害라 하드라도 韓國政府가 國民에게 損害를 끼친 境遇와 같이 韓國國民의 全損害를 賠償하도록 한다.

0175

2-2

재 무 부

재세관 391　　관리번호 100　　1962. 10.20

수신 외무부장관

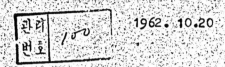

제목 한미간의 주둔군의 지위협정 교섭문제

1. 외방교 344 (62. 10. 1) 에 대한 회신입니다.

2. 미국측이 제시한 협정의 범위및 내용중 당부 소관 사항에 대한 의견을 다음과 같이 제출합니다.

가. 미국측 제안의 장비 및 보급품의 지방조달시의 제세 관세의 면제여부에 대하여는 현행 관세법제36조 5호에 주한국제 연합군용품에 대하여 면세하고 있음을 참고로 하여 주시기 바랍니다.

나. 미국측 제안의 파견국의 "써-비스" 및 시설의 이용에 있어서는 본협정에서 규정하는 구성원은 콤밋사리 및 미군표 등 사용에 대한 권리를 갖일수 있으며 구성원의 범주에 따라 변하지 않는다고 보며 를 통하여 반입하는 물품은 구성원이 일상생활에 필요한한도내 즉 상품화되지 않을정도의 수량에 한하여서만 면세할수 있는것으로 봅니다.

다. 미국측 제안의 주둔군 구성원에 내국세 및 관세에 대한 면세내용에 대해서는

(1) 주둔군 구성원이 주둔군의 구성원으로서 소득한 금액등에 대하여는 소득세를 면제하며

검토필(1966. 6. 30.)

(2) 주둔군 구성원이 한국에 입국시에 이사화물로서 반입하는 가재도구와 기타의 개인용품은 면세할수 있으며

(3) 본 협정에서 구성원으로 규정되는 사람간에 면세수입 물품의양도 양수는 무방하며

(4) 자선단체에 기증하기 위하여 수입하는 물품은 무상으로 분배될 구호에 적합한 물품에 대하여는 면세할것이며

검토필(1962. 12. 30.)

0176

2 — 1

재세관 1962. 10. 20

(5) 개인사용을 위하여 수입하는 자동차에 대한 관세는 한국인에게 양도하지 않는다는 조건으로만 면세함. 끝

보통문서로 재분류(협정체결시)

재무부장관 김 세

2 — 2

0177

국 방 부

국군무 2319 62. 11. 12

수신 외무부장관

제목 한미간의 주한 미국군대 지위협정체결 실무자 회의에 제시할 토지 및 시설에 관한 조항

1962 년 9 월 20 일부터 실시중인 한미간의 주한 미국군대 지위협정체결 실무자회의에 제시할 국방부 소관사항인 토지 및 시설에 관한 조항 (전문 6 조 14 항)을 별첨과 같이 제출합니다.

유첨 : 1, 토지및 시설에 관한 조항 1 부

2. 토지및 시설제공의 접충 경위서 1 부 끝.

장 박 병

접수 16. 12260 '62 11. 14 외무부

발송 16. 968 4295 11 13 국방부

Chai

0178

미합중국 군대 지위 협정중

토지및 시설에 관한 조항

(초안)

0179

제 4 조

1. 대한민국정부는 대한민국과 미합중국간의 상호방위 조약 제 4 조에 따라 미합중국에 대하여 한국내의 시설과 구역의의 사용을 허여한다. 개개의 시설및 구역에 대한 협정은 본협정 제 조에 규정된 합동위원회를 통하여 양정부가 채결하여야 한다.

2. 본협정의 발효시에 미합중국이 사용하는 시설과 구역은 본협정의 목적을 위하여 본협정에 의하여 미합중국에게 허여된 시설및 구역으로 간주한다. 본항의 목적을 위하여 미합중국이 본협정의 발효시에 사용하고 있는 모든 시설과 구역은 합동위원회를 통하여 양정부가 조사결정 한다.

3. 본협정에서 말한 시설과 구역은 당해 시설및 구역의 운영에 필요한 현재 설비 비품 및 정착물을 포함한다.

0180

제 5 조

1. 미합중국정부는 본협정에 의하여 미합중국에게 허여되는 시설및 구역의 취득을 위하여 지급된 전액을 대한민국정부에 보상하여야 한다 본액의 목적을 위하여 보상금액및 기타의 협정은 합동위원회를 통하여 양정부가 합의한다 위에 말한 지불은 미합중국 "달라"로 행한다

2. 미합중국정부는 대한민국에 부담을 지우지 않고 본 협정에 의하여 허여된 시설및 구역의 유지 부수하는 모든 비용을 부담한다.

3. 미합중국정부는 미합중국군대가 1950 년 7 월 한국에 주둔한 이후 본협정발효시기까지 한국의 토지 및 시설의 사용에 따르는 보상금 및 임대료를 대한민국정부에 지불할것을 합의하며 차 보상금및 임대료는 합동위원회를 통하여 양정부가 조사 결정한다.

※ 제5조 3항 추가신설조항

0181

제 6 조

1. 대한민국정부및 미합중국정부는 어느 일방 정부의 요청이 있을때에는 제4조 1항에서 말한 협정을 검토하여야 하고 당해시설및 구역을 대한민국에 반환하거나 또는 새로이 시설및 구역을 재공할것을 합의할수 있다.

2. 미합중국이 사용하는 시설및 구역은 본협정의 목적을 위하여 더 필요하지 않게된 경우에는 언제든지 대한민국정부에 조속히 반환하여야 한다. 미합중국정부는 위에 말한 반환을 위하여 시설및* 구역의 필요성을 끊임없이 검토할것에 동의 한다.

0182

제 7 조

1. 미합중국이 시설및 구역을 임시적으로 사용하지 않고 있을때에는 한국당국 또는 국민이 이를 임시적으로 사용할것을 합동위원회를 통하여 결정할수 있다.

2. 한정된 시간동안 미합중국이 사용할 시설및 구역에 대하여는 합동위원회가 당해 시설및 구역에 대한 협정에 본협정의 규정이 적용될 범위를 명기 하여야 한다.

0183

제 8 조

1. 미합중국정부는 시설및 구역내에서 이의 설치, 운영, 경호및 관리를 위하여 필요한 모든 조치를 취할수있다.

대한민국정부는 시설및 구역의 지원, 경호 및 관리를 위한 미합중국군대의 시설및 구역의 출입의 편의를 도모하기 위하여 미합중국정부의 요청과 합동위원회를 통한 양정부간의 협의에 의하여 이들 시설및 구역에 인접하거나 또는 그 근방의 토지 영수 및 공간에 있어서 관계법령의 범위내에서 필요한 조치를 취할수 있다.

미합중국정부도 또한 합동위원회를 통한 양정부간의 협의에 따라서 위의 목적은 위하여 필요한 조치를 취할수있다.

2. 미합중국정부는 대한민국영역내에의, 영역으로 부터의 또는 영역내의 항해, 항공, 통신, 또는 육상교통을 불필요하게 방해하는 방법에 의하여 1항에서 언급된 조치를 취하지 않을것에 동의한다.

미합중국정부가 사용하는 전파, 방사장치의 주파수 전력및 이에 유사한 사항에 대한 모든 문제는 양정부 당국간의 협의에 의하여 해결 한다.

3. 미합중국정부가 사용하고 있는 시설및 구역에 있어서의 작업은 공공의 안전에 대하여 타당한 고려를 행하고 실시 하여야 한다.

0184

제 9 조

1. 미합중국정부는 본협정의 종료로서 또는 그전에 시설및 구역을 대한민국정부에 반환함에 있어서 당해시설및 구역을 그들이 미합중국에 제공되었을때의 상태로 회복하거나 또는 그 회복의 대신 대한민국정부에 보상할 책임을 지지 않는다. 단, 미합중국의 사용으로 인하여 개인재산이 극심한 파괴를 당한 경우에는 미합중국정부는 대한민국정부의 요청이 있으면 이의 회복 또는 그에 대신하는 보상에 관하여 적절한 고려를 해하여야 한다.

2. 대한민국정부는 본협정의 종료시 또는 그 전의 시설및 구역의 반환시에 당해 시설및 구역에 가하여진 개량, 또는 그곳에 남겨진 건물, 공작물, 공급품, 또는 기타의 물자에 대하여 미합중국정부에 보상할 의무를 지지 않는다.

0185

土地및施設提供의折衝経緯書

0186

(一) 土地및 施設提供의 芍衝經緯

(1) 國際聯合軍이 韓國財産을 使用할수 있는 法的根據로서는 大韓民國과 統一司令部間의 經濟調整에關한 協定 및 第三條 13項에依據 徵發에關한 特別措置令의 規定에依하여 徵發提供하여 왔던것입니다 大韓民國과 統一司令部의 代理인 美國間에 覺書와 議事錄이 相互交換됨으로서 1952年5月24日 釜山에서 韓國代表 財務部長官 白斗鎭 美國政府代表 美國大統領 特使 「마이야」가 署名함으로서 同日字로 發效하게되었던것이다 ~~이를 俗稱「[illegible] 協定」이라고 하며~~ 第3條 第13項에 依하면 韓國政府는 徵發에關한 特別措置令의 規定한바에 따라 駐韓UN軍에게 財産을徵發하여 提供하게된 法的根據라 할수있다

「마이야 協定」 第3條第13項

「第3條 大韓民國은 다음과 같은 責任을 진다

第13項 韓國國民을 除外한 統一司令部의 個人 또는 機關에 對하여 前記國際聯合의 諸決議에依하여 附與되어있거나 또는 弦伯 双方또는 一方의 關係機關에

0187

依하여 公式또는 非公式으로 協定된 特权 免除 施設(便宜)를 附與한다 」

(2) UN軍이 使用中인 徵發財産과 補償金 1950年6月27日부터 1961年12月31日까지 約12個年间에 UN軍이 使用한 徵發財産 数量및 要補償額은

土地	1.201.991.231 坪	5.594.286.496 [20]원
建物	3.398.159 坪	2.763.938.267 [20]원
物資	91.646 点	33.963.937 원
計		8.392.189.700 [20]원
		$485.024.551 —

(3) UN軍에 徵發提供한 財産의 補償対策

(가) 國際联合軍에게 徵發提供된 経偉

6.25動乱 以后 國際联合軍이 作战上 必要로하는 用役및 不動産은 韓國法令 「徵發에関한特別措置令」을 適用하여 韓國陸軍參謀總長과 國際联合軍 司令官间의 作战任務遂行上 協議에依하여 陸軍參謀總長이 徵發하여 提供하여 왔으며 1954年 7月15日字로 國際联合軍 使用財産에 関한業務를

0188

陸軍으로부터 國防部에 移管되였다 UN軍의 不動產 使用要請은 戒嚴令이 解除된 以后에도 繼續됨으로 合法徵發은 하지 않고 있으나 財產所有者의 同意가 있을때만 特別히 使用承認하여 提供하고 있다

(나) 用役및 不動產使用料의 対美折衝經緯

(1) 1951年 5月17日字로 「콜터」將軍이 李大統領에게 보내온 公翰에는 美軍을 包含한 國際聯合軍은 公共用役과 物資及 施設等의 使用料 清算関係를 后日 韓國政府와의 協議下에 解決하도록 美國陸軍省과 財務省의 指示가 있었다고 하였음

(2) 1953年 8月7日 李大統領과 Dulles 美國務長官은 共同聲明을 通하여 「우리兩國政府는 韓美相互防衛条約이 發効하게된 以后 美國이 韓國에 駐屯하게할 軍隊의 地位 그리고 또한 우리들의 共同事業을 遂行하는데 必要한 韓國側施設과 人員의 使用에関한 協約을 即時 相議 하게될것이다 그동안 한편으로 韓國은 繼續 UN軍司令部와 協力할것이며 韓國에있는 UN軍의 地位와 그들에対한 韓國側 施設및

0180

「人員의 使用은 現在대로 継續될것이다」라고 闡明함으로서 UN軍의 法的地位와 韓國側施設 및 人員의 使用에対한 協定이 곧 締結될것을 宣言하고있다

(3) 1954年 8月5日 韓國経済使節団의 渡美時 145,322,706,070원 (1954.6.30 現在)을 要求折衝하여 美國朝野의 輿論을 喚起시켜 이를 調査하고저 美國政府関係官들이 来韓目的으로 日本東京에 到着한바 때마침 油類騒動으로 美側関係官은 来韓을 中止하고 歸國하게 되었다

(4) 1955年 5月23日 孫元一將軍의 渡美時 167,953,529,360圜 (1955.5.30 現在)을 要求했다

(5) 1955年 9月16日字로 「라자스」將軍(國際聯合軍參謀長)이 金顯哲 財務長官에게 보내온 公翰에依하면 清算関係를 3段階로 提案하여 왔다

(가) 1段階 休戰까지의 (1953.7.27) 戰乱期

(나) 2段階 休戰期間부터 (1953.7.27) 韓國政府 関係部処와 協定을 締結하는 날까지의 期間

(다) 3段階 協定締結日로부터의 期間

以上 3段階로 나누어서 休戰期間以前에것은 清算不可能하나

0180

協定締結日부터의것은 淸算可能 하다고 示唆하였다

(6) 1955年12月15日 財務部長官室에서 國際聯合軍이 使用한 電氣 水道 不動産等의 補償에對하여 韓美間会議를 開催할것을 美側에要請했다 (美國代表 하모니 將軍)

(7) 1956年6月18日 「하모니」 將軍이 (國際聯合軍司令部參謀長) 이 金顯哲 財務長官에게 보내온公翰에 依하면 不動産의 使用料 淸算을 削除할것을 提案하여 왔으나 이에 對하여 韓國側은

(8) 1956年8月7日字로 金顯哲 財務長官이 「하모니」 將軍에게 보낸 公翰에는 아래와같이 提案하였다

(가) 休戰期間以前의 모든 使用料淸算은 後日에 協議할것을 前提로 保留

(나) 不動産 使用料 淸算은 後日 協議키로 保留

(9) 1956年9月9日 美8軍司令官에게 앞으로 UN軍이 必要한 財産을 獲得할時에는 使用料를 支拂하지 않는限 獲得 할수 없을것이며 現在까지 使用中인 財産의 補償도 負担 하여야 한다는 協議文을 発送한바 美8軍司令官 「하이트」 將軍은 1956年9月22日字로 UN軍司令部에서

0191

詳細한 回信을 받도록 要請한바 있었다

(10) 1956年 11月 25日 UN軍司令官 「렘니쳐」 將軍으로부터 回答에 依하면 高位決定을(聯合國參戰國間의 協議對象) 하기 爲하여 美陸軍省에 上申하였다고 함

(11) 1957年 1月 17日字로 極東軍司令官에게 再次要請한바 1957年 4月 16日字로 不可하다는 回信이 왔다

(12) 1957年 3月 15日 金用雨長官 渡美時 76,843,372,236 환 1955年 12月 31日 現在 을 要求했음

(13) 1957年 11月 26日 曺正煥 外務部長官은 駐韓美國軍의 地位에關한 協定을 購買 課稅 關稅에關한 協定 請求權 淸算協定 駐屯軍이 使用하는 施設및 地域에 關한 協定 出入國에關한 協定 刑事裁判管轄에關한 協定으로 分離하여 締結할것과 이에対한 交涉開始를 提議하였으며 美側도 이에 應할것을 同意했다

(二) 土地및 施設使用에關한 補償의 問題点

(1) 現在까지의 公翰또는 渡美使節을 通한 折衝方法은 結果的으로 何等의 成果를 보지 못하였으며 이러한 非公式的 理由는 韓國은 休戰協定으로因한

0192

準戰時狀態에 있다고 主張하고있음

(2) 1955年 9月16日字로 「라자스」將軍(國際聯合參謀長)이 金顯哲 財務長官에보낸 公翰中에 美國의公式的 態度를밝히고 現在까지使用하고있는 모든土地및 施設 使用料 그리고 賃貸料等을 淸算할수 없다는 [illegible] [illegible] 表現이였던것이다 協定締結日부터의것은 淸算可能하다고 示唆함으로서 韓美行政協定締結日 以前의 期間을 休戰期間으로 看做하고 準戰時狀態를 핑게로 大韓民國이 此使用料를 負担해야 한다는 固執을 하고있다

(三) 土地및 施設使用에関한 補償要求의 理論的背景

(1) 駐韓國際聯合軍은 1950年6月27日 및 7月7日의 UN安全保障理事会 決議에依하여 派遣된 友好国의 軍隊로서 相互安全保障을為한 共同防衛에 臨하고있다

(2) 駐韓UN軍은 実際上美國의 主導下에 있으며 1950年7月15日字로 李大統領이 駐韓國際聯合司令官에게 作戰指揮权을 移譲함으로서 韓國의 軍事的防衛는 駐韓UN軍司令部가 맡고있다

0193

(3) 1953年 8月 8日 韓美相互防衛條約 第四條에 依據 美軍을 大韓民國의 領土內와 그 周辺에 配置하는 权利를 許與함으로서 美軍의 韓國駐屯이 長久化되고 軍事基地 및 財産使用에 関한 法的問題가 発生하지 않을수 없다

(4) 韓美相互防衛条約 假調印当時 「李 덜레스」 共同声明에는 두가지의 両國協議事項을 천명했다
첫째. 本條約이 発効한 直后 駐韓美軍의 身分 施設 用役等에 関한 行政協定을 迅速히 交涉 한다는 것이며
둘째. 本条約이 発効하는 그날까지 韓國軍의 指揮权을 UN軍司令官의 麾下에 두며 그리하여 指揮权은 1954年 1月 17日 와신톤 合意議事錄에 依하여 再確認되었으나 大韓民國의 权益事項인 行政協定은 其后 8年이 지난 今日까지 履行되고 있지못하다

(5) 1952年 5月 24日 發効된 大韓民國과 統一司令部間의 經濟調整에関한 協定 第三条 第十三項에 依據하여 UN軍의 土地 및 施設使用을 為한 徵発에関한 特別措置令으로서 規定한바 있으나 徵発 財産에 対한 補償問題는 合意한바 없다 그러나 同協定의 前文에 나타난

0194

立法精神을 考察하면 UN軍徵発財産에対한 補償은 美國政府가 負担하여야할것으로 解釈된다 그理由를 説明하면

(가) 同協定前文「1950年7月7日 UN安全保障理事会의 決議에 依하여 大韓民國에 軍事兵力과 其他援助를 供與하는 会員國家가 如斯한 兵力과援助를 美合衆國管理下의 統一司令部에 提供할것을 建議한바 있고」라고 規定함으로서 美國이 實質的으로 UN軍을 主導하게되고 美國을비롯한 参戦國16個國은 美軍將校인 UN軍司令官의 指揮에 들어갔던것이다 이로서 UN統一司令部의 管理및 指揮权을 美國의責任下에 行使하게되었다

(나) 同協定前文에「大韓民國의 主权을 侵略함이 없이 國際联合總司令部의 軍事兵力의 有効한 支援을保障하고 韓國國民의 苦難을 救済하며 大韓民國의 健全한 経済를 樹立 維持하기為하여 統一司令部와 大韓民國과의 経済問題를 調整함이 要望됨으로」라고 規定되어있다

0195

大韓民國은 1948年12月12日字 UN總会의 決議에 依하여 承認된 完全한主权과 独立을갖인 合法的政府인 것이다 그러므로 駐韓美軍의 軍事兵力의 有効한 支援은 어디까지나 大韓民國의 主权을侵害않은 範囲内에서 이루어져야함을 意味한다 大韓民國의 主权은 憲法 第二条에 뚜렷이 明示된바같이 严然히 大韓民國의 國民에있고 國民으로부터 由来하고 있다 美軍의 土地및 施設使用에関한 支援도 이와같은 主权的保障에서 離脱될수 없을것이다 우리나라 憲法 第15条 2項을 紹介한다면 「------ 國民의 財産을 使用 收用 또는 制限함에는 法律의 定하는바에 依하여 相当한 補償을 支給 함으로서 行한다」 라고 規定하고있다 大韓民國政府는 國民으로부터 土地 或은 施設을 徵発하여 UN軍에 提供하였지만 이는 어디까지나 非常時 韓國의 徵発에関한 法律에 基礎하고 있고 憲法 15條에 明示된 補償에関한 合憲的 救済節次가 履行되지 않으면 안될것이다 다음 同協定 前文에 「韓國 國民의 苦難을 救済하며 大韓民國의 健全한 経済를 樹立維持하기爲하여 」의 規定을

0196

미루어본다면 美軍의 軍事的 支援뿐만 아니라 經濟的 支援을 함으로서 韓國國民의 当面한 苦難을 救濟케하고 大韓民國의 經濟安全을 爲하여 努力함을 意味할것이다. 大韓民國은 美國으로부터 莫大한 軍事的 經濟的 援助에 依存하고 있다는 現実로볼때 韓國에 있어 莫大한量의 土地와 施設을 無償으로 使用하고 있다함은 政府財政的 負担과 韓國의 國民經濟를 威脅하는 結果가 되고 있는것이다. 駐韓美軍의 駐屯意義는 韓國을 共産侵略과 威脅에서 救出하고 韓國의 安全保障과 極東平和維持의 達成에 있는以上 韓國自身의 負担으로 莫大한 損失을 当하고 있는 美軍의 土地및 施設使用에関한 補償 問題는 解決되어져야 할것이다.

0197

주둔군 지위협정 초안에 대한 관계당국 의견

1. 농 림 부: 별다른 의견이 없음.
2. 보 사 부: 이의 없음.
3. 내 무 부: 별 의견이 없음.
4. 체 신 부: 원칙적으로 찬성임.
5. 법 무 부: 형사재판권 (가) 초안 12조 5항 라 호 "...대한민국에 의하여 기소가 제기될 때까지 미합중국이 계속해서 구금한다" 를 "...대한민국정부의 신병인도요청이 있을 때까지 미합중국이 계속해서 구금한다"로 개정할 것.

(나) 초안 12조 9항 마호 "...자신을 위하여 강제적절차에 의하여 증인을 획득할 권리"를 "...자신을 위하여 대한민국 법률의 정하는바에 의하여 증인을 획득할 권리"로 개정할 것

(다) 한국측이 관할권을 포기한 사건 및 공무집행중의 사건으로서 미군에서 재판하는 경우 한국측 요청이 있을 시에는 한국정부 대표를 동 재판에 입회케 함을 허용하는 지의 규정을 신설할 것.

(라) 미국측이 제 1 차적 관할권에 의하여 범인을 체포한 경우라도, 이를 한국정부에 통고하여야 하며 또 한국정부가 제 1 차적 관할권에 의한 것인지 그 여부를 밝힐 필요가 있다고 인정되어 범인심문의 요청을 할 시에는 미국측은 한국수사관헌이 구금된 그 범인을 심문함을 허용해야 한다는 지의 규정을 신설할 것.

(마) 미국측에 제 1 차적 관할권이 없는 자에 대하여는 영내에서의 체포는 물론 그 사건에 관계된 수색, 압수 기타 강제처분을 한국측이 할수 있다는 지의 규정을 신설할 것.

(바) 미국측은 한국정부의 요구가 있을 시에는 언제든지

0198

한국법의 정하는 바에 의하여 미군인을 참고인 또는
증인으로 출두케함에 협조해야한다는 지의 규정을 신설
할것.

(사) 미군에 파견되어 근무에 복하고 있는 한국군
(예 카투사)은 공무집행중이거나 아니거나 또는 영내
이거나 아니거나를 불문하고 그의 범죄에 관한 그에
대한 관할권은 한국측에 있다는 지의 규정을 신설할 것.

민사청구권(까)초안 제 13 조는 미국군대의 공무집행중
의 불법행위에 대하여는 우리나라 민사재판권이 미치지
못한다고 하여 미주둔군의 치외법권을 인정하고 있는 바,
나토협정 9조, 미일협정 9 조의 예에 따른 것이라고는
하나 전시에 있어서 작전 또는 그 목적수행을 위한
공무집행중의 불법행위에 국한시킴이 가할 것으로 사료됨.

(나) 미군에 파견 근무하는 한국군(예카투사)의 공무
집행중의 불법행위에 대한 보상책임은 미군측에 귀속
된다는 지의 규정을 신설할 것.

6. 문교부: 이의가 없음

7. 경제기획원: (1) 제 16 조 3 항(미군견응판매소설치에 관하여)
한국내에서 허가되지 않는자에 대한 동 판매소 물자의
판매 및 취급을 금지하는 미당국의 행정적조치에 한국
정부 또는 관헌에 의한 한미합동취체의 법적근거를 삽입할것.

(2) 제 16 조에 추가하여 미군당국이 주둔군 영외에서
대한민국 국민 또는 비대한민국국민으로 하여금 한국
정부의 허가 없이 택시영업 등 기타 이에 유사한 영업
행위를 못하게 하는 규정을 두도록 할 것.

(3) 제 5 조 본조항에 추가하여 미군당국이 임시 또는
영구적으로 사용 또는 관리의 책임을 지고 있는 대한민국
또는 대한민국 국민의 재산에서 발생한 손해에 대하여도

0199

이를 배상할 책임을 질것이며 이 배상책임은 가능하면 6.25 당시 미군이 사용한 재산에 대하여도 대한민국정부 또는 국민이 소정의 절차에 따라 소청한 분 부터 소급 배상 토록 할것.

8. 교 통 부: (1) 제 10 조 미합중국 및 기타 외국의 선박 및 항공기로서 미합중국에 의하여 미합중국을 위하여 또는 미합중국의 관리하에 본협정의 목적을 위하여 위에서 항공기의 범위가 결정되어 있지 않으며, 다음과 같은 경우를 고려하여 이의 명시가 필요하다고 사료 됨.

(가) 미군의 비국고활동에 의하여 사용되는 비군용항공기가 본조항이 규정하는 항공기의 범위내에 들수 있는가의 문제. 현재 미8 군내에 비국고활동의 일부로서 후라잉 클럽이 있어 민간기(미국연방항공청에 등록되어 있음)를 사용하고 있으며 이는 우리나라항공법 103 조의 위반으로서 이를 미 8군 당국에 통고한 바 8군에서는 이 항공기의 소유와 운영이 한미원조협정에 규정한 통합사령부의 기능수행에 필요한 것으로 해석한다는 의견이 있었음. 이러한 경우 국제민간항공조약 제 3 조에 규정한 국가항공기와 민간항공기의 정의는 범위를 규정하는데 도움이 될것이며 국가항공기는 민간항공국제기관에 등록되지 않으며 민간항공법의 적용을 받지 않음. 따라서 제 10 조의 항공기는 원칙적으로 국가항공기에 한하고 기타 항공기는

0200

대한민국의 민간항공에 관한 모든 법규의 대상이 되어야 할 것임.

(나) 본조에서 말한 선박 및 항공기의 출입은 국내항구간의 출입을 포함한다고 하나 이 경우 역시 민간항공기의 경우 항공법 103 조에 위반하는 결과가 됨.

(2) 제 11 조 협조 및 통합을 도모하는데 필요한 절차는 1 차적으로 대한민국에서 제정시행되는 절차에 따라 2 차적으로 우리나라에서 제정시행되는 절차가 없는 경우 국제민간항공기구에서 제정한 표준과 권고된 방식이 우리나라에 부적당하거나 없을 경우 양 정부간의 협의에 의하여 정해져야 할 것으로 사료됨.

(3) 항공교통관리는 항공교통관제라고 함이 좋을 것임.

(4) 제 10 조 대한민국 항구에 출입하는 선박으로서 입항료를 면제하는 선박의 범위를 제 2 항에서 "공간용선계약에 의한 선박을 제외한 기타의 용선계약(나용선계약, 운송계약 및 시간계약)에 의한 선박"으로 규정하고 있으나 이는 다음과 같은 사유로서 수정이 필요하다고 생각 됨.

(가) 선박의 제공을 계약의 내용으로 하여 선박관리비용의 일체를 용선자가 부담하는 나용선계약에 의한 선박이나 선박경비중 선비를 공제한 운항비(항비포함)을 용선자가 부담하는 정기용선계약에 의한 선박은 미합중국의 관리하에 본협정의 목적을 위하여 운항되는 선박으로 보고 입항료를 면제할수 있으나, (나) 개개의 화물의 운송을 계약내용으로 하는 운송계약이나 선복 즉 운송용역의 제공을 계약내용으로 하는 항해(구간)용선계약에 있어서는 선박이 용선자의 관리하에 있는 것이 아니고 항비도 선주부담으로 하는 것이므로 입항료를 징수하여도 미군국고지출에 영향이 없는 것인바 여사한 운송계약에 의하여 운항하는 선박을 미합중국의 관리하에 운항하는 선박으로는 볼수 없으며 그 입항료는 마땅히 부과되어야 할 것임. (다) 따라서 제 2 항의 입항료가 면제되는 선박의 범위는 나용선계약과 정기용선계약에 의한 선박으로 한정함이 타당한 것으로 생각됨.

0201

9. 국 방 부: 10 조 3 항의 "적당한 요율의 안내료"를 이 협정의 적용을 받지 않는 일반선박이 같은 조건 아래서 지불하는 액과 동일한 액의 안내료로 할 것.

10. 재 무 부: (1) 제 18 조 5 항에 대하여: 동 항에 의하면 미국 내에서 미국군을 위하여 미정부와 계약한 자가 한국에 일시로 체류하는 동안에 한국에서 갖게될 동산의 보유, 사용, 사망에 의한 이전등에 대하여 미국군인과 동일하게 면세토록 되어 있는 바, 군인 아닌 계약자에게 까지 여사한 면세권을 줄 필요는 없다고 생각 됨.

(2) 제 18 조 6 항에 대하여: 전기한 계약자는 다시 그들의 계약에서 발생한 소득에 대하여도 한국의 조세(소득세)를 부과 받지 않는다 하였으나 비록 미군을 위한 미국정부와의 계약으로 인한 소득이라 할지라도 그 경제행위가 한국내에서 행하여지는 이상 한국 과세권에 복종하여야 함.

(3) 대한민국 정부는 군표의 사용금지 조치로서 압수된 군표 또는 본 협정 체결시에 있어서 대한민국정부가 압수보유중인 군표는 미합중국 국고에 귀속시킬 것을 신설하여야 함.

(4) Bank of America 의 영업내용이 한국의 금융 및 외환 제도에 배치되지 않도록 한국정부의 승인 받는 조문을 신설하여야 함.

12. 법 제 처: 본 협정의 체결로 인하여 대한민국의 미합중국에 대하여 부담하게 됨 의무에 관하여는 이미 우리 국내법에 의하여 인정된 것(예 본 협정 제 3 조 제 2 항(a)의 규정에 의하여 대한민국이 지는 미합중국 군대 구성원 군속 및 그 가족에 대하여 외국인의 등록 및 관리에 관한 대한민국 법령의 적용으로 부터 면제 시켜줄 의무는 입국, 출국과 등록에 관한 법률 제 1 조 단서의 규정에 의하여 인정되었음) 대한민국과 미합중국간에 이미 체결된 조약에 의하여 인정된 것(예 본

0202

협정 제 4 조의 규정에 의하여 대한민국이 미합중국에 대하여 가지는 시설 및 지역의 사용을 허용할 의무에 대하여는 1954 년 대한민국과 미합중국간의 상호방위조약 제 4 조의 규정에 의하여 인정되었음) 및 일반국제법상 인정된 것 (예 본 협정 제 12 조의 규정에 의하여 대한민국 내에 있는 미합중국 군대 구성원 및 군속이 특정 군무집행중에 행한 작위 또는 부작위로 인한 범죄에 대하여 미합중국 군당국의 제 1 차적 재판권을 인정하여야 하는 의무 단 이설이 있음) 등이 있으며 그 이외의 의무도 본 협정은 본 협정 제 27 조의 규정에 의하여 대한민국 정부로 부터의 헌법절차에 따르는 비준의 통고가 미합중국 정부에 접수된 날로 부터 발효하게 되어 있으며 비준 공포된 국제조약은 헌법 제 7 조 제 1 항의 규정에 의하여 국내법과 동일한 효력을 가지므로 본 협정이 국내법과 저촉되거나 본 협정의 시행을 위하여 새로운 입법을 할 필요가 없는 것으로 생각됨(단 본 협정의 시행에 있어서 변잡을 피하기 위하여 현행 국내법의 관계규정을 개정하는 것은 별 문제 임).

13. 정 무 국: 제 4 조 1 항에서 대한민국 정부는 대한민국과 미합중국간의 상호방위조약 제 4 조에 따라, 미합중국에 대하여 한국내의 시설과 구역의 사용을 허용한다고 규정하고 또한 제 4 조 2 항에서 행정협정의 발효시에 미합중국이 사용하는 시설과 구역은, 본 협정의 목적을 위하여 본 협정에 의하여 미합중국에게 허여된 시설및 구역으로 간주한다고 규정한데 관하여 동 규정상으로 볼때 제 4 조 2 항에 의하여 미합중국에게 허여될 시설 및 구역의 범위를 좀더 명확히 규정함이 좋을 것으로 사료됨. 예를 들면 현재 미국군대가 사용중에 있는 시설 및 구역은 1950 년 7 월 26 일자 징발에 관한 특별 조치령에 의거하여 국방부가 징발하여 이들을 유엔군이 사용

0203

할 것을 승인한것도 있을 것이고 1948 년 9 월 11 일자로서 서명된 재정 및 재산에 관한 최초협정에 의거하여 사실상 미 8 군당국이 사용하는 재산(예를 들면 내자 아파-트) 등 등도 있을 것이니 미국군대가 사용중에 있는 시설과 구역은 미군측이 최초에 사용케된 근거가 무엇에 의한 것이든 간에 행정협정 발효시에 사용하는 것은 모다 제 4 조 2 항의 시설 및 구역으로 간주되어 합동심의위원회의 조사대상이 되도록 함이 좋을 것으로 사료됨.

14. 통 상 국: 1. 일반의견: 본 협정에 있어서는 (1) 미군이 주둔한 이래 우리나라(국민을 포함)가 체험한 막심하고 부당한 피해사실에 비추어 국가이익(국민을 포함함)을 고려하여 미군의 지위를 가능한 한 우리나라의 법질서하에 가져와야 된다는 점.

(2) 국제연합 안전보장 이사회 결의 및 한미 상호 방위조약에 의하여 우리나라에 주둔하고 있는 미군의 적절한 군사 활동과 직무수행에 지장을 주어서는 안된다는 점.

(3) 미국이 우리나라와 정치적으로 가장 밀접한 우호관계에 있으며, 군사적, 경제적으로 우리나라를 많이 원조하고 있다는 점.

(4) 미국이 본협정의 체결교섭을 지연시키고 있다는 점 (체결가능성의 문제)

(5) 우리가 제안하는 입장임으로 교섭경과에서 미국측의 수정을 각오하여야 한다는 점. 등의 여러가지가 고려되어야 할 것인데 귀국에서 작성한 협정초안은 대체로 이상 제점을 고려하면서도 상기 (1)에 중점을 두어 접수국의 이익을 가장 많이 반영시키고 있는 "1960 년의 미일간의 주둔군지위협정" 과 " NATO 조약 기구 가맹국간의 주둔군 지위협정"에 가가운 방향으로 되어 있어 그 내용이 대단히 잘되었다고 본다.

(2) 조항별 의견: 전기 1 의 (1) 및 (5) 의 입장에서 특히 경제문제에 관련하여 극히 부분적인 조항별 의견은 다음과 같다.

0204

대표부에 의하여 미군에게 부여된 특권과 면제 : (가) 본 협정 초안 설명서에 의하면 상금 그 효력이 있는 소위 "마이야협정 3 조 13 항"과 본 협정과의 관계에 관하여는 본 협정 발효후 이에 관한 명시적 규정을 두기 위하여 앞으로 적기에 미국측과 교섭하도록 하고, 본 협정에서는 이에 관한 규정을 두지 않았다. 이는 전기 1 의 (4)를 고려한 것이라고 사료되나 "마이야 협정 3 조 13 항"이 본 협정과 관계 없이 유효하게 살게되면 본 협정의 효과가 많이 제한될 것이며, 특히 관세 면제로 인하여 막심한 손해를 가져온 과거 경험을 생각하여 이 기회에 사실상 통일사령부의 대부분을 구성하는 미군의 특권과 면제의 범위를 제한하기 위하여 양 협정의 관계를 명문으로 해결함이 좋을 것이다. (나) "미국군사고문단 설치에 관한 협정"에 의하여 미국군사 고문단에게 부여되는 외교관과 동일한 특권과 면제에 관하여도 상기와 같은 이유로 이 기회에 제한하는 방향으로 양 협정의 관계를 명문으로 해결함이 좋을 것이다.

(2) 초안 14 조 : 초안 14 조 3 항에 의하면 미군 구성원, 군속 및 그 가족에게 탁송되는 사용재산 중 "이들이 처음 한국에 도착할 때 수입하는 자재 도구"와 "미군 사우편국을 통하여 우송되어오는 합리적인 양의 의복 및 가정용품"에 대하여 관세를 면제할 것을 규정하고 있는데 이들의 일상 생활에 소요되는 가재도구 기타의 상용물자에 대하여 관세를 면제함은 타당하다. 다만 처음 수입하는 가재도구가 가재도구로서 인정되는 범위인가 아닌가 하는 것과 미군사 우편국을 통하여 우송되어 오는 의복 및 가정용품의 양이 합리적인가 아닌가 하는 것은 우리 세관의 검열을 거쳐 세관장의 재량으로 판단되어야 하는데 이들의 재산이 세관 검열을 거치게 되는가가 분명치 않다. 물론 초안 14 조 1 항

0205

후단에 우리세관의 일반적 검열권을 규정하고 있으므로 이들 문자를 동조 5 항에 의한 면제대상 이외로 보아 검열의 대상이 되는 것으로 해석되기는 하나, 동조 5 항에 의하면 "명령에 의하여 출입국하는 미군부대" 라고만 하여 "이들이 처음 한국에 도착할때 수입하는 가재도구" 역시 "명령에 의하여 출입국하는 미군부대가 처음 한국에 도착할 때 수입하는 가재도구"라고도 오해될 가능성이 있으며, "미군사우편국을 통하여 우송되어 오는 가정용품"에 관하여도 동조 5항에서 규정한 "군사 우편을 이용하는 공용우편물"은 아니라 하여도 과거 실제로 미군사우편물(공용, 사용이고 간에)에 대하여 우리 세관당국에서 어느 정도 검열권을 가지고 있는 가가 의문임을 생각할 때 좀더 그 규정 방식을 상세하게 하는 것이 좋지 않을 까 한다.

동조 3 항 및 5 항은 미일협정(1960) 11 조의 3 항 및 5 항을 참작하여 작성된듯 하나, 미군에 의한 또는 미군과 한국인이 결탁한 밀수행위는 우리나라가 일본의 경우보다 심하며, 이로 인한 국내경제의 악영향을 생각할 때 동조 3 항의 물자가 세관의 검열대상이 되도록 보다 명확한 규정으로 하여, 가령 동조 5 항의 "명령에 의하여 출입국하는 미군부대"를 "명령에 의하여 출입국하는 미군부대의 휴대품" 으로 국한한다든가, 또는 미군사우편국을 통하여 우송되는 가정용품 등에 관하여는 초안 21 조 2 항과 같은 규정에 기치지 말고 보다 적극적으로 군사우편국을 통한 사용(私用) 가정용 우편물은 한국세관의 검열을 받어야 한다고 규정함이 좋을 것이다.

(3) 초안 15 조 1 항: 동 15 조 1 항은 미군이 한국내에서 보유, 사용 또는 이전하는 재산에 대하여 조세 또는 유사한 과징금을 과하지 않음을 규정하고 있는 바, "이전"이 "미군 상호간의 이전"을 뜻한다면 동조 3 항과 같이 이를 상호간의 이전"이라고 명시하여 오해를 남기지 않음이 좋을 것이다.

0206

(4) 초안 16 조 4 항 : 동 16 조 4 항은 미군의 사용을 위하여 미군 PX 등 기관이 수입하는 상품의 양을 합리적인 범위에 국한하도록 규정하고 있는데 이에 관하여도 전기 2, (2) 와 같은 이유로 우리 세관당국의 검열을 기할수 있도록 보다 구체적인 규정이 있어야 할 것이다.

(5) 초안 17 조 : 동조는 미군 자체의 소비를 위하여 필요한 물품과 그들이 필요로 하는 역무의 현지구매에 관한 규정인 바, 우리 초안에는 미일협정 (1960) 12 3 항과 같은 규정이 없으므로 미군의공인 조달기관이 적당한 증명서에 의하여 한국 내에서 공용으로 조달하는 자재, 수품 및 역무에 대하여 한국의 조세가 면제 되지 않는 것으로 해석된다. 우리나라는 현재 경제개발 5 개년계획에 의하여 산업개발과 병행하여 수출진흥에 전력을 다하고 있으며 미군의 공용 현지 조달에 있어서는 우리나라가 항상 일본과 경쟁하는 입장에 있어 우리가 미군에 판매할수 있는 물자중 많은 것을 일본에게 빼앗겨 왔다는 경험에 비추어 미군의 한국물자 구매의욕을 고취시키기 위하여 미군의 공용 현지 조달에 한해서는 한국의 일정 범위의 조세 면제를 고려함이 좋을 것이다.

0207

기 안 용 지

자 체 통 제		기안처	미주과 강석재	전화번호	근거서류접수일자
과장	국장	차관보좌관	차관	장관	
관계관 서명					
기안 년월일	1962. 10. 10	시행 년월일		보존 년한	영	정서	기장
분류 기호		전체 통제		종결	
경유 수신 참조	건의		발신		
제목	미주둔군 지위협정 제3차 회의 개최				

10월 10일 14:00 시에 개최될 미주둔군 지위협정 제 3차 실무 교섭회의에서는 9월 28일 제 2차 회의에서 양측이 각각 제시한바 있는 교섭 범위 및 내용에 대한 상호 의견 교환과 토의순위를 결정 하기로 되어 있는바 우리측은 별안과 여히 미국측안에 대한 우리측의 일반적 견해를 피력하고 토의순위 결정에 있어서는 차기회의에서는 우선 아래문제중에서 합의를 보는 문제부터 토의하도록 제의코저 건의하오니 재가하여 주시기 바랍니다.

아 래

차기회의 토의순위: 용어의 정의, 출입국 관리, 및 관세문제중 합의 보는 문제를 토의함.

유첨: 미국측안에 대한 우리측의 일반적 견해 (안) ... 1부. 끝

문서로 재분류 (1966.12.31 ...) 1966. 2.30

1966. 12. 31 에 예고문에 의거 일반문서로 재분류됨

0208

승인양식 1—1—3 (1112-040-016-018) (190mm×260mm16절지)

1964 년 9 월 30 일 미주과 직권으로 파기문서로 재분류

18-1

미국측 안에 대한 우리측의 일반적 견해 (안)

1. 토지 및 시설문제

미국측안은 토지 및 시설에 대한 보상문제를 전연 언급하지 않고 있음. 그러나 이보상 문제를 둘러싼 쌍방의 의견차이는 충분히 알려져 있는 바이며 이러한 실질적 의견차이를 내포하는 중요한 사항을 협정교섭의 토의 사항에서 뺄수는 없는것임. 따라서 보상문제를 토의의 대상으로 삼는다는데 대하여는 우선 미국측도 이의가 없을것으로 생각됨.

2. 인적 범위

미국측안은 군인, 군속, 군계약자 및 그들의 가족이외에도 출장 기타 공용으로 잠정적으로 입국하는 군인등에 대한 규정도 포함시킬것을 제의하고 있는데 이는 우리측으로서도 별반 이의가 없음.

3. 공의물 및 용역

공의물 및 용역에관한 충분한 보장을 미국측이 받기를 원하는 입장에서 이사항에 관한 규정을 포함할것을 미국측이 제의하고 있는데 필요한 범위 내에서 이문제를 토의하는데는 이의가 없음.

4. 형사 행정

형사행정 문제에 관하여는 형사 재판관할권 문제와 일괄해서 토의하는 것이 매우 적절할 것으로 생각됨.

5. 미국측안의 결론

미국측은 그 제안의 결론에서 양국간에 현존하는 공식 또는 비공식 약정 등의 원칙을 살려 앞으로의 협정에 융합하는것이 어떠냐는 질문을 제기하였는데 우리들 실무자 교섭의 이의는 현존하는 제 약정의 비현실성과 그부적합성을 인정하고 현실에 적합한 새로운 협정을 마련하는데 그 목적이 있는것으로 생각됨.

6. 기타

미국측이 (양) (현재까지) 제시한 교섭범위 및 내용에 포함되지않은 기타 문제들도 토의에추가 내지 삭제할수 있음

0209

18-2

Background Paper
E-9
October 10, 1962

STATUS OF FORCES ~~[illegible]~~ MAJOR TOPICS

1. PREAMBLE

2. DEFINITIONS

3. FACILITIES AND AREAS

4. AIR TRAFFIC CONTROL AND NAVIGATIONAL AIDS

5. JOINT COMMITTEE

6. ENTRY AND EXIT OF PERSONS

7. CUSTOMS AND DUTIES

8. VEHICLE, VESSEL & AIRCRAFT ACCESS TO PORTS AND AIRPORTS, ACCESS OF VEHICLES AND PERSONNEL TO FACILITIES AND AREAS

9. UTILITIES AND SERVICES

10. MILITARY PAYMENT CERTIFICATES

11. APO's AND MAILING

12. ENROLLMENT AND TRAINING OF RESERVISTS

13. MEASURES TO INSURE SAFETY AND SECURITY OF US ARMED FORCES, ITS MEMBERS, DEPENDENTS, AND PROPERTY

14. METEOROLOGICAL AND RELATED SERVICES

15. VEHICLE AND DRIVER LICENSES; MARKINGS

16. CURRENCY CONTROLS

17. NONAPPROPRIATED FUND ACTIVITIES

18. RESPECT FOR LOCAL LAW

19. CRIMINAL JURISDICTION AND ADMINISTRATION

20. CLAIMS

21. TAXES

22. LOCAL (OFF SHORE) PROCUREMENT OF SUPPLIES, MATERIALS AND CONSTRUCTION

23. CONTRACTUAL DISPUTES

24. ARMED FORCES CONTRACTORS

21-5 0210

25. LABOR

26. NATIONAL APPROVAL, EFFECTIVE DATE, AND IMPLEMENTING LEGISLATION TO BRING AGREEMENT INTO FORCE

27. REVISION OR AMENDMENT OF AGREEMENT

28. DURATION AND TERMINATION OF AGREEMENT

보통문서로 재분류(1966.12.31.)

1964 년 9 월 30일 미주과 직권으로 예고문 로재

1966,12,31,에 예고문에 의거 일반문서로 재분류됨

0211

21-6

자체 통제		기안처	조약과 이창범	전화번호	근거서류접수일자

	수석대표		차관보 보좌관		차관	장관
					무재	

관계관 서명	미주과장: 조약과장:	기획조정관:

기안 년월일	1962. 10. 10	시행 년월일		보존 년한	10	정서	기장
분류 기호	외방교 348	전체 통제	검열 1962.10. 통제관	종결			
경유 수신 참조	국가재건최고회의의장 (외무국방위원장 참조) 내각수반			발신	외무부장관		

제목: 한미간의 주둔군지위협정 체결을 위한 제3차 실무자회의 보고

1962. 10. 10. 오후 2시부터 동 3시 10분 까지 외무부회의실에서 개최된 표기 협정 체결을 위한 한미 양국 실무자회의 결과를 별지와 같이 보고 합니다.

유첨: 회의 보고서 끝.

1962, 10, 15에 예고문에 의거 일반문서로 재분류됨

첨부물에서 분리되면 보통문서로 재분류

관리번호 62-625

1964년 9월 30일 미주과 직권으로 재분류

4-1

승인양식 1-1-3 (1112-040 016 018) (190mm×260mm16절지)

0212

한미간의 주둔군지위협정 실무자회의

보 고 서

1. 시일: 1962. 10. 10. 오후 2 시부터 동 3 시 10분 까지

2. 장소: 외무부 회의실

3. 참석자: 한국측: 신 관 섭 (재무부 세관국장) (수석대표대리)

박 근 (외무부 미주과장)

이 남 구 (국방부 군무과장)

지 성 구 (외무부 공보관)

신 정 섭 (외무부 2 등서기관)

이 창 범 (외무부 3 등서기관)

강 석 제 (" ")

미국측:

Mr. Philip C. Habib	Counselor of the Embassy for Political Affairs
Brig.Gen. J.D. Lawlor	Deputy Chief of Staff 8th Army
Col. G.G. O'Connor	" "
Capt. R.M. Brownlie	Assistant Chief of Staff USN/K
Mr. William J. Ford	First Secretary of the Embassy
Mr. Benjamin A. Fleck	First Secretary of the Embassy
Lt.Col.R.E. Miller	Staff Officer,JAG 8th Army
Lt.Col.G.T.Suderman	Staff Officer, J-5 USAF/K
Mr. Robert A. Lewis	Second Secretary and Consul of the Embassy

4. 토의사항: (1) 협정에 포함될 범위 및 내용에 관하여 의견을 교환하였으며 지난번 회의에서 제시한 우리측 안에 미국측이 새로운 몇가지 항목을 추가한 포괄적인 협정의 범위 및 내용을 제시하였음.

(2) 이에 대하여 양측간에 의견교환이 있었으며 우리측은 원칙적으로 이에 동의하고 다만 미국측 제의 제 13 항

0213

4-2

미국문 88-12(5)

0214

에서 규정한 주둔군, 기타 인원과 재산의 안전에 대한 보장조치에 관하여는 우리측은 여사한 항목은 협상의 독립된 대상이 될수 없으며 특히 입법조치에 관한 일반적 의무부과문제는 본 협정의 적절한 대상이 되지 않는 점을 지적하고 이 항목의 제외를 요구하였으나 합의에 이르지 못하였음으로 일단 보류키로 합의하고, 기타 항목을 채택하였음.

(3) 다음으로 차기 회의에서 토의할 의제에 관하여 양측의 의견교환이 있었는데 미국측은 먼저 협정의 전문, 용어의 정의, 그리고 합동위원회의 설치 및 구성에 관한 문제부터 토의 하자고 제의하였는바, 우리측은 합동위원회 대신 출입국 관리문제를 우선 토의하자고 제의하여 토론이 전개되었으며 결국 협정의 전문, 용어의 정의, 및 출입국관리문제를 차기회의에서 토의하기로 합의함.

5. 중요합의사항: (1) 미국측이 제시한 협정의 범위 및 내용에 관하여 13 항만을 보류하고 합의함. (별첨 1 참조)

(2) 차기 회의의 의제로서 협정의 전문, 용어의 정의 및 출입국관리 문제를 토의하기로 합의 함.

6. 기타 사항: (1) 차기 회의시일: 1962. 10. 19. 오후 2 시

(2) 차기회의 의제: (가) 협정의 전문

(나) 용어의 정의

(다) 출입국 관리

(3) 신문발표: 별지 참조(별첨2)

끝

0215

4-3

미일 88-12

0216

별첨 1

STATUS OF FORCES AGREEMENT - MAJOR TOPICS

1. Preamble
2. Definitions
3. Facilities and Areas
4. Air Traffic Control and Navigational Aids
5. Joint Committee
6. Entry and Exit of Persons
7. Customs and Duties
8. Vehicle, Vessel & Aircraft Access to Ports and Airports, Access of Vehicles and Personnel to Facilities and Areas
9. Utilities and Services
10. Military Payment Certificates
11. APO's and Mailing
12. Enrollment and Training of Reservists
13. Measures to Insure Safety and Security of US Armed Forces, Its Members, Dependents, and Property
14. Meteorological and Related Services
15. Vehicle and Driver Licenses; Markings
16. Currency Controls
17. Nonappropriated Fund Activities
18. Respect for Local Law
19. Criminal Jurisdiction and Administration
20. Claims
21. Taxes
22. Local (off shore) Procurement of Supplies, Materials and Construction
23. Contractual Disputes
24. Armed Forces Contractors
25. Labor
26. National Approval, Effective Date, and Inplementing Legislation to bring Agreement into Force
27. Revision or Amendment of Agreement
28. Duration and Termination of Agreement

1966.12.31에 예고문에 의거 일반문서로 재분류됨

일반문서로 재분류(1966.12.31)

1-4

0217

0218

보도자료 제 71호

별첨 2 10월 10일

대한민국 외무부와 주한미국대사관의
공동발표

오늘의 회담에서는 대표들은 주둔군 지위 협정의 범위와 내용에 관한 토의를 계속하였다. 대표들은 앞으로의 회담에서 교섭될 주둔군 지위 협정에 포함시키게 될 주요제목에 관하여 원칙적인 합의에 도달하였다.

대표들은 다음번 회담에서는 동건 협정의 서문, 협정에 사용될 용어의 정의에 관한 조항 그리고 인원의 출입국에 관한 조항에 관하여 세부적이고 구체적인 토의를 할것을 결정하였다.

다음 회담은 10월 19일 오후 2시로 결정하였다.

0219

4-5

미분 88-12

0220

별첨 2

JOINT STATEMENT

At today's meeting, the negotiators continued their discussion regarding the scope and content of a Status of Forces agreement. Agreement was reached in principle on the major topics to be included in the agreement which will be negotiated at subsequent meetings.

The negotiators decided to take up for detailed and concrete discussion at the next meeting the preamble to the proposed agreement, the article which defines the terms to be used in the agreement, and the article governing entry and exit of persons.

The next meeting was scheduled for Oct. 19 at 2 P.M.

0221

4-6

비보 88-12(5)

0222

담당 과장 국장 차관 장관 | 10월 12일 | 조약과 | 양고재

CONFIDENTIAL

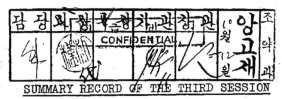

SUMMARY RECORD OF THE THIRD SESSION
STATUS FORCES NEGOTIATIONS

October 10, 1962

I. Time and Place: 2:00 to 3:10 p.m. on October 10, 1962 at Conference Room of the Ministry of Foreign Affairs

II. Attendants:

ROK Side:

Mr. Shin, Kwan Sup	Director Bureau of Customs Ministry of Finance
Mr. Pak, Kun	Chief, America Section Ministry of Foreign Affairs
Col. Lee, Nam Koo	Chief, Military Affairs Section Ministry of National Defense
Mr. Chi, Sung Koo	Press Officer Ministry of Foreign Affairs
Mr. Shin, Chung Sup (Rapporteur)	2nd Secretary Ministry of Foreign Affairs
Mr. Lee, Chang Bum	3rd Secretary Ministry of Foreign Affairs
Mr. Kang, Suk Jae (Interpreter)	3rd Secretary Ministry of Foreign Affairs

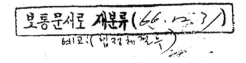

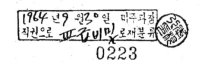

보통문서로 재분류(66.12.31)

1964년 9월 30일 미주과장 직권으로 비밀로 재분류

0223

US Side:

Mr. Philip C. Habib	Counselor of the Embassy for Political Affairs
Brig. Gen. J.D. Lawlor	Deputy Chief of Staff 8th Army
Mr. William J. Ford	First Secretary of the Embassy
Col. G.G. O'Connor	Deputy Chief of Staff 8th Army
Capt. R.M. Brownlie	Assistant Chief of Staff USN/K
Col. W.A. Solf	Staff Judge Advocate 8th Army
Mr. Benjamin A. Fleck (Rapporteur and Press Officer)	First Secretary of the Embassy
Mr. Robert A. Lewis	Second Secretary and Consul of the Embassy
Lt. Col. G.T. Suderman	Staff Officer, J-5 USAF/K
Lt. Col. R.E. Miller	Staff Officer, JAG 8th Army

III. Gist of Talks:

a. Further U.S. Comments on Scope and Content

1. Mr. Shin Kwan-sup, presiding in the absence of Messrs. Chin Pil-shik and Yi Kyung-ho, asked whether the U.S. side had any comments to make on the Korean side's presentation of scope and content at the previous meeting.
Mr. Habib replied that the two sides appeared to be in general agreement. However, he noted that the Korean side had included sub-headings in the outline which it had presented,

0224

5-2

some of which might be construed as setting forth a position in regard to the particular subjects to which they pertained. The U.S. side believed that at this stage in the negotiations, the negotiators should be considering only the major topics which should be included in the agreement and should not be considering substantive sub-headings.

2. With regard to the remarks made by Mr. Chin at the previous meeting, Mr. Habib stated the U.S. side was puzzled by Mr. Chin's apparent belief that some conflict exists between the granting of privileges and immunities to the sending state's forces and the upholding of the laws and regulations of the receiving state. Mr. Habib pointed out that it has always been the policy of U.S. forces stationed in another country to respect the laws of that government. In Korea particularly, he pointed out, the policy of the U.S. forces has been to render all possible assistance to the local law enforcement agencies.

3. Mr. Habib then relinquished the floor to Lt. Colonel Miller, who presented a list of major topics for consideration. Miller pointed out that the list contained 28 headings, compared with 16 headings in the Korean outline. This, he said, was due to the separation of certain of the items in the Korean outline into two or more separate headings and the elevation of certain of the Korean sub-headings to the status of major topics. Miller pointed out that two topics not included in the Korean outline were included in the U.S. list: (a) the obligation of the receiving state to enact such legislation, and take such other action as may be necessary, to provide for the security and safety of the U.S. armed forces their civilian and military members,

0225

their dependents and their property (Item 13), and (b) the obligation of sending state personnel to respect the laws of Korea and to conduct themselves in a manner consistent with the spirit of the agreement (Item 18).

b. Discussion

4. Replying to Mr. Habib, Mr. Shin stated that the granting of privileges and immunities to the sending state's forces involved modification and exceptions in the existing laws and regulations of the Korean government. The problem, therefore, was a delicate one on which the Korean side would elaborate its views on this matter at a later date. Turning to the list presented by Lt. Col. Miller, Mr. Shin asked for clarification of Item 13.

5. Lt. Col. Miller explained that basically Item 13 represented an assurance that the necessary legislation or other actions required by the SOFA would be carried out by the ROKG. Mr. Habib added that this was a standard feature in status of forces agreements. It was a statement of intent on the part of the receiving state and an assurance to the sending state.

6. Mr. Shin then suggested that Item 13 be incorporated with Item 26. Mr. Habib pointed out that they were not concerned with the same subject. He said Item 13 covered a major substantive topic and, the other items on the list, did not necessarily represent a specific article. Mr. Shin stated that the measures implied in Item 13 were covered by Item 3(f) of the Korean outline. He said that the phrasing of Item 13 carried an implication of interfering with and limiting the legislative authority of the ROKG. Dr. Pak Kun suggested that these measures be dealt with as appropriate

0226

5-4

during the detailied negotiation of other major items.

7. Mr. Habib emphasized the belief of the U.S. side that Item 13 constituted a major subject. He agreed, however, that the manner in which it would be handled would be determined in the subsequent negotiations, during which he was certain that the U.S. side would be able to convince the Korean side of the relevance and importance of this item.

8. Mr. Shin then pointed out that Item 16(d) of the Korean outline (provision for abrogation of existing agreements incompatible with the SOFA) was not included in the U.S. list. Mr. Habib replied that the SOFA would, of course, take precedence over previous relevant agreements. Mr. Shin stated that the two delegations appeared to be in agreement with regard to the major topics included in the U.S. list, with the exception of Item 13, regarding which the Korean side wished to reserve its position. Mr. Habib agreed.

9. Mr. Shin then referred to the presentation made at the previous meeting by Lt. Col. Miller, in which Miller had referred to existing agreements between the Republic of Korea and the U.S. Armed Forces. These agreements, Mr. Shin stated, were reached under specific circumstances existing in the past which no longer exist and, in the view of the Korean side, will be superseded by the SOFA because of changed conditions. Mr. Habib replied that the SOFA may supersede only those agreements which are relevant to the SOFA. He explained that the SOFA being negotiated would pertain to, and be relevant to, United States armed forces (as distinct from UNC forces from other countries).. He said this subject would be discussed more fully at a later date. Mr. Shin agreed, and indicated that the Korean side would reserve further comment on the views of the U.S. side

0227

5-5

regarding scope and content until detailed discussion of specific articles is begun.

c. <u>Agenda for Next Meeting</u>

10. Mr. Habib suggested that negotiation of specific articles be commenced at the next meeting. As an appropriate beginning, he suggested consideration of the preamble, definitions article, and if time should permit, the article regarding the establishment of a joint committee. Mr. Shin suggested that the preamble might be left until the concluding stage of the negotiations. He said the Korean side agreed to a discussion of the definitions article but would prefer to discuss the article governing entry and exit of persons rather than the joint committee article.

11. Mr. Habib pointed out that the preamble was not just an ordinary preamble; it is the fundamental basis on which the SOFA is erected. It sets the tone for the entire agreement and makes clear that the SOFA was negotiated on the basis of the Mutual Security Treaty between the two governments. He requested the Korean side to reconsider. He said that the U.S. side had no objection to discussing entry and exit but felt it appropriate to consider the joint committee article first, inasmuch as the joint committee is referred to throughout a SOFA and the negotiators should know to what they are referring when discussing the activities of the joint committee in regard to specific articles. Mr. Shin agreed to a discussion of the preamble but requested that entry and exit should be taken up instead of the joint committee article, which could come later. It was then agreed that the agenda for the next meeting shoudl be as follows:

0228

5-6

a. Preamble

b. Definitions

c. Entry and Exit

12. The next meeting was scheduled for October 19 at 2:00 p.m.

보통문서로 재분류(1966. 12. 31)

1966. 12. 31.에 예고문에 의거 일반문서로 재분류됨

0229

5-7

7. 제4차 회의, 10.19

0230

기 안 용 지

자체 통제		기안처	미주과 강석재	전화번호	근거서류접수일자

과장	국장	차관보좌관	차관	장관		

관계관 서명	

기안 년월일	1962. 10. 12	시행 년월일		보존 년한		정서	기장
분류 기호		전체 통제		종결			

경유 수신 참조	건의	발신	

제목	미주둔군 지위협정 제4차 실무교섭회의 시간변경

10월 12일 미대사관측은 10월 19일 오후 2시에 개최하기로 합의 본 미주둔군 지위협정 제4차 실무교섭회의를 사정으로 인하여 동일 오후 3시에 개최하면 어떠한지 문의하여 왔는바 이를 수락해도 좋을것으로 사료하여 건의하오니 재가하여 주시기 바랍니다. 끝

승인양식 1—1—3 (1112—040—016—018) (190mm×260mm16절지)

0231

서 문

1. 내 용

(1) 1950 년 6 월 25 일 및 6 월 27 일자의 국제연합 안전보장이사회의 결의에 의하여 미군이 한국 영역에 주둔하였음.

(2) 1953 년 7 월 27 일의 휴전협정의 성립으로 사실상 평시상태로 복귀 하였음.

(3) 1953 년 10 월 1 일 체결된 한미상호방위 조약 제 4 조에 따라 미국군대의 한국영역에 대한 주둔을 위한 법적 근거를 마련하였음.

(4) 미군의 한국주둔은 양국간의 공동 이익과 우호관계의 증진을 위한 것이며 이들 주둔군의 지위에 관한 협정 체결은 양국이 다같이 희구하였던 것임.

2. 문제점과 우리의 태도

(1) 유엔 안전보장이사회의 결의에 언급한 것은 미군이 한국에 주둔한 시점과 그 목적을 밝히기 위한 것이며, 우리측의 입장으로서는 유엔안보이사회의 결의를 언급한 것은 주로 미군의 주둔목적 보다도 그 시점을 명백히 함으로서 토지, 시설의 사용등에 관한 보상문제를 소급해서 적용하려는 것이나, 휴전성립 이전에 있어서는 사실상 한국전역이 전투지역이었으므로 미국측이 우리측의 의도에 반대할 것은 명확하나 미군의 한국주둔목적과 그 시점은 명확히 하여야 할 것임.

(2) 휴전협정의 성립에 언급한 것은 휴전으로 열전이 종식되었고 전시하에의 긴박한 사태가 해소되었으며 모든 질서가 사실상 평시로 복귀하였음을 강조함으로서 그 당시 비상사태하에서 체결되었던 제 잠정협정 또는 약정 등을 폐기하여 현실에 적합한 협정을 체결하여야 함을 시사하기 위한 것임. 특히 본 협정에서 취급될 모든 문제는 주로 휴전 전후를 하나의 분기점으로 하여 검토가 행하여질 것이 예상됨으로 휴전성립으로 전시상태가 사실상 종결되었음을 강조하여야 할 것임.

0232

(3) 한미상호방위조약은 유엔안보이사회의 결의를 제외하면 미군의 한국주둔에 관하여 양국이 정식으로 합의한 유일한 법적 근거가 되는 것이며 주둔군지위협정 체결의 당위성을 찾을수 있는 유일한 근거가 되는 것이다. 특히 휴전의 성립으로 주한 유엔군의 임무가 어느 정도 완수된 오늘날 주한 미군의 한국주둔에 관한 법적근거는 주로 이 조약 제 4 조의 규정에 두어야 할 것이다. 현재 주한 미군의 지위가 이중의 성격 즉 안보이사회의 결의에 의하여 파견된 유엔군의 일부로서의 미군과 한미상호방위조약 제 4 조의 규정에 의하여 한국에 주둔하는 미군——을 가진것은 유엔군사령부가 한국에 존재하는 한 이를 부인할수 없겠으나 우리측 입장으로서는 가급적 현재 한국에 주둔하는 미군의 법적지위를 방위조약에 귀결시킴으로써 주둔군지위협정 교섭에 있어서 미국측이 수시로 제기할지 모를 유엔군의 특수성(미국군대의) 에 대한 논거를 ~~최소한으로~~ 제거 ~~제한~~하여야 할 것임.

(4) 끝으로 일반 협정에서 그 서문에 공식적으로 기술되는 협정체결로 인한 양국간의 유대강화나 또는 공동이익의 추구와 같은 문구의 삽입에 관하여는 쌍방이 별로 이견이 없을 것임.

3. 기 타

서문에 관하여 현행관례나 또는 기타 특기할 점이 없음.

4. 비교표 및 초안

비교표 및 초안은 별첨 참조

0233

정 의

1. 내 용

협정에서 정의에 포함될 내용은 아래와 같이 열거할수 있다.

(1) 군대구성원

(2) 군속

(3) 군대구성원 및 군속의 가족

(4) 기타

~~(5) ...~~

2. 설 명

정의는 본 협정의 적용을 받을 인적객체의 범위를 규정하는데 그 목적이 있는 것이다. 즉 누가 본 협정의 적용을 주로 받을 것인가와 본 협정의 적용을 받을 자의 범위는 어느 정도인가의 문제를 규율하는 것이다.

우리 초안에서는 인적객체를 세가지로 구분하였는데 첫째로, 군대구성원은 한국에 있는 미국 현역군인이 이에 해당되며 미국 현역군인이면 그 소속부대가 한국에 주둔해 있는지의 여부에 관계 없이 본 협정의 보호 또는 규제대상이 되는 것임. 둘째로, 군속은 미국인 문관으로서 주한 미군에 근무하는 자를 말하는데 미국인 문관이라 할지라도 그가 한국에 통상적으로 거주하는 자이면 본 협정의 규율대상이 되지 않는다. 셋째로, 가족은 전기한 구성원 및 군속의 가족을 의미하는데 주로 그들의 배우자 및 21 세 이하의 자녀와 부모 및 21 세이상의 자녀라 할지라도 그 생계의 반이상을 구성원 또는 군속에 의존하는 자를 지칭하는 것이다.

3. 문 제 점

(1) 구성원의 범위 (비공무 또는 휴가로 입국한 구성원의 지위)

(2) 군속의 범위 (미국측이 제 2 차 회의에서 제시한 ~~[illegible]~~ 적십자요원, 종교 또는 교육관계자의 지위 등)

(3) 군대구성원 및 군속의 가족의 범위

(4) 기타 정의에 포함될 사항 (이에 관하여는 미국측이 "합의지역" 또는 "작전지역" 등 인적객체이외에 물적객체에 관하여도 정의에서 규정할 것을 제의할지도 모름)

~~(5) 용어 해석~~

(5) 용어해석

0234

4. 우리 입장

(1) 정의에 있어서는 협정의 규제를 받을 인적개체만을 규정하는 것을 원칙으로 한다.

(2) 구성원, 군속 및 그들의 가족 이외에 미국측이 계약자 등 기타 인원에 관하여도 정의에서 규정할 것을 제의 하는 경우에는 이들에 관하여는 정의에 포함시킴이 없이 개개의 협정 조항에서 규정하도록 한다.

(3) 인적개체 이외에 "작전지역" "합의지역" 등 물적개체에 관하여도 정의에서 이를 규제하자고 미국측이 주장하는 경우에는, 정의에서 이를 규정하여 협정전체에 미치는 영향을 고려하여 이를 회피하도록하여야 할 것이며 부득이한 경우에는 ~~별도의 합의사항으로~~ 개々해당조항에서 취급 ~~이를 규정~~하도록 한다.

(4) 군대구성원, 군속 및 그들의 가족에 관한 정의에 관하여는 우리 초안에서 규정한 원칙에 따른다.

5. 현재 관례

없음

6. 비교표

별첨 참조

7. 초 안

별첨 참조

0235

출입국 관리

1. 내용

(1) 군대구성원, 군속 및 그들의 가족의 입국 허가

(2) 외국인 관리 및 등록으로 부터의 면제

(3) 구성원, 군속 및 그들의 가족이 출입국시 소지하여야 할 문서

(4) 신분변경에 따라 한국측이 출국을 요구하거나 추방명을 내린자의 외국으로의 수송에 대한 미국측의 책임.

(5) 비공무 또는 휴가로 입국하는 구성원에 대한 조치.

2. 설명

(1) 본 조항에서는 주둔군 및 이에 부수하는 자의 출입국 관리와 외국인 등록에 관한 사항을 규제하는 것임.

(2) 구성원, 군속 및 그들의 가족은 외국인 등록과 관리에 관한 한국 법령의 적용에서 면제를 부여한다.

(3) 군대구성원은 여권 및 사증에 관한 한국법령의 적용으로 부터 면제를 받으나 신분증명서와 출입국시에는 여행증명서를 항시 소지할 의무가 있다.

(4) 군속과 그 가족 및 군대구성원 가족은 여권에 관한 한국법령에 따라야 하며 항시 유효한 여권을 소지하여야 한다. ([illegible])

(5) 위에서 말한 자의 신분변동으로 인하여 한국측이 출국을 요구하거나 추방령을 내린 경우에는 미국측이 이자들을 한국측의 부담없이 출국시킬 의무를 부담한다.

(6) 비공무 또는 휴가로 한국에 입국하는 미국현역군인의 대우에 관한 문제는 "정의"에서 군대구성원의 범위를 어떻게 결정하느냐에 따라 좌우될 문제임.

3. 문제점

(1) 면제의 범위

(2) 구성원, 군속 및 그들의 가족이 출입국시 소지하여야 할 문서

(3) 신분변동에 따른 출국요구 및 추방문제

(4) 구성원, 군속 및 그들의 가족 이외의 자의 출입국 및 등록에 관한 면제 문제. (예: 군 계약자들)

0236

(5) 군속 그 가족 및 군대구성원 가족에 대하여 여권 및 사증에 관한 법령으로 부터의 면제를 부여하지 않았는데, 이들이 여권을 소지하여야 하느냐 또는 미군당국이 발행한 증명서의 소지로 족하느냐의 문제 (미. 일 협정에는 미측당국이 발행한 증명(서소지)로서 여권에 대치할수있도록 되어있군.)

4. 우리 입장

(1) 군대구성원, 군속 및 그 가족은 외국인 등록 및 관리에 관한 제법령으로 부터의 면제를 부여한다.

(2) 군대구성원은 엄격한 지휘계통하에 움직이는 자들이므로 여권 및 사증에 관한 모든 의무로 부터 면제를 부여하나, 신분증명서 및 여행을 증명하는 증명서를 소지토록 하여야 한다.

(3) 군속 그 가족 및 군인가족은 여권에 관한 한국법령으로 부터의 면제가 부여되지 않는다.

(4) 신분변동에 따라 출국요구 또는 추방명을 받은 자에 대하여는 미국측이 한국측에 부담을 지우지 않고 한국외로 출국시킬 의무를 부담한다.

(5) 군대구성원, 군속 및 그들의 가족 등 정의에서 규정한 인적범위 이외의 자의 출입국에 관하여는 미군 계약자 등 별개항목에서 규제한 것을 제외하고는 원칙적으로 본 협정에서 규정하지 않는다.

(5) (6) 현재 출입국에 관한 무협정상태하에서 미군이 행하고 있는 지금까지의 관례는 본 협정에서 규정할 내용자체와 상당한 거리가 있을것이 예상되는 바, 미국측이 이점 현행관행을 들어 보다 광범위한 특권과 면제를 주장할 가능성도 있으므로 이에 관하여는 지금 까지의 관례가 무협정상태하에서 미국측의 거의 일방적인 조치에 일임되어 왔음을 상기시키고 협정체결을 위한 교섭의 의의를 강조하여야 할 것임.

5. 현행 관례

출입국관리에 관한 현행관례는 지금 까지 양국간에 이에 관한 협정이 없었으므로 미군 및 그들의 가족의 출입국에 관하여는 미국측이 모든

0237

책임을 전담하고 있으며 우리측이 전혀 관여하고 있지 않는 실정임.

6. 비교표

별첨 참조

7. 초 안

별첨 참조

0238

1. 제 4 차 회의에서 문제로 남긴 제 문제점:

(1) 서문의 문제점

(가) 주한 미군의 주둔근거 문제

현재 우리나라에 주둔하고 있는 미국군대는 그 주둔근거를 기초로 할 때 이중의 법적지위를 가진다고 할수 있다. 즉, 하나는 1950 년 6 월 27 일 및 7 월 7 일자 유엔안전보장이사회의 결의에 따라 파견된 유엔군의 일부로서의 미국군대와 다른 하나는 1953 년 10 월 1 일 서명된 한미간의 상호방위조약 제 4 조에 따라 한국에 주둔하는 미군으로서 그들이 우리나라에 주둔하고 있는데는 두가지 근거를 가지고 있다고 볼수 있다. 따라서 협정의 서문에서 이들의 주둔근거를 전기한 양자를 전부 인용할것인가 또는 어느 하나만을 근거로 할것인가의 문제가 필연적으로 제기되는데 어느 것을 근거로 하나냐에 따른 장단점을 비교하면:

가. 양자를 모두 근거로 하는 경우에는 이들의 주둔시점을 1950 년으로 소급할수 있어 1950 년 이래의 법적지위를 포괄적으로 규정할 있는 장점도 있으나 반면 현재 주한 미군의 근거를 구체적으로 양자중 어느 것에 주로 둘것인가의 문제가 제기되며 또한 유엔결의에 따라 파견된 미군은 법적으로는 유엔군사령부 위하의 군대임으로 이들의 지위에 관한 지금까지의 공식 또는 비공식적인 제 약정을 어느 정도 미국측이 원용하려고 한다면 지금 교섭중인 협정의 성격이 변모될 우려가 있는 것임.

나. 유엔결의 하나만을 근거로 하는경우에는 이들의 주둔시점이 1950 년 까지 소급되는 점은 있어나 유엔결의 자체가 앞으로 항구적인 영속성이 없는 것임으로 교섭중인 협정의 근거로서는 빈약할 뿐만 아니라 유엔결의가 ~~언느 시기에~~ 그 효력을 상실하는 경우에는 본 협정의 체결 근거자체가 없어 지는 것임.

다. 한미상호방위조약 하나만을 주둔근거로 하는 경우에는 동 조약체결 이전의 주둔군지위에 관한 제 법률관계는 사실상 백지로 환원하여야 하는 문제가 제기되나 방위조약자체의 항구성에 비추어 볼때 미군의 주둔근거를 동 조약에 두는

0239

것이 ~~주둔목적 등~~ 더욱 건실한 법적근거가 될수 있다는 장점도 있다.

(나) 미국측 안의 분석

미국측이 제시한 초안에 의하면 그들은 현재 교섭중인 주둔군 지위협정의 법적근거를 상호방위조약에만 두고 있는데 미국측이 상호방위조약만을 협정의 근거로 하고 있는 의도를 분석하면:

(1) 양국간의 합의에 의하여 체결된 상호방위조약을 협정근거로 하는 것이 정통적인 입장이라는 점, 이점에 관하여는 우리나라와는 다소 사정이 다르나 일본등의 경우에도 모두 같은 입장을 취하고 있다.

(2) 유엔결의는 6.25 당시에 미군을 한국에 파견한 정당성의 근거로서는 적합할지 모르나 앞으로 계속해서 미국군대가 한국에 주둔하여야 한다는 법적인 근거로서는 ~~빈약~~불안정하다는 점.

(3) 미국측안은 협정체결의 근거로서 상호방위조약을 내세우고 있으나 현재 7가지의 미군의 주둔근거를 명시하지 않고 있음. 휴전후 지금 7가지의 미군의 주둔근거를 명시하지 않음은 현재7가지 주한미군의 주둔으로 발생한 여러가지 법률관계를 사실상 무시하려는 전략적의도가 내포되고 있을 가능성이 있다. 이는 특히 토지 시설의 보상문제에 있어서도 주둔군지위협정 체결이전에 미군이 사용한 토지 시설에 관한 제 문제는 백지로 환원시키려는 의도가 포함되어 있지 않느냐하는 점도 일단 추측할수 있다.

(4) 정치적인 이유로 미군의 주둔근거를 유엔결의에 둔다는 것은 휴전 성립 이후 사실상 유엔군의 주둔근거인 유엔결의가 어느 정도 실효성을 갖느냐의 문제와 관련하여 공산측이 주장할지도 모를 한국으로부터의 유엔군의 철수 등의 정치적인 문제가 제기되는 경우, 미군의 주둔근거를 상호방위조약에 둠으로서 이러한 문제를 미연에 방지할수 있고 주둔군 지위협정의 체결근거를 더욱 정당화하려는 의도가 있지 않느냐 하는 점도 고려할수 있다.

(2) 정의 조항에서의 문제점

(가) 1. 문제점: 주둔군지위협정에서 포함될 미국군대의 정의로서

0240

미국측은 " except for those for whom status has otherwise been provided" 조항에서 본협정의 규정을 받지 않을 자의 범위를 포괄적으로 규정하고 있는데, 미국측의 설명에 의하면 이들은 현재 다른 협정 또는 관례에 따라 규정되고 있는 자를 제외한다는 뜻이라고 함.

2. 우리측 입장: 미국측의 설명을 양해한다면 우리측으로서도 이에 이의를 제기할수는 없으나 지금 까지의 미군의 지위가 불명확했던 사실에 비추어 그 구체적인 범위에 관하여 명확한 사전양해가 있어야 할것임. 그렇지 않으면 미국측이 현존하는 제 협정을 계속원용하려고 한다면 주둔군 지위협정 체결의 의의가 사실상 없어지는 것임.

(나) 1. 문제점: 군속의 범위를 미국인에 한정하여야 한다는 우리측 주장에 대하여 미국측은 이를 검토하여 차기회의에서 이에 대한 회답을 할것을 약속하고 있는데 이문제는 양국간의 협정의 효력이 제 3 국인에게 까지도 미치느냐 하는 법률상의 문제를 떠나서도 미국과의 협정에서 미국인 아닌 제 3 국인에게 본 협정에서 규정한 제 특권과 면제를 향유하게 한다는 것은 우리측의 의도와 거리가 먼 것이라고 할 것임.

2. 우리측 입장: 이 문제는 우리측의 주장을 계속관철하는 방향으로 노력하되 미국측이 끝 까지 이에 응하지 않는 경우에는 협정자체에서는 우리측 안과 같이 규정하고 제 3 국인이 군속으로 한국에 입국하는 문제에 관하여는 합동위원회에서 구체적으로 협의하도록 하는 것이 가할 것임.

(다) 1. 문제점: 가족의 범위에 관하여 미국측이 주장하는 "or other relatives ~~dependent~~" 에 관하여는 미국측이 본협정의 규정을 원용할 목적으로 그들의 가족단위를 필요이상으로 확대 세분하지 않겠다는 점을 설명하고 있음.

2. 우리측 입장: 이 문제는 미국측 주장을 수락하여도 실제로 이러한 자들이 한국에 입국할 가능성을 고려할 때 우리측으로서는 구태여 이에 반대할 필요가 없을 것임.

0241

(3) 출입국관리 문제

(가) 1. 문제점: 군속 및 그들의 가족과 그리고 군인가족이 소지하여야 할 문서에 관하여 미국측 초안에서 규정한 "적절한 문서" 대신 우리측은 여권소지를 주장한 바 있는데 다른 나라의 협정례에서는 미국측 초안과 같이 규정한 것이 상당수 있음. (예: 미일 협정)

2. 우리측 입장 미국측이 그들의 주장을 고집하는 경우에는 여권을 소지하거나, 또는 적절한 기타 문서를 소지하거나 그들의 출입국과 관련하여 그들의 동태 및 신분을 증명하는데 충분한 것이면 우리측으로서도 구태어 여권소지를 주장하지 않아도 가할 것임. 또한 미국측 초안에서 규정한 "적절한 문서"가 여권이 제외되는 것으로는 해석할수 없음으로 이에 관하여는 미국측안을 수락하여도 가할 것임.

2. 차기 회의 의제 문제

(1) 미국측 제의 내용:

미국측은 다음 토의 의제로서 합동위원회문제를 제기하고 있으며 또한 비공식적으로 합동위원회 문제의 토의가 끝나면 다음으로는 토지 및 시설의 사용문제를 토의할 것을 시사하고 있음.

(2) 우리측 제의:

우리측으로서는 이에 대하여 다음의제로서 관세문제 또는 조세문제 토의를 주장하고, 미국측이 이에 불응하는 경우에는 위선 합동위원회문제만을 먼저 토의하고 토지 시설문제는 준비관계등을 이유로 이를 다음 회기에 토의하도록 할것을 제의할 것임.

0242

기 안 용 지

자 체 통 제		기안처	이창범	전화번호	근거서류접수일자
	수석대표		차관보 좌관	차관	장관 (후결)
관 계 관 서 명	미주과장: 조약과장:			기획조정관:	
기 안 년월일	1962. 10. 18	시 행 년월일		보존 년한	정 서 기 장
분 류 기 호		전 체 통 제		종결	
경 유 수 신 참 조	건 의			발 신	
제 목	제 4 차 주둔군 지위협정 실무자회의에 임할 우리측 태도				

10. 19. 개최되는 제 4 차 주둔군 지위협정 체결을 위한 한미실무자회의에서는 제 3 차회의에서 합의된 의제에 따라 협정의 서문, 용어의 정의, 및 출입국관리에 관한 실질적 토의가 전개될 것인바, 우리측 대표단은 별지와 같은 입장에 따라 토의에 임하고저 하며, 또한 제 3 차회의에서 우리측이 태도표명을 보류한바 있는 협정의 범위 및 내용에 관한 미국측 제의 제 13 항(주둔군 및 재산의 안전보장에 관한 조치)은 재검토한 결과 토의 의제로 하는데 대하여는 반대할 이유가 없다고 사료됨으로 이를 수락할 것을 건의 합니다.(미일협정에서도 이에 관한 조항이 포함되어 있음).

1966,12,31,에 예고문에 의거 일반문서로 재분류됨

유 첨: 우리측의 입장. 끝

1964년 9월 30일 미 국 장 직권으로 파기 비밀로 재분류 일반문서로 재분류(1966.12.31.)

25-1

승인양식 1-1-3 (1112-040-016-018) (190mm×260mm16절지)

0243

우리측 입장

서 문

1. 내용

(1) 1950 년 6 월 25 일 및 6 월 27 일 그리고 7 월 7 일자의 유엔 안전보장이사회의 결의에 따라 공산무력침략을 격퇴하기 위하여 미군이 한국 영역에 주둔하였음.

(2) 1953 년 7 월 27 일의 휴전성립에 이어 동년 10 월 1 일 서명된 한미 상호방위조약 제 4 조에서는 미군이 한국에 주둔할 권리를 대한민국이 허여하고 미국이 이를 수락한다고 규정하고 있음.

(3) 전기 방위조약 제 4 조에 따라 미군이 한국영역에 주둔하고 있음.

(4) 미군의 한국 주둔은 양국간의 공동이익과 우호관계의 증진을 위한 것이며 이들 주둔군의 지위에 관한 협정 체결은 양국이 다 같이 희구 하였던 것임.

2. 문제점과 우리의 태도

(1) 유엔안전보장이사회의 결의에 언급한 것은 미군이 한국에 주둔한 시점과 그 목적을 밝히기 위한 것이며, 우리측의 입장으로서는 유엔안보이사회의 결의를 제기한 것은 주로 미군의 주둔목적보다도 그 시점을 명백히 함으로서 토지, 시설의 사용등에 관한 보상문제를 소급해서 적용하려는 것이나, 휴전성립 이전에 있어서는 사실상 한국 전역이 전투지역이었으므로 미국측이 우리측의 의도에 반대할 것은 명확하나 미군의 한국주둔목적과 그 시점은 명확히 하여야 할 것임.

(2) 휴전협정의 성립에 언급한 것은 휴전으로 열전이 종식되었고 전시하에서의 긴박한 사태가 해소되었으며 모든 질서가 사실상 평시로 복귀하였음을 강조함으로서 그 당시 비상사태하에서 체결되었던 제 잠정협정 또는 약정 등을 폐기하여 현실에 적합한 협정을 체결하여야 함을 시사하기 위한 것임. 특히 본 협정에서 취급될 모든 문제는 주로 휴전 전후를 하나의 분기점으로 하여 검토가 행하여질 것이 예상됨으로 휴전 성립으로 전시상태가 사실상 종결되었음을 강조하여야 할 것임.

25-2

0244

4次

(3) 한미 상호방위조약은 유엔안보이사회의 결의를 제외하면 미군의 한국주둔에 관하여 양국이 정식으로 합의한 유일한 법적근거가 되는 것이며 주둔군지위협정 체결의 당위성을 찾을수 있는 유일한 근거가 되는 것이다. 특히 휴전의 성립으로 주한 유엔군의 임무가 어느 정도 완수된 오늘날 주한 미군의 한국주둔에 관한 법적 근거는 주로 이 조약 제 4 조의 규정에 두어야 할것이다. 현재 주한 미군의 지위가 이중의 성격 즉 안보이사회의 결의에 의하여 파견된 유엔군의 일부로서의 미군과 한미상호방위조약 제 4 조의 규정에 의하여 한국에 주둔하는 미군 —을 가진것은 유엔군 사령부가 한국에 존재하는 한 이를 부인할수 없겠으나 우리측 입장으로서는 가급적 현재 한국에 주둔하는 미군의 법적지위를 방위조약에 귀결 시킴으로서 주둔군 지위협정 교섭에 있어서 미국측이 수시로 제기할지 모를 유엔군의 특수성 (미국군대의)에 대한 논거를 제거하여야 할것임.

(4) 끝으로 일반 협정에서 그 서문에 공식적으로 기술되는 협정체결로 인한 양국간의 유대강화나 또는 공동이익의 추구와 같은 문구의 삽입에 관하여는 쌍방이 별로 이견이 없을것임.

3. 기타

서문에 관하여 현행관례나 또는 기타 특기할 점이 없음.

4. 초안

별첨 참조

0245

정 의

1. 내 용

협정에서 정의에 포함될 내용은 아래와 같이 열거할수 있다.

(1) 군대구성원

(2) 군속

(3) 군대구성원 및 군속의 가족

(4) 기타

2. 설 명

정의는 본 협정의 적용을 받을 인적 개체의 범위를 규정하는데 그 목적이 있는 것이다. 즉 누가 본 협정의 적용을 주로 받을 것인가와 본 협정의 적용을 받을 자의 범위는 어느 정도인가의 문제를 규율하는 것이다. 우리 초안에서는 인적개체를 세가지로 구분하였는데 첫째로, 군대구성원은 한국에 있는 미국 현역군인이 이에 해당되며 미국 현역군인이면 그 소속부대가 한국에 주둔해 있는지의 여부에 관계없이 본 협정의 보호 또는 규제대상이 되는것임. 둘째로, 군속은 미국인 문관으로서 주한 미군에 근무하는 자를 말하는데 미국인 문관이라 할지라도 그가 한국에 통상적으로 거주하는 자이면 본 협정의 규율대상이 되지 않는다. 셋째로, 가족은 전기한 구성원 및 군속의 가족을 의미하는데 주로 그들의 배우자 및 21 세 이하의 자녀와 부모 및 21 세 이상의 자녀라 할지라도 그 생계의 반 이상을 구성원 또는 군속에 의존하는 자를 지칭하는 것이다.

3. 문제점

(1) 구성원의 범위 (비공무 또는 휴가로 입국한 구성원의 지위)

(2) 군속의 범위 (미국측이 제 2 차 회의에서 제시한 적십자요원, 종교 또는 교육관계자의 지위 등)

(3) 군대구성원 및 군속의 가족의 범위

25-4

0246

(4) 기타 정의에 포함될 사항 (이에 관하여는 미국측이 "합의지역" 또는 "작전지역" 등 인적개체 이외에 물적개체에 관하여도 정의에서 규정할 것을 제의할지도 모름)

(5) 군 계약자

4. 우리 입장

(1) 정의에 있어서는 협정의 규제를 받을 인적개체만을 규정하는 것을 원칙으로 한다.

(2) 구성원, 군속 및 그들의 가족 이외에 미국측이 계약자 등 기타 인원에 관하여도 정의에서 규정할 것을 제의하는 경우에는 이들에 관하여는 정의에 포함시킴이 없이 개개의 협정 조항에서 규정하도록 한다.

(3) 인적개체 이외에 "작전지역" "합의지역" 등 물적개체에 관하여도 정의에서 이를 규제하자고 미국측이 주장하는 경우에는, 정의에서 이를 규정하여 협정 전체에 미치는 영향을 고려하여 이를 회피하도록 하여야 할것이며 부득이한 경우에는 개개 해당조항에서 취급하도록 한다.

(4) 군대구성원, 군속 및 그들의 가족에 관한 정의에 관하여는 우리 초안에서 규정한 원칙에 따른다.

5. 현행 관례

없음.

6. 초안

별첨 참조

25-5

0247

출입국 관리

1. 내 용

(1) 군대구성원, 군속 및 그들의 가족의 입국 허가

(2) 외국인 관리 및 등록으로 부터의 면제

(3) 구성원, 군속 및 그들의 가족이 출입국시 소지하여야 할 문서

(4) 신분변경에 따라 한국측이 출국을 요구하거나 추방명을 내린자의 외국으로의 수송에 대한 미국측의 책임

(5) 비공무 또는 휴가로 입국하는 구성원에 대한 조치

2. 설 명

(1) 본 조항에서는 주둔군 및 이에 부수하는 자의 출입국 관리와 외국인 등록에 관한 사항을 규제하는 것임.

(2) 구성원, 군속 및 그들의 가족은 외국인 등록과 관리에 관한 한국 법령의 적용에서 면제를 부여한다.

(3) 군대구성원은 여권 및 사증등에 관한 한국법령의 적용으로 부터 면제를 받으나 신분증명서와 출입국시에는 여행증명서를 항시 소지할 의무가 있다.

(4) 군속과 그 가족 및 군대구성원 가족은 여권에 관한 한국법령에 따라야 하며 항시 유효한 여권을 소지하여야 한다.

(5) 위에서 말한 자의 신분 변동으로 인하여 한국측이 출국을 요구하거나 추방명을 내린 경우에는 미국측이 이자들을 한국측의 부담없이 출국시킬 의무를 부담한다.

(6) 비공무 또는 휴가로 한국에 입국하는 미국현역 군인의 대우에 관한 문제는 "정의"에서 군대구성원의 범위를 어떻게 결정하느냐에 따라 좌우될 문제임.

3. 문제점

(1) 면제의 범위

(2) 구성원, 군속 및 그들의 가족이 출입국시 소지하여야 할 문서

(3) 신분변동에 따른 출국요구 및 추방문제

25-6

0248

(4) 구성원, 군속 및 그들의 가족 이외의 자의 출입국 및 등록에 관한 면제 문제 (예: 군 계약자들)

(5) 군속 그 가족 및 군대구성원 가족에 대하여는 여권 및 사증에 관한 법령으로 부터의 면제를 부여하지 않았는데, 이들이 여권을 소지 하여야 하느냐 또는 미군당국이 발행한 증명서의 소지로 족하느냐 의 문제 (미.일 협정에는 미측 당국이 발행한 증명서 소지로서 여권에 대치할수 있도록 되어있음.)

4. 우리 입장

(1) 군대구성원, 군속 및 그 가족은 외국인 등록 및 관리에 관한 제 법령으로 부터의 면제를 부여한다.

(2) 군대구성원은 엄격한 지휘계통하에 움직이는 자들이므로 여권 및 사증에 관한 모든 의무로 부터 면제를 부여하나, 신분증명서 및 여행을 증명하는 증명서를 소지토록 하여야 한다.

(3) 군속 그 가족 및 군인가족은 여권에 관한 한국법령으로 부터의 면제가 부여되지 않는다.

(4) 신분변동에 따라 출국요구 또는 추방령을 받은 자에 대하여는 미국측이 한국측에 부담을 지우지 않고 한국외로 출국시킬 의무를 부담한다.

(5) 현재 출입국에 관한 무협정 상태하에서 미군이 행하고 있는 지금까지의 관례는 본 협정에서 규정할 내용자체와 상당한 거리가 있을것이 예상되는 바, 미국측이 이점 현행관행을 들어 보다 광범위한 특권과 면제를 주장할 가능성도 있으므로 이에 관하여는 지금까지의 관례가 무협정상태하에서 미국측의 거의 일방적인 조치에 일임되어 왔음을 상기시키고 협정체결을 위한 교섭의 의의를 강조하여야 할것임.

5. 현행 관례

출입국 관리에 관한 현행관례는 지금까지 양국간에 이에 관한 협정이 없었으므로 미군 및 그들의 가족의 출입국에 관하여는 미국측이 모든

25-7

0249

책임을 전담하고 있으며 우리측이 전혀 관여하고 있지 않는 실정임.

6. 초안

별첨 참조

차기 회의에서 토의할 의제 문제

차기 회의에서 토의할 의제에 관하여 미국측과 비공식적으로 접촉한 바에 의하면 미국측은 차기 회의에서 "합동위원회 설치 문제" 와 "토지 및 시설의 사용문제" 를 토의할 것을 시사하였음. 이에 대하여 우리측은 아직 토지 및 시설문제의 토의를 위한 준비가 되어 있지 않음으로 (국방부) 다음 회의에서는 관세 및 조세 문제를 토의 하도록 제의하였으나 미국측은 합동위원회와 토지시설문제 이외의 다른 문제에 대하여는 전연 토의할 준비가 되어 있지 않음을 강조하고 있음으로 제 4 차 회의에서 미국측이 계속 합동위원회 문제와 토지 시설문제의 토의를 고집하는 경우에는 이를 수락하도록 할 것임.

2[?]-8

0250

우리측 초안

서 문

통합사령부 휘하의 미 합중국 군대가 1950 년 6 월 25 일, 1950 년 6 월 27 일 및 1950 년 7 월 7 일의 국제연합 안전보장이사회 결의에 따라 공산군의 무력공격을 격퇴하기 위하여 대한민국의 영역 내 및 그 부근에 배비되어 있으므로,

1953 년 7 월 27 일의 휴전협정의 체결에 이어 1953 년 10 월 1 일 대한민국과 미합중국간에 서명된 상호방위조약 제 4 조는 상호 합의에 의하여 결정되는 바에 따라 미합중국의 육군, 공군 및 해군을 대한민국의 영역내 및 그 주변에 배비할 권한을 대한민국이 허여하고, 또한 미합중국이 이를 수락한다고 규정하고 있으므로,

상호방위조약의 전기 조항에 따라 미합중국은 그 육군, 공군 및 해군을 대한민국 영역 내 및 그 주변에 배비하고 있으므로, 그리고:

대한민국과 미합중국은 대한민국 영역내 및 그 주변에 있어서의 미합중국의 배비를 규제하고, 또한 그럼으로써 그들 양 국가간의 긴밀한 상호이익의 유대를 공고히 할 실용적인 행정협정을 체결할 것을 희망함으로,

그러므로 대한민국과 미합중국정부는 아래와 같이 합의 하였다.

25-9

0251

정 의

본 협정에 있어서,

가. "미합중국 군대구성원"이라 함은 대한민국의 영역 내에 있을때의 미 합중국의 육군, 해군 또는 공군에 속하는 인원으로서, 현역으로 복무하고 있는 자를 말한다.

나. "군속"이라 함은 미 합중국의 국적을 가진 문관으로서 대한민국에 있는 미 합중국 군대에 고용되거나, 또는 근무하거나, 또는 이에 수반하는 자를 말한다. 단, 대한민국에 통상 거주하는 자 및 제 18 조에서 말한 자는 제외한다. 이 협정의 적용에 관한 한, 미 합중국 및 대한민국의 이중 국적자로서, 미 합중국이 대한민국에 보낸 자는 미 합중국 국민으로 간주한다.

다. "가족"이라 함은 다음의 자를 말한다. 즉

(1) 배우자 및 21 세 미만의 자녀

(2) 부모 및 21 세 이상의 자녀로서, 그 생계비의 반액 이상을 미 합중국 군대의 구성원 또는 군속에 의존하는 자.

25-10

0252

입국과 출국

1. 본조의 규정에 따른것을 조건으로 하여, 미 합중국은 미합중국 군대구성원, 군속 및 그 가족인 자를 대한민국에 입국시킬수 있다.

2. (가) 미 합중국 군대구성원은 여권 및 사증에 관한 대한민국 법령의 적용으로 부터 면제된다. 미 합중국 군대 구성원, 군속 및 그 가족은 외국인의 등록 및 관리에 관한 대한민국 법령의 적용으로 부터 면제된다. 단, 이들은 대한민국 내에서 영구적인 거소 또는 주소를 요구할 권리를 취득하는 것으로 간주되지 않는다.

(나) 군속, 그 가족 및 미합중국 군대구성원의 가족은 대한민국에 입국하거나 대한민국으로부터 출국함에 있어서, 또는 대한민국에 있는 동안, 그들의 신분을 기재한 여권을 소지하여야 한다.

3. 미 합중국 군대구성원은 대한민국에 입국 또는 대한민국으로 부터 출국함에 있어서 하기의 문서를 소지하여야 한다:

(가) 미 합중국 군당국이 발행한 성명, 생년월일, 계급과 군번 및 군의 구분을 기재하고 사진을 첨부한 신분 증명서

(나) 개인 또는 집단이 미 합중국 군대 구성원으로서 가지는 지위 및 명령된 여행을 증명하는 미 합중국 군당국이 발행한 개별적 또는 집단적 여행 명령서

미 합중국 군대 구성원은 대한민국에 있는 동안의 신분을 증명하기 위하여, 전기의 신분증명서를 소지하여야 한다. 신분증명서는 대한민국의 적절한 당국이 요구하면 이를 제시하여야 한다.

4. (가) 본 조 1 항의 규정에 의하여 한국에 입국한 자가, 그 신분의 변경으로 인하여 전항에 규정된 여사한 입국의 권리를 갖지 못하게 된 경우에는, 미 합중국 당국은 한국 당국에 이를 즉시 통고하여야 하며, 또한 그자가 한국으로 부터 출국할 것을 한국 당국이 요구한 경우에는, 대한민국 정부에 부담을 지우지 않고 상당한 기간내에 그 자를 한국으로 부터 수송할 책임을 진다.

25-11

0253

(나) 대한민국 정부가 미 합중국 군대구성원 또는 군속을 그 영역으로부터 퇴거 시킬것을 요구하고 또는 미 합중국 군대의 전 구성원, 또는 전 군속에 대하여, 또는 미합중국 군대구성원, 군속, 전 구성원 또는 전 군속의 가족에 대하여 퇴거명령을 내린 경우에는, 미 합중국 당국은 그 자를 자국의 영역내에 받아 들이거나, 그 밖에 그를 대한민국 외로 퇴거시키는데 대하여 책임을 진다. 본 항의 규정은 대한민국 국민이 아닌 자로서 미 합중국 군대의 구성원 또는 군속으로서 또는 미 합중국 군대 구성원 또는 군속이 되기 위하여 대한민국에 입국한 자 및 이러한 자의 가족에 대하여 만 적용한다.

25-12

0254

Definition

In this Agreement the expression --

(a) "members of the United States forces" means the personnel on active duty belonging to the land, sea or air armed services of the United States of America when in the territory of the Republic of Korea.

(b) "civilian component" means the civilian persons of United States nationality who are in the employ of, serving with, or accompanying the United States forces in the Republic of Korea, but excludes persons who are ordinarily resident in the Republic of Korea or who are mentioned in Article XVIII. For the purposes of this Agreement only, dual nationals, Korean and United States, who are brought to the Republic of Korea by the United States shall be considered as United States nationals.

(c) "dependents" means

(i) Spouse, and children under 21;

(ii) Parents, and children over 21, if dependent for over half their support upon a member of the United States forces or civilian component.

25-13

0255

Entry and Exit

1. The United States may bring into the Republic of Korea persons who are members of the United States forces, the civilian components, and their dependents, subject to the provisions of this Article.

2. (a) Members of the United States forces shall be exempt from laws and regulations of the Republic of Korea governing the passport and visa. Members of the United States forces, the civilian component, and their dependents shall be exempt from laws and regulations of the Republic of Korea governing the registration and control of aliens, but shall not be considered acquiring any right to permanent residence or domicile in the Republic of Korea.

(b) Members of the civilian component, their dependents, and the dependents of the members of the United States forces shall be in possession of passports with their status described therein, upon their entry into or departure from or while in the Republic of Korea.

3. Upon entry into or departure from the Republic of Korea members of the United States forces shall be in possession of the following documents:

(a) personal identity card issued by the authorities of the United States forces showing name, date of birth, rank and number, service, and photograph; and

(b) individual or collective travel order issued by the authorities of the United States forces certifying to the status of the individual or group as a member or members of the United States forces and to the travel ordered.

For the purpose of their identification while in the Republic of Korea, members of the United States forces shall be in possession of the foregoing personal identity card

25-14

0256

which must be presented on demand of the appropriate authorities of the Republic of Korea.

4. (a) If any person brought into the Republic of Korea under paragraph 1 of this Article is, by reason of alteration in his status, no longer entitled to such admission provided for in the foregoing paragraphs, the United States authorities shall immediately notify the authorities of the Republic of Korea and shall, if such person be required by the authorities of the Republic of Korea to leave the Republic of Korea, be responsible for the transportation from the Republic of Korea of such person within a reasonable time at no cost to the Government of the Republic of Korea.

(b) If the Government of the Republic of Korea has requested the removal from its territory of a member of the United States forces or the civilian component or has made an expulsion order against an ex-member of the United States forces or of the civilian component or against a dependent of a member or ex-member, the United States authorities shall be responsible for receiving the person concerned within its own territory or otherwise disposing of him outside the Republic of Korea. This paragraph shall apply only to persons who are not nationals of the Republic of Korea and have entered the Republic of Korea as members of the United States forces or the civilian component or for the purpose of becoming such members, and to the dependents of such persons.

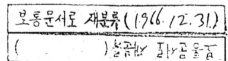

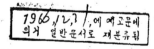

보통문서로 재분류(1966.12.31.)

1966.12.31.에 예고문에 의거 일반문서로 재분류됨

0257

October 19, 1962

ARTICLE I

DEFINITIONS

In this Agreement the expression

(a) "members of the United States armed forces" means the personnel on active duty belonging to the land, sea or air armed services of the United States of America when in the territory of the Republic of Korea except for those for whom status has otherwise been provided.

(b) "civilian component" means the civilian persons who are in the employ of, serving with, or accompanying the United States armed forces in the Republic of Korea, but excludes persons who are ordinarily resident in the Republic of Korea or who are mentioned in paragraph of Article

Agreed upon (c) "dependents" means

(1) Spouse and children under 21;

(2) Parents, and children over 21, or other relatives dependent for over half their support upon a member of the United States armed forces or civilian component.

0258

PREAMBLE

"Whereas the United States of America has disposed its armed forces in and about the territory of the Republic of Korea pursuant to the resolutions of the United Nations Security Council of June 25, 1950, June 27, 1950, and July 7, 1950, and pursuant to Article IV of the Mutual Defense Treaty between the United States of America and the Republic of Korea signed on October 1, 1953,

Therefore, the United States of America and the Republic of Korea, in order to strengthen the close bonds of mutual interest between their two countries, have entered into this Agreement regarding facilities and areas and the status of United States armed forces in the Republic of Korea in terms as set forth below:"

0259

October 19, 1962

ENTRY AND EXIT

1. The United States may bring into the Republic of Korea persons who are members of the United States armed forces, the civilian component, and their dependents, subject to the provisions of this Article. The Government of the Republic of Korea will be notified at regular intervals, in accordance with procedures to be agreed between the two Governments, of numbers and categories of persons entering and departing.

反対解釈

2. Members of the United States armed forces shall be exempt from Korean passport and visa laws and regulations. Members of the United States armed forces, the civilian component, and their dependents shall be exempt from Korean laws and regulations on the registration and control of aliens, but shall not be considered as acquiring any right to permanent residence or domicile in the territory of the Republic of Korea.

3. Upon entry into or departure from the Republic of Korea members of the United States armed forces shall be in possession of the following documents:

(a) personal identity card showing name, date of birth, rank and service number, service, and photograph; and

(b) individual or collective travel order certifying to the status of the individual or group as a member or members of the United States armed forces and to the travel ordered.

0260

For purposes of their identification while in the Republic of Korea, members of the United States armed forces shall be in possession of the foregoing personal identity card which must be presented on request to the appropriate Korean authorities.

4. Members of the civilian component, their dependents, and the dependents of members of the United States armed forces shall be in possession of appropriate documentation issued by the United States authorities so that their status may be verified by Korean authorities upon their entry into or departure from the Republic of Korea, or while in the Republic of Korea.

5. If the status of any person brought into the Republic of Korea under paragraph 1 of this Article is altered so that he would no longer be entitled to such admission, the United States authorities shall notify the Korean authorities and shall, if such person be required by the Korean authorities to leave the Republic of Korea, assure that transportation from the Republic of Korea will be provided within a reasonable time at no cost to the Government of the Republic of Korea.

6. If the Government of the Republic of Korea has requested the removal from its Territory of a member of the United States armed forces or civilian component or has made an expulsion order

0261

against an ex-member of the United States armed forces or the civilian component or against a dependent of a member or an ex-member, the authorities of the United States shall be responsible for receiving the person concerned into its own territory or otherwise disposing of him outside the Republic of Korea. This paragraph shall apply only to persons who are not national of the Republic of Korea ordinarily resident in the Republic of Korea and have entered the Republic of Korea as members of the United States armed forces or civilian component or for the purpose of becoming such members, and to the dependents of such persons.

0262

October 19, 1962

PREAMBLE

The United States of America and the Republic of Korea, pursuant to Article IV of the Mutual Defense Treaty between the United States of America and the Republic of Korea signed at Washington on October 1, 1953, have entered into this Agreement regarding facilities and areas and the status of United States armed forces in the Republic of Korea in terms as set forth below:

보통문서로 재분류(1966.12.31.)

1966,12,31,에 예고문에 의거 일반문서로 재분류됨

1964년 9월30일 미주과장 직권으로 예고문 로재분류

0263

PK

October 19, 1962

ARTICLE I

DEFINITIONS

In this Agreement the expression

(a) "members of the United States armed forces" means the personnel on active duty belonging to the land, sea or air armed services of the United States of America when in the territory of the Republic of Korea except for those for whom status has otherwise been provided. e.g. attaché of Embassy KMAG personnel

"Third state nationality"

(b) "civilian component" means the civilian persons who (of the U.S. nationality) (dual nationality) are in the employ of, serving with, or accompanying the United States armed forces ~~in the Republic~~ of Korea, but excludes persons who are ordinarily resident in the Republic of Korea or who are mentioned in paragraph of Article (Armed forces contractors)

If a third state national is employed, the be given the same privileges & immunity. U.S.-Japan

Agreed minutes.

(c) "dependents" means

(1) Spouse and children under 21;

(2) Parents, and children over 21, or other relatives dependent for over half their support upon a member of the United States armed forces or civilian component.

0264

PK

October 19, 1962

ENTRY AND EXIT

(OK) 1. The United States may bring into the Republic of Korea persons who are members of the United States armed forces, the civilian component, and their dependents, subject to the provisions of this Article. The Government of the Republic of Korea will be notified at regular intervals, in accordance with procedures to be agreed between the two Governments, of numbers and categories of persons entering and departing.

J.C.

(OK) 2. Members of the United States armed forces shall be exempt from Korean passport and visa laws and regulations. Members of the United States armed forces, the civilian component, and their dependents shall be exempt from Korean laws and regulations on the registration and control of aliens, but shall not be considered as acquiring any right to permanent residence or domicile in the territory of the Republic of Korea.

(OK) 3. Upon entry into or departure from the Republic of Korea members of the United States armed forces shall be in possession of the following documents:

JC or agreed minutes to provide for U.S. military police a law enforcement personnel they should carry bilingual card

(a) personal identity card showing name, date of birth, rank and service number, service, and photograph; and

(b) individual or collective travel order certifying to the status of the individual or group as a member or members of the [redacted] armed forces and to the travel ordered.

0265

For purposes of their identification while in the Republic of Korea, members of the United States armed forces shall be in possession of the foregoing personal identity card which must be presented on request to the appropriate Korean authorities.

4. Members of the civilian component, their dependents, and the dependents of members of the United States armed forces shall be in possession of appropriate documentation issued by the United States authorities so that their status may be verified by Korean authorities upon their entry into or departure from the Republic of Korea, or while in the Republic of Korea.

5. If the status of any person brought into the Republic of Korea under paragraph 1 of this Article is altered so that he would no longer be entitled to such admission, the United States authorities shall notify the Korean authorities and shall, if such person be required by the Korean authorities to leave the Republic of Korea, assure that transportation from the Republic of Korea will be provided within a reasonable time at no cost to the Government of the Republic of Korea.

6. If the Government of the Republic of Korea has requested the removal from its Territory of a member of the United States armed forces or civilian component or has made an expulsion order

0266

against an ex-member of the United States armed forces or the civilian component or against a dependent of a member or an ex-member, the authorities of the United States shall be responsible for receiving the person concerned into its own territory or otherwise disposing of him outside the Republic of Korea. This paragraph shall apply only to persons who are not ordinarily resident in the Republic of Korea and have entered the Republic of Korea as members of the United States armed forces or civilian component or for the purpose of becoming such members, and to the dependents of such persons.

change of words

0267

우리측이 미측에 제시한 초안

Preamble

Whereas the United States forces were originally disposed in and about the territory of the Republic of Korea pursuant to the resolutions of the United Nations Security Council of June 25, 1950, June 27, 1950 and July 7, 1950 to repel the Communist armed attack;

Whereas, the Article IV of the Mutual Defense Treaty between the Republic of Korea and the United States of America signed on October 1, 1953, following the conclusion of the Armistice Agreement on July 27, 1953, states that the Republic of Korea grants, and the United States of America accept, the right to dispose United Stated land, air and sea forces in and about the territory of the Republic of Korea as determined by mutual agreement;

Whereas, pursuant to the aforesaid provision of the Mutual Defense Treaty, the United States of America has disposed its ~~land, air and sea~~ armed forces in and about the territory of the Republic of Korea, and;

Whereas the Republic of Korea and the United States of America are desirous of providing for practical administrative arrangements which shall govern the disposition of the United States forces in and about the territory of the Republic of Korea ~~in order to~~ and will thereby strengthen the close bonds of mutual interests between their two countries; (rephrase)

Therefore, the Government of the Republic of Korea and of the United States of America have agreed as follows:

Res. 1950 – 1953 (MDT) (F & A)

① UN 군도 cover 된고

보통문서로 재분류 (1966. 12. 31.)

1966, 12, 31에 예고문에 의거 일반문서로 재분류됨

0268

분제시

Definition

In this Agreement the expression --

(a) "members of the United States forces" means the personnel on active duty belonging to the land, sea or air armed services of the United States of America when in the territory of the Republic of Korea.

(b) "civilian component" means the civilian persons of United States nationality who are in the employ of, serving with, or accompanying the United States forces in the Republic of Korea, but excludes persons who are ordinarily resident in the Republic of Korea or who are mentioned in Article XVIII. For the purposes of this agreement only, dual nationals, ~~Korean and United States~~, who are brought to the Republic of Korea ~~by the United States~~ shall be considered as United States nationals.

다

(c) "dependents" means

(i) Spouse, and children under 21;

(ii) Parents, and children over 21, if dependent for over half their support upon a member of the United States forces or civilian component.

Skills
3rd states nationals

NATO

Japan
Joint Committee admitted

보통문서로 재분류(1966.12.31)

1966.12.31에 예고문에 의거 일반문서로 재분류됨

1964년7월30일 미주 직권으로 비밀 로재

0269

불제시

Entry and Exit

1. The United States may bring into the Republic of Korea persons who are members of the United States forces, the civilian component, and their dependents, subject to the provisions of this Article.

2. (a) Members of the United States forces shall be exempt from laws and regulations of the Republic of Korea governing the passport and visa. Members of the United States forces, the civilian component, and their dependents shall be exempt from laws and regulations of the Republic of Korea governing the registration and control of aliens, but shall not be considered acquiring any right to permanent residence or domicile in the Republic of Korea.

(b) Members of the civilian component, their dependents, and the dependents of the members of the United States forces shall be in possession of passports with their status described therein, upon their entry into or departure from or while in the Republic of Korea.

3. Upon entry into or departure from the Republic of Korea members of the United States forces shall be in possession of the following documents:

(a) personal identity card issued by the authorities of the United States forces showing name, date of birth, rank and number, service, and photograph; and

(b) individual or collective travel order issued by the authorities of the United States forces certifying to the status of the individual or group as a member or members of the United States forces and to the travel ordered.

For the purpose of their identification while in the Republic of Korea, members of the United States forces

0270

shall be in possession of the foregoing personal identity card which must be presented on demand of the appropriate authorities of the Republic of Korea.

4. (a) If any person brought into the Republic of Korea under paragraph 1 of this Article is, by reason of alteration in his status, no longer entitled to such admission provided for in the foregoing paragraphs, the United States authorities shall immediately notify the authorities of the Republic of Korea and shall, if such person be required by the authorities of the Republic of Korea to leave the Republic of Korea, be responsible for the transportation from the Republic of Korea of such person within a reasonable time at no cost to the Government of the Republic of Korea.

(b) If the Government of the Republic of Korea has requested the removal from its territory of a member of the United States forces or the civilian component or has made an expulsion order against an ex-member of the United States forces or of the civilian component or against a dependent of a member or ex-member, the United States authorities shall be responsible for receiving the person concerned within its own territory or otherwise disposing of him outside the Republic of Korea. This paragraph shall apply only to persons who are not nationals of the Republic of Korea and have entered the Republic of Korea as members of the United States forces or the civilian component or for the purpose of becoming such members, and to the dependents of such persons.

보통문서로 재분류(1966. 12. 31)

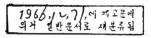

1966, 12, 31,에 예고문에 의거 일반문서로 재분류됨

0271

기 안 용 지

자체 통제		기안처	이 창범	전화번호	근거서류접수일자
	수석대표	본부관		차관	장관
관계관 서명	미주과장: 조약과장:		기획조정관:		
기안 년월일		시행 년월일	검열 1962.10.22	보존 년한	정서기장
분류 기호	외정무	전체 통제			
경유 수신 참조	국가재건최고회의 의장 (참조: 외무국방위원장) 내각수반	발신	외무부장관		
제목	주둔군지위협정 체결을 위한 제 4 차 실무자회의 보고				

1962. 10. 19. 오후 3 시부터 동 4 시 50분 까지 외무부에서 개최된 표기문제에 관한 제 4 차 실무자회의에서 토의된 내용을 별지와 같이 보고 합니다.

유 첨: 제 4 차 실무자회의 보고서 끝.

보통문서로 재분류 (1966. 12. 31.)

1966. 12. 31. 에 예고문에 의거 일반문서로 재분류됨

6-1

1964 년 9 월 30 일 미주과

승인양식 1-1-3 (1112-040 016-018) (190mm×260mm16절지)

0272

제 4 차

주둔군 지위협정 실무자 회의 보고

1962. 10. 20.

1. 일 시: 1962. 10. 19. 오후 3시—4시 50분 까지

2. 장 소: 외무부 회의실

3. 참석자: 한국측: 교섭대표단 전원(노신영, 지성구, 이경훈 세대표 공무관계로 불참)

미국측: 교섭대표단 전원

4. 토의사항:

(1) 제 3 차회의에서 합의한 바에 따라 협정의 서문, 용어의 정의 및 출입국관리에 관한 문제를 순차적으로 토의함.

(2) 먼저, 협정의 서문에 관하여는 미국측이 그들의 초안을 제시하였으며, 이에 대하여 우리측은 우리초안을 제시하였음. 우리측은 우리초안에 대하여 설명하고 기본적인 정신에 있어서는 양측초안이 상이한 바 없음을 강조 함.

협정의 서문에 관하여는 양측이 각각 상대방의 초안을 검토한 후 다음 회의에서 그 입장을 표명하기로 함.

(3) 출입국관리 문제에 관하여는 미국측이 그 초안을 제시하였으며 우리측은 우리초안과 내용에 대차 없으므로 미국초안을 중심으로 토의를 전개하였음. 우리측은 먼저 미국측 초안에서 규정한 "except for those for whom status has otherwise been provided. " 에 대한 설명을 요구하였는데 이에 대하여 미국측은 이는 미국대사관 무관 또는 군사고문단 등 다른 관례 또는 기존협정에서 규정된 자는 제외하자는 뜻이라고 설명하였음. 이에 대하여 우리측은 재검토한 후 우리측 태도를 다음회의에서 표명할 것임을 약속함.

(4) 다음 용어의 정의문제와 관련하여 한미 양국의 이중국적자에 관하여 우리측이 질문한데 대하여 미국측이 한국법이나 미국법에서 타국적을 취득하면 다른 국적을 상실하게 되어 있으므로 이 문제는 발생할 여지가 없음을 설명하였으며 우리측은 이를 양해 함.

0273

6-2

0274

(5) 다음으로 우리측은 용어의 정의에 있어서 "군속"을 "미국인" 고용인으로 한정할것을 제의한데 대하여 양측간에 상당한 논의가 전개되었는데, 미국측은 제 3 국인을 고용하는 것은 그들이 가진 기술이 미국인이나 한국인으로 부터는 얻을수 없는 경우가 있기 때문이며 또한 정의에서는 단지 군속의 정의만을 규정하는 것이며 이들이 향유할 특권이나 면제를 규정하자는 것이 아님을 강조하였음. 이에 대하여 우리측은 군속은 미국인 고용인에 한한다는 규정을 삽입할 것을 재차 강조하고 이 문제에 대하여는 다음 회의에서 우리측의 태도표명과 함께 재검토하기로 함.

(6) 다음으로 우리측은 "부양가족" 중에서 미국측안에서 규정한 "..or other relatives dependent.... " 은 우리측안에는 없는 것이라고 설명한데 대하여 미국측은 이는 실제적인 표현인 것이며 불필요하게 가족단위를 파괴~~할 의도는 없으며~~ 하는 일이 없도록 처의 부모 또는 형제들도 부양하여야할 실제적인 경우가 있음을 강조하였음. 이에 대하여 우리측은 다음회의에서 우리측 태도를 밝힐 것임을 약속함.

(7) 출입국관리문제에 관하여 미국측이 그들의 초안을 제시하였는데 우리측이 준비한 초안과 내용에 있어서 ~~거의 동일함으로~~ 대차가 없음으로 미국측안을 중심으로 토의하였음. 이 문제에 대하여는 ~~우리측은 우리초안과 같은 내용에 대하여는 미국측안에 동의하고~~ 다만 군속, 그들의 가족 및 군인가족이 소지하여야 할 "적절한 문서" 대신에 이들이 여권을 소지하도록 할것을 제의한데 대하여 미국측은 이를 검토후 다음회의에서 회답하겠다고 약속함.

(8) 출입국관리 문제에 관하여는 양측간에 별반 이견이 없었으나 단지 이 조항의 시행과 관련하여 행정적문제 및 기술적인 문제에 관하여는 양측이 앞으로 별도의 합의의사록이나 합동위원회를 통하여 구체적인 문제를 결정하도록 할것에 합의함.

5. 중요합의사항:

(1) 협정의 서문에 관하여 양측이 제시한 초안을 상호 검토하여 차기 회의에서 각자의 입장을 제시하기로 함.

0275

미문 88-11

0276

(2) 정의에 관하여, 미국측 초안에 대하여(는) ~~원칙적으로 합의하고 다만~~ 우리측이 제시한 몇가지 문제(토의사항 참조)에 관하여 다음회의에서 계속 토의 하기로 함.

(3) 출입국관리에 관하여는 미국측이 제시한 초안이 우리측 초안과 내용에 있어 (대차 없음으로) ~~동일함으로~~ 이를 중심으로 토의한 결과 미국측 초안에서 기술된 "적절한 문서" 대신 "여권"으로 대치할 것을 제의한 우리측 제안에 대하여 미국측이 검토후 통고할 것을 약속하고 (기타 문제에 관한) 이 조항에 관하여는 쌍방이 ~~완전히~~ 합의에 도달함.

(4) 출입국관리 문제에 관하여 이를 구체적으로 시행함에 있어서는 합동위원회를 통하여 또는 별도의 합의의사록에서 행정적인 그리고 기술적인 문제에 관하여 양측이 다시 세칙을 규정하자는데 대하여 합의 함.

6. 기타사항:

(1) 차기회의 일자: 1962. 11. 1. 오후 2 시

(2) 차기회의 의제: 제 4 차 회의에서(의) 의제 중 합의에 도달하지 못한 문제를 계속해서 토의하며 시간이 있으면 합동위원회 문제를 토의할 것인지에 관하여(그런데) 별도로 (협)의하기로 함.

7. 참고자료:

미국측이 제의한 협정초안 (서문, 정의 및 출입국관리조항) 별첨참조.

보통문서로 재분류(1966. 12. 31.)

1966, 12, 31, 에 예고문에 의거 일반문서로 재분류됨

0277

6-4

미완 88-11

0278

PREAMBLE

The United States of America and the Republic of Korea, pursuant to Article IV of the Mutual Defense Treaty between the United States of America and the Republic of Korea signed at Washington on October 1, 1953, have entered into this Agreement regarding facilities and areas and the status of United States armed forces in the Republic of Korea in terms as set forth below:

0279

6-5

비문 88-11

0280

DEFINITIONS

In this Agreement the expression

(a) "members of the United States armed forces" means the personnel on active duty belonging to the land, sea or air armed services of the United States of America when in the territory of the Republic of Korea except for those for whom status has otherwise been provided.

(b) "civilian component" means the civilian persons who are in the employ of, serving with, or accompanying the United States armed forces in the Republic of Korea, but excludes persons who are ordinarily resident in the Republic of Korea or who are mentioned in paragraph of Article

(c) "dependents" means

(1) Spouse and children under 21;

(2) Parents, and children over 21, or other relatives dependent for over half their support upon a member of the United States armed forces or civilian component.

0281

6-6

미문 88-11

0282

ENTRY AND EXIT

1. The United States may bring into the Republic of Korea persons who are members of the United States armed forces, the civilian component, and their dependents, subject to the provisions of this Article. The Government of the Republic of Korea will be notified at regular intervals, in accordance with procedures to be agreed between the two Governments, of members and categories of persons entering and departing.

2. Members of the United States armed forces shall be exempt from Korean passport and visa laws and regulations. Members of the United States armed forces, the civilian component, and their dependents shall be exempt from Korean laws and regulations on the registration and control of aliens, but shall not be considered as acquiring any right to permanent residence or domicile in the territory of the Republic of Korea.

3. Upon entry into or departure from the Republic of Korea members of the United States armed forces shall be in possession of the following documents:

(a) personal identity card showing name, date of birth, rank and service number, service, and photograph; and

(b) individual or collective travel order certifying to the status of the individual or group as a member or members of the United States armed forces and to the travel ordered.

For purposes of their identification while in the Republic of Korea, members of the United States armed forces shall be in possession of the foregoing personal identity card which must be presented on request to the appropriate Korean authorities

0283

6-7

미원 88-11

0284

4. Members of the civilian component, their dependents, and the dependents of members of the United States armed forces shall be in possession of appropriate documentation issued by the United States authorities so that their status may be verified by Korean authorities upon their entry into or departure from the Republic of Korea, or while in the Republic of Korea.

5. If the status of any person brought into the Republic of Korea under paragraph 1 of this Article is altered so that he would no longer be entitled to such admission, the United States authorities shall notify the Korean authorities and shall, if such person be required by the Korean authorities to leave the Republic of Korea, assure that transportation from the Republic of Korea will be provided within a reasonable time at no cost to the Government of the Republic of Korea.

6. If the Government of the Republic of Korea has requested the removal from its Territory of a member of the United States armed forces or civilian component or has made an expulsion order against an ex-member of the United States armed forces or the civilian component or against a dependent of a member or an ex-member, the authorities of the United States shall be responsible for receiving the person concerned into its own territory or otherwise disposing of him outside the Republic of Korea. This paragraph shall apply only to persons who are not ordinarily resident in the Republic of Korea and have entered the Republic of Korea as members of the United States armed forces or civilian component or for the purpose of becoming such members, and to the dependents of such persons.

0285

보통문서로 재분류(1966.12.31)

1966.12.31에 예고문에 의거 일반문서로 재분류됨

6-8

미주문 88-11(7)

0286

SUMMARY RECORD OF THE FOURTH SESSION
STATUS FORCES NEGOTIATIONS

October 19, 1962

I. Time and Place: 3:00 to 4:50 p.m. on October 19, 1962 at Conference Room of the Ministry of Foreign Affairs

II. Attendants:

ROK Side:

Mr. Chin, Pil Shik	Director Bureau of Political Affairs Ministry of Foreign Affairs
Mr. Shin, Kwan Sup	Director Bureau of Customs Ministry of Finance
Mr. Yi, Kyung Ho	Director Bureau of Legal Affairs Ministry of Justice
Mr. Pak, Kun	Chief, America Section Ministry of Foreign Affairs
Col. Lee, Nam Koo	Chief, Military Affairs Section Ministry of National Defense
~~Mr. Chi, Sung Koo~~	Press Officer Ministry of Foreign Affairs
Mr. Shin Chung Sup (Rapporteur)	2nd Secretary Ministry of Foreign Affairs
Mr. Lee, Chang Bum	3rd Secretary Ministry of Foreign Affairs
Mr. Kang, Suk Jae (Interpreter)	3rd Secretary Ministry of Foreign Affairs

담 당	과 장	국 장	차 관	장 관	10월 26일

1964 년 9 월 30 일 미주과장 직권으로 로 재분류

0287

7-1

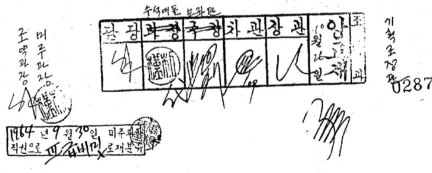

US Side:

Mr. Philip C. Habib	Counselor of the Embassy for Political Affairs
Brig. Gen. J.D. Lawlor	Deputy Chief of Staff 8th Army
Mr. William J. Ford	First Secretary of the Embassy
Col. G.G. O'Connor	Deputy Chief of Staff 8th Army
Capt. R.M. Brownlie	Assistant Chief of Staff USN/K
Mr. Benjamin A. Fleck (Rapporteur and Press Officer)	First Secretary of the Embassy
Mr. Robert A. Lewis	Second Secretary and Consul of the Embassy
Lt. Col. G.T. Suderman	Staff Officer, J-5 USAF/K
Lt. Col. R.E. Miller	Staff Officer, JAG 8th Army

III. Gist of Talks:

a. Further ROK Comment on Scope and Content

1. Before proceeding to the agreed agenda, Mr. Chin stated that he wished to refer to the discussion at the previous meeting concerning Item 13 on the U.S. list of major topics. He said the Korean side wished to state its agreement to the inclusion of Item 13 in the U.S. list, in regard to which both sides were now in complete agreement. The U.S. side welcomed this statement.

0288

7-2

b. Preamble

2. Both sides then tabled drafts of the Preamble. It was agreed that these would be discussed at the next meeting, after each side had the opportunity to study the other's draft.

c. Definitions Article

3. Colonel Solf introduced the U.S. draft of the definitions article. Mr. Chin suggested that, since the difference was small between the Korean draft and the U.S. draft, the U.S. draft serve as the basis for discussion.

4. Mr. Chin asked for clarification of the phrase "except for those for whom status has otherwise been provided" in sub-paragraph (a). Colonel Solf replied that this phrase was included in order to clarify the fact that certain U.S. military personnel, i.e. the military attaches at the Embassy and the members of the Military Assistance Advisory Group, were not covered by the provisions of the SOFA. He pointed out that the MAAG personnel came under the provisions of the MAAG Agreement of January 26, 1950. Mr. Chin stated that the Korean side would study this matter and discuss at the next meeting.

5. There followed a discussion of the question of dual nationality. Colonel Solf pointed out that dual nationality was not specifically mentioned in the U.S. draft because this draft was based on the criterion of residence rather than of of nationality. It provided for the exclusion of persons ordinarily resident in the Republic of Korea. Also, Colonel Solf added, the nationality laws of both the Republic of Korea and the United States provide for the loss of nationality when a national voluntarily acquires another nationality.

0289

7-3

Therefore, it did not seem necessary to introduce the question of dual nationality in the context of this agreement. Mr. Chin pointed out that Korean wives of U.S. military personnel would pose no problems since they are dependents within the meaning of subparagraph (c). Mr. Chin stated that he believed the discussion showed that the question of dual nationality was not a problem.

6. Mr. Chin then indicated that the Korean side desired to confine the civilian component to American citizens. He proposed the insertion of the phrase "of U.S. nationality" immediately after the words "civilian persons" in the first line of subparagraph (b).

7. Colonel Solf replied that the article under discussion is solely one of definitions; it does not convey any rights or privileges. Nor does it establish pre-requisites for employment. He suggested that many of the questions which the Korean side might have concerning this matter might more appropriately be discussed in connection with other articles. He pointed out that in the past, the U.S. armed forces in Korea have hired a relatively small number of third state nationals because they had specific skills not otherwise available. He stated that this had been done in the interests of both the U.S. forces and the ROKG. In the case of these people, he added, there should be no discrimination in regard to privileges or rights.

8. Mr. Chin replied that the Korean side wished to limit the civilian component to U.S. nationals and wished to preclude aliens residing in Korea from enjoying the privileges and immunities granted to the U.S. forces. Mr. Habib reinterated that the article under discussion had no relation to later

0290

7-4

articles covering the terms of employment of members of the civilian component. He said that the U.S. position was that if third state nationals are employed by the U.S. forces, they should be included in the definition of the civilian component. He pointed out that aliens resident in Korea are excluded by the terms of the U.S. draft. Colonel Solf said he wished to add one further point for the consideration of the Korean side. The SOFA with the Philippines, the NATO SOFA (with respect to nationals of other NATO countries), and an administrative arrangement by the Joint Committee operating under the Japanese SOFA, all provide for the admission of third state nationals as members of the civilian component. Mr. Habib added that this was a practical matter; that persons whose skills were not available either in the U.S. or in Korea should not be discriminated against in regard to privileges and immunities. Mr. Chin replied that the Korean side believed all the necessary skills were available either among U.S. nationals or Korean nationals. Mr. Habib said the key word was "availability". It was then agreed to discuss the matter further at the next meeting.

d. Definition of Dependents (subparagraph (c))

9. Moving on to subparagraph (c), Mr. Chin stated that the Korean side had not included in its draft any mention of "other relatives". Mr. Habib replied that this was another practical matter and that, in effect, the paragraph was a definition of the family unit. Colonel Solf explained that the intention in this instance was to avoid any unnecessary breaking up of the family unit. Parents-in law and dependent brothers or sisters should not be excluded. He added that the criterion in the U.S. draft was very similar to that found in the U.S. tax laws, i.e. the dependent must rely for more than

0291

7-5

50% of his support on the sponsor. Mr. Chin replied that he understood the U.S. position and was in general agreement. However, he suggested that discussion of this paragraph be continued at the next meeting.

e. Entry and Exit

10. Mr. Habib then briefly introduced the U.S. draft of the entry and exit article, which was distributed to the negotiators. After reading the draft, the Korean side, without comment, agreed to the text of paragraphs 1, 2, 3, 5, and 6.

11. With regard to paragraph 3, Mr. Habib pointed out that there would be much work for the Joint Committee in the field of documentation. This, he assured the negotiators, was the case in all status of forces agreements. It was handled sometimes by an Agreed Minute to the agreement, sometimes through administrative arrangements made by the Joint Committee. Referring to subparagraph (a), he said the U.S. would expect action which would provide that:

a. U.S. law enforcement personnel (MPs, SPs, etc.) should carry bilingual identity cards to be shown on request when the bearer is in the performance of his duty;

b. the U.S. armed forces would furnish to the Korean authorities, on request, a description of the various uniforms worn by members of the U.S. forces in Korea and sample copies of the identification cards.

With regard to the last sentence of paragraph 3, Mr. Habib proposed that the negotiators reach an understanding that the identity cards be displayed upon request but not surrendered. He suggested that the form of such an understanding could be determined during subsequent negotiations.

0232

12. Mr. Chin replied that the Korean side fully understood the necessity for technical arrangements to implement paragraphs 1 and 3. He indicated that either an Agreed Minute or action by the Joint Committee would be acceptable to the Korean side.

13. Referring to paragraph 4, Mr. Chin suggested that since the persons referred to in the paragraph are civilians rather than military personnel, the word "passports" should be inserted in place of the words "appropriate documentation". Mr. Habib replied that the U.S. side would study this suggestion and reply at the next meeting.

14. With respect to paragraph 6, Mr. Habib suggested that the negotiators reach an understanding that following a notice of change of status pursuant to paragraph 5, the responsibilities of the U.S. under paragraph 6 shall arise only if the expulsion order is issued within a reasonable time after the notice under paragraph 5 is given. Mr. Chin agreed to such an understanding, the terms of which could be worked out later on.

f. Agenda for Next Meeting

15. Mr. Chin stated that in his opinion the negotiators had made great progress in that day's meeting. He suggested that an Agreed Minute be prepared, setting forth the specific items agreed upon. Mr. Habib replied that the U.S. side believed it would be preferable to record agreement article by article rather than paragraph by paragraph. Mr. Chin agreed.

16. Mr. Habib proposed that the negotiators continue their fruitful discussion at the next meeting and seek to reach full agreement. Then, if time permitted, they might go on to consider the article establishing the Joint Committee.

0293

7-7

Mr. Chin agreed to continuation of discussion on the three articles already tabled but stated that the Korean side wished to reserve its position with regard to discussion of the Joint Committee article.

17. It was agreed to hold the next meeting on November 1 at 2:00 p.m.

보통문서로 재분류(1966.12.31.)

1966.12.31.에 예고문에 의거 일반문서로 재분류됨

0294

정/리/보/존/문/서/목/록					
기록물종류	문서-일반공문서철	등록번호	913 9586	등록일자	2006-07-27
분류번호	741.12	국가코드	US	주제	
문서철명	한.미국 간의 상호방위조약 제4조에 의한 시설과 구역 및 한국에서의 미국군대의 지위에 관한 협정 (SOFA) 전59권. 1966.7.9 서울에서 서명 : 1967.2.9 발효 (조약 232호) *원본				
생산과	미주과/조약과	생산년도	1952 - 1967	보존기간	영구
담당과(그룹)	조약	조약	서가번호	--	
참조분류					
권차명	V.15 실무교섭회의, 제5-9차, 1962.11-12월				
내용목차	1. 제5차 회의, 11.1 (p.2~34) 2. 제6차 회의, 11.14 (p.35~82) 3. 제1-6차 회의 종합보고 (1차) (p.83~90) 4. 제7차 회의, 11.26 (p.91~149) 5. 제8차 회의, 12.4 (p.150~209) 6. 제9차 회의, 12.14 (p.210~298) * 일지 : 1953.8.7 이승만 대통령-Dulles 미국 국무장관 공동성명 - 상호방위조약 발효 후 군대지위협정 교섭 약속 1954.12.2 정부, 주한 UN군의 관세업무협정 체결 제의 1955.1월, 5월 미국, 제의 거절 1955.4.28 정부, 군대지위협정 제의 (한국측 초안 제시) 1957.9.10 Hurter 미국 국무차관 방한 시 각서 수교 (한국측 제의 수락 요구) 1957.11.13, 26 정부, 개별 협정의 단계적 체결 제의 1958.9.18 Dawling 주한미국대사, 형사재판관할권 협정 제외 조건으로 행정협정 체결 의사 전달 1960.3.10 정부, 토지, 시설협정의 우선적 체결 강력 요구 1961.4.10 장면 국무총리-McConaughy 주한미국대사 공동성명으로 교섭 개시 합의 1961.4.15, 4.25 제1, 2차 한.미국 교섭회의 (서울) 1962.3.12 정부, 교섭 재개 촉구 공한 송부 1962.5.14 Burger 주한미국대사, 최규하 장관 면담 시 형사재판관할권 문제 제기 않는 조건으로 교섭 재개 통고 1962.9.6 한.미국 간 공동성명 발표 (9월 중 교섭 재개 합의) 1962.9.20~ 1965.6.7 제1-81차 실무 교섭회의 (서울) 1966.7.8 제82차 실무 교섭회의 (서울) 1966.7.9 서명 1967.2.9 발효 (조약 232호)				

마/이/크/로/필/름/사/항				
촬영연도	*롤 번호	화일 번호	후레임 번호	보관함 번호
2006-11-22	I-06-0067	10	1-298	

0001

1. 제5차 회의, 11.1

0002

기 안 용 지

자 체 통 제		기안처	미주과 강석재	전화번호	근거서류접수일자

과장	국장	차관보좌관	차관	장관		

관계관 서명	조약과장

기안 년월일	1962. 10. 24	시행 년월일		보존 년한	병	정서	기장
분류 기호		전체 통제		종결			
경유 수신 참조	건 의		발신				
제목	미 주둔군 지위협정 실무교섭대표 변경						

미 주둔군 지위협정 실무교섭 회의 한국측 대표를 아래와 같이 변경하고저 건의하오니 재가하여 주시기 바랍니다.

아 래

1. 전 조약과장을 교섭대표직으로부터 해임하고 신임 조약과장 오 원용 서기관을 교섭대표로 임명케한다.
2. 한국측 기록작성자로서 그동안 자진적극적으로 임무수행하여온 조약과 신 정섭 2등서기관을 미주과 이 경훈 2등 서기관으로 교체케 한다. 끝

승인양식 1-1-3 (1112-040-016-018) (190mm×260mm16절지)

0003

기 안 용 지

자체 통제		기안처	미주과 이경훈	전화번호	근거서류접수일자

과장	수석대표		보좌관		차관	장관

관계관 서명	조약과장 　 기획조정관

기안 년월일	1962. 11. 1.	시행 년월일		보존 년한		정서 기장
분류 기호	외정무 2253	전체 통제				

경유 수신 참조	국가재건최고회의 의장 (참조 : 외무국방위원장) 내각수반	발신	외무부장관
제목	주둔군 지위협정 체결을위한 제5차교섭 회의 보고		

1962.11.1. 하오 2시부터 동3시 30분 까지 외무부에서 개최된 표기문제에 관한 제5차 교섭회의에서 토의된 내용을 별지와 같이 보고 합니다.

유첨 : 제5차 교섭회의 보고서 .... 부

보통문서로 재분류(1966. 12. 31.)

1966.12.31.에 예고문에 의거 일반문서로 재분류됨

1964년 9월 30일 미주과 직권으로 대외비로 재분류

승인양식 1—1—3 (1112—040—016—018) (190mm×260mm16절지)

8-1

0004

의 무 부

외정무 1962. 11. 2.

수 신 국가재건최고회의 의장

참 조 외무국방위원장

제 목 주둔군 지위협정 체결을위한 제5차 교섭회의 보고

1962. 11. 1. 하오 2시부터 동 3시 30분까지 외무부에서 개최된 표기문제에 관한 제 5 차 교섭회의에서 토의된 내용을 별지와같이 보고합니다.

유첨 : 제 5 차 교섭회의 보고서 2부. 끝

의 무 부 장 관 최 덕 신

0005

1-5

외 무 부

의정무 1962. 11. 2.

수 신 내각수반

제 목 주둔군 지위협정 체결을위한 제5차 교섭회의 보고

1962. 11. 1. 하오 2시부터 동 3시 30분까지 외무부에서 개최된 조기문제에 관한 제 5 차 교섭회의에서 토의된 내용을 별지와 같이 보고합니다.

유첨 : 제 5 차 교섭회의 보고서 1부, 끝

외 무 부 장 관 최 덕 신

0006

8-6

제 5 차

한미간 주둔군지위 협정 실무자회의

보 고 서

1. 시 일 : 1962. 11. 1. 하오 2시부터 동 3시 30분까지

2. 장 소 : 외무부 회의실

3. 참석자 : 한국측 : 이 경 호 (법무부 법무국장) (수석대리)

박 근 (외무부 미주과장)

오 원 용 (외무부 조약과장)

이 남 구 (국방부 군무과장)

지 성 구 (외무부 공보관)

이 경 훈 (외무부 2등서기관)

신 정 섭 (" ")

강 석 재 (외무부 3등서기관)

미국측 : 교섭대표단 전원

4. 토의사항 : (1) 협정의 서문, 용어의 정의, 출입국관리 및 합동위원회에 관한 문제를 순차적으로 토의함.

(2) 협정의 서문에 관하여 우리측은 우리측 초안대로 주한미국 군대가 한미간 방위조약에 의거해서 뿐만아니라 유엔안전보장 이사회의 결의에 의거하여 한국영토에 배치되고 있다는점도 언급한데 대하여 미국측은 고려하여 보겠다고 하였음.

(3) 용어의 정의 토의에있어 우리측은 미국군대 구성원의 정의에관하여 미국측안에서 규정한"except for those for whom status has otherwise been provided."라는 부분을 구체적으로 어떤 조약인지를 명시하자고 제시함. 이에대하여 미국측은 다음에 다시 토의하자고 하였음.

0007

8-2

外交 88-9(3)

0003

(4) 용어의 정의토의에 있어 우리측은 "civilian persons" 다음에 "미국의 국적을 가진" 이라는 문구를 삽입 할것을 제의하자 미국측은 이것도 후에다시 토의 하자고 하였음.

(5) 출입국 관리문제에 관하여 지난회의에서 문제가된 군속, 그들의 가족 및 군인가족이 소지하여야 할 "적절한 문서" 대신에 "여권" 을 소지하도록 할것을 우리측이 제의한데 대하여 미국측은 "적절한 문서" 라는 용어가 "여권" 이라는 용어보다 더욱 포괄적임으로 미국측안대로 하자고 주장하였음. 이에대하여 우리측은 "여권" 으로하되 예외적인 규정에 관해서는 합동위원회 에서 정하자고 주장하자 미국측은 이문제를 다음에 다시 토의하자고 하였음.

(6) 출입국관리에 관련된 조항에 대한 합의의사록 미국측 안을 제시하자 우리측은 특히 동안의 4 항에관하여는 추후 검토후 다음회의에서 답변하겠다고 하고 추가할 사항이 있으면 추가하겠다고 하였음.

(7) 합동위원회에 관한 양국간의 초안을 교환한후 양측은 양측안의 차의점에관한 의견교환을 하였음.

(8) 한국측은 관세문제를 미국측은 토지 및 시설문제를 차기회의에서 토의하자고 주장하였음.

5. 기타 사항 :

(1) 차기회의 일자 : 1962. 11. 13. 하오 2 시

(2) 차기회의 의제 : 제5차 회의에서 토의된 의제중 합의에 도달하지 못한사항과 그때 까지 양측수석대표간에 합의된 기타의제

0009

→

-ʃ-3

外院 88-9

0010

7. 참고자료 : 미국측이 제의한 협정초안 (출입국 관리에 관한 합의 의사록 및 합동위원회) ...... 별첨참조

보통문서로 재분류 (1966.12.31.)

(. .) 일반문서로 재분류

19 . . . 에 예고문에 의거 일반문서로 재분류됨

0011

f-4

0012

a. Introduction of New Korean Participants

1. Before beginning substantive discussion, Mr. Yi Kyung-ho, acting as Chief Negotiator for the Korean side, introduced Mr. O Won-yong, newly appointed Chief of the Treaty Section in the International Relations Bureau of the Foreign Ministry, and Mr. ~~Yi~~ Lee Kyung-~~hun~~ Hom, Second Secretary in the America Section of the Ministry's Political Affairs Bureau.

I. Preamble

2. Turning to the topics discussed at the last meeting, Mr. Yi said that the principal difference in the two drafts of the Preamble was that the Korean draft referred to the UN Resolutions and the U. S. draft omitted any such reference. Mr. Habib agreed but suggested that further discussion regarding the Preamble be deferred ~~untis~~ until the following meeting, in as much as the U. S. side was awaiting word from Washington. Mr. Yi agreed.

3. Mr. Habib asked whether the Korean side had any purpose on proposing the reference to the UN Resolutions other than that of providing historical background. Mr. YI replied that the purpose was to make clear that the U. S. forces, whether operating as U. S. forces or as members of the United Nations Command, would come under the provisions of the SOFA. Mr. Habib stated that the U. S. side would consider this position for discussion at the next meeting.

C. Definitions

4. Mr. Yi, referring to subparagraph (a) of the U. S. draft of the definitions article, said that the phrase "except those for whom status has otherwise been provided" was too vague and that the Korean side would prefer that the matter be handled in some other fashion, perhaps by means of an agreed minute. Mr. Habib replied that the negotiators might find the use of agreed minutes advantageous and desirable, not only in this

0013

9-8

case but also in regard to other items. He asked whether the Korean side had any specific language to suggest. Mr. Yi replied ~~in the negative~~ he did not have any specific language to suggest at the moment, but suggested that the phrase be worded more precisely in the form of an agreed minute. It was then agreed to defer further discussion of the definitions article until the next meeting.

d. Entry and Exit

5. Turning to the entry and exit article, Mr. Yi asked for comment by the U. S. side on the Korean suggestion that the word "passports" be substituted for "appropriate documentation" in paragraph 4. Mr. Habib asked the Korean side to reconsider its proposal. He pointed out that the term "appropriate documentation" is a much broader term than "passports". It would include the latter whereas "passports" would not include "appropriate documentation". The language in the U. S. draft would meet the Korean needs and would permit the U. S. authorities to take care of any contingencies that might arise with respect to people not entitled to a U. S. passport. In practice, he said, any problem arising in this connection would probably be settled by the Joint Committee. He also pointed out that Korean dependents of U. S. personnel could not be issued U. S. passports.

6. Mr. Yi suggested that both sides agree in principle that passports should be issued to members of the civilian component and that exceptional cases should be considered by the Joint Committee. Mr. Habib replied that there would be little the Joint Committee could do, since the U. S. authorities could not issue passports to aliens. He suggested that the more general phrasing "appropriate documentation" be adopted because it would be more useful and would make this article of the SOFA easier to administer. After several more exchanges in which each side reiterated its position, it was decided to postpone further discussion of this question until

9-7

0014

the next meeting.

7. Mr. Habib then tabled the draft texts of four Agreed Minutes to the entry and exit article, setting forth ~~explixity~~ explicitly the various matters agreed to in principle at the previous meeting. Mr. Yi said the Agreed Minutes appeared to be acceptable but the Korean side would like to have time to consider them, particularly the fourth one (which ~~xx~~ refers to the responsibilities of the U. S. and Korean governments under paragraphs 5 and 6 of the article).

2. Joint Committee

8. Mr. Habib then suggested that the negotiators next consider the article establishing the Joint Committee. Mr. Yi suggested that this article be considered along with the customs and duties article at the next meeting. Mr. Habib indicated that the U. S. side might not be quite ready to discuss the customs article at the next meeting and suggested instead discussion of the areas and facilities articles. When Mr. Yi replied that the Korean side would not be ready to discuss areas and facilities, it was agreed that the chairmen of the two negotiating teams should meet privately before the next meeting in order to draw up an agenda.

~~K~~9. It was then decided to go ahead with consideration of the Joint Committee article and both sides tabled drafts. Mr. Habib pointed out the following differences in language:

a. In paragraph 2, the references to the two governments are reversed in the first sentence and simplieifed in the final sentence of the Korean draft.

b. The additional phrase at the end of the first sentence in paragraph 1 of the U. S. draft refers to another article not yet tabled which will deal with communications facilities. The relevance of this phrase will become clear to the Korean side, he added, when the facilities and areas articles are discussed. He said this was a purely technical matter and had no other relevance.

0015

9-10

c. The Korean draft speaks of "diplomatic" channels in paragraph 3 rather than "appropriate" channels. The U.S. side, Mr. Habib indicated, believes that "appropriate" is a better and more useful word.

d. The Korean draft does not include the final sentence of paragraph 1 of the U.S. draft relating to the particular functions of the Joint Committee in connection with facilities and areas.

10. Mr. Yi commented that there appeared to be general agreement between the two drafts, with only minor points of difference. He pointed out that the Korean draft contained the insertion of the words "interpretation and" immediately before the word "implementation" in the first sentence of paragraph 1. Mr. Habib replied that the Joint Committee has no power to "interpret" the SOFA; it consults and "implements" the agreement but it does not interpret. The two governments are the interpreting agencies. Mr. Yi ~~promised a further explanation of the Korean side's draft at the next meeting.~~ suggested that discussion of this matter be continued at the next meeting.

11. Mr. Yi said he did not understand the necessity for the additional phrase in the U.S. draft (see para. 9b above). Mr. Habib replied that it would become clear when the ~~facilite~~ facilities and areas articles are discussed, at which time the necessity for special arrangements covering communications would emerge. He asked the Korean side to reserve their comments on this point until that time. Mr. Yi agreed.

12. Mr. Habib asked for Korean views on the final sentence of Paragraph 1 in the U.S. draft which did not appear in the Korean draft. Mr. Yi replied that the Korean side questioned the necessity for specific stipulation of this aspect of the Joint Committee's functions. Mr. Habib said the U.S. side believed this sentence referred to one of the most important of the Joint Committee's functions and should therefore be included. He asked if the Korean side found anything in it which was inconsistent with their view of the Joint Committee. Mr. Yi replied that this function of the Committee would be spelled out in the facilities and areas articles and that there was

a-11

no ~~xxx~~ need to repeat it here.

13. Mr. Yi then referred to the use of "diplomatic" as opposed to "appropriate" channels. He said the Korean side intended a precise and specific reference to diplomatic channels. He asked what the term "appropriate" meant. Mr. Habib suggested that the Joint Committee should be permitted to decide what channels should be used. Perhaps the Embassy and the Ministry of Foreign Affairs would not necessarily always be the right channel. Perhaps they ~~x~~ should not be involved in every little detail of SOFA implementation. Therefore, use of the word "appropriate" would be more suitable. Mr. Yi suggested further discussion of this point at the next meeting. ~~Mr. Habik Agreed.~~ 1966.12.31.에 예고문에 의거 일반문서로 재분류됨

14. ~~XX~~ It was decided to hold the next meeting on November 13 at 2:00 p.m. 보통문서로 재분류 (1966. 12. 31.)

0017

Agreed Minutes to Article

(Entry and Exit)

1. With regard to Paragraph 3(a), United States Armed Forces law enforcement personnel (such as MP, SP, AP, CID and CIC), who engage in military police activities in the Republic of Korea, will carry a bilingual identity card containing the bearer's name, position, and the fact that he is a member of a law enforcement agency. This card will be shown upon request to persons concerned when the bearer is in the performance of duty.

2. The United States Armed Forces will furnish, upon request, to Korean authorities the form of the identification cards of the members of the United States Armed Forces, the civilian component, and their dependents and descriptions of the various uniforms of the United States Armed Forces in the Republic of Korea.

3. The final sentence of Paragraph 3 means that members of the United States Armed Forces will display their identity cards upon request but will not be required to surrender them to Korean authorities.

4. Following a change of status pursuant to Paragraph 5, the responsibilities of the United States authorities under Paragraph 6 shall arise only if the expulsion order is issued within a reasonable time after the notice under Paragraph 5 has been communicated to the Korean authorities.

0018

明 88-10(2)

0019

SOF B-7

ARTICLE (VII)

1. A Joint Committee shall be established as the means for consultation between the Government of the United States and the Government of the Republic of Korea on all matters requiring mutual consultation regarding the implementation of this Agreement ~~unless otherwise provided for~~ except where otherwise provided for. (In particular, the Joint Committee shall serve as the means for consultation in determining the facilities and areas in the Republic of Korea which are required for the use of the United States in carrying out the purposes of this Agreement.)

2. The Joint Committee shall be composed of a representative of the Government of the United States and a representative of the Government of the Republic of Korea, each of whom shall have one or more deputies and a staff. The Joint Committee shall determine its own procedures, and arrange for such auxiliary organs and administrative services as may be required. The Joint Committee shall be so organized that it may meet immediately at any time at the request of the representative of either the Government of the United States or the Government of the Republic of Korea.

3. If the Joint Committee is unable to resolve any matter, it shall refer that matter to the respective Governments for further consideration through appropriate channels.

1966. 12. 31 에 예고문에 의거 일반문서로 재분류됨

보통문서로 재분류 (1966. 12. 31.)

0020

8-5

마이크 88-10(2)

0021

1. A Joint Committee shall be established as the means for consultation between the two Governments on all matters requiring mutual consultation regarding the interpretation and implementation of this Agreement.

2. The Joint Committee shall be composed of a representative of the Government of the Republic of Korea and a representative of the Government of the United States, each of whom shall have one or more deputies and a staff. The Joint Committee shall determine its own procedures, and arrange for such auxiliary organs and administrative services as may be required.

The Joint Committee shall be so organized that it may meet immediately at any time at the request of the representative of either Government.

3. If the Joint Committee is unable to resolve any matter, it shall refer that matter to the respective Governments for further consideration through diplomatic channels.

보통문서로 재분류(1966. 12. 31.)

1966. 12. 31. 에 예고문에 의거 일반문서로 재분류됨

1964 년 9 월 30 일 직권으로 파기 비밀로 재분류

8-11

0022

SUMMARY RECORD OF THE FIFTH SESSION
STATUS FORCES NEGOTIATIONS

November 1, 1962

I. Time and Place : 2:00 to 3:10 p.m. on November 1, 1962 at Conference Room of the Ministry of Foreign Affairs

II. Attendants:

ROK Side:

Mr. Yi, Kyong Ho	Director Bureau of Legal Affairs Ministry of Justice
Mr. Pak, Kun	Chief, America Section Ministry of Foreign Affairs
Mr. O, Won Yong	Chief, Treaty Section Ministry of Foreign Affairs
Col. Lee, Nam Koo	Chief, Military Affairs Section Ministry of National Defense
Mr. Chi, Sung Koo	Press Officer Ministry of Foreign Affairs
Mr. Lee, Kyung Hoon (Rapporteur)	2nd Secretary Ministry of Foreign Affairs
Mr. Shin, Chung Sup	2nd Secretary Ministry of Foreign Affairs
Mr. Kang, Suk Jae (Interpreter)	3rd Secretary Ministry of Foreign Affairs

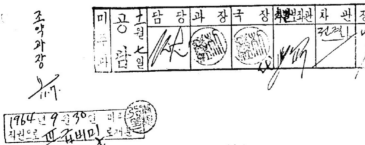

0023

9-1

US Side:

Mr. Philip C. Habib	Counselor of the Embassy for Political Affairs
Brig. Gen. J.D. Lawlor	Deputy Chief of Staff 8th Army
Mr. William J. Ford	First Secretary of the Embassy
Col. G.G. O'Connor	Deputy Chief of Staff 8th Army
Capt. R.M. Brownlie	Assistane Chief of Staff USN/K
Col. W.A. Solf	Staff Judge Advocate 8th Army
Mr. Benjamin A. Fleck (Rapporteur and Press Officer)	First Secretary of the Embassy
Mr. Robert A. Lewis	Second Secretary and Consul of the Embassy
Lt. Col. R.E. Miller	Staff Officer, JAG 8th Army
(Lt. Col. G.T. Suderman)	Staff Officer, J-5 USAF/K

III. Gist of Talks:

a. Introduction of New Korean Participants

1. Before beginning substantive discussion, Mr. Yi Kyung-ho, acting as Chief Negotiator for the Korean side, introduced Mr. O Won-yong, newly appointed Chief of the Treaty Section in the International Relations Bureau of the Foreign Ministry, and Mr. Lee Kyung Hoon, Second Secretary in the America Section of the Ministry's Political Affairs Bureau.

b. Preamble

2. Turning to the topics discussed at the last meeting, Mr. Yi said that the principal difference in the two drafts of the Preamble was that the Korean

0024

9-2

draft referred to the UN Resolutions and the U.S. draft omitted any such reference. Mr. Habib agreed but suggested that further discussion regarding the Preamble be deferred until the following meeting, in as much as the U.S. side was awaiting word from Washington. Mr. Yi agreed.

3. Mr. Habib asked whether the Korean side had any purpose on proposing the reference to the UN Resolutions other than that of providing historical background. Mr. Yi replied that the purpose was to make clear that the U.S. forces, whether operating as U.S. forces or as members of the United Nations Command, would come under the provisions of the SOFA. Mr. Habib stated that the U.S. side would consider this position for discussion at the next meeting.

c. Definitions

4. Mr. Yi referring to subparagraph (a) of the U.S. draft of the definitions article, said that the phrase "except those for whom status has otherwise been provided" was too vague and that the Korean side would prefer that the matter be handled in some other fashion, perhaps by means of an agreed minute. Mr. Habib replied that the negotiators might find the use of agreed minutes advantageous and desirable, not only in this case but also in regard to other items. He asked whether the Korean side had any specific language to suggest. Mr. Yi replied he did not have any specific language to suggest at the moment, but suggested that the phrase be worded more precisely in the form of an agreed minute. It was then agreed to defer further discussion of the definitions article until the next meeting.

d. Entry and Exit

5. Turning to the entry and exit article, Mr. Yi asked for comment by the U.S. side on the Korean suggestion that the word "passports" be substituted for "appropriate documentation" in paragraph 4. Mr Habib asked the Korean side to reconsider its proposal. He pointed out that the term "appropriate documentation" is a much broader term than "passports". It would include the latter whereas "passports" would not include "appropriate documentation". The language in the U.S. draft would meet the Korean needs and would permit the U.S. authorities to take care of any contingencies that might arise with respect to people not entitled to a U.S. passport. In practice, he said, any problem arising in this connection would probably be settled by the Joint Committee. He also pointed out that Korean dependents of U.S. personnel could not be issued U.S. passports.

6. Mr. Yi suggested that both sides agree in principle that passports should be issued to members of the civilian component and that exceptional cases should be considered by the Joint Committee. Mr. Habib replied that there would be little the Joint Committee could do, since the U.S. authorities could not issue passports to aliens. He suggested that the more general phrasing "appropriate documentation" be adopted because it would be more useful and would make this article of the SOFA easier to administer. After several more exchanges in which each side reiterated its position, it was decided to postpone further discussion of this question until the next meeting.

0026

9-4

7. Mr. Habib then tabled the draft texts of four Agreed Minutes to the entry and exit article, setting forth explicitly the various matters agreed to in principle at the previous meeting. Mr. Yi said the Agreed Minutes appeared to be acceptable but the Korean side would like to have time to consider them, particularly the fourth one (which refers to the responsibilities of the U.S. and Korean governments under paragraphs 5 and 6 of the article).

e. Joint Committee

8. Mr. Habib then suggested that the negotiators next consider the article establishing the Joint Committee. Mr. Yi suggested that this article be considered along with the customs and duties article at the next meeting. Mr. Habib indicated that the U.S, side might not be quite ready to discuss the customs article at the next meeting and suggested instead discussion of the areas and facilities articles. When Mr. Yi replied that the Korean side would not be ready to disuuss areas and facilities, it was agreed that the chairmen of the two negotiating teams should meet privately before the next meeting in order to draw up an agenda.

9. It was then decided to go ahead with considerat-ion of the Joint Committee article and both sides tabled drafts. Mr. Habib pointed out the following differences in language:

a. In paragraph 2, the references to the two governments are reversed in the first sentence and simplified in the final sentence of the Korean draft.

0027

9-5

b. The additional phrase at the end of the first sentence in paragraph 1 of the U.S. draft refers to another article not yet tabled which will deal with communications facilities. The relevance of this phrase will become clear to the Korean side, he added, when the facilities and areas articles are discussed. He said this was a purely technical matter and had no other relevance.

c. The Korean draft speaks of "diplomatic" channels in paragraph 3 rather than "appropriate" channels. The U.S. side, Mr. Habib indicated, believes that "appropriate" is a better and more useful word.

d. The Korean draft does not include the final sentence of paragraph 1 of the U.S. draft relating to the particular functions of the Joint Committee in connection with facilities and areas.

10. Mr. Yi commented that there appeared to be general agreement between the two drafts, with only minor points of difference. He pointed out that the Korean draft contained the insertion of the words "interpretation and" immediately before the word "implementation" in the first sentence of paragraph 1. Mr. Habib replied that the Joint Committee has nor power to "interpret" the SOFA; it consults and "implements" the agreement but it does not interpret. The two governments are the interpreting agencies. Mr. Yi suggested that discussion of this matter be continued at the next meeting.

11. Mr. Yi said he did not understand the necessity for the additional phrase in the U.S. draft (see para. 9b above). Mr. Habib replied that it would become clear when the facilities and areas articles are discussed, at which time the necessity for special arrangements covering communications would emerge. He asked the Korean side to reserve their comments on this point until that time. Mr. Yi agreed.

0028

9-6

12. Mr. Habib asked for Korean views on the final sentence of Paragraph 1 in the U.S. draft which did not appear in the Korean draft. Mr. Yi replied that the Korean side questioned the necessity for specific stipulation of this aspect of the Joint Committee's functions. Mr. Habib said the U.S. side believed this senternce referred to one of the most important of the Joint Committee's functions and should therefore be included. He asked if the Korean side found anything in it which was inconsistent with their view of the Joint Committee. Mr. Yi replied that this function of the Committee would be spelled out in the facilities and areas articles and that there was no need to repeat it here.

13. Mr. Yi then referred to the use of "diplomatic" as opposed to "appropriate" channels. He said the Korean ~~said~~ side intended a precise and specific reference to diplomatic channels. He asked what the term "appropriate" meant. Mr. Habib suggested that the Joint Committee should be permitted to decide what channels should be used. Perhaps the Embassy and the Ministry of Foreign Affairs would not necessarily always be the right channel. Perhaps they should not be involved in every little detail of SOFA implementation. Therefore, use of the word "appropriate" would be more suitable. Mr. Yi suggested further discussion of this point at the next meeting.

14. It was decided to hold the next meeding on November 13 at 2:00 p.m.

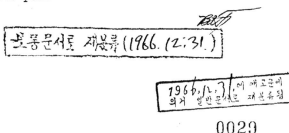

0029

노무조항 한국측 개정안

(개정부분을 밑 줄로 표시함)

1. 미합중국군대와 ____ 조에 규정된 기관들(이후 고용주라 함)은 본협정에 따라 민간인(이후 고용인이라 함)을 고용할수 있다. 그와같은 민간인은 대한민국국민이여야 한다.

2. 제 1 항에 규정된 고용주는 가능한 최대한도로 대한민국 당국의 원조를 얻어 채용하고 고용하여야 한다. 고용주는 각별히 필요한대로 채용고용 및 행정은 직접 행할수 있다. 고용주가 고용인의 직접채용을 행할 경우 미합중국 군사당국은 노동행정에 필요한 관계정보를 대한민국 노동청에 제공하여야 한다.

3. 본조의 규정 혹은 미합중국군대의 군사상의 필요성에 상반되지 않는 한도내에서 임금 및 제수당에 관한 것과 같은 고용과 업무의 조건, 고용인의 보호와 후생을 위한 조건, 보상 그리고 노동관계에 관한 고용인의 권리는 대한민국 법령에 정하여진 것과 일치하여야 한다.

4. 고용주는 고용인의 불평을 정당하고 정기에 해결하기 위한 조처(措處)를 보지한다.

5. (가) 대한민국이 노동력을 배정하는 조치(措置)를 취할 경우 미합중국군대는 대한민국국군이 향유하는 것보다 불리하지 않은 고용특권이 부여되어야 한다.

(나) 전쟁, 사변 또는 이에 준하는 사태와 같은 국가위기에 처하여 미합중국군대의 임무수행에 긴요한 기술을 습득한 고용인은 미합중국군대의 요청으로 대한민국 병역 또는 기타 강제노역으로부터 연기를 받을수 있다. 미합중국군대는 그와 같이 긴요하다고 생각되는 고용인의 명단을 사전에 대한민국에 제출하여야 한다.

6. 미합중국정부는 ____ 조에 언급된 계약자가 본협정에 의한 그들의 활동에 있어서 한국인을 가능한 최대한도로 고용하고 계약자가 그들의 고용인을 위하여 설정한 고용 조건, 보상 및 노사관계관력가 대한민국의 법령에 정하여진 것과 일치하도록

0030

7. 군속은 고용의 한계와 조건에 관련하여 한국법령을 규정에 따르지 아니한다.

합의의사록

1. 미합중국군대의 개인구성원, 군속 및 그의 가족에 의한 가사사용인의 고용은 적용될수 있는 한국법령 그리고 추가하여 미합중국군대가 공포한 임금표와 관리조치에 의하여 운용되어야 한다.

2. 대한민국의 법령에 정하여진 것에 일치하도록 한다는 미합중국의 약속은 미합중국정부가 국제법에 의한 그들의 면제를 포기하는 것을 의미하지 아니한다.

3. 고용주는 대한민국의 소득세법령에 규정된 원천 과세액을 공제하고 대한민국정부에 납부하여야 한다.

4. 대한민국정부가 제2항에 의거하여 제공한 원조에 소요된 직접경비에 대하여 보상받아야 한다는 것으로 양해 한다.

5. 제5항에 규정된 "군사상의 필요성"에 의하여 고용주가 취한 행위와 조치는 한국노동법령에 상반할 경우 사전에 합동위원회에 협의를 위하여 회부되어야 하며 그의 결정에 따라야 한다.

6. 미합중국군대의 기존절차의 이용을 통하여 해결 될수 없는 고용주와 어떤 고용인 혹은 노동조합간의 분쟁에 관하여는 다음과 같은 방법으로 해결을 성취하여야 한다:

(가) 분쟁은 대한민국 보건사회부 노동청에 알선을 위하여 회부되어야 한다.

(나) 전기 (가)의 절차에 의하여 분쟁이 해결되지 않을 경우, 그분쟁은 합동위원회에 그분쟁을 해결하기 위한 중재를 위하여 회부되어야 하며 그합동위원회는 이사건을 노동분과위원회 혹은 특별히 지정된 위원회에 회부할수 있다.

0031

(다) 분쟁이 전기절차에 의하여 해결되지 않을 경우 합동위원회는 그분쟁을 해결한다. 합동위원회의 결정은 구속력을 가진다.

(라) 분쟁이 전기 (가), (나) 및 (다)항의 절차에 의하여 취급되고 있는 기간중에는 고용인 단체 혹은 고용인은 한국노동법령의 규정에 위반하여 정상적 업무 요건을 해하는 행위를 자행하지 못한다.

(마) 승인된 고용인 단체 혹은 고용인이 분쟁에 관한 합동위원회의 결정에 불복하거나, 혹은 한국노동법령의 규정에 위반하여 해결절차 진행중 정상적 업무요건을 해하는 행위를 자행함은, 대한민국 관계 법에 의하여 부여된 권리와 보호의 박탈을 초래하는 원인으로 간주한다.

0032

Revised Korean Draft of Labor Article

(The underlined parts are modifications)

1. The United States armed forces and the organizations provided for in Article ____ (hereinafter referred to as "employer") may employ civilian personnel (hereinafter referred to as "employee") under this Agreement. Such civilian personnel shall be nationals of the Republic of Korea.

2. The employers provided for in Paragraph 1 shall recruit and employ to the maximum extent practicable with the assistance of the authorities of the Republic of Korea. The employers may accomplish such recruitment, employment and administration directly as may be essentially required. In case employers accomplish direct recruitment of employees, the United States military authorities shall provide such relevant information as may be required for labor administration to the Office of Labor Affairs of the Republic of Korea.

3. To the extent not inconsistent with the provision of this article or the military requirements of the United States armed forces, the conditions of employment and work, such as those relating to wages and supplementary payments, the conditions for the protection and welfare of employees, compensations, and the rights of employees, concerning labor relations shall conform with those laid down by the legislation of the Republic of Korea.

4. Employers will maintain procedures designed to assure the just and timely resolution of employee grievances.

5. (a) Should the Republic of Korea adopt measures allocating labor, the United States Armed Forces shall be accorded employment privileges no less favorable than those enjoyed by the armed forces of the Republic of Korea.

0033

(b) In the event of a national emergency such as war, hostilities, or other imminent situations, the employees who have acquired skills essential to the mission of the United States Armed Forces may, upon request of the United States Armed Forces, be deferred from Republic of Korea military service or other compulsory services. The United States armed forces shall in advance furnish to the Republic of Korea lists of those employees deemed essential.

6. The United States Government shall ensure that the contractors referred to in Article _____ employ the Korean personnel to the maximum extent practicable in connection with their activities under this Agreement and the conditions of employment, compensation, and labor-management practices established by the contractors for their employees conform with those laid down by the legislation of the Republic of Korea.

7. Members of the civilian component shall not be subject to Korean laws or regulations with respect to their terms and conditions of employment.

AGREED MINUTES

1. The employment of a domestic by an individual member of the United States armed forces, civilian component or dependent thereof shall be governed by applicable Korean legislation and in addition by wage scales and control measures promulgated by the United States armed forces.

2. The undertaking of the United States to conform with those laid down by the legislation of the Republic of Korea does not imply any waiver by the United States Government of its immunities under international law.

0034

3. Employers shall withhold from the pay of their employees, and pay over to the Government of the Republic of Korea, withholdings required by the income tax legislation of the Republic of Korea.

4. It is understood that the Government of the Republic of Korea shall be reimbursed for direct costs incurred in providing assistance made pursuant to Paragraph 2.

5. Any action and measures, to be taken by the employers on the account of "military requirements" provided for in Paragraph 3, ~~and to be~~ whenever inconsistent with the Korean labor legislation, shall be referred in prior for consultation to the Joint Committee and be subject to the decision thereof.

6. With regard to any dispute between the employers and any employees or labor unions which cannot be settled through the use of existing procedures of the United States Armed Forces, settlement shall be accomplished in the following manner:

(a) The dispute shall be referred to the Office of Labor Affairs, Ministry of Health and Social Affairs, Republic of Korea, for conciliation.

(b) In the event that the dispute is not settled by the procedures described in (a) above, the dispute shall be referred to the Joint Committee, which may refer the matter to the Labor Sub-Committee or specially designated Committee for arbitration to resolve the dispute.

(c) In the event that the dispute is not settled by the procedures outlined above, the Joint Committee will resolve the dispute. The decisions of the Joint Committee shall be binding.

0035

(d) During the period in which a dispute is being handled by the procedures mentioned in paras (a), (b) and (c) above, neither employee organizations nor employees shall indulge in any practice disruptive of normal work requirements in violation of the provisions laid down in the Korean labor legislation.

(e) Failure of any recognized employee organization or employee to abide by the decision of the Joint Committee on any dispute, or indulging in practice disruptive of normal work requirements during settlement procedure in violation of the provisions laid down in the Korean labor legislation, shall be considered cause for the depriviation of the rights and protection accorded by the relevant laws of the Republic of Korea.

0036

Revised Korean Draft of Labor Article

(The underlined parts are modifications)

1. The United States armed forces and the organizations provided for in Article _____ (hereinafter referred to as "employer") may employ civilian personnel (hereinafter referred to as "employee") under this Agreement. Such civilian personnel shall be nationals of the Republic of Korea.

2. The employers provided for in Paragraph 1 shall recruit and employ to the maximum extent practicable with the assistance of the authorities of the Republic of Korea. The employers may accomplish such recruitment, employment and administration directly as may be required. In case employers accomplish direct recruitment of employees, the United States military authorities shall provide such relevant information as may be required for labor administration to the Office of Labor Affairs of the Republic of Korea.

3. Except as may otherwise be mutually agreed, the conditions of employment and work, such as those relating to wages and supplementary payments, the conditions for the protection and welfare of employees, compensations, and the rights of employees, concerning labor relations shall conform with those laid down by the legislation of the Republic of Korea.

4. Employers shall insure the just and timely resolution of employee grievances.

5. (a) Should the Republic of Korea adopt measures allocating labor, the United States Armed Forces shall be accorded allocation privileges no less favorable than those enjoyed by the armed forces of the Republic of Korea.

0037

(b) In the event of a national emergency such as war, hostilities, or other imminent situations, the employees who have acquired skills essential to the mission of the United States Armed Forces may, upon request of the United States Armed Forces, be deferred from Republic of Korea military service or other compulsory services. The United States armed forces shall in advance furnish to the Republic of Korea lists of those employees deemed essential.

6. Members of the civilian component shall not be subject to Korean laws or regulations with respect to their terms and conditions of employment.

AGREED MINUTES

1. The undertaking of the United States to conform with those laid down by the legislation of the Republic of Korea does not imply any waiver by the United States Government of its immunities under international law.

2. Employers shall withhold from the pay of their employees, and pay over to the Government of the Republic of Korea, withholdings required by the income tax legislation of the Republic of Korea.

3. It is understood that the Government of the Republic of Korea shall be reimbursed for direct costs incurred in providing assistance pursuant to Paragraph 2.

4. In case where it is impossible for the employers to conform, on account of the military requirements of the United States Armed Forces, with the Korean labor legislation under the provisions of Paragraph 3, the matter shall in advance be referred to the Joint Committee for mutual agreement.

The Republic of Korea will give due consideration to the military requirements of the United States Armed Forces.

0038

5. With regard to any dispute between the employers and any employees or labor unions which cannot be settled through the use of existing procedures of the United States Armed Forces, settlement shall be accomplished in the following manner:

(a) the dispute shall be referred to the Office of Labor Affairs of the Republic of Korea, for conciliation.

(b) In the event that the dispute is not settled by the procedures described in (a) above, the dispute shall be referred to a special ~~ly~~ committee designated by the Joint Committee for ~~mediation to resolve the dispute~~ further conciliation efforts.

(c) In the event that the dispute is not settled by the procedures outlined above, the Joint Committee will resolve the dispute. The decisions of the Joint Committee shall be binding.

(d) During the period in which a dispute is being handled by the procedures mentioned in paras (a), (b) and (c) above, neither employee organizations nor employees shall indulge in any practice disruptive of normal work requirements.

The above provisions shall not be interpreted to prejudice in any way the Article 14 of the Korean Labor Dispute Law.

(e) Failure of any recognized employee organization or employee to abide by the decision of the Joint Committee on any dispute, or indulging in practice disruptive of normal work requirements in violation of the provisions of Paragraph (d) above, shall be considered cause for the depriviation of the rights and protection accorded by the relevant laws of the Republic of Korea.

0039

2. 제6차 회의, 11.14

0040

재 무 부

재세관 10472 1962. 11. 5

수신 외무부장관

참조 정무국장

제목 한미행정협정 실무자회의 대표 보좌원 선정

한미 행정 협정 실무자 회의의 우리나라 대표로 당부 세관국장 재경 이사관 신 관 섭의 보좌요원을 다음과 같이 선정 하였기 그들이 실무자회의에 대표를 수행하여 보좌하도록 조처하여 주시기 바랍니다.

1. 재무부 세관국 관세과장 재경서기관 박봉진
2. 재무부 세관국 기 획 과 행정사무관 이종확
3. 재무부 세관국 감 시 과 행정 주사 이 재 섭. 끝

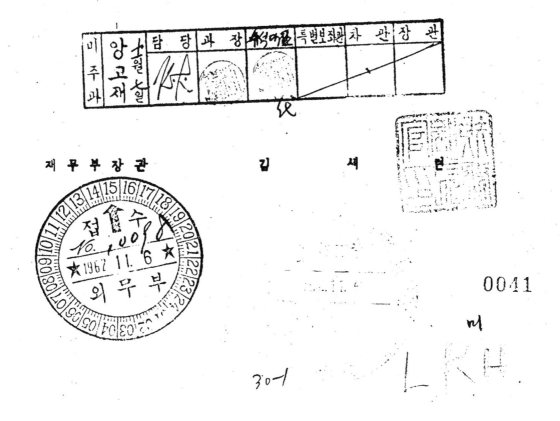

미주과	양고재 월 일	담당	과장	국장	특별보좌관	차관	장관

재 무 부 장 관 김 세 련

접수 No. 10098 1962 11. 6 외무부

0041

제목 : 한미 행정협정 제 6 차 교섭회의 개최시간 변경

1962. 11. 8. 하오 주한미대사관 "후렉" 1 등서기관은 미주과장을 방문하고 오는 11. 13. 하오 2시에 개최키로한 한미행정협정 제 6 차 교섭회의를 주한8 군측 사정으로 동일 하오 3시에 개최함이 좋겠다고 제시하여왔기 그렇게하자고 답하였음.

미 주 과 장　　　　박　　　근

0042

부 전 지

수 신 19 . . .

제 목
요 약

정무국장과 Habib 참사관의 회담

일시 : 1962.11.12, 15시

장소 : 정무 국장실

목적 : 6차 회의의 의제 점검

Habib의 발언 요지

1. 제6차 회의를 11월 13일 13시로 하자.
2. 다음 의제는 Custom 좋다.
3. 동시에 Entry & Exit 를 끝내자
4. 제7次 회의는 다음 주에 하자
5. 제7次에는 토지. 시설 문제를 하자.

관계부처

협 조 처

전화번호 주
부

발 신( )

승인양식 1-24 (1112-040-032-023) (130mm×190mm 32절지)

0043

제 6 차 한미간의 주둔군지위협정 교섭을 위한
실무자회의에 임할 우리측 입장

1. 의 제: 제 6 차 회의 의제로서는 제 5 차 회의에서 합의에 도달하지 못한 협정의 서문, 정의 및 출입국관리에 관한 문제를 계속 토의하고 또한 양측 수석대표간의 비공식적인 회합에서 합의를 본 관세문제를 토의 할 것임.

2. 우리측 입장:

(1) 출입국관리 문제에 있어서 지난번 회의에서 합의를 보지 못한 군속, 동가족 및 군인가족이 소지할 문서를 passports 로 하느냐 또는 미국측이 제의한 ~~other~~ appropriate documentation 으로 하느냐의 문제에 관하여는 미국측이 계속하여 자기측 주장을 고집하는 경우에는 이를 수락하도록 한다.

(2) 관세문제에 있어서는 이미 작성된 우리측 초안의 원칙에 따라 다음과 같은 입장에서 교섭을 진행할 것임.

(가) 미군구성원, 군속 및 그들의 가족은 본 협정에 별도의 규정이 없는 한, 우리나라의 세관당국이 집행하는 법령에 복종하여야 한다. 이는 미일협정이나 나토협정에서도 규정하고 있는 조항으로서 주둔군은 주둔국에서 일정한 범위의 특권과 면제를 향유함이 인정된다는 국제법상의 원칙을 규정한 것이며 파견국은 본 협정에서 명시적으로 규정한 이상의 면제를 주장할수 없도록 한 것이다.

(나) 한국의 세관당국은 한국법령에서 규정한 일반적 조건에 따라, 미군구성원, 군속 및 그들의 가족을 수색, 조사하고 그 물품을 압수할수 있다. 단, 예외적으로 명령에 의하여 출입국하는 미국부대, 공식봉인이 날인된 공문서 및 군사우편을 통한 공용우편물 및 미국정부의 선하증권에 의하여 운송되는 군사화물은 세관검사가 면제된다. 이 규정은 위에서 말한 관세법규의 집행을 담당하는 우리 세관당국이

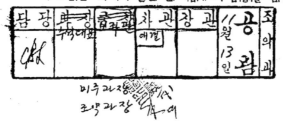

담 당	~~과 장~~ 수석대표	~~국 장~~ 국과관	차 관	장 관	11월 13일 공람	조약과
(signature)			대결			

미주과장 (signature)
조약과장 (signature)

0044

그 업무를 합리적으로 수행하는데 필요한 절차적 규정이다.

세관당국의 검사권을 명문으로 규정한 예는 나토협정 뿐이고 미일협정은 우리초안과 동일한 범위의 통관검사의 면제를 규정하고 있다.

(다) 면세의 범위로서 미군 또는 세출외 자금기관이 공용을 위하여, 또는 그 구성원, 군속 및 그들의 가족의 사용을 위하여 수입하는 물자는 미군당국이 발행한 증명서를 제출하고 관세를 면제한다.

이는 미군의 주둔을 인정한 이상 미군의 활동과 유지에 필요한 공용 물자와 미군당국이 구성원, 군속 및 그들의 가족의 사용을 위하여 공급하여야하는 물자에 대하여는 면세한다는 원칙을 천명한 것이다.

(라) 미군구성원, 군속 및 그 가족이 사용할 재산에 대하여 원칙적으로 관세를 부과하나, 이들이 처음 한국에 도착할때 수입하는 가재도구와 군사우편을 통하여 우송되어 오는 합리적인 양의 의복 및 가정용품에 대하여는 관세를 면제하여 준다.

여기서 말하는 합리적인 양이라고 함은 그 물품의 양이 상행위를 위한 것이 아님을 충분히 인정할수 있는 정도 의 양을 말하는 것으로 해석하여야 한다. 미일협정이 우리초안과 동일한 규정을 두고 있다.

(마) 다 항 및 라항에서 관세를 면제함은 전기물자의 수입시에 국한하는 것임. 즉, 관세를 이미 지불한 물자를 국내에서 구입하는 경우 이미 지불한 관세를 상환한다는 것을 의미하는 것이 아님. 이에 관하여는 미일협정만이 우리초안과 동일한 규정을 두고 있고 다른 협정에서는 이러한 규정이 없다.

(바) 면세로 수입한 물품은 관세의 부과 없이 재수출할수 있으며, 양국이 인정하는 경우를 제외하고는, 물품을 수입함에 있어 관세를 면제 받을 권리가 없는 자에게 매각이나 선물형식으로 국내에서 이를 처분 하지 못한다. 특히 본항 후단의 규정은 미국측이 이러한 관세에 관한 특권을 남용하여 수입한 물자를 국내에서 자의로 처분 또는 선사함은 우리나라의 관세제도를 문란케하는것일뿐 더러 우리나라 경제에 미치는 악영향을 미연에 방지하기 위한 규정인 것임.

0045

(사) 끝으로 관세조항의 시행에 있어서 부여된 특권을 남용함을 방지하는데 필요한 조치를 미군당국이 취하여야 하며, 관세법의 조사, 범칙물자의 압수, 관세 또는 벌금의 징수사무에 관하여 한국당국에 대하여 필요한 원조를 제공하는 동시에 미군용부두, 비행장등에 세관검사를 위하여 파견되는 한국세관원에 대하여 모든 가능한 원조를 제공하도록 한다.

우리나라가 그 주권의 한 속성으로서 행하는 관세법규 또는 기타의 재정법규의 집행에 있어서 미군당국의 적극적인 협조 없이는 그 원할한 성과를 기할수 없으므로, 본 협정에 의하여 상당한 특권을 허여받은 구성원등에 대한 한국당국의 관세사무에 관하여 미군당국이 적극적으로 이에 파견되는 세관원에 대한 원조제공이 요청되는 것이다. 미일협정과 나토협정에서는 우리초안과 거의 동일한 규정을 두고 있다.

3. 미국측이 제의한 출입국 관리에 관한 합의 의사록

제 5 차 회의에서 이미 미국측 제의에 대하여 원칙적으로 동의한 바 있으며 그 후 재검토한 결과 제 4 항에서 규정한 *within a reasonable time* 에 관하여만 그 의의가 모호함으로 이를 구체적으로 확정할 필요가 있다고 사료 함.

0046

Customs Duties

1. Except as provided expressly to the contrary in this Agreement, members of the United States forces, the civilian component, and their dependents shall be subject to the laws and regulations administered by the customs authorities of the Republic of Korea. In particular the customs authorities of the Republic of Korea shall have the right, under the general conditions laid down by the laws and regulations of the Republic of Korea, to search members of the United States forces, the civilian component and their dependents and to examine their luggage, and to seize articles pursuant to such laws and regulations.

2. All materials, supplies and equipment imported by the United States forces or by the organizations provided for in Article ______ exclusively for the official use of the United States forces or those organizations or for the use of members of the United States forces, the civilian component and their dependents shall be permitted entry into Korea free from customs duties and other such charges. When such materials, supplies and equipment are imported, a certificate issued by the authorities of the

32-8

0047

United States forces in the form to be determined by the Joint Committee shall be submitted to the customs authorities of the Republic of Korea.

3. Property consigned to and for the personal use of members of the United States armed forces, the civilian component and their dependents, shall be subject to customs duties except that no such duties or charges shall be paid with respect to:

(a) Furniture, household goods and other personal effects for their private use imported by the members of the United States forces, the civilian component and their dependents at time of their first arrival in Korea.

(b) Reasonable quantities of clothing and household goods which are mailed into the Republic of Korea through the United States military post offices.

(c) Vehicles and parts imported by members of the U.S. armed forces or civilian component <u>within two months</u> after their first arrival in Korea for the private use of themselves or their dependents.

4. The exemption granted in paragraphs 2 and 3 shall apply only to cases of importation of goods and shall not be interpreted as refunding customs duties and domestic excises collected by the customs authorities

0043

32-9

at the time of entry in cases of purchases of goods on which such duties and excises have already been collected.

5. Customs examination shall be exempted only in the following cases:

(a) Units of the United States forces under orders entering or leaving the Republic of Korea;

(b) Official documents under official seal;

(c) Official mail in United States military postal channels;

√ (d) Military cargo shipped on a United States Government bill of lading.

6. Goods imported free from customs duties and other such charges pursuant to paragraph 2 and 3 above:

(a) May be re-exported free from customs duties and other such charges;

(b) Shall not be disposed of in the Republic of Korea, by way of either sale or gift, to person not entitled to import such goods free from duty, except as such disposal may be authorized on conditions agreed between the authorities of the Republic of Korea and the United States.

7. (a) The authorities of the United States forces, in cooperation with the authorities of the Republic of Korea, shall take such steps as are necessary to prevent

0049

abuse of the privileges granted to the United States forces, members of such forces, the civilian component, and their dependents in accordance with this Article.

(b) In order to prevent offenses against customs and fiscal laws and regulations, the authroties of the Republic of Korea and of the United States forces shall assist each other in the conduct of inquiries and the collection of evidence.

(c) The authorities of the United States forces shall render all assistance within their power to ensure that articles liable to seizure by, or on behalf of, the customs authorities of the Republic of Korea are handed to those authorities.

(d) The authorities of the United States forces shall render all assistance within their power to ensure the payment of duties, taxes and penalities payable by members of the United States forces or the civilian component, or their dependents.

(e) The authorities of the United States forces shall provide all practicable assistance to the customs officials dispatched to military controlled piers and airports for the purpose of customs inspection.

0050

8. Vehicles and articles belonging to the United States armed forces seized by the customs authorities of the Government of the Republic of Korea in connection with an offense against its customs or fiscal laws or regulations shall be handed over to appropriate authorities of the force concerned.

ARTICLE (Customs)

1. Save as provided in this Agreement, members of the United States armed forces, the civilian component, and their dependents shall be subject to the laws and regulations administered by the customs authorities of the Republic of Korea.

2. All materials, supplies and equipment imported by the United States armed forces, including their authorized procurement agencies and their non-appropriated fund organizations provided for in Article , for the official use of the United States armed forces or for the use of the members of the United States armed forces, the civilian component, and their dependents, and materials, supplies and equipment which are to be used exclusively by the United States armed forces or are ultimately to be incorporated into articles or facilities used by such forces, shall be permitted entry into the Republic of Korea; such entry shall be free from customs duties and other such charges. Appropriate cartification shall be made that such materials, supplies and equipment are being imported by the United States armed forces, including their authorized procurement agencies and their non-appropriated fund organizations provided for in Article ,

0052

32-13

or, in the case of materials, supplies and equipment to be used exclusively by the United States armed forces or ultimately to be incorporated into articles or facilities used by such forces, that delivery thereof is to be taken by the United States armed forces for the purposes specified above. The exemptions provided in this paragraph shall extend to materials, supplies and equipment imported by the United States armed forces for the use of other armed forces in Korea which receive logistical support from the United States armed forces.

3. Property consigned to and for the personal use of members of the United States armed forces, the civilian component, and their dependents, shall be subject to customs duties and other such charges, except that no duties or charges shall be paid with respect to:

(a) Furniture, household goods, and personal effects for their private use imported by the members of the United States armed forces or civilian component when they first arrive to serve in the Republic of Korea or by their dependents when they first arrive for reunion with members of such forces or civilian component;

0053

32-14

(b) Vehicles and parts imported by members of the United States armed forces or civilian component for the private use of themselves or their dependents;

(c) Reasonable quantities of personal effects and household goods of a type which would ordinarily be purchased in the United States for the private use of members of the United States armed forces, civilian component, and their dependents, which are mailed into the Republic of Korea through United States military post offices.

4. The exemptions granted in paragraphs 2 and 3 shall apply only to cases of importation of goods and shall not be interpreted as refunding customs duties and domestic excises collected by the customs authorities at the time of entry in cases of purchase of goods on which such duties and excises have already been collected.

5. Customs examination shall not be made in the following cases:

(a) Members of the United States armed forces under orders entering or leaving the Republic of Korea;

(b) Official documents under official seal and mail in United States military postal channels;

0054

32-15

(c) Military cargo consigned to the United States armed forces, including their authorized procurement agencies and their non-appropriated fund organizations provided for in Article.

6. Except as such disposal may be authorized by the United States and Korean authorities in accordance with mutually agreed conditions, goods imported into the Republic of Korea free of duty shall not be disposed of in the Republic of Korea to persons not entitled to import such goods free of duty.

7. Goods imported into the Republic of Korea free from customs duties and other such charges pursuant to paragraphs 2 and 3, may be re-exported free from customs duties and other such charges.

8. The United States armed forces, in cooperation with Korean authorities, shall take such steps as are necessary to prevent abuse of privileges granted to the United States armed forces, members of such forces, the civilian component, and their dependents in accordance with this Article.

9. (a) In order to prevent offenses against laws and regulations administered by the customs authorities

0055

32-16

of the Government of the Republic of Korea, the Korean authorities and the United States armed forces shall assist each other in the conduct of inquiries and the collection of evidence.

(b) The United States armed forces shall render all assistance within their power to ensure that articles liable to seizure by, or on behalf of, the customs authorities of the Government of the Republic of Korea are handed to those authorities.

(c) The United States armed forces shall render all assistance within their power to ensure the payment of duties, taxes, and penalties payable by members of such forces or of the civilian component, or their dependents.

(d) Vehicles and articles belonging to the United States armed forces seized by the customs authorities of the Government of the Republic of Korea in connection with an offense against its customs or fiscal laws or regulations shall be handed over to the appropriate authorities of the forces concerned.

0056

32-17

AGREED MINUTES TO ARTICLE (Customs)

1. The quantity of goods imported under paragraph 2 by non-appropriated fund organizations of the United States armed forces for the use of the members of the United States armed forces, the civilian component, and their dependents shall be limited to the extent reasonably required for such use.

2. Paragraph 3(a) does not require concurrent shipment of goods with travel of owner nor does it require single loading or shipment. In this connection, members of the United States armed forces or civilian component and their dependents may import free of duty their personal and household effects during a period of six months from the date of their first arrival.

3. The term "military cargo" as used in paragraph 5(c) is not confined to arms and equipment but refers to all cargo consigned to the United States armed forces, including their authorized procurement agencies and their non-appropriated fund organizations provided for in Article.

4. The United States armed forces will take every practicable measure to ensure that goods will not be imported into the Republic of Korea by or for the members of the United States armed forces, the civilian component,

0057

32-18

or their dependents, the entry of which would be in violation of Korea customs laws and regulations. The United States armed forces will promptly notify the Korean customs authorities whenever the entry of such goods is discovered.

5. The Korean customs authroities may, if they considger that there has been an abuse or infringement in connection with the entry of goods under Article , take up the matter with the appropriate authorities of the United States armed forces.

6. The words "The United States armed forces shall render all assistance within their power," etc., in paragraph 9(b) and (c) refer to reasonable and practicable measures by the United States armed forces authorized [by United States law and service regulations.]

재분류(1966. 12. 31.)

1966.12.31.에 예고문에 의거 일반문서로 재분류됨

32-19

0058

PRESS RELEASE

SOFA 6th meeting

November 14, 1962

Reached full agreement on the text of draft article on entry and exit procedures. This approved article will be incorporated in the final text of the Status of Forces Agreement.

In addition, drafts were exchanged and discussion was begun on the article dealing with customs and duties. Discussion of this article as well as other articles previously discussed will be continued at next meeting, which is scheduled for ~~Novembe~~ Monday, November 26 at 2.00 P.M.

0059

軍人身分協定 合意

美、從前態度바꿔? 韓美行協實務會議

…UPI報道…

【서울十四日発UPI東洋=本社特約】韓国과 美国의 実務者들은 韓国法廷에게 軍營밖에서 犯罪를저지른 美軍人을 裁判할 權利를주는 協定에 暫定的合意를보았다고 韓国外務部는 十四日말하였다

軍人身分協定은 英国「터키」日本및美軍이 駐屯하고있는 其他여러나라에서의協定과 비슷한것이 될것으로 期待되고있다 새로운協定은 兩国代表들의 正式調印과美国上院의批准이 있어야한다

同協定은 韓国政府가 오랫동안 締結을要求해온것이나 美国은 韓国이 民政復歸가될때까지 身分協定을맺지않겠다고 主張해왔다

出入條項完結

韓・美行政協定第六次実務者会議는 十四日下午三時부터 外務部에서 續開되어 出入国條項에 完全合意를보는한편 關稅條項에관한 雙方의 草案을 交換했다

合意된內容일지라도 行政協定案이 全體的으로 作成될때까지는 발표는 保留되리라 한다

第七次会議는 오는 二十六日 열린다

韓国日報 11/15

공보관이 UPI에 정정 의뢰 함 11/15

0060

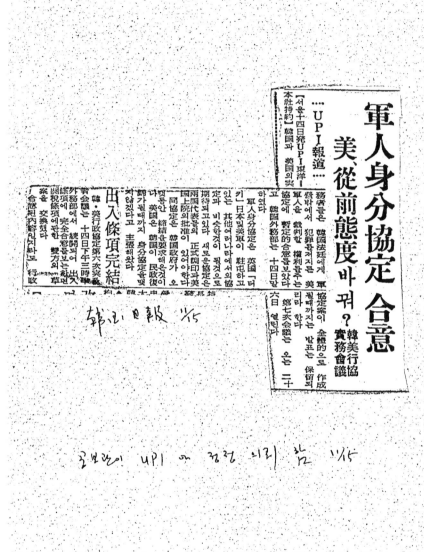

Agreed [redacted] Article

(Entry and Exit)

1. With regard to Paragraph 3(a), United States Armed Forces law enforcement personnel (such as MP, SP, AP, CID and CIC), who engage in military police activities in the Republic of Korea, will carry a bilingual identity card containing the bearer's name, position, and the fact that he is a member of a law enforcement agency. This card will be shown upon request to persons concerned when the bearer is in the performance of duty.

2. The United States Armed Forces will furnish, upon request, to Korean authorities the form of the identification cards of the members of the United States Armed Forces, the civilian component, and their dependents and descriptions of the various uniforms of the United States Armed Forces in the Republic of Korea.

3. The final sentence of Paragraph 3 means that members of the United States Armed Forces will display their identity cards upon request but will not be required to surrender them to Korean authorities.

4. Following a change of status pursuant to Paragraph 5, the responsibilities of the United States authorities under Paragraph 6 shall arise only if the expulsion order is issued within a reasonable time after the notice under Paragraph 5 has been communicated to the Korean authorities.

for further study

92-20

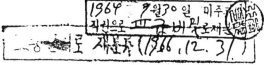

1. A Joint Committee shall be established as the means for consultation between the two Governments on all matters requiring mutual consultation regarding the interpretation and implementation of this Agreement.

2. The Joint Committee shall be composed of a representative of the Government of the Republic of Korea and a representative of the Government of the United States, each of whom shall have one or more deputies and a staff. The Joint Committee shall determine its own procedures, and arrange for such auxiliary organs and administrative services as may be required.
The Joint Committee shall be so organized that it may meet immediately at any time at the request of the representative of either Government.

3. If the Joint Committee is unable to resolve any matter, it shall refer that matter to the respective Governments for further consideration through diplomatic channels.

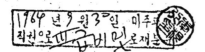

32-21

0062

AGREED MINUTES TO ARTICLE (Customs)

1. The quantity of goods imported under paragraph 2 by non-appropriated fund organizations of the United States armed forces for the use of the members of the United States armed forces, the civilian component, and their dependents shall be limited to the extent reasonably required for such use. Non-appropriated fund organizations referred to in paragraph 2 shall be permitted to import such materials, supplies and equipment only with non-appropriated fund.

2. Paragraph 3 (a) does not require concurrent shipment of goods with travel of owner nor does it require single loading or shipment. In this connection, members of the United States armed forces or civilian component and their dependents may import free of duty their personal and household effects during a period of three months from the date of their first arrival. The quantity of such personal and household effects shall be limited to reasonable amount.

3. The term "military cargo" as used in paragraph 5 (c) is not confined to arms and equipment but refers [redacted]ned to the United

States armed forces

4. The United States armed forces will take every practicable measure to ensure that goods will not be imported into the Republic of Korea by or for the members of the United States armed forces, the civilian component, or their dependents, the entry of which would be in violation of Korean customs laws and regulations. The United States armed forces will promptly notify the Korean customs authorities whenever the entry of such goods is discovered.

5. The Korean customs authorities may, if they consider that there has been an abuse or infringement in connection with the entry of goods under Article , take up the matter with the appropriate authorities of the United States armed forces.

6. The words "The United States armed forces shall render all assistance within their power," etc., in paragraph 9 (b) and (c) refer to reasonable and practicable measures by the United States armed forces. (deleted)

보통문서로 재분류(1966.12.31.)

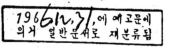

1966.12.31.에 예고문에 의거 일반문서로 재분류됨

0064

기 안 용 지

자 체 통 제	(차)	기안처	미주과 / 채의석	전화번호	근거서류접수일자

	과장	국장	차관보좌관	차관	장관
	/14	(전)	15	대결	15

관계관 서명	조약과장

기안 년월일	62. 11. 15	시행 년월일		보존 년한	정서 (차)	기장
분류 기호	387	전체 통제				
경유 수신 참조	~~내각수반~~ 외무국방위원장 국가재건최고회의의장			발신	장관	
제목	주둔군지위협정체결을 위한 제6차교섭회의보고					

1. 1652.11.14 하오 3시30분부터 동 4시40분까지 외무부에서 개최된 표기문제에 관한 제6차 교섭회의에서 토의된 내용을 별첨과 같이 보고합니다.

2. 유첨: 제6차교섭회의보고서 1부. 끝

1966.12.31에 예고문에 의거 일반문서로 재분류됨

보통문서로 재분류(1966.12.31)

1964년 9월 30일 미주과 직권으로 비밀로 재분류

승인양식 1-1-3 (1112-040-016-018) (190mm×260mm16절지)

0065

외 부

외정부 1962. 11. 15.

수 신 국가재건최고회의 의장

참 조 외무국방위원장

경 유 내각수반

제 목 주둔군 지위협정 체결을 위한 제6차 교섭회의 보고

1. 1962. 11. 14. 하오 3시 30분부터 동 4시 40분까지 외무부에서 개최된 표기문제에 관한 제6차 교섭회의에서 토의된 내용을 별첨과같이 보고합니다.

2. 유첨 : 제6차 교섭회의 보고서 1부, 끝

보통문서로 재분류(1966. 12. 31.)

외 무 부 장 관 최 덕 신

1966, 12, 31에 예고문에 의거 일반문서로 재분류됨

0066

10-1

기 안 용 지

자 체 통 제	(채)	기안처	미주과 채 의 석	전화번호		근거서류접수일자	
과 장	국 장		차 관		장 관	내각 수반	
(채)	(서명)	(서명)					
관계관 서 명							
기 안 년월일	1962. 11. 21.	시 행 년월일		보존 년한		정 서	기 장
분 류 기 호	외정무 391	전 체 통 제		종결		(채)	
경 유 수 신 참 조	국가재건최고회의 의장 외무국방위원장			발 신		장 관	
제 목	주둔군 지위협정 체결을위한 제6차 교섭회의 회의록 송부 (가제목 : 감메기)						

1. 외정무 387 (62. 11.15) 의 연호입니다.

2. 연호로 보고한바 있는 주둔군 지위협정체결을 위한 제6차 교섭회의의 영문 회의록을 별첨과같이 송부합니다.

3. 유첨 : 동회의록 1부. 끝

보통문서로 재분류 (1966.12.31)

1966.12.31 에 예고문에 의거 일반문서로 재분류됨

0067

승인양식 1-1-1 (1112-010-016-016) (190mm×260mm16절지)

1964 년 9 월 30 일 미주과 직권으로 비밀 해제

외 무 부

외정무 1962. 11. 21.

수 신 국가재건최고회의 의장

참 조 외무국방위원장

제 목 주둔군 지위협정 체결을위한 제6차 교섭회의 회의록송부

1. 외정무 387 (62. 11.15.)의 연호입니다.

2. 연호로 보고한바 있는 주둔군 지위협정체결을 위한 제6차 교섭회의의 영문 회의록을 별첨과같이 송부합니다.

3. 유첨 : 동회의록 1부, 끝

외 무 부 장 관 최 덕 신

0068

12-2

기 안 용 지

자체 통제	(서명)	기안처	미주과 채의석	전화번호	근거서류접수일자
과장	국장	차관보	차관	장관	내자 수반
(서명) 11/21	(서명)	(서명)	대결 / 후열		
관계관 서명					
기안 년월일	1962. 11. 21.	시행 년월일		보존 년한	정서 (서명) 기장 (서명)
분류 기호	외정무 391	전체 통제		종결	
경유 수신 참조	주 미 대 사			발신	장 관
제목	주둔군지위 협정 체결을위한 제6차 교섭회의 회의록송부 (기재록 : 갈매기)				

1. 1962. 11. 14. 하오 3시 30분부터 4시 40분 까지 외무부에서 개최된 표기문제에 관한 제6차 교섭회의 영문회의록을 별첨과 같이 송부하니 참조하시기 바랍니다.

2. 유첨 : 동 회의록 1부. 끝

1966, 12, 31 에 예고문에 의거 일반문서로 재분류됨.

보통문서로 재분류(1966. 12. 31.)

0069

승인양식 1-1-1 (1112-040-016-016) 13-1 (190mm×260mm16절지)

1964년 9월30일 미주과장 직권으로 비밀로 재분류

외 무 부

외정무 1962. 11. 21.

수 신 : 주 미 대 사

제 목 : 주둔군지위 협정체결을 위한 제6차 교섭회의 회의록 송부

1. 1962. 11. 14. 하오 3시 30분부터 4시 40분까지 외무부에서 개최된 표기문제에 관한 제 6 차 교섭회의 영문회의록을 별첨과 같이 송부하니 참조하시기 바랍니다.

2. 유첨 : 동 회의록 1부. 끝

외 무 부 장 관 최 덕 신

0070

제 6 차

한미간 주둔군 지위협정실무자 회의

보 고 서

1. 시 일 : 1962. 11. 14. 하오 3시 30분부터 동 4시 40분 까지

2. 장 소 : 외무부 회의실

3. 참석자 : 한국측 : 진 필 식 (외무부정무국장, 수석대표)

주 문 기 (법무부 법무과장)

박 봉 진 (재무부 관세과장)

이 남 구 (국방부 군무과장)

신 정 섭 (외무부 2등서기관)

채 의 석 (" ")

강 석 재 (" 3등서기관)

이 창 범 (" ")

미국측 : 교섭대표단 전원

4. 토의사항 :

(1) 출입국 관리문제에 대하여 완전한 합의를보고 합동위원회, 관세에 관한 문제를 순차적으로 토의함.

(2) 우리측은 출입국 관리문제중 미국측이 전번 회의에서 제출한바 있는 합의의사록 제4항의 "within reasonable time " 에 대한 설명을 요구하자 미국측은 동역의 뜻은 6개월, 1년 또는 1년 6개월~~도 될수있으나~~ 등 구체적인것은 합동위원회 에서 합리롭게 정하도록 제의하여 우리측은 이를 받아드림.

(3) 동출입국 관리문제중 미국측은 지난번 회의에서 미결된바 있는 "적절한 문서" (appropriate documentation)에 언급하여 특히 미국정부는 특정한 범주에 속하는자에는 미국의 여권을 발급

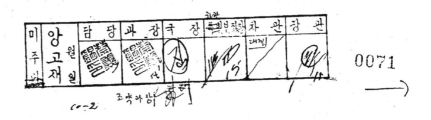

미주	양 고 재 월 일	담 당	과 장	국 장	차관보	차 관	장 관

0071

관문 88-8(9)

0072

할수 없기때문에 "적절한 문서"의 발급으로 해결할수 있는점에서 동어는 "여권" 보다더 포괄적인것을 주장함. 이에대하여 우리측은 "적절한문서"의 기재사항을 "여권"기재사항과 동일하게하고, 또한 동기재사항은 합동위원회의 합의하에서 규정할것이며, "적절한문서" 자체가 여권이 아니다" 라는 조건이라면 미측안을 받아드리겠다고 함. 이에대하여 미국측은 우리측 제안을 받아드림과동시에 이문제에대한 토의기록을 토대로 합동위원회에서 처리하도록 하자고함.

(4) 합동위원회 문제에 대하여 미국측은 미국측이 제시한 합동위원회안 제 1 항중 " unless otherwise provided for" 를"except where otherwise provided " 로 정정해줄것을 요청하고, 합동위원회 문제는 다음회의에 토의할것을 제외하여 우리측은 동제의를 받아드림.

(5) 다음에는 관세문제에 들어가 미국측은 자기들 안을 우리측에 배부하고 설명하였으며 우리측은 우리측안을 배부하여 주었음. 이에대한 토의는 서로 상대방안을 검토하여 다음회의에서 축조 토의하기로 합의함.

5. 기타사항

(1) 차기회의 일자 : 1962. 11. 26. 하오 2시

(2) 차기회의 의제 : 6차 회의까지 합의에 도달못한 서문, 용어의 정의, 합동위원회와 관세문제

6. 참고자료 : 미국측이 제의한 협정초안 (관세문제)

보통문서로 재분류(1966. 12. 31.)

1966. 12. 31.에 예고문에 의거 일반문서로 재분류됨

0073

10-3

미문 88-8

0074

美口側案

ARTICLE (Customs)

1. Save as provided in this Agreement, members of the United States armed forces, the civilian component, and their dependents shall be subject to the laws and regulations administered by the customs authorities of the Republic of Korea.

2. All materials, supplies and equipment imported by the United States armed forces, including their authorized procurement agencies and their non-appropriated fund organizations provided for in Article , for the official use of the United States armed forces or for the use of the members of the United States armed forces, the civilian component, and their dependents, and materials, supplies and equipment which are to be used exclusively by the United States armed forces or are ultimately to be incorporated into articles or facilities used by such forces, shall be permitted entry into the Republic of Korea; such entry shall be free from customs duties and other such charges. Appropriate cartification shall be made that such materials, supplies and equipment are being imported by the United States armed forces, including their authorized procurement agencies and their non-

0075

10-4

비문 88-8

0076

appropriated fund organizations provided for in Article

, or, in the case of materials, supplies and equipment to be used exclusively by the United States armed forces or ultimately to be incorporated into articles or facilities used by such forces, that delivery thereof is to be taken by the United States armed forces for the purposes specified above. The exemptions provided in this paragraph shall extend to materials, supplies and equipment imported by the United States armed forces for the use of other armed forces in Korea which receive logistical support from the United States armed forces.

3. Property consigned to and for the personal use of members of the United States armed forces, the civilian component, and their dependents, shall be subject to customs duties and other such charges, except that no duties or charges shall be paid with respect to:

(a) Furniture, household goods, and personal effects for their private use imported by the members of the United States armed forces or civilian component when they first arrive to serve in the Republic of Korea or by their dependents when they first arrive for reunion with members of such forces or civilian component;

0077

10-5

미문 88-8

0078

(b) Vehicles and parts imported by members of the United States armed forces or civilian component for the private use of themselves or their dependents;

(c) Reasonable quantities of personal effects and household goods of a type which would ordinarily be purchased in the United States for the private use of members of the United States armed forces, civilian component, and their dependents, which are mailed into the Republic of Korea through United States military post offices.

4. The exemption granted in paragraphs 2 and 3 shall apply only to cases of importation of goods and shall not be interpreted as refunding customs duties and deoestic excises collected by the customs authorities at the time of entry in cases of purchase of goods on which such duties and excises have already been collected.

5. Customs exemination shall not be made in the following cases:

(a) Members of the United States armed forces under orders entering or leaving the Republic of Korea;

0079

10-6

미문 88-8

0080

(b) Official documents under official seal and mail in United States military postal channels;

(c) Military cargo consigned to the United States armed forces, including their authorized procurement agencies and their non-appropriated fund organizations provided for in Articles .

6. Except as such disposal may be authorized by the United States and Korean authorities in accordance with mutually agreed conditions, goods imported into the Republic of Korea free of duty shall not be disposed of in the Republic of Korea to persons not entitled to import such goods free of duty.

7. Goods imported into the Republic of Korea free from customs duties and other such charges pursuant to paragraphs 2 and 3, may be re-exported free from customs duties and other such charges.

8. The United States armed forces, in cooperation with Korean authorities, shall take such steps as are necessary to prevent abuse of privileges granted to the United States armed forces, members of such forces, the civilian component, and their dependents in accordance with this Article.

0081

10-17

미문 88-8

0082

9. (a) In order to prevent offense against laws and regulations administered by the customs authorities of the Government of the Republic of Korea, the Korean authorities and the United States armed forces shall assist each other in the conduct of inquiries and the collection of evidence.

(b) The United States armed forces shall render all assistance within their power to ensure that articles liable to seizure by, or on behalf of, the customs authorities of the Government of the Republic of Korea are handed to those authorities.

(c) The United States armed forces shall render all assistance within their power to ensure the payment of duties, taxes, and penalties payable by members of such forces or of the civilian component, or their dependents.

(d) Vehicles and articles belonging to the United States armed forces seized by the customs authorities of the Government of the Republic of Korea in connection with an offense against its customs or fiscal laws or regulations shall be handed over to the appropriate authorities of the forces concerned.

10-8

0083

비문 88-8

0084

AGREED MINUTES TO ARTICLE \ (Customs)

1. The quantity of goods imported under paragraph 2 by non-appropriated fund organizations of the United States armed forces for the use of the members of the United States armed forces, the civilian component, and their dependents shall be limited to the extent reasonably required for such use.

2. Paragraph 3(a) does not require concurrent shipment of goods with travel of owner nor does it require single loading or shipment. In this connection, members of the United States armed forces or civilian component and their dependents may import free of duty their personal and household effects during a period of six months from the date of their first arrival.

3. The term "military cargo" as used in paragraph 5(c) is not confined to arms and equipment but refers to all cargo consigned to the United States armed forces, including their authorized procurement agencies and their non-appropriated fund organizations provided for in Articles .

4. The United States armed forces will take every practicable measure to ensure that goods will not be

0085

10-8

외문 88-8

0086

imported into the Republic of Korea by or for the members of the United States armed forces, the civilian component, or their dependents, the entry of which would be in vielation of Korean customs laws and regulations. The United States armed forces will promptly notify the Korean customs authorities whenever the entry of such goods is discovered.

5. The Korean customs authorities may, if they consider that there has been an abuse or infringement in connection with the entry of goods under Article , take up the matter with the appropriate authorities of the United States armed forces.

6. The words "The United States armed forces shall render all assistance within their power", etc., in paragraph 9(6) and (c) refer to reasonable and practicable measures by the United States armed forces authorized by United States law and service regulations.

1966.12.31.에 예고문에 의거 일반문서로 재분류됨

보통문서로 재분류(1966.12.31.)

0087

10-10

명문 88-8(97)

0088

SUMMARY RECORD OF THE SIXTH SESSION
STATUS FORCES NEGOTIATION

November 14, 1962

I. Time and Place : 3:30 to 4:40 p.m. November 14, 1962 at Conference Room of the Ministry of Foreign Affairs

II. Attendants:

ROK Side :

Mr. Chin, Pil Shik	Director Bureau of Political Affairs Ministry of Foreign Affairs
Col. Lee, Nam Koo	Chief, Military Affairs Section Ministry of National Defense
Mr. Chu, Mun Ki	Chief, Legal Affairs Section Ministry of Justice
Mr. Pak, Pong Chin	Chief, Customs Duty Section Ministry of Finance
Mr. Chai, Eui Sok	2nd Secretary Ministry of Foreign Affairs
Mr. Shin, Chung Sup	2nd Secretary Ministry of Foreign Affairs
Mr. Kang, Suk Jae	3rd Secretary Ministry of Foreign Affairs
Mr. Lee, Chang Bum	3rd Secretary Ministry of Foreign Affairs

US Side:

Mr. Philip C. Habib	Counselor of the Embassy for Political Affairs
Brig. Gen. J.D. Miller	Deputy Chief of Staff 8th Army
Mr. William J. Ford	First Secretary of the Embassy
Col. G.G. O'Connor	Deputy Chief of Staff 8th Army
Capt. R.M. Brownlie	Assistance Chief of Staff

미주과	공람	담당	과장	국장	차관	장관
	11월 21일					

조약과장

1964년 9월 30일 미주과장 직권으로 재분류

11-1

Col W.A. Solf	Staff Judge Advocate 8th Army
Mr. Benjamin A. Fleck= (Rapporteur and Press Officer)	First Secretary of the Embassy
Mr. Robert A. Lewis	Second Secretary and Consul of the Embassy
Lt. Col. R.E. Miller!	Staff Officer, JAG 8th Army

III. Gist of Talks:

a. Introduction of New Korean Participants

1. Before beginning substantive discussion, Mr. Chin introduced several members of the Korean side participating in the hegotiations for the first time. They were: Mr. CHU Mun-ki, Chief of the Legal Affairs Section of the Justice Ministry's Bureau of Legal Affairs, substituting for Mr. YI Kyung-ho; Mr. PAK Pong-chin, Chief of the Customs Duty Section of the Finance Ministry's Bureau of Customs, substituting for Mr. SIN Kwan-sop; and Mr. CHAE Eui-sok, Second Secretary in the America Section of the Foreign Ministry's Political Affairs Bureau, substituting as Rapporteur for Mr. YI Kyung-hun and as Press Officer for Mr. CHI Sung-ku.

2. As neither side wished to make additional comments at this meeting regarding the Preamble or the Definitions article, it was agreed to postpone further discussion of these articles until the next meeting.

b. Entry and Exit

3. Turning to the entry and exit article, Mr. Habib asked if the Korean side had any comment to make

0090

11-2

on the draft agreed minutes tabled by the U.S. side at the previous meeting. Mr. Chin replied that there was no disagreement regarding the first three minutes but requested clarification of the phrase "within a reasonable time" in the fourth minute. Mr. Habib replied by suggesting that the SOFA should establish general principles, leaving to the Joint Committee the detailed implementation of those principles. Thus "a reasonable time" is a principle the implementation of which should be worked out in detail by the Joint Committee. He pointed out that "a reasonable time" would be a period of time which both sides believe to be reasonable. Mr. Chin stated that the Korean side accepted the agreed minutes, with the understanding that the Joint Committee will decide the exact meaning of the phrase "within a reasonable time" in the fouth minute. It was agreed that the joint agreed summary of the meeting should record this understanding for the guidance of the Joint Committee.

4. Mr. Habib then reminded the negotiators of the difference of opinion which had developed at the previous meeting regarding the phrase "appropriate documentation" in pargraph 4 of the U.S. draft article. He said the U.S. side still believed that this phrase was more appropriate and more useful than the word "passports" which the Korean side wished to use. For the purposes of this article, and irrespective of any specific wording in any other article, "appropriate documentation" was better, for the simple reason that

0091

the United States authorities cannot issue passports to Korean dependents of U.S. citizens or to other persons of non-U.S. nationality who would be permitted enty into Korea under the provisions of the SOFA. In no way, he continued, would this language affect or detract from anything said in any other article of the agreement.

5. Mr. Chin stated that the Korean side had considered the matter but still held the view that since the majority of persons entering Korea under the provisions of this article could be U.S. passport bearers and only a small minority would not have U.S. passports, the word "passports" should be used and an agreed minute drafted to cover the exceptional cases.

6. Mr. Habib pointed out that a passport by itself does not necessarily contain sufficient information to verify the status of the bearer. While the passport indicates the bearer to be a U.S. citizen, other documentation would be necessary to indicate his status as a member of the civilian component or as a dependent. Therefore, "appropriate documentation" would more satisfactorily meet the need of the Korean side for documentary verification. He pointed out that this was another good example of a case in which the SOFA should establish a basic principle and leave the details to be worked out by the Joint Committee.

7. Mr. Habib pointed out that if the documentation issued did not verify the status of the bearers in a manner satisfactory to the Korean authorities, the Joint Committee obviously would consider the matter.

0092

11-4

In answer to questions by Mr. Chin, Mr. Habib stated that persons of U.S. nationality falling under the provisions of paragraph 4 would ordinarily carry documentation including passports and other identifying papers such as indentity cards or written orders. This documentation would be sufficiently detailed to permit the Korean authorities to verify their status. Mr. Chin stated that the Korean side agreed to the use of "appropriate documentation", with the understanding that such documentation must include sufficient information to permit themKorean authorities to verify the status of the bearer. It was then agreed to accept the U.S. draft of the entry and exit article, together with the four agreed minutes, as the text to be incorporated into the final SOFA. Mütual congratulations were thereupon exchanged.

c. Joint Committee

8. Referring to the U.S. draft of the Joint Committee article tabled at the previous meeting, Mr. Habib reported a slight grammatical error in the first sentence of paragraph 1. He said the final phrase of the sentence should read "except where otherwise provided" instead of "unless otherwise provided for". Upon Mr. Habib's statement that the U.S. side had no substantive comment to make at this time, it was agreed to defer further discussion of this article.

d. Customs and Duties

9. The U.S. draft of the customs and duties article was introduced by Mr. Ford, who pointed out

that the negotiators, having just completed consideration of the entry and exit of persons, were now turning their attention to the entry and exit of things. He called attention to the fact that the U.S. draft explicitly states that the persons subject to its provisions shall be subject to the customs laws and regulations of Korea, with certain specific exceptions.

10. Emphasizing that the article provides the basis for facilitating the successful accomplishment of the sending state's mission, Mr. Ford stated that perhaps the most important feature of the article is that the privileges and immunities which it confers have a considerable impact upon the morale of the troops and other persons who share its benefits. He pointed out that the article provides for the entry free of customs duties of materials, equipment, and supplies imported by and for the use of the U.S. armed forces and their agencies. However, property consigned to, and for the personal use of individuals covered by the article would be subject to duties, with the exception of: (a) furniture, household goods, and personal effects imported when the individuals first arrive in Korea; (b) vehicles and parts for private use; and (c) reasonable quantities of personal effects and household goods for private use imported through U.S. military post offices.

11. Mr. Ford also pointed out that the draft article provides that customs examination shall not be made in the case of official documents, mail, and

0094

11-6

~~and~~ military cargo. In addition, the article provides that any disposal of goods imported into Korea shall be effected only in accordance with conditions agreed upon between the authorities of Korea and the United States. He also referred to the provision that goods imported free from customs duties and similar charges may be re-exported from Korea free of any customs or similar charges.

12. Concluding his introduction of the draft article, Mr. Ford mentioned the necessity for prevention of the abuse of privileges granted therein. He pointed out that the draft provides that the U.S. armed forces, in cooperation with the Korean authorities, shall take necessary steps to prevent such abuse. Such cooperation extends to mutual assistance in conducting investigations of suspected abuses, and the rendering of assistance to ensure payment of duties and other fees.

13. At the conclusion of Mr. Ford's remarks, the U.S. draft of the article and related agreed minutes was tabled. After reading the U.S. draft, Mr. Chin remarked that it and the Korean draft were based on similar principles, with perhaps some minor points of difference with regard to the classification of goods. He then tabled the Korean draft and suggested that both sides consider the two drafts and be prepared to discuss them, paragraph by paragraph, at the next meeting.

0095

11-7

14. After a quick persual of the Korean draft, Mr. Habib remarked that upon first examination, there did appear to be broad areas of agreement. However, he detected a number of differences of substantial importance. It was agreed to discuss this article, paragraph by paragraph, at the next meeting.

15. It was agreed to hold the next meeting on November 26 at 2:00 p.m.

보통문서로 재분류(1966.12.31.)

1966.12.31.에 예고문에 의거 일반문서로 재분류됨

0096

11-8

3. 제1-6차 회의 종합보고

0097

美駐屯軍地位協定締結
交涉會議 綜合報告 (1次~6次)

一. 經緯

美駐屯軍地位協定 締結을 爲한 韓美間 實務者交涉은 1962年 9月 28日 第一次會議를 開催하였으며 現在까지 第六次會議를 가졌다.

二. 討議範圍 및 題目

實務交涉會議에서는 먼저 協定에 包含될 事項의 範圍와 題目에 對하여 다음과 같은 28個의 題目에 合意하였다.

(1) 序文
(2) 用語의 定義
(3) 土地 및 施設
(4) 航空統制 및 航海補助施設 問題
(5) 合同委員會
(6) 出入國管理
(7) 關稅業務
(8) 船舶 및 航空機 出入問題
(9) 公益物 및 用役問題
(10) 軍票
(11) 軍事郵便施設 및 軍郵行政
(12) 豫備役訓練 問題

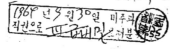

0098

32-1

미국문 107-1(17)

0099

(13) 美軍人家族 및 財産의 安全問題
(14) 氣象 및 其他関聯된 業務
(15) 車輛 및 運転免許問題
(16) 貨幣統制 問題
(17) 非戰斗機関活動問題
(18) 法規遵守問題
(19) 刑事裁判管轄权 問題
(20) 請求权 問題
(21) 租税問題
(22) 現地調達問題
(23) 契約上의 紛争
(24) 軍契約者 問題
(25) 勞務問題
(26) 協定의 批准発効 및 施行에 関한 事項
(27) 協定의 改正 및 修正
(28) 協定의 有効期間 및 滿了事項

三. 討議事項

前記 討議範囲 및 題目中 第六次會議까지 討議된 事項은 아래와 같다.

(1) 序文
(2) 用語의 定義
(3) 出入国管理
(4) 合同委員會
(5) 関税業務

0100

32-2

미운 1017-1

0101

四. 內容

(1) 序文

序文에 있어서 美側案은 다만 協定締結根據로서 韓美防衛條約 第四條를 들고 있는데 反하여 韓國側案은 美軍이 UN決議에 依據하여 韓國에 駐屯케된 歷史的 背景을 併記하고 있다.

兩側案의 이러한 相違点에 關해서는 現在 美國側은 美國政府의 訓令을 기다리고 있는 中인바 여기에는 實質的인 難点이 없으리라고 보고 있음.

(2) 用語의 定義

用語의 定義에 關한 條文草案은 三個項으로 成立되고 있으며 "美軍隊 構成員" (members of the United States armed forces) "軍屬" (civilian components) 및 家族(dependents) 으로 區分하여 定義하고 있는바 大体的인 合意에 이르렀다. 다만 "軍屬"의 定義에 있어서 美側案은 美國國籍所有者뿐만 아니라 第三國人도 包含할수 있도록 主張하고 있는데 對해서 韓國側案은 美國國籍所有者에만 限하자고 主張하고 있음. 이에 關해서 美國側은 美國政府의 訓令을 기다리고 있음.

(3) 出入國管理

出入國管理問題에 關해서는 實質的으로 意見의 差異가 없었음으로 完全合意에 到達했으며 이 部分은 美日行政協定의 該當 該當部分과 內容이 꼭 같은바 條文草案은 6個項

0102

미:문 1077

0103

으로 成立되었다. 同 6個項의 內容은 大略 다음과 같다.

가. 第一項은 韓國領域에 出入하는 美軍人, 軍屬 및 家族의 人員數를 美國当局은 定期的으로 韓國政府에 通告할것을 規定하고 있다.

나. 第二項은 美軍人은 韓國政府의 旅券 및 査證에 関한 規定에 따르지 않으며 軍人 軍屬 및 家族은 外國人登録法에서 除外되나 永住权을 取得하는것이 아님을 規定하고 있다.

다. 第三項은 美軍이 韓國領域에 出入時 身分証明書와 旅行命令書를 所持할것을 規定하고 있다.

라. 第四項은 軍屬 및 그 家族과 美軍人家族들은 그들의 身分을 確認할수 있는 適切한 文書를 所持할것을 規定하고 있다.

마. 第五項은 美國은 万若 規制対象人員의 身分의 变更이 發生할 境遇 이를 韓國政府에 通告할것과 韓國政府가 그러한 人員의 退去를 要求할 境遇 美國側이 이에 應할것을 規定하고 있다.

바. 第六項은 美軍人 軍屬 및 家族으로서 入國한 者가 그 身分이 变更된 後 韓國

0104

→

미·문 107-1

0105

政府에 依하여 強制退去令을 받은
境遇 美國側은 그 者의 退去에 責任
질것을 規定하고 있다.

(4) 合同委員會

合同委員會에 關한 兩側의 條文草案은
그 內容에 있어서 大體로 類似하나 表現方法에
있어서 若干의 差異가 있으므로 앞으로 이를 調整
하는 일은 困難視되지 않음.

(5) 關稅業務

이 問題에 對하여는 第五次會議에서
双方의 協定案을 交換하였으며 第七次會議
(11月26日)에서 逐條討議하기로 하였는바
우리側의 內容을 보면 다음과 같다.

가. 美軍隊構成員, 軍屬 및 그 家族은 別途
規定이 없는限 大韓民國 稅關當局의
法令에 服從해야 한다.

나. 美軍隊構成員, 軍屬 및 家族등의 使用을
爲하여 輸入되는 資材, 供給品 및 備品은
關稅를 賦課하지 않는다.

다. 美國에서 託送되는 私用物品에는 關稅를
賦課하나 다음 物品에 對해서는 例外로
한다.

最初로 韓國에 到着할때 搬入한
家具, 家庭用品, 個人用品, 美軍事郵便局
을 通하여 郵送되는 被服類, 家庭用品,
韓國到着后 三個月以內에 搬入한
自動車 및 附屬品

0106

→

미·문 1077

0107

라. 稅關檢査 免除事項

命令으로 움직이는 美軍部隊, 公式封印된 公文書, 公用郵便物, 美國船荷証券으로 運送되는 軍事貨物

마. 関稅免除로 輸入된 物品은 韓國에서 処分할수 없다.

바. 美軍当局은 大韓民國의 稅関業務에 모든 援助를 提供한다.

美國側案은 大体的으로 우리側案과 類似하나 다음 몇가지 点에 差異가 있다.

가. 免除範囲에 있어 "認可된 調達機関"에 依한 輸入品은 免除된다고 規定하고 있다.

나. 稅関檢査 免除條項中 美側案은 우리側案의 " units of U. S. armed forces" 代身 " members of ...." 로 되어 있고 " official mail " 代身에 그냥 " mail" 로 되어 있으며 또한 우리 案의 " on a U. S. Governmen bill of lading " 句節은 두지 않고 있다.

다. 美側案에는 美軍이 管理하는 埠頭, 飛行場에 派遣되는 稅関公務員에 対한 援助 提供의 規定이 明示되어 있지 않다.

그러나 그같이 両側案에 若干의 相異点이 있으나 다음 會議에서 逐條審議時 調整될것이다.

0108 →

미-문 1071

0100

五. 來週에는 美側의 要求에 따라 土地 및 施設內容가 討議될것이다.

六. 展望

지금까지의 交涉會議는 美國側의 積極的이고 協助的인 態度로 比較的 順調롭게 進行되었음을 보아 앞으로도 一般的으로 잘 進行될것으로 思料되나 다만 刑事裁判管轄權 內容과 土地施設內容中 補償內容에 對해서는 相當한 差異가 予想되며 特히 後者에 對해서는 美側이 全혀 考慮하지 않고 있는것으로 判斷됨.

보통문서로 재분류(1966.12.31.)

1966.12.31.에 예고문에 의거 일반문서로 재분류됨

1964년9월30일 미주과장 직권으로 예고문 로재분류

~~문서로 재분류(협정체결후)~~

32-7

0110

미주문 1074 (7)

0111

4. 제7차 회의, 11.26

0112

주둔군 지위협정 제7차 교섭회의 토의사항

관세문제에 관한 미국측 초안 검토

1. 우리초안과의 실질적인 차이점 :

(1) 제1항 전단의 규정은 내용이 동일하나 우리초안 1 항 후단에서 규정한 미군, 군속 및 그들의 가족에대한 수색권, 휴대품 조사권 및 법칙물자의 압수권에 관한 규정이 없다.

(2) 면세범위에 관하여 미국초안은 미국군대, 세출외자금 기관 이외에 미군이 "인가한 조달기관" 에 의한 수입물품도 면세 된다고 규정하여 "인가된 조달기관" 이라는 구절을 명시하고있다. 또한 면세되는 물자로서미국의 병참보급을 받는 주한유엔군의 사용을 위하여 미군이 수입하는 물자에 대하여도 면세된다는 규정을 두고있다.

(3) 제 3 항 및 제 4 항의 규정은우리 초안과 실질적인 차이점이없다

(4) 세관검사 면제에 관한 조항중, (a)항에서 미국초안은"Members of the U.S. armed forces" 라고 규정하여 우리초안의 "Units of the United States forces" 의 규정과 상이하며, (b)항에서 official mail 대신 단지 mail 이라고만 규정하고 있으며 또한 (c)항에서 우리초안이 규정한 on a U.S. Government bill of lading 이라는 구절을 두지않았다.

(5) 미국초안 6, 7, 8, 및 9항은 우리초안과 실질적인 차이점이없다.

(6) 미국초안에서는 우리초안 7항 (e)에서 규정한 미군이 관리하는 부두 또는 비행장에 파견되는 세관공무원에 대한 원조 제공의 규정이 명시되지 않았다.

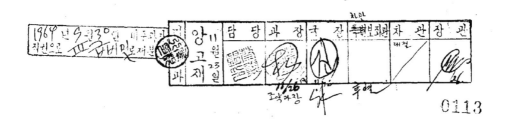

기안	11월 23일	담당	과장	국장	차관보	차관	장관
고재						대결	

1966년 5월 30일 예고문에 의거 일반문서로 재분류

11/26 조약과장 후결

0113

2. 미국측 초안에대한 검토:

(1) 우리초안 1 항 후단에서 규정한 미군, 군속 및 그들의 가족에 대한 수색권, 휴대품 조사권 및 법칙물자의 압수권에 관한 규정은 원칙적으로 본조에서 별단의 규정이없는 한 우리나라의 세관법규가 적용된다는 원칙적 규정에 비추어 미군이 우리 세관 당국의 업무수행에 충분한 편의와 원조를 제공한다는 것을 보장한다면 이규정을 구태어 두지않아도 소기의 목적을 달성할수 있을것으로 생각됨.

(2) 미국측 초안 2항에서 규정한 면세로서 물품을 수입할수 있는 기관으로서 authorized procurement agencie를 명시하고 있는데 이문제는 미군의 대행기관이라고 생각되는 조달기관에 의한 수입물품은 이들물품이 전적으로 미군을위하여 사용되는 것이며 물품을 수입다는 기관자체의 문제보다도 수입물품이 어떻게 처리되느냐에 따라 면세의 범위가 결정되는 우리 초안의 근본적인 취지에서 볼때 이들 기관이 수입하는 물품을 미군자체가 수입하는 것이로 간주할수도 있으나 이러한 기관의 수효와 그성질에 따라서 면세문제도 달라질수 있을것이며 동기관의 남용으로 한국경제에 악영향을 미칠우려가 있으므로 이러한 조달기관의 인가 또는 지정에 관하여는 사전에 우리 정부와 협의하여 합의를 보도록 하는 보장을 얻어야할것이며 이러한 보장이없는 한 이규정을삭제할것을 주장할것이다. 그러나 미측에서 고집하는 경우에는 미.일 협정에 동구절이 있음에 감하여 이를받아 드린다. 다만 합의의사록에non-appropriated fund organizations이 수입하는 물건은 non-appropriated fund 로 수입할것을 제의한다.

0114

우리측 3항 (b)중 자동차 및 부속품의 면세는 한국 처음 도착후 3개월 이내에만 한다고 수정함. (원안에는 2개월로 되어있음.)

(3) 세관검사 면제에 관한 미국초안 중, "Units of US armed forces" 대신 "Members of US armed forces" 라고 규정한 부분은 미군이 부대단위로서 입국하는경우는 물론 개개인이 개별적으로 입국하는 경우에도 검사를 면제한다는 규정인데, 이는 1952년의 미일간의 협정의 조항과 같은데, 밀수행위등은 주로 개별적으로 입국하는 미군에 의하여 자행된다는 점에 비추어 이를 방지하기 위하여서도 개별적으로 입국하는 미군에 대하여는 세관검사를 할수있도록 우리측 초안을 계속 주장하여야 할것임. (Units 와 Members 의 의의 해석에 대하여는 국방부에서 더 연구할것임) 또한 (b)항에서 규정한 official mail 대신 mail 이라는 규정은 APO를 통한 모든 우편물은 세관검사를 면제한다는 뜻인데 위에서 말한바와 같은이유로 사적인 우편물에 대하여는 세관검사를 할수있는 권한을 우리 세관당국이 가져야할것이므로 official mail 을 주장할것임. (c) 항에서는 on a US Government bill of lading 이라는 구절이 없는데 미국정부의 선하증권이 없는 군사화물에 대하여 일률적으로 세관검사를 면제함은 세관검사의 면제조항을 규정한 본항의 실질적인 의의를 없에는것이라고 생각됨으로 우리측 안을 주장할것임. 미.일 협정도 우리안과 같은 구정을 두고있음.

(4) 우리측 초안에서 규정한 미군이 관리하는 부두또는 비행장에 파견되는 우리나라의 세관공무원에 대한 원조제공에 관한 규정은

33-3

0115

미군이 관리하는 부두 또는 비행장의 특수한 성격을 고려하여 이규정을 삽입토록하는것이 가할것으로 생각됨. 따라서 동규정은 미측의 9항 (d)로, (d)는 (e)로 할것임.

3. 미국측이 제의한 합의의사록에 대한 검토

(1) 미국군대 구성원, 군속 및 그들의 가족의 사용을위하여 미군 또는 그기관이 면세로 수입하는 물품의 양은 이러한 사용을 위하여 필요한 합리적인 범위에 국한한다는 규정은 "합리적" 이라는 용어가 다소 애매하기는 하나 전반적으로 이규정은 별반 이의가 없는것으로 생각됨.

(2) 제2항에서 규정한 6개월동안의 기간은 주한 미군의 한국에서의 근무기간이 1 년임을고려할때 너무 장기간이라고 생각되며 본조에서 규정한 면세의 취지가 그들이 한국에 최초로 도착 한때 또는최초로 채류하는데 필요한 물품에 한하여 면세 한다는점에 비추어 이기간은 다소 단축되어야할것임. 따라서 우리측은 3개월을 주장할것이나 미측이 6개월을 고집하는 경우에는 수입품의 량을 합리적으로 제한할것을 조건으로하여 이를 받아드린다. ~~이와관련하여 출입국관리 문제에서 미군이 최초로 한국에도착한 일자를 알기위하여는 미군당국이 이에 관하여 한국정부 당국에 대하여 정기적으로 통고하여야 한다는 규정을 합의의사록에 두어야 할것이다.~~

(3) 동 제 3 항중 군사화물은 미국정부의 선하증권에 의하여 선적되는것에 한하여야 하며, 또한 미국군대가 인가한 조달 기관 또는 세출외 자금기관에 송부되는 군사화물은 군사 화물의 개념에서 제외되어야 할것이므로 미국측의 초안의 "including their authorized procurement...." 이하는 삭제하여야 할것이다.

0116

(4) 제 4 항 및 5 항의 규정에 대하여는 별반 의견이 없는 것으로 생각됨.

(5) 제 6 항에서 규정한 "autherized by United States law and...." 이하의 구절은 미국측이 필요한 원조제공을 회피하는 구실로서 그들의 법규를 인용할수도 있는모호한 규정이므로 이를 삭제하는것이 가할것으로 생각됨.

33-5

0117

1. Save as provided in this Agreement, members of the United States armed forces, the civilian component, and their dependents shall be subject to the laws and regulations administered by the customs authorities of the Republic of Korea.

2. All materials, supplies and equipment imported by the United States armed forces, including their authorized procurement agencies and their non-appropriated fund organizations provided for in Article , for the official use of the United States armed forces or for the use of the members of the United States armed forces, the civilian component, and their dependents, and materials, supplies and equipment which are to be used exclusively by the United States armed forces or are ultimately to be incorporated into articles or facilities used by such forces, shall be permitted entry into the Republic of Korea; such entry shall be free from customs duties and other such charges. Appropriate certification shall be made that such materials, supplies and equipment are being imported by the United States armed forces, including their authorized procurement agencies and their non-appropriated fund organizations provided for in Article , or, in the case of materials, supplies and equipment to be used exclusively by the United States armed forces or ultimately to be incorporated into articles or facilities used by such forces, that delivery thereof is to be taken by the United States armed forces for the purposes specified above. The exemptions provided in this paragraph shall extend to materials, supplies and equipment imported by the United States armed forces for

0118

the use of other armed forces in Korea which receive logistical support from the United States armed forces.

3. Property consigned to and for the personal use of members of the United States armed forces, the civilian component, and their dependents, shall be subject to customs duties and other such charges, except that no duties or charges shall be paid with respect to:

(a) Furniture, household goods, and personal effects for their private use imported by the members of the United States armed forces or civilian component when they first arrive to serve in the Republic of Korea or by their dependents when they first arrive for reunion with members of such forces or civilian component;

(b) Vehicles and parts imported by members of the United States armed forces or civilian component for the private use of themselves or their dependents;

期間問題

(c) Reasonable quantities of personal effects and household goods of a type which would ordinarily be purchased in the United States for the private use of members of the United States armed forces, civilian component, and their dependents, which are mailed into the Republic of Korea through United States military post offices.

4. The exemptions granted in paragraphs 2 and 3 shall apply only to cases of importation of goods and shall not be interpreted as refunding customs duties and domestic excises collected by the customs authorities at the time of entry in cases of purchase of goods on which such duties and excises have already been collected.

0119

5. Customs examination shall not be made in the following cases:

(a) Members of the United States armed forces under orders entering or leaving the Republic of Korea;

(b) Official documents under official seal and mail in United States military postal channels;

(c) Military cargo consigned to the United States armed forces, including their authorized procurement agencies and their non-appropriated fund organizations provided for in Article .

6. Except as such disposal may be authorized by the United States and Korean authorities in accordance with mutually agreed consitions, goods imported into the Republic of Korea free of duty shall not be disposed of in the Republic of Korea to persons not entitled to import such goods free of duty.

7. Goods imported into the Republic of Korea free from customs duties and other such charges pursuant to paragraphs 2 and 3, may be re-exported free from customs duties and other such charges.

8. The United States armed forces, in cooperation with Korean authorities, shall take such steps as are necessary to prevent abuse of privileges granted to the United States armed forces, members of such forces, the civilian component, and their dependents in accordance with this Article.

9. (a) In order to prevent offenses against laws and regulations administered by the customs authorities of the Government of the Republic of Korea, the Korean authorities and the United States armed forces shall assist

0120

each other in the consuct of inquiries and the collection of evidence.

(b) The United States armed forces shall render all assistance within their power to ensure that articles liable to seizure by, or on behalf of, the customs authorities of the Government of the Republic of Korea are handed to those authorities.

(c) The United States armed forces shall render all assistance within their power to ensure the payment of duties, taxes, and penalties payable by members of such forces or of the civilian component, or their dependents.

(d) Vehicles and articles belonging to the United States armed forces seized by the customs authorities of the Government of the Republic of Korea in connection with an offense against its customs or fiscal laws or regulations shall be handed over to the appropriate authorities of the forces concerned.

0121

AGREED MINUTES TO ARTICLE (Customs)

activities

1. The quantity of goods imported under paragraph 2 by non-appropriated fund organizations of the United States armed forces for the use of the members of the United States armed forces, the civilian component, and their dependents shall be limited to the extent reasonably required for such use.

2. Paragraph 3(a) does not require concurrent shipment of goods with travel of owner nor does it require single loading or shipment. In this connection, members of the United States armed forces or civilian component and their dependents may import free of duty their personal and household effects during a period of six months from the date of their first arrival.

3. The term "military cargo" as used in paragraph 5(c) is not confined to arms and equipment but refers to all cargo consigned to the United States armed forces, including their authorized procurement agencies and their non-appropriated fund organizations provided for in Article ___.

4. The United States armed forces will take every practicable measure to ensure that goods will not be imported into the Republic of Korea by or for the members of the United States armed forces, the civilian component, or their dependents, the entry of which would be in violation of Korean customs laws and regulations. The United States armed forces will promptly notify the Korean customs authorities whenever the entry of such goods is discovered.

0122

agreed. 5. The Korean customs authorities may, if they consider that there has been an abuse or infringement in connection with the entry of goods under Article , take up the matter with the appropriate authorities of the United States armed forces.

6. The words "The United States armed forces shall render all assistance within their power," etc., in paragraph 9(b) and (c) refer to reasonable and practicable measures by the United States armed forces (authorized by United States law and service regulations.)

0123

財務部案

76-70

0124

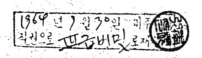

관 세 조 항

1. 관세관계 제법령의 적용

가. 미합중국 군대 구성원,군속 및 그가족은 본 협정에 명백히 반대의 규정이 있는 경우를 제외하고 대한민국 세관당국이 집행하는 법령에 복종하여야한다.

나. 본 협정에서 규정된 관세에관한 면제특전은 군사목적의 수행을 원활이 하는데 있는바 만약 특정군사 시설 및 구역내에서의 대한민국 관세법상의 이유로 관세경찰권을 행사할 사유가 발생할때에는 미합중국 군당국은 협조하여야 한다.

다. 미합중국 군대구성원 군속및 그가족이 대한민국에 또는 대한민국으로부터 입출국할때에 대한민국 세관은 그들의 휴대품을 조사하고 필요할때에는 수색을 함과 동시에 범칙물품을 압수할 권한을 갖는다.

2. 관세면제특전 및 증명

가. 다음의 물품은 관세 및기타 과징금을 면제한다.

(1) 미합중국 군대가 수입하는 공용품

(2) 미합중국 군당국이 허가하고 규제하는 미군판매소, PX ,식당보급소 사교크럽 극장 및 기타의 세출외 자금에 의하여 운영되는 기관이 수입하는자용품.

(3) 미합중국 군대 구성원 군속 및 그가족의 사용을 위하여 또는 그들에게 판매하기 위하여 전기 (2) 항에서 말한 제기관 또는 미합중국 군대가 수입하는 물품.

나. 전항의 물품은 자재공급품 및 비품등으로서 미합중국 군기관이 직접 수입

하는 [redacted]이며 이의 수입자는 미합중국 군대 및 미합중국군대의 공인 조달기관 이다.

다. 전항의 사실은 합동위원회에서 결정된 소정 양식에 의하여 미합중국 군당국이 발행하는 증명서를 첨부하여 대한민국 세관에 신고하여야만 한다.

(1) 세관에대한 신고는 미합중국 군기관의 명의와 책임하에 행하여야 한다.

(2) 따라서 수입행위에 대하여 제3자의 개입이나대리는 인정하지않는다.

라. 대한민국 정부가 공인하는 자선단체에 증여하기 위하여 수입하는 자선용 구호물품에 대한 관세및 과징금은 면제 한다.

마. 미합중국 군대의 구성원 및 군속이 사용으로 수입하는 자동차에 대하여 그들이 최초로 한국에 도착할때 반입하는 경우에 한하여 관세및제세를 면제한다. 단 본인이 도착한날로 부터 2개월 내에 한국내에 반입되어야 한다.

3. 재 산 반 입

가. 원칙적으로 미합중국 군대의 구성원군속 및 그가족의 사용재산의 반입에 대하여는 관세를 부과한다. 단 다음 경우에는 관세및 과징금을 면제한다.

(1) 미합중군 군대의 구성원군속 및 그가족이 한국에 최초로 도착할때에 반입하는 그들 개인의 사용에 공하는 가구 가정용품 및 기타 개인용품.

(2) 미합중국 군사우체국을 통하여 한국에 우송되는 합리적인 양의 의복류와 가정용품.

4. 수입물품의 관세불반대

가. 미합중군 군대 또는 미합중국 정부의 세출외자금에 의하여 운영되는

36-12

0126

군인용 판매기관 등이 한국내에서 본 협정에 의하여 관세및 국징금을 면제받는 것은 당해 물품 수입시에 한한다.

나. 관세및국징금이 이미 납부된 수입물품을 한국내에서 미합중국군 또는 미합중국 정부의 세출외자금에 의하여 운영되는 제기관이 공용으로 구매조달한 경우에도 당해 관세및국징금을 반려하지는 않는다.

~~이는 일반의 국산품 보다 수입품이 유리한 특권을 받게되는 결과로서 야기되는 일반국내 제조업에 대한 부당한 압박이 되는 까닭이다.~~

다. 미합중국 군대 구성원군속 및 그가족이 사용하고저 하는 물품을 한국내에서 관세및국징금을 이미 납부한 수입품을 구매한 경우에도 전항과 같이 당해 관세및 국징금을 반려하지 않는다.

5. 세관검사의 면제

가. 수출입 물품에 대하여 세관에서 필요로하는 모든 검사는 본 협정에 의하여 다음의 경우에 한하여 면제 한다.

(1) 명령에 의하여대한민국에 출입국하는 미합중국 군대의 부대

(2) 미합중국군대의 공문서로서 공식봉인으로 공용인이 표시된것.

(3) 미합중국 군사우편 선로상에 있는 공용우편물

(4) 미합중국 정부의 선하증권에 의하여 미합중국 군대 앞으로 운송되는 군사화물

그러나 본 협정에서의 세관검사의 면제는 본래의 수출입신고 및 수출입면허절차 까지를 면제하는것은 아니다.

나. 명령에 의하여 대한민국에 출입국하는 미합중국 군대의 부대및 구성원

36-13

의 휴대품에 대하여는 각각 그지휘관 및 본인의 구두신고에 의하여 사정을 감안하고 세관검사를 면제하며 공용의 봉인이 있는 공문서에 대하여는 그의 공용의 표시를 확인하고 세관검사를 면제한다.

다. 미합중국 정부의 선하증권에 의하여 미합중국 군대 앞으로 운송되는 군사화물은 합동위원회에서 결정한 소정 양식에 의거 미합중군 군대가 수입 신고를 하고 정부 선하증권 사본 또는 이에 대치할 미합중국 군대수송부의 증명서를 첨부하여 세관검사를 면제한다.

라. "미합중국 정부의선하증권" 이라 함은 미합중국 정부가 발행하는 것을 말하며 선박회사가 미합중군 정부를 위하여 발행하는것은 포함하지않는다.

마. 본 협정에서 "군사화물" 이라 함은 무기및비품에 한정하는 것이 아니고 합중국정부의 선하증권에 의하여 미합중군 군대 앞으로 운송되는모든 화물을 말하며 미합중국 정부의 타의 기관앞으로 운송되는 화물은 이와 구별되어야 한다.

바. 대한민국 세관당국이 필요하다고 인정하는 경우에는 미합중국 군대의 군인용 판매기관 등 앞으로 미합중국 정부의 선하증권에 의하여 운송되는 화물에 대하여 검사를 한다.

6. 관세면제물품의 양도의제한및 동물품양수시의관세징수

가. 미합중국 군대 또는 미합중국 정부의 세출외 자금에 의하여 운영되는 군인용 판매기관 등 과 미합중국군대의 구성원,군속 및 그가족이 본 협정에 의하여 관세및기타의 과징금을 면제받고 수입한 물품은

(1) 재 수출할수 있으며 0128

(2) 한미 양당국의 합의한 조건에 처분을 인정하는 경우를 제외

36-14

— 4 —

하고는 본 협정 기타 대한민국 법령에 의거 관세및과징금의 면제특권이 부여된 이외의자에게 한국내에서 매각 증여 등 형식으로 처분하지 못한다.

나. 미합중국 군대의 구성원 군속 및그가족인 자가 제대 사직 이혼등 이유로 일반인이 되었을때에는 본인이 구성원 군속 및그가족으로 있을 당시에 소유하든 면세물품을 계속 소유하고있는한 본 협정의 효력이 있다.

다. 본 협정에 의하여 면세 수입된 물품에 대한 양도의 제한이나 소정절차와 이행을 요함은 미합중국 군대의 구성원 군속 및 그가족 등이 직접 수입한 물품에 한정되는것이 아니고 미합중국 군대로부터 지급된 물품 군인용 판매기관 등에서 구입한 면세물품 등을 양도하는경우에도 적용된다.

마. 본 협정에 의하여 면세된 물품을 무단 양도하였을 때에는 한국 관세법에 의하여 처벌된다.

7. 미합중국군 당국의 협조

가. 미합중국군 당국은 대한민국 당국과 협력하여 본 협정에서 미합중국 군대 그 구성원 군속및 그가족에게 허여한 특권의 남용을 방지하는데 필요한 조치를 취하여야 한다.

나. 미합중국군 당국은 관세및 세관법령에 관한 위반행위를 대한민국 당국이 조사실시 및 증거의수집을 하는데 대하여 협조하여야 한다.

양당국은 본항의 위반행위를 방지하는데 필요한 계속적인 정보의 교환은 물론 법위반의 잠재적 요소가 농후한 군인용판매기관 등에 대한 수시적인 조사를 실시하고 위반 증거 수집에 상호 협조한다.

다. 미합중국 군당국은 대한민국 세관당국에 의하여 또는 기타 대한민국

36 15

0129

관헌에 의하여 압수된 물품이 한국 세관측으로 인도되도록 가능한 모든 원조를 하여야 한다.

라. 미합중국군 당국은 미합중국 군대 구성원 군속 또는 그가족이 납부하여야할 관세조세 및 벌금의 납부를 확보하기 위하여 가능한 모든 원조를 제공 하여야 한다.

마. 미합중국 군 당국은 세관검사의 목적을 위하여 군대가 관리하는 부두와 비행장에 파견된 세관공무원에게 모든 실제적 원조를 제공하여야한다.

일반문서로 재분류(1966.12.31.)

1966.12.31.에 예고문에 의거 일반문서로 재분류됨

- 6 -

0130

62.11.26

Press Release

At today's meeting, the negotiators continued to discuss the Preamble and began detailed discussion of the article on customs and duties. Considerable progress and substantial agreement in some respect were achieved.

It was agreed to continue discussion of these and other articles at the next meeting which is scheduled for December 4 at 2:00 p.m.

0131

3K-4

1962.11.26

1962.11.26.
提案

ARTICLE (Customs)

2. All materials, supplies and equipment imported by the United States armed forces, including their authorized procurement agencies and their non-appropriated fund organizations provided for in Article , for the official use of the United States armed forces or for the use of forces logistically supported by the United States armed forces or for the use of the members of the United States armed forces, the civilian component, or their dependents shall be permitted entry into the Republic of Korea free from customs duties and other such charges. Similarly, materials, supplies and equipment which are imported by others than the United States armed forces but are to be used exclusively by the United States armed forces and/or forces logistically supported by the United States armed forces or are ultimately to be incorporated into articles or facilities to be used by such forces shall be permitted entry into the Republic of Korea free from customs duties and other such charges. Appropriate certification shall be made by the United States armed forces with respect to the importation of materials, supplies and equipment for the foregoing specified purposes.

0132

ARTICLE (Customs)

2. All materials, supplies and equipment imported by the United States armed forces, including their authorized procurement agencies and their non-appropriated fund organizations provided for in Article , for the official use of the United States armed forces or for the use of forces logistically supported by the United States armed forces or for the use of the members of the United States armed forces, the civilian component, or their dependents shall be permitted entry into the Republic of Korea free from customs duties and other such charges. Similarly, materials, supplies and equipment which are imported by others than the United States armed forces but are to be used exclusively by the United States armed forces and/or forces logistically supported by the United States armed forces or are ultimately to be incorporated into articles or facilities to be used by such forces shall be permitted entry into the Republic of Korea free from customs duties and other such charges. Appropriate certification shall be made by the United States armed forces with respect to the importation of materials, supplies and equipment for the foregoing specified purposes.

0133

ARTICLE (Customs)

1. Save as provided in this Agreement, members of the United States armed forces, the civilian component, and their dependents shall be subject to the laws and regulations administered by the customs authorities of the Republic of Korea.

agreed

2. All materials, supplies and equipment imported by the United States armed forces, including their authorized procurement agencies and their non-appropriated fund organizations provided for in Article , for the official use of the United States armed forces or for the use of the members of the United States armed forces, the civilian component, and their dependents, and materials, supplies and equipment which are to be used exclusively by the United States armed forces or are ultimately to be incorporated into articles or facilities used by such forces, shall be permitted entry into the Republic of Korea; such entry shall be free from customs duties and other such charges. Appropriate certification shall be made that such materials, supplies and equipment are being imported by the United States armed forces, including their authorized procurement agencies and their non-appropriated fund organizations provided for in Article , or, in the case of materials, supplies and equipment to be used exclusively by the United States armed forces or ultimately to be incorporated into articles or facilities used by such forces, that delivery thereof is to be taken by the United States armed forces for the purposes specified above. The exemptions provided in this paragraph shall extend to materials, supplies and equipment imported by the United States armed forces for the use of other armed forces in Korea which receive logistical support from the United States armed forces.

activities

exclusively

under the unified command

agreed

0134

3. Property consigned to and for the personal use of members of the United States armed forces, the civilian component, and their dependents, shall be subject to customs duties and other such charges, except that no duties or charges shall be paid with respect to:

(a) Furniture, household goods, and personal effects for their private use imported by the members of the United States armed forces or civilian component when they first arrive to serve in the Republic of Korea or by their dependents when they first arrive for reunion with members of such forces or civilian component;

(b) Vehicles and parts imported by members of the United States armed forces or civilian component for the private use of themselves or their dependents;

(c) Reasonable quantities of personal effects and household goods of a type which would ordinarily be purchased in the United States for the private use of members of the United States armed forces, civilian component, and their dependents, which are mailed into the Republic of Korea through United States military post offices.

4. The exemptions granted in paragraphs 2 and 3 shall apply only to cases of importation of goods and shall not be interpreted as refunding customs duties and domestic excises collected by the customs authorities at the time of entry in cases of purchase of goods on which such duties and excises have already been collected.

0135

5. Customs examination shall not be made in the following cases:

(a) Members of the United States armed forces under orders entering or leaving the Republic of Korea;

(b) Official documents under official seal and mail in United States military postal channels;

(c) Military cargo consigned to the United States armed forces, including their authorized procurement agencies and their non-appropriated fund organizations provided for in Article .

6. Except as such disposal may be authorized by the United States and Korean authorities in accordance with mutually agreed conditions, goods imported into the Republic of Korea free of duty shall not be disposed of in the Republic of Korea to persons not entitled to import such goods free of duty.

우리 草案 6項과 同一.

7. Goods imported into the Republic of Korea free from customs duties and other such charges pursuant to paragraphs 2 and 3, may be re-exported free from customs duties and other such charges.

8. The United States armed forces, in cooperation with Korean authorities, shall take such steps as are necessary to prevent abuse of privileges granted to the United States armed forces, members of such forces, the civilian component, and their dependents in accordance with this Article.

0136

9. (a) In order to prevent offenses against laws and regulations administered by the customs authorities of the Government of the Republic of Korea, the Korean authorities and the United States armed forces shall assist each other in the conduct of inquiries and the collection of evidence.

(b) The United States armed forces shall render all assistance within their power to ensure that articles liable to seizure by, or on behalf of, the customs authorities of the Government of the Republic of Korea are handed to those authorities.

(c) The United States armed forces shall render all assistance within their power to ensure the payment of duties, taxes, and penalties payable by members of such forces or of the civilian component, or their dependents.

(d) Vehicles and articles belonging to the United States armed forces, seized by the customs authorities of the Government of the Republic of Korea in connection with an offense against its customs or fiscal laws or regulations shall be handed over to the appropriate authorities of the forces concerned.

우리側草案
第7項e項의規定 — insertion agreed
無.

0137

AGREED MINUTES TO ARTICLE (Customs)

1. The quantity of goods imported under paragraph 2 by non-appropriated fund organizations of the United States armed forces for the use of the members of the United States armed forces, the civilian component, and their dependents shall be limited to the extent reasonably required for such use.

2. Paragraph 3(a) does not require concurrent shipment of goods with travel of owner nor does it require single loading or shipment. In this connection, members of the United States armed forces or civilian component and their dependents may import free of duty their personal and household effects during a period of six months from the date of their first arrival.

3. The term "military cargo" as used in paragraph 5(c) is not confined to arms and equipment but refers to all cargo consigned to the United States armed forces, including their authorized procurement agencies and their non-appropriated fund organizations provided for in Article .

4. The United States armed forces will take every practicable measure to ensure that goods will not be imported into the Republic of Korea by or for the members of the United States armed forces, the civilian component, or their dependents, the entry of which would be in violation of Korean customs laws and regulations. The United States armed forces will promptly notify the Korean customs authorities whenever the entry of such goods is discovered.

0138

5. The Korean customs authorities may, if they consider that there has been an abuse or infringement in connection with the entry of goods under Article , take up the matter with the appropriate authorities of the United States armed forces.

6. The words "The United States armed forces shall render all assistance within their power," etc., in paragraph 9(b) and (c) refer to reasonable and practicable measures by the United States armed forces, authorized by United States law and service regulations.

deletion agreed

0130

기 안 용 지

자체 통제		기안처	미주과 강석재	전화번호	근거서류접수일자

	과장	국장	차관보좌관	차관	장관
	11/27				11/28

관계관 서명	~~기획조정관~~
기안 년월일	1962. 11.27
시행 년월일	
보존 년한	
정서기장	
분류 기호	외정무 397
전체 통제	
검열	1962.11.27 종결
경유 수신 참조	~~국가재건최고회의 총무처장~~ 의장 외무국방 위원장
발신	장관
제목	주둔군 지위협정 체결교섭회의 제7차회의 보고서 송부

(가제목: 갑 메 기)

1. 1962. 11. 26. 하오 2시부터 4시 10분까지 외무부에서 개최된 주둔군 지위 협정에 관한 제7차 교섭회의의 보고서를 별첨과 같이 송부합니다.
2. 유첨: 제7차 교섭회의 보고서 1부. 끝

보통문서로 재분류(1966. 12. 31)

1966.12.31에 예고문에 의거 일반문서로 재분류됨

승인양식 1-1-3 (1112-040-016-018) RET (190mm×260mm16절지)

1964년 9월 30일 미주과 직권으로 IIIㄱ급비밀로 재분류

외 무 부

외정무 . 1962. 11. 28.

수 신 국가재건최고회의 의장

~~경 유 국가재건최고회의 총무처장~~

참 조 외무국방위원장

제 목 주둔군 지위협정체결 교섭회의 제7차회의 보고서 송부

(가제목 : 갑 메 기)

1. 1962. 11. 26. 하오 2시부터 4시 10분까지 외무부에서 개최된 주둔군 지위협정에 관한 제7차 교섭회의의 보고서를 별첨과 같이 송부합니다.

2. 유첨 : 제7차 교섭회의 보고서 1부. 끝

외 무 부 장 관 최 덕 신

0141

14-8

제 9 차

한미간 주둔군 지위협정 실무자 회의

보 고 서

1. 시 일 : 1962. 11. 26. 하오 2시부터 4시 10분까지

2. 장 소 : 외무부 회의실

3. 참석자 : 한국측 : 진 필 식 (외무부 정무국장)

이 경 호 (법무부 법무국장)

박 근 (외무부 미주과장)

박 봉 진 (재무부 관세과장)

이 남 구 (국방부 군무과장)

신 정 섭 (외무부 2등서기관)

채 의 석 (외무부 2등서기관)

강 석 재 (외무부 3등서기관)

이 창 범 (외무부 3등서기관)

미국측 : 교섭대표단 전원

4. 토의사항 :

(1) 서문에관한 토의를 계속한후 관세문제에 관하여 축조토의 함.

(2) 서문에관하여 우리측은 미군대가 당초 유엔결의에 의거하여 한국에 주둔케된 사실을 삽입할것을 계속 주장하였음.

가. 우리측은 그이유로서 미군대는 그주둔 근거가 유엔결의에 의거하거나 또한 상호 방위조약 제4조에 의거하거나에 불구하고 모두 주둔군지위 협정에 의하여 규제되어야 하기 때문이라고 말하고 따라서 어떠한 미군대의 군사행동이 통합사령부의 이름으로 수행되고있다는 이유로서 본협정에서 제외된다든가 본협정의 적용에 있어서 예외가될수 없다는 점을 명백히 하였음.

0142

14-2

0143

나. 미국측은 통합사령부를 위한 어떠한 교섭도 할수 없으며 다만 미국군대의 지위에관한 협정을 교섭하고 있다고 주장하고 본 주둔군 지위협정의 어떠한 부분도 통합사령부 휘하에있는 다른나라 군대에 관계되는것이 아니며 오직 미국군대에 한하여 규제하는것이라고 설명하였음.

다. 우리측은 이에관하여 물론 다른나라에서 파견된 유엔군은 협정의 대상에서 당연히 제외되는것이며, 다만 미군에 관한한 통합사령부 휘하군으로서의 행동이건 또는 주한미 8군으로서의 행동이건 관계없이 모든 미군대 구성원의 지위나 사용하는 토지 및 시설문제를 본협정에 의하여 규제한다는 점을 재차 강조하고 미국측이 이점을 수락할 것을 요청함.

라. 미국측은 이와같은 우리측입장을 이해한다고 말하고, 여기에대한 충분한 검토를한후 미국측의 태도를 알려주겠다고 답변함.

마. 미국측은 이와관련하여 미군이 방위조약 제4조 및 유엔결의에 의거하여 주둔케된사실을 밝힌 별첨과같은 서문의 새로운 수정안을 제시하였는바 우리측은 이를 검토한후 다음회의에서 계속 토의하기로 함.

(3) 관세문제에 관한 토의내용은 다음과같음.

가. 제 1 항에있어서 우리측은 우리측 초안의 후단구절을 삭제할것에 동의하고 "별도규정이 없는한 미군대 구성원, 군속 및 그가족은 한국세관 당국 규정에 따라야 한다" 는 내용의 미국측안에 합의하였음.

0144

14-3

미북 88-7

0145

나. 제 2 항에 있어서 미국측은 원안대신 더욱 간략하게 작성된 수정안을 제출하였음. 우리측은 "인가된 조달기관" (authorized procurement agencies) 에 대하여 그 정확한 의미를 문의하였든바 미국측은 "인가된 조달기관" 은 미군대 행정기관의 일부를 구성하는 군대 수입 기관이라고 하였으며 특권 남용을 방지하기 위해서 관세조항에서 양측이 상호 협력한다는 별도 조항이 있음을 언급하였다. 우리측은 미국측이 새로 제시한 수정안을 검토한후 다음회의에서 계속 토의키로 하였다.

다. 제 3 항에 있어서는 서문 조항과 (a) (c)항에 대해서는 미국측안대로 합의하였으나, (b)항의 자동차 및 부속품의 면세 조치는 미군 구성원, 군속 및 가족의 한국 도착후 3 개월간으로 한다는 우리측안에 관하여 미국측은 수송 기간을 고려하여 6 개월간으로 해야한다고 주장하고 있는바 이문제는 다음회의에서 계속 토의하기로 함.

라. 제 4 항은 양측안이 동일함으로 그대로 채택키로 합의함.

마. 제 5 항의 세관검사 면제대상으로 우리측안은 한국영역에 출입하는 미군대 " Units " 로 규정하고 있으며 미국측 안에는 " members " 로 규정하고 있는바 이용어에 관련하여 미국측은 주한 미국군대는 대부분이 개인별로 교체되고 있다는 사실에 언급하고 개인으로 출입하는 미군대 구성원은 모두 세관검세 면제 대상이 되어야 한다고 설명하였음. 한국측은 이문제를 검토하여 보겠다고 말하고 다음 회의에서 계속 토의키로 제의하였음.

0146

14-4

미문 88-7

0147

5. 기타사항 :

(1) 차기회의 일자 : 1962. 12. 4. 하오 2시

(2) 차기회의 의제 : 관세문제를 계속 토의키로 함.

6. 참고자료 :

미국측이 제의한 서문 및 관세문제 제 2 항 수정안 사본

보통문서로 재분류(1966. 12. 31.)

1966.12.31.에 예고문에 의거 일반문서로 재분류됨

0148

14-5

[illegible] 88-7

0149

美側修正案

PREAMBLE

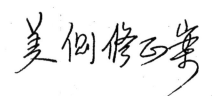

"Whereas the United States of America has disposed its armed forces in and about the territory of the Republic of Korea pursuant to the resolutions of the United Nations Security Council of June 25, 1950, June 27, 1950, and July 7, 1950, and pursuant to Article IV of the Mutual Defense Treaty between the United States of America and the Republic of Korea signed on October 1, 1953.

Therefore, the United States of America and the Republic of Korea, in order to strengthen the close bonds of mutual interest between their two countries, have entered into this Agreement regarding facilities and areas and the status of United States armed forces in the Republic of Korea in terms as set forth below:"

0150

14-6

미원 88-7

0151

美側修正案 留保

ARTICLE (Customs)

(2.) All materials, supplies and equipment imported by the United States armed forces, including their authorized procurement agencies and their non-appropriated fund organizations provided for in Article , for official use of the United States armed forces or for the use of forces logistically supported by the United States armed forces or for the use of the members of the United States armed forces, the civilian component, or their dependents shall be permitted entry into the Republic of Korea free from customs duties and other such charges. Similarly, materials, supplies and equipment which are imported by others than the United States armed forces but are to be used exclusively by the United States armed forces and or forces logistically supported by the United States ammed forces or are ultimately to be incorporated into articles or facilities to be used by such forces shall be permitted entry into the Republic of Korea free from customs duties and other such charges. Appropriate certification shall be made by the United Stated armed forces with respect to the importation of materials, supplies and equipment for the foregoing specified purposes.

보통문서로 재분류(1966.12.31)

0152

1966.12.31.에 예고문에 의거 일반문서로 재분류됨

미국문 88-7(6)

0153

Customs Duties

1. Except as provided expressly to the contrary in this Agreement, members of the United States forces, the civilian component, and their dependents shall be subject to the laws and regulations administered by the customs authorities of the Republic of Korea. In particular the customs authorities of the Republic of Korea shall have the right, under the general conditions laid down by the laws and regulations of the Republic of Korea, to search members of the United States forces, the civilian component and their dependents and to examine their luggage, and to seize articles pursuant to such laws and regulations.

2. All materials, supplies and equipment imported by the United States forces or by the organizations provided for in Article ______ exclusively for the official use of the United States forces or those organizations or for the use of members of the United States forces, the civilian component and their dependents shall be permitted entry into Korea free from customs duties and other such charges. When such materials, supplies and equipment are imported, a certificate issued by the authorities of the

0154

15-121

United States forces in the form to be determined by the Joint Committee shall be submitted to the customs authorities of the Republic of Korea.

3. Property consigned to and for the personal use of members of the United States armed forces, the civilian component and their dependents, shall be subject to customs duties except that no such duties or charges shall be paid with respect to:

(a) Furniture, household goods and other personal effects for their private use imported by the members of the United States forces, the civilian component and their dependents at time of their first arrival in Korea.

(b) Reasonable quantities of clothing and household goods which are mailed into the Republic of Korea through the United States military post offices.

(c) Vehicles and parts imported by members of the U.S. armed forces or civilian component within two months after their first arrival in Korea for the private use of themselves or their dependents.

4. The exemption granted in paragraphs 2 and 3 shall apply only to cases of importation of goods and shall not be interpreted as refunding customs duties and domestic excises collected by the customs authorities

0155

15-18

at the time of entry in cases of purchases of goods on which such duties and excises have already been collected.

5. Customs examination shall be exempted only in the following cases:

(a) Units of the United States forces under orders entering or leaving the Republic of Korea;

(b) Official documents under official seal;

(c) Official mail in United States military postal channels;

(d) Military cargo shipped on a United States Government bill of lading.

6. Goods imported free from customs duties and other such charges pursuant to paragraph 2 and 3 above:

(a) May be re-exported free from customs duties and other such charges;

(b) Shall not be disposed of in the Republic of Korea, by way of either sale or gift, to person not entitled to import such goods free from duty, except as such disposal may be authorized on conditions agreed between the authorities of the Republic of Korea and the United States.

7. (a) The authorities of the United States forces, in cooperation with the authorities of the Republic of Korea, shall take such steps as are necessary to prevent

0156

15-14

abuse of the privileges granted to the United States forces, members of such forces, the civilian component, and their dependents in accordance with this Article.

(b) In order to prevent offenses against customs and fiscal laws and regulations, the authroties of the Republic of Korea and of the United States forces shall assist each other in the conduct of inquiries and the collection of evidence.

(c) The authorities of the United States forces shall render all assistance within their power to ensure that articles liable to seizure by, or on behalf of, the customs authorities of the Republic of Korea are handed to those authorities.

(d) The authorities of the United States forces shall render all assistance within their power to ensure the payment of duties, taxes and penalities payable by members of the United States forces or the civilian component, or their dependents.

(e) The authorities of the United States forces shall provide all practicable assistance to the customs officials dispatched to military controlled piers and airports for the purpose of customs inspection.

0157

15-18

8. Vehicles and articles belonging to the United States armed forces seized by the customs authorities of the Government of the Republic of Korea in connection with an offense against its customs or fiscal laws or regulations shall be handed over to appropriate authorities of the force concerned.

0158

15-16

ARTICLE (Customs)

1. Save as provided in this Agreement, members of the United States armed forces, the civilian component, and their dependents shall be subject to the laws and regulations administered by the customs authorities of the Republic of Korea.

2. All materials, supplies and equipment imported by the United States armed forces, including their authorized procurement agencies and their non-appropriated fund organizations provided for in Article , for the official use of the United States armed forces or for the use of the members of the United States armed forces, the civilian component, and their dependents, and materials, supplies and equipment which are to be used exclusively by the United States armed forces or are ultimately to be incorporated into articles or facilities used by such forces, shall be permitted entry into the Republic of Korea; such entry shall be free from customs duties and other such charges. Appropriate certification shall be made that such materials, supplies and equipment are being imported by the United States armed forces, including their authorized procurement agencies and their non-appropriated fund organizations provided for in Article ,

0159

5-17

or, in the case of materials, supplies and equipment to be used exclusively by the United States armed forces or ultimately to be incorporated into articles or facilities used by such forces, that delivery thereof is to be taken by the United States armed forces for the purposes specified above. The exemptions provided in this paragraph shall extend to materials, supplies and equipment imported by the United States armed forces for the use of other armed forces in Korea which receive logistical support from the United States armed forces.

3. Property consigned to and for the personal use of members of the United States armed forces, the civilian component, and their dependents, shall be subject to customs duties and other such charges, except that no duties or charges shall be paid with respect to:

(a) Furniture, household goods, and personal effects for their private use imported by the members of the United States armed forces or civilian component when they first arrive to serve in the Republic of Korea or by their dependents when they first arrive for reunion with members of such forces or civilian component;

0160

5-18

(b) Vehicles and parts imported by members of the United States armed forces or civilian component for the private use of themselves or their dependents;

(c) Reasonable quantities of personal effects and household goods of a type which would ordinarily be purchased in the United States for the private use of members of the United States armed forces, civilian component, and their dependents, which are mailed into the Republic of Korea through United States military post offices.

4. The exemptions granted in paragraphs 2 and 3 shall apply only to cases of importation of goods and shall not be interpreted as refunding customs duties and domestic excises collected by the customs authorities at the time of entry in cases of purchase of goods on which such duties and excises have already been collected.

5. Customs examination shall not be made in the following cases:

(a) Members of the United States armed forces under orders entering or leaving the Republic of Korea;

(b) Official documents under official seal and mail in United States military postal channels;

0161

5-18

(c) Military cargo consigned to the United States armed forces, including their authorized procurement agencies and their non-appropriated fund organizations provided for in Article.

6. Except as such disposal may be authorized by the United States and Korean authorities in accordance with mutually agreed conditions, goods imported into the Republic of Korea free of duty shall not be disposed of in the Republic of Korea to persons not entitled to import such goods free of duty.

7. Goods imported into the Republic of Korea free from customs duties and other such charges pursuant to paragraphs 2 and 3, may be re-exported free from customs duties and other such charges.

8. The United States armed forces, in cooperation with Korean authorities, shall take such steps as are necessary to prevent abuse of privileges granted to the United States armed forces, members of such forces, the civilian component, and their dependents in accordance with this Article.

9. (a) In order to prevent offenses against laws and regulations administered by the customs authorities

0162

6-20

of the Government of the Republic of Korea, the Korean authorities and the United States armed forces shall assist each other in the conduct of inquiries and the collection of evidence.

(b) The United States armed forces shall render all assistance within their power to ensure that articles liable to seizure by, or on behalf of, the customs authorities of the Government of the Republic of Korea are handed to those authorities.

(c) The United States armed forces shall render all assistance within their power to ensure the payment of duties, taxes, and penalties payable by members of such forces or of the civilian component, or their dependents.

(c) Vehicles and articles belonging to the United States armed forces seized by the customs authorities of the Government of the Republic of Korea in connection with an offense against its customs or fiscal laws or regulations shall be handed over to the appropriate authorities of the forces concerned.

0163

15-21

AGREED MINUTES TO ARTICLE (Customs)

1. The quantity of goods imported under paragraph 2 by non-appropriated fund organizations of the United States armed forces for the use of the members of the United States armed forces, the civilian component, and their dependents shall be limited to the extent reasonably required for such use.

2. Paragraph 3(a) does not require concurrent shipment of goods with travel of owner nor does it require single loading or shipment. In this connection, members of the United States armed forces or civilian component and their dependents may import free of duty their personal and household effects during a period of six months from the date of their first arrival.

3. The term "military cargo" as used in paragraph 5(c) is not confined to arms and equipment but refers to all cargo consigned to the United States armed forces, including their authorized procurement agencies and their non-appropriated fund organizations provided for in Article.

4. The United States armed forces will take every practicable measure to ensure that goods will not be imported into the Republic of Korea by or for the members of the United States armed forces, the civilian component,

0164

15-22

or their dependents, the entry of which would be in violation of Korea customs laws and regulations. The United States armed forces will promptly notify the Korean customs authorities whenever the entry of such goods is discovered.

5. The Korean customs authroities may, if they considger that there has been an abuse or infringement in connection with the entry of goods under Article , take up the matter with the appropriate authorities of the United States armed forces.

6. The words "The United States armed forces shall render all assistance within their power," etc., in paragraph 9(b) and (c) refer to reasonable and practicable measures by the United States armed forces authorized by United States law and service regulations.

보통문서로 재분류(1966. 12. 31)

1966.12.31.에 예고문에 의거 일반문서로 재분류됨

0165

15-28

SUMMARY RECORD OF THE SEVENTH SESSION
STATUS FORCES NEGOTIATION

November 26, 1962

I. Time and Place : 2:00 to 4:10 p.m. November 26, 1962 at Conference Room of the Ministry of Foreign Affairs

II. Attendants:

ROK Side:

Mr. Chin, Pil Shik	Director Bureau of Political Affairs Ministry of Foreign Affairs
Col. Lee, Nam Koo	Chief, Military Affairs Section Ministry of National Defense
Mr. Yi, Kyung Ho	Director Bureau of Legal Affairs Ministry of Justice
Mr. Pak, Kun	Chief, America Section Ministry of Foreign Affairs
Mr. Pak, Pong Chin	Chief, Customs Duty Section Ministry of Finance
Mr. Chai, Eui Sok	2nd Secretary Ministry of Foreign Affairs
Mr. Shin, Chung Sup	2nd Secretary Ministry of Foreign Affairs
Mr. Kang, Suk Jae	3rd Secretary Ministry of Foreign Affairs
Mr. Lee, Chang Bum	3rd Secretary Ministry of Foreign Affairs

US Side:

Mr. Philip C. Habib	Counselor of the Embassy for Political Affairs
Brig. Gen. J.D. Miller	Deputy Chief of Staff 8th Army
Mr. William J. Ford	First Secretary of the Embassy
Col. G.G. O'Connor	Deputy Chief of Staff 8th Army

0166

1964 년 9 월 30 일 예고문에 의거 일반문서로 재분류됨

15-1

Capt. R.M. Brownlie	Assistance Chief of Staff USN/K
Col. W.A. Solf	Staff Judge Advocate 8th Army
Mr. Benjamin A. Fleck (Rapporteur and Press Officer)	First Secretary of the Embassy
Mr. Robert A. Lewis	Second Secretary and Consul of the Embassy
Lt. Col. R.E. Miller	Staff Officer, JAG 8th Army
Lt. Col. W.A. Burt	J-5
Mr. Campen	Interpreter

Introduction of New U.S. Participant

1. Before beginning substantive discussion, Mr. Habib introduced Lt. Col. W.A. Burt, J-5, who has replaced Lt. Col. G.T. Sudermann as an Alternate Member of the U.S. negotiating team. Mr. Habib also welcomed back Mr. Campen, who had not been able to participate in the last several meetings.

Preamble

2. The negotiators then began substantive discussion by resuming their consideration of the tabled drafts of the Preamble. Mr. Habib stated that the U.S. side had carefully considered both drafts and continued to prefer the simple statement that it had submitted. Fundamentally, he said, the Preamble should be a statement of the basis for the presence of the U.S. forces in Korea and the U.S. side believed its draft was a satisfactory statement of this kind, whereas the Korean draft was lengthy, involved,

0167

15-2

and in some respects repetitive. Both drafts were attempting to accomplish the same purpose but the Korean draft was unduly complex. Mr. Habib then asked Mr. Chin to indicate the most outstanding feature of the Korean draft in comparison with the U.S. draft.

3. Mr. Chin replied that an important purpose of the Preamble was stated in the U.S. draft. However, the Korean side wished to state in the Preamble the fact that the presence of the U.S. forces in Korea is based on both the UN resolutions and the Mutual Defense Treaty. Therefore, even though the wording of the Korean draft was not perfect and could be altered, the Korean side desired a text similar to that which they had drafted. ~~Therefore, even though the wording of the Korean draft was not perfect and could be altered, the Korean side desired a text similar to that which they had drafted~~.

4. Mr. Habib stated that the U.S. side had recognized and carefully considered the desire of the Korean side to include in the Preamble some reference to the historical background. There was one thing that needed to be absolutely clear -- that the present negotiations were concerned solely with the U.S. forces and not with United Nations forces. Mr. Habib pointed out that the Korean side had agreed in earlier discussions that whatever agreement emerged from the negotiations would have no bearing on the United Nations forces. With that understanding, he said, the U.S. side was willing to take under consideration the desire of the Korean side to include in the Preamble some reference to the historical background.

0168

15-8

5. Mr. Habib went on to say that there were two items in the Korean draft which were not found in the U.S. draft: (a) the reference to the United Nations resolutions, and, (b) an expression of the desire to strengthen the bonds of mutual interest between our two countries. The U.S. side, he said, wished to submit a new draft which incorporated these two points but was less complex than the Korean draft. At this point he tabled a revised U.S. draft.

6. Mr. Chin replied that the Korean side agreed that what was being negotiated was an agreement covering the status of U.S. forces in Korea. It had nothing to do with the forces of any other nation. Nor did it have any relevancy to the forces of other countries serving as part of the United Nations Command. The U.S. forces, he continued, will be subject to the providions of the SOFA whether they are in Korea under the provisions of the UN resolutions or the provisions of the ROK-US Mutual Defense Treaty. In this respect, he said, he could see no difference between the UN Resolutions and the Mutual Defense Treaty. Therefore, there should be no difference in treatment, regardless of whether the U.S. forces were here as U.S. forces or as components of the unified command.

7. Mr. Habib reiterated that the SOFA is concerned with the status of the U.S. armed forces in Korea. It has no relevance to the forces of any other country or to the unified command per se. He again stated that the U.S. negotiating team was not authorized to negotiate on behalf of the unified command established under the UN Security Council resolutions.

0169

15-4

8. Mr. Chin replied that the Korean side agreed that the SOFA would apply to no other forces in the unified command except the U.S. forces. He repeated that the SOFA will govern U.S. forces whether or not those forces are components of the unified command. Mr. Habib replied that this was exactly what the U.S. draft stated. He asked for the views of the Korean side on the revised U.S. draft which had just been tabled.

9. Commenting on the revised draft, Mr. Chin stated that the purposes and objectives of the U.S. forces are the same, whether or not the presence of those forces in Korea is based upon the UN resolutions or upon the Mutual Defense Treaty. Therefore, in order to make sure that the SOFA will facilitate those purposes and objectives, there should be no exceptions for U.S. forces serving as components of the unified command. Facilities and areas used by U.S. components of the unified command would therefore come under the provisions of the SOFA. Elaborating on Mr. Kang's interpretation of Mr. Chin's remarks Dr. Pak said that the fundamental objective of the SOFA is to facilitate the fulfillment of the purposes and objectives of the UN resolutions and the Mutual Defense Treaty. Therefore, there should be no discrimination in regard to U.S. forces stationed in Korea under one or the other.

10. Mr. Habib replied that there is nothing in the U.S. draft Preamble regarding the objectives or purposes of either the UN resolution or the Mutual Defense Treaty. The Preamble merely states that the SOFA covers U.S. forces stationed in the Republic of Korea "pursuant to" the resolutions and the Treaty.

0170

15-5

11. Mr. Chin replied that consequently, any agreement between the Republic of Korea Government and ~~the~~ the unified command concerning the status and facilities and areas of the forces of the unified command will apply to the forces of other nations but not to the U.S. component. Mr. Habib said that the U.S. side understood the position of the Korean side and would take it under consideration. Mr. Chin said that if a clear understanding could be reached on that point, the Korean side would have no difficulty in finalizing the wording of the Preamble. He suggested that the discussion be continued at the next meeting, and Mr. Habib agreed.

Customs and Duties

Paragraph 1

12. Turning to the drafts of the customs and duties article which had been tabled at the previous meeting, Mr. Chin suggested paragraph by paragraph discussion. Mr. Habib agreed. He stated that the U.S. draft of Paragraph 1 was a clear and unequivocal statement and the U.S. side saw no reason to go beyond it. Mr. Chin said there was no fundamental difference in the two drafts and that the purpose and main points were the same. He suggested that the second sentence of the Korean draft be deleted, to which Mr. Habib agreed. Mr. Habib expressed the view that the phraseology in the U.S. draft of the first sentence was more precise and specific. Mr. Chin stated that the U.S. draft of Paragraph 1 was acceptable to the Korean side in as much as the content of the drafts of both sides is basically the same.

0171

15-6

Paragraph 2

13. Turning to Paragraph 2, Mr, Chin asked for an explanation of the phrase "including their authorized procurement agencies and their non-appropriated fund organizations". Mr. Habib replied that the U.S. side realized that their draft of Paragraph 2 was cumbersome and somewhat difficult to understand. He wished, therefore, to submit a revised version of this paragraph. At this point he tabled a new draft of Paragrah 2. He stated that the new version was simpler and more readily understood.

14. In reply to Mr. Chin's request for clarification, Colonel Solf pointed out that the word "including" in the U.S. draft means that the authorized procurement agencies are a part of the U.S. armed forces. In effect this is no different from the wording of the Korean draft, except that use of the word "including" clarifies the position of the agencies. The scope of the U.S. draft is thus no larger than that of the Korean draft.

15. Mr. Chin inquired whether "authorized procurement agencies" included civilian companies. Mr. Habib replied that they did not. He pointed out that civilian companies were covered in the second sentence of the revised U.S. draft which refers to items "imported by others than the United States armed forces" for the exclusive use of the U.S. armed forces. An example, he said, would be the importation by a civilian contractor of materials to be used in the construction of a radar tower. Clearly such materials should enter free of duty.

0172

15-7

16. Mr. Chin said that he would like to have further discussion of the second sentence in the U.S. draft. It was agreed to continue discussion of this sentence at the next meeting.

17. Turning to the question of certification Mr. Chin pointed out that the third sentence of the revised U.S. draft called for "appropriate certification" whereas the second sentence of the Korean draft was more precise in referring to "a certificate issued ... in the form to be determined by the Joint Committee".

18. Mr. Habib recalled that in previous meetings a similar discussion had been held regarding the same point in another article. He said that "appropriate certification" obviously has to be acceptable to both sides in order to be appropriate. The U.S. side saw no necessity for spelling out specifically in the agreement what is "appropriate". Both side agreed that all procedural matters such as this might be left for later determination by the Joint Committee, rather than specified in the Agreement.

Paragraph 3

19. Mr. Habib pointed out that the introductory sentence in the two drafts of paragraph 3 was identical, except that the U.S. draft includes the phrase "and other such charges". Mr. Chin agreed that there was no real difference. He asked, however, whether "other such charges" included charges by civilian firms, such as storage charges, unloading charges, charges by customs brokers, et. Mr. Habib replied that the phrase referred only to governmental charges and not to charges by private companies. It was agreed to discuss this point at the next meeting.

0173

15-8

20. Mr. Chin expressed agreement to the U.S. draft of subparagraph (a). When Mr. Habib inquired whether this included agreement to the Agreed Minute #2 in the U.S. draft Mr. Chin suggested that the Agreed Minutes be discussed separately and Mr. Habib agreed.

21. Mr. Chin pointed out that the only difference between the U.S. draft of subparagraph (b) and the Korean draft of subparagraph (c) was that a time limit of two months was specified in the Korean draft. He suggested that the limit be changed to three months. Mr. Habib stated that a time limit created a problem with regard to the importation of spare parts. There was also the problem arising from the fact that it took some time for vehicles to arrive in Korea from the United States. This was not only true of vehicles belonging to members of the U.S. armed forces but had also been the experience of Embassy personnel. Mr. Chin replied that he recognized the difficulty with regard to parts. However, he thought a three month limit on vehicles would be appropriate since he understood that personnel of the U.S. armed forces leave Korea after one year of service here. Mr. Habib replied that this was not true in all cases. There was considerable variation in the lengths of tours of duty here, particularly in the case of members of the civilian component. It was agreed that this matter should be discussed further at the next meeting.

0174

15-8

22. Mr. Chin stated that the Korean side agreed to the U.S. draft of subparagraph (c).

Paragraph 4

23. Mr. Habib pointed out that the two drafts of Paragraph 4 were identical, except that the U.S. draft read "exemptions" where the Korean draft read "exemption". Mr. Chin stated that the Korean side agreed to the U.S. draft.

Paragraph 5

24. With respect to paragraph 5, Mr. Habib stated that the introductory sentence in the U.S. draft was a more specific statement than the corresponding sentence in the Korean draft of the exemptions to be granted from customs examination. Mr. Chin replied that the Korean side would study this matter for discussion at the next meeting.

25. Mr. Habib pointed out that in subparagraph (a) the U.S. draft used the word "members" instead of "units", inasmuch as the great bulk of the personnel of the U.S. armed forces entered Korea as individuals and not in organized units. He explained that the word "unit" had a specific connotation, denoting an organized body of troops forming a component of the U.S. forces. He pointed out that the operative phrase in subparagraph (a) was the phrase "under orders".

26. At this point it was decided to adjourn the meeting, which had then been in session for over two hours. The next meeting was scheduled for Tuesday, December 4, at 2:00 p.m.

0175

15-10

27. Summary of Points of Agreement - The following of the text of the U.S. draft of the customs and duties article were agreed upon for inclusion in the final text of the Agreement:

Paragraph 1

Paragraph 3, subparagraph (a)

Paragraph 3, subparagraph (c)

Paragraph 4

보통문서로 재분류(1966.12.31)

미주과	양 12월 3일 고재	담 당	과 장	국 장	차관보	차 관	장 관
						후결	

1966.12.31.에 예고문에 의거 일반문서로 재분류됨

0176

15-11

5. 제8차 회의, 12.4

0177

기 안 용 지

자 체 통 제		기안처	미주과 강 석 재	전화번호	근거서류접수일자

과 장	국 장	차관보	차 관		장 관	내각 수반
(서명) 12/3	(서명)	(서명)			(서명) 3.	

관계관 서 명	기획조정관 (서명)

기 안 년월일	1962. 12. 3.	시 행 년월일		보존 년한		정 서	기 장
분 류 기 호	외정무	전 체 통 제		종결			

경 유 수 신 참 조	건 의	발 신	

제 목 제 8 차 주둔군 지위협정 실무자회의에 임할 우리측 태도

12. 4. 개최되는 제8차 주둔군지위협정 체결을 위한 실무자 회의에서는 제 7 차 회의에 이에 서문 및 관세업무에 관한 토의를 계속하고 비행기 선박의 출입 및 항해통제와 기상업무~~에 관한~~문제에 관한 양국초안을 제시 토의키로 되어있는바 이에관련하여 우리측 실무교섭자는 12. 1. 회합을갖고 제8차 실무자회의에 대한 우리측 대표단 입장을 별첨과같이 취하기로 결정하였아오니 이를 재가하여 주시기 바랍니다.

유첨 : 비행기. 선박출입 및 항해 통제와 기상업무에 관한 우리측안

보통문서로 재분류(1966. 12. 31.)

끝

1966.12.3 ,에 예고문에 의거 일반문서로 재분류됨

36-1

1966년 3월30일 미주국장 직권으로 III급비밀로재분류

~~승인양식 1-1-1~~ (1112 - 040 - 016 - 016) (190mm×260mm16절지)

0178

1. 서 문

가. 문제점

주한미군은 1953. 10. 1. 조인된 한.미 상호방위조약 제4조에 의거하여 한국에 주둔하고 있다는점에 관해서는 한미 양국의 서문초안에서 다같이 일치하고있으나 현재까지 다음과같은 우리측 주장에대해서는 합의를 보지못하였던 것임.

(1) 미군은 상호방위조약외에 1950년 6월 25일 및 6월 27일 그리고 7월 7일자의 유엔안전보장 이사회결의에 따라 한국영역에 주둔하였다는 사실. (이사실에 의거하여 주한 미군은 유엔군으로서 행동하든 미제 8군으로서 행동하든 다같이 주둔군지위 협정의 적용을받는다는 원칙)

(2) 미군의 한국주둔은 양국간의공동 이익과 우호관계의 증진을 위한것이라는 점

나. 입장

제 7차 주둔군 지위협정 실무자회의에서 미국측은 위와같은 우리측의 계속적인 주장을 고려에 넣은새로운 수정안을 제의 하여왔는바 표현상 약간의 차이가 있으나 근본적이며 실질적인 내용에 있어서는 우리측의 주장이 반영되었다고 사료됨으로 미국측의 수정안을 수탁키로 한다.

2. 관세문제

가. 미국측 초안 제 2 절

미국측초안의 제2절은 "미군대의 공적사용과 군대구성원. 군속 및 가족이 사용할 공인된 조달기관 및 비세출자금 기관으로 수입된 모든물자, 보급품 및 장비와 또한 배타적으로 미군대에 의하여 사용되거나 혹은 미군에 의하여 사용되고있는

36-2

0179

물자 및 시설에 궁극적으로 통합될 모든물자, 보급품 및 장비는 통관세 기타 수수료가 면제되어 수입이 허가된다 (미일협정과 동일)는 점을 골자로하고 그에 부수되는 증명 서류 문제들을 규제하고 있는바 그 체제와 표현이 너무 복잡하고 어색함으로 미국측은 제 7 차 실무회의시 새로운 수정안을 제출하였는바 내용에 있어서 실질적인 차이는 없음.

나. 문제점

미국측안의 원안과 수정안에 있어서의 문제점은 다음과같음.

(1) 비세출자금 기관

미군대의 공적 사용과 미군대구성원 군속 및 그 가족에 의하여 사용될 모든물자는 비세출자금 기관을 포함한 미군대에 의하여 수입할수 있는바 비세출자금기관의 기능, 자금형성, 자금범위 및 비세출자금 기관의 써-비스를 이용할수있는 대상인원의 범위등에 대하여 확실한 것을 알수없음으로 이에대한 설명을 요구하기로 함.

(2) 기타 수입기관

공인된 조달기관 및 비세출 자금기관을 포함한 미군대에 의한 수입외에도 미군에 의하여 배타적으로 사용되거나 미군이 사용하는 물자 및 시설에 궁극적으로 통합될 모든 물자는 관세가 면제되며 수입이 허가된다고 규제하고 있는바 미국측 원안에는 물자의 용도를 기준으로 하고 수입기관에 대해서는 언급이 없으나 수정안에선 ". . . imported by others ..."라고 하여 미군대 이외의 수입기관에 의하여 수입되는 물건이라도 궁극적으로 미군대가 사용하는 물자라면 누구나가 수입할수 있도록 되어있음. 이에관한 미국측의 입장을 더욱 상세히 설명하도록 요구하기로 함.

36-3

0180

다. 입장

미국측의 제 2 절에대한 안은 원안과 수정안 2 개의안이 있는바 우리측은 다음과같은 비교분석 결과로 미국측의 원안을 수락하도록 한다.

(1) 원안에는 미군에 의하여 배타적으로 수입되거나 혹은 미군이 사용하는 물자 및 시설에 궁극적으로 사용될 물자에대한 수입기관을 명시하지 않고 있으나 오히려 수정안은 ...by others ... 라고 명백히 자구를 첨가함으로서 어떠한 기관일지라도 물자의 사용목적만 합법적이면 수입할수 있도록 명시적으로 규정되어 있으며.

(2) 수입물자의 증명문제에 있어서 수정안은 막연히 적절한 증명을 하도록 규정하고 있으나 원안은 수입물자에 관한 증명을 더구체적으로 규정하고 있으며, (1) 미군대의 공적 사용과 미군대 구성원, 군속 및 가족에 의하여 사용될 공인된 조달기관 및 비세출자금 기관을 포함한 미군대에 의하여 수입된 물품과 (2) 미군대에 의하여 배타적으로 사용되거나 혹은 미군대가 사용하는 물자 및 시설에 궁극적으로 통합될 물자로 구분하여 각각 증명토록 규정되고 있음.

다. 자동차 및 부속품에 대한 관세면제에 관한 문제점및 입장

우리측은 자동차 및 부속품이 소유자 입국후 3개월내에 도착하여야 면세조치를 해주기로 규정하기 원하고 있는데 대하여 미국측은 그기간을 6개월로 연장하기를 원하고있음. 이문제에 대하여는 재무부 ~~세관당국의 의견이 확정될때까지 우선 2개월을 계속 주장하여 보도록 한다~~ 장관의 동의를 얻는대로 그 기간을 완화하기로 한다.

364

0181

마. 세관검사 면제에 있어서의 문제점과 입장

세관검사 면제대상중 미군대구성원과 우편물에 관하여서 면제 특례의 남용방지를 위하여 우리측을 미군대 구성원에 있어서는 "units" 로 입국할 경우에만 면제케하고 "members 로 입국할 경우에는 세관검사를 하도록하며 또한 우편물에 있어서도 " official mail 만을 면제하기로 계속 주장하기로 함.

3. 비행기 및 선박의 출입과 항해통제 및 기상업무조항의 문제점과입장

가. 이문제에 대하여 미국측 수석대표는 한국측 수석대표에게 미국측안은 미.일협정 내용과같은 안을 가지고 나올것이라고 사전에 암시하여온바 있음.

나. 따라서 우리측안과 내용에있어서 실제적인차이가 없을것으로 전망되며 이문제에 관하여 아래와같은 입장을 취한다.

(1) 우리측안 제 1 절 후단에 미.일협정에서 규정하고 있는바 "본협정에서 면제되지 아니하는 화물 및 여객이 선박 및 비행기에 탑승하고있을 경우 한국당국에 이를 통고하여 그들의 출입국은 한국법율과 규정에따라야 한다" 이라는 구절을 삽입토록 한다.

(2) 우리측 제 2 절에있는 선박의 구분은 합의의사록에서 규정토록 한다.

(3) 우리측안에는 ~~규정되어 있지않으나~~ 당연한일로서 규정되어 있지않으나 미.일협정에 규정되고 있는 다음과같은 조항을 미국측이 희망한다면 이를 수락하여도 무방하다.

"제 1 구절에서 기술한 선박 및 비행기, 장갑차를 포함한 미국정부 소유 차량 및 미군대 구성원,

0182

36-5

군속 및 그가족은 미군대가 사용하는 시설 및 토지간 및 그러한 시설 및 토지와 한국 항만 및 비행장간의 출입 및 이동이 허용된다. 미군대 차량에의한 시설 및 토지간의 그러한 출입 및 이동은 통과세 기타 부과금에서 면제된다.

(4) 우리측안에는 가상. 기후 및 지진업무에 대한 한미양국 간의 협조에 관하여 항해통제 조항에서 규제하고 있으나 만약 미국측이 이를 별도 규정할것을 원한다면 수락할것임.

366

0183

ARTICLE (Access by Aircraft and Vessel)

1. United States and foreign vessels and aircraft operated by, for, or under the control of the Government of the United States for the purpose of this Agreement shall be accorded access to any port or airport of the Republic of Korea free from toll or landing charges. When cargo or passengers not accorded the exemptions of this Agreement are carried on such vessels and aircraft notification shall be given to the apprpriate Korean authorities, and their entry into and departure from the Republic of Korea shall be according to the laws and regulations of the Republic of Korea.

2. When the vessels mentioned in paragraph 1 enter Korean ports, appropriate notification shall be made to the appropriate Korean authorities. Such vessels shall have freedom from compulsory pilotage. If, however, a pilot is taken, pilotage shall be paid for at appropriate rates.

36-7

0184

AGREED MINUTES TO ARTICLE (ACCESS BY AIRCRAFT AND VESSEL)

1. The vessels mentioned in paragraph 1 include chartered vessels (bare boat charter, voyage charter and time charter,), except space chartered vessels.

36-8

0185

ARTICLE (CONTROL OF NAVIGATIONS ~~AND METEOROLOGICAL SERVICES~~)

I. All civil and military air traffic control and communications systems shall be developed in close coordination between the two Governments and shall be integrated to the extent necessary for mutual security interests. Procedures, and any subsequent changes thereto, necessary to effect this coordination and integration will be established by arrangements between the appropriate authorities of the two Governments.

2. Lights and other aids to navigation of vessels and aircraft placed or established in the facilities and areas in use by the United States and in territorial waters adjacent thereto or in the vicinity thereof shall conform to the system in use in the Republic of Korea. The Republic of Korea and United States authorities which have established such navigation aids shall notify each other of their positions and characteristics and shall give advance notification before making any changes in them or establishing additional navigation aids.

3. The Governments of the Republic of Korea and the United States shall cooperate in meteorological services through exchanges of meteorological observations, climatological information and seismographic data in accordance with arrangements between the appropriate authorities of the two Governments.

36-9

0186

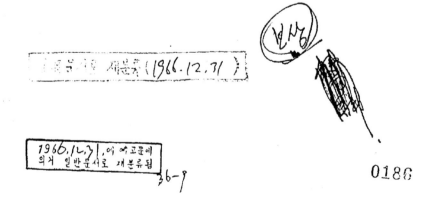

1962. 12. 4.
8次会議에서
美國側이 手交.

ARTICLE (Access by Aircraft and Vessel)

1. United States and foreign vessels and aircraft operated by, for, or under the control of the Government of the United States for the purpose of this Agreement shall be accorded access to any port or airport of the Republic of Korea free from toll or landing charges. When cargo or passengers not accorded the exemption of this Agreement are carried on such vessels and aircraft notification shall be given to the appropriate Korean authorities, and their entry into and departure from the Republic of Korea shall be according to the laws and regulations of the Republic of Korea.

2. When the vessels mentioned in paragraph 1 enter Korean ports, appropriate notification shall be made to the appropriate Korean authorities. Such vessels shall have freedom from compulsory pilotage. If, however, a pilot is taken, pilotage shall be paid for at appropriate rates.

0187

<u>AGREED MINUTES TO ARTICLE</u> (Access by Aircraft and Vessel)

I. The vessels mentioned in paragraph 1 include chartered vessels (bare boat charter, voyage charter and time charter,), except space chartered vessels.

0188

Agreement between ROK and U.S.

ARTICLE X

1. United States and foreign vessels and aircraft operated by, for, or under the control of the Government of the United States for the purpose of this Agreement shall be accorded access to any port or airport of the Republic of Korea free from toll or landing charges.

{Agreed Minute} 2. The vessels mentioned in paragraph 1 of this Article include chartered vessels (bare boat charter, voyage charter and time charter,), except space chartered vessels.

3. When the vessels menioned in paragraph 1 enter Korean ports, appropriate notification shall be made to the appropriate Korean authorities. Such vessels shall have freedom from compulsory pilotage. If, however, a pilot is taken, pilotage shall be paid for at appropriate rates.

0189

ARTICLE XI

1. All civil and military air traffic control and communications systems shall be developed in close coordination between the two Governments and shall be integrated to the extent necessary for mutual security interests. Procedures, and any subsequent changes thereto, necessary to effect this coordination and integration will be established by arrangements between the appropriate authorities of the two Governments.

2. Lights and other aids to navigation of vessels and aircraft placed or established in the facilities and areas in use by the United States and in territiorial waters adjacent thereto or in the vicinity thereof shall conform to the system in use in the Republic of Korea. The Republic of Korea and United States authorities which have established such navigation aids shall notify each other of their positions and characteristics and shall give advance notification before making any changes in them or establishing additional navigations aids.

0190

Agreement between U.S. and Japan

ARTICLE V

1. United States and foreign vessels and aircraft operated by, for, or under the control of the United States for official purposes shall be accorded access to any port or airport of Japan free from toll or landing charges. When cargo or passengers not accorded the exemptions of this Agreement are carried on such vessels and aircraft notification shall be given to the appropriate Japanese authorities, and their entry into and departure from Japan shall be according to the laws and regulations of Japan.

2. The vessels and aircraft mentioned in paragraph 1, United States Government-owned vehicles including armor, and members of the United States armed forces, the civilian component, and their dependents shall be accorded access to and movement between facilities and areas in use by the United States armed forces and between such facilities and areas and the ports or airports of Japan. Such access

0191

to and movement between facilities and areas by United States military vehicles shall be free from toll and other charges.

3. When the vessels mentioned in paragraph 1 enter Japanese ports, appropriate notification shall, under normal conditions, be made to the proper Japanese authorities. Such vessels shall have freedom from compulsory pilotage, but if a pilot is taken pilotage shall be paid for at appropriate rates.

ARTICLE VI

1. All civil and military air traffic control and communications systems shall be developed in close coordination and shall be integrated to the extent necessary for fulfillment of collective security interests. Procedures, and any subsequent changes thereto, necessary to effect this coordination and integration will be established by arrangement between the appropriate authorities of the two Governments.

2. Lights and other aids to navigation of vessels and aircraft placed or established in the facilities and areas in use by United States armed

0192

3. The Governments of the Republic of Korea and the United States shall cooperate in meteorological services through exchanges of meteorological observations, climatological information and seismographic data in accordance with arrangements between the appropriate authorities of the two Governments.

0193

forces and in territorial waters adjacent thereto or in the vicinity thereof shall conform to the system in use in Japan. The United States and Japanese authorities which have established such navigation aids shall notify each other of their positions and characteristics and shall give advance notification before making any changes in them or establishing additional navigation aids.

ARTICLE VII

The United States armed forces shall have the use of all public utilities and services belonging to, or controlled or regulated by the Government of Japan, and shall enjoy priorities in such use, under conditions no less favorable than those that may be applicable from time to time to the ministries and agencies of the Government of Japan.

ARTICLE VIII

The Government of Japan undertakes to furnish the United States armed forces with the following meteorological services in accordance with arrangements

0194

between the appropriate authorities of the two Governments:

(a) Meteorological observations from land and ocean areas including observations from weather ships.

(b) Climatological information including periodic summaries and the historical date of the Meteorological Agency.

(c) Telecommunications service to disseminate meteorological information required for the safe and regular operation of aircraft.

(d) Seismographic data including forecasts of the estimated size of tidal waves resulting from earthquakes and areas that might be affected thereby.

0195

Draft proposed by Korean side.

Customs Duties

1. Except as provided expressly to the contrary in this Agreement, members of the United States forces, the civilian component, and their dependents shall be subject to the laws and regulations administered by the customs authorities of the Republic of Korea. In particular the customs authorities of the Republic of Korea shall have the right, under the general conditions laid down by the laws and regulations of the Republic of Korea, to search members of the United States forces, the civilian component and their dependents and to examine their luggage, and to seize articles pursuant to such laws and regulations.

2. All materials, supplies and equipment imported by the United States forces or by the organizations provided for in Article ____ exclusively for the official use of the United States forces or those organizations or for the use of members of the United States forces, the civilian component and their dependents shall be

0196

permitted entry into Korea free from customs duties and other such charges. When such materials, supplies and equipment are imported, a certificate issued by the authorities of the United States forces in the form to be determined by the Joint Committee shall be submitted to the customs authorities of the Republic of Korea.

3. Property consigned to and for the personal use of members of the United States forces, the civilian component and their dependents, shall be subject to customs duties, except that no such duties or charges shall be paid with respect to:

(a) Furniture, household goods and other personal effects for their private use imported by the members of the United States forces, the civilian component and their dependents at time of their first arrival in Korea..

(b) Reasonable quantities of clothing and household goods which are mailed into the Republic of Korea through the United States military post offices.

4. The exemption granted in paragraphs 2 and 3

0197

shall apply only to cases of importation of goods and shall not be interpreted as refunding customs duties and domestic excises collected by the customs authorities at the time of entry in cases of purchases of goods on which such duties and excises have already been collected.

5. Customs examination shall be exempted only in the following cases:

(a) Units of the United States forces under orders entering or leaving the Republic of Korea;

(b) Official documents under official seal;

(c) Official mail in United States military postal channels;

(d) Military cargo shipped on a United States Government bill of lading.

6. Goods imported free from customs duties and other such charges pursuant to paragraphs 2 and 3 above:

(a) May be re-exported free from customs duties and other such charges;

(b) shall not be disposed of in the Republic of Korea, by way of either sale or gift, to person

0198

not entitled to import such goods free from duty, except as such disposal may be authorized on conditions agreed between the authorities of the Republic of Korea and the United States.

7. (a) The authorities of the United States forces, in cooperation with the authorities of the Republic of Korea, shall take such steps as are necessary to prevent abuse of the privileges granted to the United States forces, members of such forces, the civilian component, and their dependents in accordance with this Article.

(b) In order to prevent offenses against customs and fiscal laws and regulations, the authorities of the Republic of Korea and of the United States forces shall assist each other in the conduct of inquiries and the collection of evidence.

(c) The authorities of the United States forces shall render all assistance within their power to ensure that articles liable to seizure by, or on behalf of, the customs authorities of the Republic of Korea are handed to those authorities.

0199

(d) The authorities of the United States forces shall render all assistance within their power to ensure the payment of duties, taxes and penalities payable by members of the United States forces or the civilian component, or their dependents.

(e) The authorities of the United States forces shall provide all practicable assistance to the customs officials dispatched to military controlled piers and airports for the purpose of customs inspection.

0200

3. (c) Vehicles and parts imported by members of the U.S. armed forces or civilian component within two months after their first arrival in Korea for the private use of themselves or their dependents.

0201

8. Vehicles and articles belonging to the United States armed forces seized by the customs authorities of the Government of the Republic of Korea in connection with an offense against its customs or fiscal laws or regulations shall be handed over to appropriate authorities of the force concerned.

0202

1962.12.4.
美國側提案

ARTICLE

1. All civil and military air traffic control and communications systems shall be developed in close coordination and shall be integrated to the extent necessary for the operation of this Agreement. Procedures, and any subsequent changes thereto, necessary to effect this coordination and integration will be established by arrangement between the appropriate authorities of the two Governments.

2. The United States is authorized to establish, construct and maintain aids to navigation for vessels and aircraft, both visual and electronic as required, throughout the Republic of Korea and in the territorial waters thereof. Such navigation aids shall conform generally to the system in use in Korea. The United States and Korean authorities which have established navigation aids shall duly notify each other of their positions and characteristics and shall give advance notification where practicable before making any changes in them or establishing additional navigation aids.

~~through~~ the agreement bet. ROK. US.

through the arrangement between the appropriate authorities of the two Governments

accept (our position)

communication systems.

0203

外62.12.4.

ARTICLE

1. United States and foreign vessels and aircraft operated by, for, or under the control of the United States for official purposes shall be accorded access to any port or airport of Korea free from toll or landing charges. When cargo or passengers not accorded the exemptions of this Agreement are carried on such vessels and aircraft, notification shall be given to the appropriate Korean authorities, and their entry into and departure from Korea shall be according to the laws and regulations of Korea.

2. The vessels and aircraft mentioned in paragraph 1, United States Government-owned vehicles including armor, and members of the United States armed forces, the civilian component, and their dependents shall be accorded access to and movement between facilities and areas in use by the United States armed forces and between such facilities and areas and the ports or airports of Korea. Such access to and movement between facilities and areas by United States military vehicles shall be free from toll and other charges.

3. When the vessels mentioned in paragraph 1 enter Korean ports, appropriate notification shall, under normal conditions, be made to the proper Korean authorities. Such vessels shall have freedom from compulsory pilotage, but if a pilot is taken pilotage shall be paid for at appropriate rates.

Under Normal conditions -

0204

AGREED MINUTES TO ARTICLE

1. "United States and foreign vessels...operated by, for, or under the control of the United States for official purposes" mean United States public vessels and chartered vessels (bare boat charter, voyage charter and time charter). Space charter is not included. Commercial cargo and private passengers are carried by them only in exceptional cases.

2. The Korean ports mentioned herein will ordinarily mean "open ports".

3. An exception from making the "appropriate notification" referred to in paragraph 3 will apply only in unusual cases where such is required for security of the United States armed forces or similar reasons.

4. The laws and regulations of Korea will be applicable except as specifically provided otherwise in this Article.

0205

0206

기 안 용 지

자 체 통 제		기안처	미주과 이경훈	전화번호	근거서류접수일자
과장	수석대표		보좌관	차관	장관
				전결	
관계관 서 명	조약과장		기획조정관		
기안 년월일	1962. 12. 4.	시행 년월일		보존 년한	정서 기장
분류 기호	외정무405	전체 통제			
경유 수신 참조	국가재건최고회의 의장 (참조 : 외무국 방위원장) 내각수반	발신	외무부장관		
제 목	주둔군 지위협정 체결을위한 제 8 차 교섭회의 보고				

1962. 12. 4. 하오 2시 30분부터 동 4시 35분 까지 중앙청 외무부장관실에서 개최된 표기문제에 관한 제 8 차 교섭회의에서 토의된 내용을 별지와같이 보고합니다.

유첨 : 제 8 차 교섭회의 보고서 .... 부, 끝

보통문서로 재분류(1966. 12. 31.)

1966.12.31.에 예고문에 의거 일반문서로 재분류됨

승인양식 1-1-3 (1112-040-016-018) (190mm×260mm16절지)

1964년 9월 30일 미주과 직권으로 김비밀 조재

16-1

외 무 부

외정무 1962. 12. 5.

수 신 국가재건최고회의 의장

참 조 외무국방위원장

제 목 주둔군 지위협정 체결을위한 제 8 차 교섭회의 보고

1962. 12. 4. 하오 2시 30분부터 동 4시 35분까지 중앙청 외무부장관실에서 개최된 표기문제에 관한 제 8 차 교섭회의에서토의된 내용을 별지와같이 보고합니다.

유첨 : 제 8 차 교섭회의 보고서 2 부. 끝

파기하라 : 분필요시

외 무 부 장 관 최 덕 신

170

0207

16-8

외 무 부

외정무 1962. 12. 5.

수 신 내각수반

제 목 주둔군 지위협정 체결을위한 제 8 차 교섭회의 보고

1962. 12. 4. 하오 2시 30분부터 동 4시 35분 까지 중앙청 외무부장관실에서 개최된 표기문제에 관한 제 8 차 교섭회의에서 토의된 내용을 별지와같이 보고합니다.

유첨 ; 제 8 차 교섭회의 보고서 1부. 끝.

파기일자 : 분필요시

외 무 부 장 관 최 덕 신

0208

19-9

제 8 차

한미간 주둔군지위 협정 실무자 회의

보 고 서

1. 시 일 : 1962. 12. 4. 하오 2시 30분부터 동 4시 35분까지

2. 장 소 : 중앙청 외무부장관실

3. 참석자 : 한국측 : 진 필 식 (외무부 정무국장, 수석대표)

이 경 호 (법무부 법무국장)

박 근 (외무부 미주과장)

오 원용 (외무부 조약과장)

박 봉 진 (재무부 관세과장)

이 남 구 (국방부 군무과장)

지 성 구 (외무부 공보관)

이 경 훈 (외무부 2등서기관)

신 정 섭 (")

강 석 재 (외무부 3등서기관)

이 창 범 (")

미국측 : 교섭대표단 전원 ("후렐"대표 제외)

4. 토의사항 :

(1) 협정의서문, 관세, 선박 및 항공기의 출입, 그리고 항해 및 항공의 통제와 기상문제를 순차적으로 토의함.

(2) 협정의서문에 관한 토의에 있어서 미국측은 본협정의 적용범위에 관하여 주한미군사 고문단과 주한미대사관 시종무관을 제외한 모든 미군 즉 유엔군의 구성원으로서의 미군이나 상호방위조약에 의거하여 주둔하고있는 미군이냐를 막론하고 모든 미군에 적용된다는것을 명백히 인정한다는 성명이 있었으며 따라서

0209

16-2

明文 88-6(6)

0210

우리측은 미국측이 제시한 서문에관한 2개의 안중 미국군대가 한국에 주둔하게된 근거가 한미간 상호방위조약에 의해서 뿐만아니라 유엔안전보장 이사회의 결의에도 의거한것이라는 점을 규정한 수정안을 받아드리기로 하고 서문에 완전 합의함.

(3) 관세문제의 토의에있어서 미국측이 제2항에 관하여 2 개의 안을 제시한바 우리측은 원안을 원칙적으로 받아드리되 동 2항의 최종구절중 " other armed forces"의 어구에 대하여는 막연함으로 합의의사록등에 좀더 상세히 규정할것을 제의하자 미국측은 이는 미국군대로부터 병참지원을 받는 "카추사", 유엔군산하 각군을 말하는것이라고 주장하면서 한국측에서 구체적인 안을 제시해주기 바란다고 하였기 우리측은 이를 다음회의에서 제시하기로 하였음.

(4) 관세문제와 관련하여 세관검사 면제에관한 5항 (a)에 있어서 우리측안은 한국에 출입하는 미군대 "units" 에만 세관 검사를면제해 주기로 규정하고 있는데 반하여 미국측안은 "members" 에 대한 면제를 규정하고 있는바 우리측은 본항은 관세의 면제규정이 아니라 관세검사에 관한 규정으로 미국 군인이 개별적으로 한국영역에 출입하는것에 대하여는 세관 검사를함이 좋을것이라고 한데대하여 미국측은 주한미군대가 개별적으로 교대되는점을 강조하면서 미국군대 구성원은 단체로건 개별적으로건 세관검사의 면제대상이 되어야한다고 주장하여 이문제는 다음회의에 다시토의키로 함.

(5) 같은 세관검사 면제에관하여 5항 (b)에서 우리측안은 공용 우편물 "official mail" 을 면제하기로 규정한데 반하여 미국측안은 모든 "우편물" (mail)에 대한면제를 규정하고 있는바 우리측은 미국측안은 이특권의 남용의 방지를 어렵게 할

0211

→

16-3

0212

가능성이 있으니 우리측안을 받아드릴것을 요구하자 미국측은 고려해보겠다고 하였음.

(6) 동 세관검사 면제에관한 5항 (c)에 있어서 우리측안을 "미합중국 정부의 선하증권에 의하여 운송되는 군사화물"을 면제대상으로 규정하는데 대하여 미국측안은 "......미국군대가 승인한 조달기관 및 세출외 자금기관을 포함한 미국군대에 운송된 화물"로 규정한바, 미국측은 과거에는 군사화물을 미국정부의 선하 증권으로서 운송했으나 지금은 수속이 변경되어 대부분 정부선하 증권아닌 다른 선하증권으로 들어오고 있다고 주장하였기 우리측은 동미국측 설명을기록에 남길것을 요구하고 이문제를 다음회의에 다시 토의키로 함.

(7) 관세문제에 있어 한국의 관세법령 위반방지 조항인 미국측안 9 항에관하여 우리측은 체제상 및 론리적으로보아 우리측안 7 항 (e)를 미국측안 9항 (c) 다음에 삽입시키자고 주장한데 대하여 미국측은 고려하겠다고 하였음.

(8) 선박 및 항공기의 출입문제와 항해 및 항공의 통제와 기상 문제에관한 양측의초안을 교환하고 이에대한 양측의 설명이 있었음.

5. 중요합의 사항:

(1) 협정의 서문에관하여 합의함

(2) 관세문제에 관한 미국측안의 6,7,8 항에 합의함

6. 기타사항:

(1) 차기회의 일자 : 1962. 12. 14. 하오 2 시

(2) 차기회의 의제 : 제8차 회의에서 합의에 도달치못한 사항과 차기회의시까지 양측수석대표 간에 합의된 사항

7. 참고자료 : 미국측이 제의한 협정초안 (선박과 항공기의 출입 및 항해용(에) [redacted])

1966.v.7, 에 예고문에 의거 일반문서로 재분류됨

보통문서로 재분류(1966.12.31)

16-4

0213

0214

1. United States and foreign vessels and aircraft operated by, for, or under the control of the United States for official purposes shall be accorded access to any port or airport of Korea free from toll or landing charges. When cargo or passengers not accorded the exemptions of this Agreement are carried on such vessels and aircraft, notification shall be given to the appropriate Korean authorities, and their entry into and departure from Korea shall be according to the laws and regulations of Korea.

2. The vessels and aircraft mentioned in paragraph 1, United States Government-owned vehicles including armor, and members of the United States armed forces, the civilian component, and their dependents shall be accorded access to and movement between facilities and areas in use by the United States armed forces and between such facilities and areas and the ports or airports of Korea. Such access to and movement between facilities and areas by United States military vehicles shall be free from toll and other charges.

3. When the vessels mentioned in paragraph 1 enter Korean ports, appropriate notification shall, under normal conditions, be made to the proper Korean authorities. Such vessels shall have freedom from compulsory pilotage, but if a pilot is taken pilotage shall be paid for at appropriate rates.

0215

16-5

비보88-6

0216

AGREED MINUTES TO ARTICLE

1. "United States and foreign vessels...operated by, for, or under the control of the United States for official purposes" mean United States public vessels and chartered vessels (bare boat charter, voyage charter and time charter). Space charter is not included. Commercial cargo and private passengers are carried by them only in exceptional cases.

2. The Korean ports mentioned herein will ordinarily mean "open ports".

3. An exception from making the "appropriate notification" referred to in paragraph 3 will apply only in unusual cases where such is required for security of the United States armed forces or similar reasons.

4. The laws and regulations of Korea will be applicable except as specifically provided otherwise in this Article.

0217

16-6

미문 88-6

0218

communication deleted (why?)

ARTICLE

1. All civil and military air traffic control shall be developed in close coordination and shall be integrated to the extent necessary for the operation of this Agreement. Procedures, and any subsequent changes thereto, necessary to effect this coordination and integration will be established by arrangement between the appropriate authorities of the two Governments.

2. The United States is authorized to establish, construct and maintain aids to navigation for vessels and aircraft, both visual and electronic as required, throughout the Republic of Korea and in the territorial waters thereof. Such navigation aids shall conform generally to the system in use in Korea. The United States and Korean authorities which have established navigation aids shall duly notify each other of their positions and characteristics and shall give advance notification where practicable before making any changes in them or establishing additional navigation aids.

qualifying phrase

일반문서로 재분류(1966.12.31.)

1966.12.31에 예고문에 의거 일반문서로 재분류됨

0219

16-7

외과문 88-6 (6)

0220

DEFINITIONS ARTICLE

AGREED MINUTE

With regard to Article 1(a), the expression "members of the United States armed forces" does not include personnel on active duty belonging to the United States land, sea or air armed services for whom status has otherwise been provided such as personnel for whom status is provided in the Military Advisory Group Agreement signed on January 26, 1950, and personnel of service attache offices in the Embassy of the United States of America.

for example.

0221

→

18-8

明定 88-5(10)

0222

DEFINITIONS ARTICLE

PROPOSED ADDITIONAL SENTENCE TO SUBPARAGRAPH (b)

For the purposes of the Agreement only, dual nationals, i.e. persons having both United States and Korean nationality, who are brought into the Republic of Korea by the United States shall be considered as United States nationals.

0223

18-9

미원 88-5

0224

DEFINITIONS ARTICLE

AGREED MINUTE

With regard to subparagraph (b), it is recognized that persons possessing certain skills, not readily available from United States or Korean sources, who are nationals of third states may be brought into Korea by the United States armed forces solely for employment by the United States armed forces. Such persons, and third state nationals who are employed by, serving with, or accompanying the United States armed forces in Korea when this agreement becomes effective, shall be considered as members of the civilian component.

0225

18-10

→

미문88-5

0226

A

ARTICLE

1. (a) The United States is granted, under Article IV of the Mutual Defense Treaty, the use of facilities and areas in the Republic of Korea. Agreements as to specific facilities and areas shall be concluded by the two Governments through the Joint Committee provided for in Article   of this Agreement. "Facilities and Areas" include existing furnishings, equipment and fixtures, wherever located, used in the operation of such facilities and areas.

(b) The facilities and areas of which the United States has the use at the effective date of this Agreement shall be considered as facilities and areas agreed upon between the two Governments in accordance with sub-paragraph (a) above.

2. At the request of either Government, the Governments of the United States and the Republic of Korea shall review such arrangements and may agree that such facilities and areas or portions thereof shall be returned to the Republic of Korea or that additional facilities and areas may be provided.

3. The facilities and areas used by the United States shall be returned to the Republic of Korea under such conditions as may be agreed through the Joint Committee whenever they are no longer needed for the purposes of this Agreement and the United States agrees to keep the needs for facilities and areas under continual observation with a view toward such return.

0227

18-11

미북 88-5

0228

4. (a) When facilities and areas are temporarily not being used and the Government of the Republic of Korea is so advised, the Government of the Republic of Korea may make, or permit Korean nationals to make, interim use of such facilities and areas provided that it is agreed between the two Governments through the Joint Committee that such use would not be harmful to the purposes for which the facilities and areas are normally used by the United States armed forces.

(b) With respect to facilities and areas which are to be used by United States armed forces for limited periods of time, the Joint Committee shall specify in the agreements covering such facilities and areas the extent to which the provisions of this Agreement shall apply.

0229

18-12

비문 88-5

(4) [illegible]

0230

B

ARTICLE

1. Within the facilities and areas, the United States may take all the measures necessary for their establishment, operation, safeguarding and control. In an emergency, measures necessary for their safeguarding and control may also be taken in the vicinity thereof. In order to provide access for the United States armed forces to the facilities and areas for their support, safeguarding and control, the Government of the Republic of Korea shall, at the request of the United States armed forces and upon consultation between the two Governments through the Joint Committee, take necessary measures within the scope of applicable laws and regulations over land, territorial waters and airspace adjacent to, or in the vicinities of the facilities and areas. The United States may also take necessary measures for such purposes upon consultation between the two Governments through the Joint Committee.

2. (a) The United States agrees not to take the measures referred to in paragraph 1 in such a manner as to interfere unnecessarily with navigation, aviation, communication, or land travel to or from or within the territories of the Republic of Korea.

(b) All questions relating to telecommunications including radio frequencies for electromagnetic radiating devices, or like matters, shall continue to be resolved expeditiously in the utmost spirit of coordination and cooperation by arrangement between the designated military communications authorities of the two Governments.

(c) The Government of the Republic of Korea shall, within the scope of applicable laws, regulations and agreements, take all reasonable measures to avoid or eliminate interference with electromagnetic radiation sensitive devices, telecommunications devices, or other apparatus required by the United States armed forces.

0231

18-13

미분 88-5

0232

3. Operations in the facilities and areas in use by the United States armed forces shall be carried on with due regard for the public safety.

8-14

0233

미운 88-5

0234

D

ARTICLE

1. It is agreed that the United States will bear for the duration of the Agreement without cost to the Republic of Korea all expenditures incident to the maintenance of the United States armed forces in the Republic of Korea, except those to be borne by the Republic of Korea as provided in paragraph 2.

2. It is agreed that the Republic of Korea will furnish for the duration of this Agreement without cost to the United States and make compensation where appropriate to the owners and suppliers thereof all facilities and areas and rights of way, including facilities and areas jointly used such as those at airfields and ports as provided in Articles II and III. The Government of the Republic of Korea assures the use of such facilities and areas to the United States Government and will hold the United States Government as well as its agencies and employees harmless from any third party claims which may be advanced in connection with such use.

3. [Use of public utilities and services to be inserted later.]

0235

8-15

미분 88-5

0236

ARTICLE

1. The United States is not obliged, when it returns facilities and areas to the Republic of Korea on the expiration of this Agreement or at an earlier date, to restore the facilities and areas to the condition in which they were at the time they became available to the United States armed forces, or to compensate the Republic of Korea in lieu of such restoration.

2. All removable facilities erected or constructed by or on behalf of the United States at its expense and all equipment, materials and supplies brought into or procured in the Republic of Korea by or on behalf of the United States in connection with the construction, development, operation, maintenance, safe-guarding and control of the facilities and areas will remain the property of the United States Government and may be removed from the Republic of Korea.

3. The foregoing provisions shall not apply to any construction which the Government of the United States may undertake under special arrangements with the Government of the Republic of Korea.

보통문서로 재분류(1966. 12. 31.)

1966.12.31. 에 예고문에 의거 일반문서로 재분류됨

0237

8-16

외문 88-5

0238

Agreed Minute to Definition of Terms

(우리측 안)

Members of the United States armed forces referred to in Paragraph (a) exclude the military attaché to the Embassy of the United States of America and those for whom status has been provided for in the Agreement between the Government of the Republic of Korea and the Government of the United States of January 26, 1950 regarding the establishment of a United States Military Advisory Group to the Republic of Korea, as amended by the exchange of Notes between the Foreign Minister of the Republic of Korea and the Charge D'Affairs of the Embassy of the United States dated October 21, 1960.

보통문서로 재분류(1966. 12. 31.)

1966.12.31.에 예고문에 의거 일반문서로 재분류됨

8-17

0239

미국문 88-5(10)

0240

Joint Agreed Summary
D-8
December 4, 1962

SUBJECTS: 1. Preamble
2. Customs and Duties
3. Introduction of Two Articles

PLACE: Capitol Building

DATE: December 4, 1962 (2.30~4.35)

PARTICIPANTS:

Republic of Korea	United States
CHIN P'il-sik	Philip C. Habib
YI Kyung-ho	Brig. General J. D. Lawlor, USA
SHIN Kwan-sup	William J. Ford
Colonel YI Nam-ku, ROKA	Colonel G. G. O'Connor, USA
PAK Kun	Captain R. M. Brownlie, USN
SHIN Chung-sup	Colonel W. A. Solf, USA
~~CHAE Dai-sek~~ LEE Kyung-Hoon	Robert A. Lewis
YI Chang-bum	Lt. Colonel R. E. Miller, USA
KANG Suk-che (Interpreter)	Lt. Colonel W. A. Burt, USA
O Won-yong	Kenneth Campen (Interpreter)

Introduction

1. Mr. CHIN P'il-sik, Korean Chief Negotiator, opened the eighth meeting of the Status of Forces negotiations and suggested beginning with further discussion on the Preamble.

Preamble

2. Mr. Habib opened the substantive discussion by stating that the U.S. side preferred the original preamble tabled by the U.S. at a previous meeting. Mr. Habib noted that under Korean urging a revised version had been tabled by the U.S. and that this revision took into account Korean desire to include reference to relevant UN resolutions.

3. In answer to a Korean question on the applicability of SOFA to U.S. Armed Forces personnel, the U.S. side made this statement: "Within the scope of the matters agreed to, the provisions of the SOF will apply to U.S. Armed Forces and their members, while in the Republic of Korea without regard to whether they are in the Republic of Korea pursuant to the resolutions of the United Nations Security Council or pursuant to the Mutual Defense Treaty. They will not, however, apply to members of the U.S. Armed Forces for whom status is provided in the MAAG Agreement signed on January 26, 1950 and personnel of service attache offices in the Embassy of the United States." He then asked if this statement answered the question raised at the previous meeting by the Korean side regarding the applicability of SOFA to the U.S. Armed Forces. It was also noted that applicability

0241

14. Mr. Habib stated that he wished to make a general statement on the customs article before turning to other business. The U.S. side would like to have an understanding incorporated in the negotiating record or otherwise to the effect that Korean authorities would act promptly in clearing items through customs. Mr. Chin replied by stating that the Korean authorities will cooperate to the extent possible so as not to cause unnecessary delay in clearing items through customs.

15. Captain R. M. Brownlie, USN, introduced two articles dealing with Landing Rights for Vessels and Aircraft and Civil and Military Air Traffic Control. The articles were tabled.

16. Dr. PAK Kun introduced two articles on the same subject. Dr. Pak noted that the Korean draft on Civil and Military Air Traffic Control included meteorological services whereas the U.S. draft did not. Mr. Habib replied that the U.S. side envisaged a separate article on meteorological services. Dr. Pak stated that although included, the Korean side would have no objection to separating meteorological services if the U.S. side found it necessary. Mr. Habib agreed to consider the suggestion. It was agreed to study the drafts further and to continue discussion at a subsequent meeting.

17. It was agreed to hold the next meeting on December 14, 1962 at 1400 hours.

보통문서로 재분류(1966. 12. 31.)

0244

17-12

JOINT SUMMARY RECORD OF THE 8TH SESSION
STATUS FORCES NEGOTIATION

December 4, 1962

I. Time and Place : 2:30 to 4:35 p.m. December 4, 1962
in the Capitol Building

II. Attendants:

ROK Side:

Mr. Chin, Pil Shik	Director Bureau of Political Affairs Ministry of Foreign Affairs
Mr. Yi, Kyung Ho	Director Bureau of Legal Affairs Ministry of Justice
Mr. Shin, Kwan Sup	Director Bureau of Costums Duty Ministry of Finance
Col. Lee, Nam Koo	Chief, Military Affairs Section Ministry of National Defense
Mr. Pak, Kun	Chief, America Section Ministry of Foreign Affairs
Mr. O, Won Yong	Chief, Treaty Section Ministry of Foreign Affairs
Mr. Shin, Chung Sup	2nd Secretary Ministry of Foreign Affairs
Mr. Lee, Kyung Hoon	2nd Secretary Ministry of Foreign Affairs
Mr. Lee, Chang Bum	3rd Secretary Ministry of Foreign Affairs
Mr. Kang, Suk Jae	3rd Secretary Ministry of Foreign Affairs

U.S. Side:

Mr. Philip C. Habib	Counselor of the Embassy for Political Affairs
Brig. Gen. J.D. ~~Miller~~ Lowder	Deputy Chief of Staff 8th Army
Mr. William J. Ford	First Secretary of the Embassy

미주과	안고재	담당	과장	국장	특별보좌관	차관	장관

Col. G.G. O'Connor	Deputy Chief of Staff 8th Army
Capt. R.M. Brownlie	Assistant Chief of Staff USN/K
Col. W. A. Solf	Staff Judge Advocate 8th Army
Mr. Robert A. Lewis	Second Secretary and Consul of the Embassy
Lt. Co. R.E. Miller	Staff Officer, JAG 8th Army
Lt. Col. W.A. Burt	J-5
Kenneth Campen	Interpreter

Introduction

1. Mr. CHIN Pil-sik, Korean Chief Negotiator, opened the eighth meeting of the Status of Forces negotiations and suggested beginning with further discussion on the Preamble.

Preamble

2. Mr. Habib opened the substantive discussion by stating that the U.S. side preferred the original preamble tabled by the U.S. at a previous meeting. Mr. Habib noted that under Korean urging a revised version had been tabled by the U.S. and that this revision took into account Korean desire to include reference to relevant UN resolutions.

3. In answer to a Korean question on the applicability of SOFA to U.S. Armed Forces personnel, the U.S. side made this statement: "Within the scope of the matters agreed to, the provisions of the SOF will apply to U.S. Armed Forces and their members, while in the Republic of

0246

17-2

Korea pursuant to the resolutions of the United Nations Security Council or pursuant to the Mutual Defense Treaty. They will not, however, apply to members of the U.S. Armed Forces for whom status is provided in the MAAG Agreement signed on January 26, 1950 and personnel of service attache offices in the Embassy of the United States." He then asked if this statement answered the question raised at the previous meeting by the Korean side regarding the applicability of SOFA to the U.S. Armed Forces. It was also noted that applicability of SOFA to U.S. personnel was set forth in the definitions article. Mr. Chin replied that the Korean side understood the U.S. position and that the revised preamble was acceptable.

4. It was agreed to accept the revised preamble tabled by the U.S. side at the seventh meeting. Both sides so noted.

Customs and Duties

5. Mr. Chin opened the discussion on customs and duties article by stating that the Korean side wished to work from the original draft on paragraph two tabled by the U.S. side at the sixth meeting rather than from the revised draft of paragraph 2 tabled at the seventh meeting. Mr. Chin stated that he preferred the original draft because it is better divided into categories and more detailed. Mr. Habib agreed to discuss paragraph 2 of the original draft with the understanding that the revised paragraph 2 be kept in mind for subsequent discussion.

6. Mr. Chin stated that the Korean side was ready to accept the original paragraph 2 tabled by the U.S. side but be requested clarification of the phrase in the

0247

final sentence "~~for the~~ use of other armed forces in Korea which receive logistical support from the U.S. Armed Forces." Mr. Habib stated that the phrase referred to Katusas and other armed forces receiving logistical support from the U.S. and that clearly the U.S. should not pay customs duty on materials brought in to support armed forces dependent on U.S. for support. Mr. Chin acknowledged the explanation by stating that the Korean side had no objection to the duty-free entry of such supplies but that the Korean side wished to have spelled out exactly who these forces are. Mr. Habib pointed out that the operative clause "who receive logistical support" defines who these forces are. Mr. Chin stated that the wording is too flexible and that the Korean side desired wording either in the text or in an agreed minute which would specify that such forces were, for example, a "component of the United Command, etc." Mr. Habib requested the Korean side to submit suggested wording at the next meeting, after which it could be considered. Mr. Chin agreed.

7. Mr. Chin asked if the U.S. side had anything to add to previous discussion on paragraph three(b). Mr. Habib replied in the negative.

8. Attention was then turned to paragraph five where the previous meeting had broken off. The Korean side agreed to the introductory sentence of paragraph five of the U.S. draft.

9. On paragraph five(a), Mr. Chin raised the question of specifying "members" of armed forces in the

0248

17-4

U.S. draft as opposed to "units" of armed forces in the Korean draft and the fact that the Japanese SOFA provides for units. Mr. Habib replied that the change to members was made to fit the practicality of the situation in Korea where troops arrive as individuals under orders rather than as units. Mr. Habib stated that the implementation of the Japanese SOFA was actually on the basis of members of the armed forces rather than units. Moreover, a U.S.-ROK SOFA should be based on actual conditions which exist and the wording of other agreements may not be relevant. Mr. Habib stated that if the U.S. side agreed to units, then individual members of the armed forces entering Korean would be subject to customs examination. Mr. Chin then asked if the U.S. side intended exemption to apply to original entry and final departure or did it include departures and entry for leave purposes. Mr. Habib answered by stating that exemption applied to any member of the amred forces entering or leaving Korea under orders. Mr. Chin replied that the Korean position was that members entering Korea as individuals may abuse customs privileges. Mr. Habib stated that there were adequate safeguards in paragraph eight to prevent abuses.

Mr. Habib suggested that the discussion on this paragraph be postponed until the Korean side has studied the matter further. Mr. Chin agreed.

10. On paragraph five(b), Mr. Chin noted that the Korean draft only included official mail and did not include other mail in the U.S. military postal channels as did the U.S. draft. Mr. Habib replied that mail

0249

17-5

for servicemen in Korea without their families was an important morale factor and that the U.S. side wished to provide for the prompt and unimpeded delivery of such mail. Mr. Chin gave assurance that private mail would be quickly cleared through customs and stated that in the Korean view only official mail should be customs exempt. Both sides agreed to discuss the Korean position at a future meeting.

11. Mr. Chin requested an explanation of the differences in the Korean draft and the U.S. draft on paragraph five(c). Mr. Habib replied that the basic difference was that the U.S. draft provided for exemption of military cargo consigned to the U.S. Amred Forces wherease the Korean draft provided for exemption on military cargo shipped on a government bill of lading; the reason for the change in the U.S. draft was simply that a large part of the military cargo no longer was shipped on a government bill of lading as had been done in the past. Mr. Chin noted that in the Korean view there was a difference in cargo consigned to the U.S. Armed Forces and cargo consigned to a non-appropriated fund activity. Mr. Chin stated that the Korean side wished to have cargo consigned to non-appropriated fund activities subject to customs examination and related this request to the desire to limit imports of goods for such activities to reasonable amounts only. It was agreed to discuss this subject further at a later meeting.

12. Mr. Chin noted that paragraphs six, seven and eight in the U.S. draft coincide in substance with the

0250

17-6

Korean draft; therefore, he accepted these three paragraphs of the U.S. draft. Mr. Habib agreed.

13. Mr. Chin requested that paragraph seven(e) of the Korean draft be inserted as paragraph nine(d) of the U.S. draft and that paragraph nine(d) of the U.S. draft be made paragraph nine(e). Mr. Chin agreed to accept paragraph nine of the U.S. draft if this insertion was made. Mr, Habib agreed to consider this proposal and to answer at a subsequent meeting.

14. Mr. Habib stated that he wished to make a general statement on the customs article before turning to other business. The U.S. side would like to have an understanding incorporated in the negotiating record or otherwise to the effect that Korean authorities would act promptly in clearing items through customs. Mr. Chin replied by stating that the Korean authorities will cooperate to the extent possible so as not to cause unnecessary delay in clearing items through customs.

15. Captain R.M. Brownlie, USN, introduced two articles dealing with Landing Rights for Vessels and Aircraft and Civil and Military Air Traffic Control. The articles were tabled.

16. Dr. PAK Kun introduced two articles on the same subject. Dr. Pak noted that the Korean draft on Civil and Military Air Traffic Control included meteorological services whereas the U.S. draft did not. Mr. Habib replied that the U.S. side envisaged a separate article on meteorological services. Dr. Pak stated that although included, the Korean side would have no objection to

0251

17-9

separating meteorlogical services if the U.S. side found it necessary. Mr. Habib agreed to consider the suggestion. It was agreed to study the drafts further and to continue discussion at a subsequent meeting.

17. It was agreed to hold the next meeting on December 14, 1962 at 1400 hours.

보통문서로 재분류(1966. 12. 31.)

0252

17-8

6. 제9차 회의, 12.14

0253

기 안 용 지

자 체 통 제		기안처	미주과 이경훈	전화번호	근거서류접수일자
과 장	수석대표	차관보	차관	장관	
관계관 서 명	조약과장 기획조정관				
기 안 년월일	1962. 12. 13	시 행 년월일		보존 년한	정 서 기 장
분 류 기 호		전 체 통 제		종결	
경 유 수 신 참 조	건 의			발 신	
제 목	제9차 주둔군 지위협정 체결 교섭회의에 임할 우리측 태도				

12. 14. 개최될 제9차 주둔군 지위 협정 체결 한미간 교섭 회의에서는 용어의 정의, 합동위원회, 선박및 항공기의 출입과 항해통제문제를 토의하고 시설및 토지에관 양국측 초안을 교환할 예정이온바 이에 관련하여 우리측 교섭실무자는 12. 13일 회합을 갖고 제8차회의에서 취할 우리측 태도를 별첨과 같이 결정하였아오니 재가하여 주시기바랍니다.

유첨: 제9차 주둔군 지위 협정 체결 교섭회의에 임할 우리측 태도.

일반문서로 재분류(1966.12.31)

19 에 예고문에 의거 일반문서로 재분류됨

39-1

승인양식 1-1-3 (1112-040-016-018) (190mm×260mm16절지)

0254

I. 용어의 정의

1. 미국군대 구성원의 정의에관하여 미국측은 "따로 신분이 규정된 군대구성원을 제외한다" 는 일반적 예외규정을 두도록 제시한데 대하여 우리측은 다음과같은 열거적 예외 규정으로 ~~대~~하도록 한다. "~~except for~~ the military ~~service~~ attache to the Embassy of the United States of America and those for whom status has been provided for in the Agreement between the Government of the Republic of Korea and the Government of the United States of January 26, 1950, as amended by the exchange of Notes

Members of the U.S. armed forces ~~referred to~~ in Paragraph a ~~of~~ exclude
합의의사록에 규정
regarding the establishment of a U.S. Military Advisory Group to R.O.K.
between the Foreign Minister of the R.O.K. and the Charge D'Affaires of the Embassy of the United States dated October 21, 1960,

2. 미국측은 군소의 정의에 있어서 국적을 막론하고 미군의 고용된 민간인을 군속으로 규정하자고 하는데 대하여 우리측은 미국국적을 가진 민간인만을 군속의 범주에 포함시키도록 계속 주장한다.

3. 미국측은 가족의 범주안에 군인에게 생계의 반이상을 의존 하고있는 기타 친척도 포함시키도록 제의한데대하여 우리는 이를 수락하여 준다.

II. 선박 및 항공기의 출입문제

1. 미국소유 및 미국이 사용하는 외국선박 및 항공기의 출입에 관한 규정에 있어서 미국측 초안은 형식적으로나 실질적으로나 우리측 초안과 동일하다. 단지 입국에대한 통고 의무에 관한 미국측 초안 제 3 항에서 미국측은 " under normal conditions" 라는 단서를 붙이고 있어 미국측이 통고 의무 회피의 구실로 삼지않을가 하는 우려도있으나 미국측이 제의한 Agreed Minutes 에서 통고의무가 배제되는 경우에관한 상세한 규정을두고 있으므로 실질적인 효과에는 큰 영향이 없을것으로 생각됨.

9次

39-2

0255

2. 이상으로보아 본 조항에관하여는 다음과같은 입장을 취한다

(1) 미국측안 (1) 및 (2)항을 수락한다.

(2) 미국측안 (3) 항에대한 설명을 요구한후 이를 수락한다.

(3) 본조항에 대한 미국측 Agreed minutes 도 수락한다.

III. 항공교통 관제문제

1. 본 문제에 관하여도 우리측초안과 미국측 초안간에 실질적인 큰 차이는 없다.

2. 다만 아래와같이 몇가지 차이점이 있으나 이에대하여 다음과 같은 입장을 취한다.

(1) 모든 항공교통 통제에대한 한미간의 상호협조 의무에 관한 상방의초안 (1)항에 있어서 우리측 초안에서는 통신체제 (communication system) 도 모든 항공교통 통제와같이 한미간에 상호협조의무를 갖게 하였는데 미국측 초안에는 이것이 삭제되어 있음. 이문제에 대하여는 미국측에 우선 삭제에대한 이유를 문의하고 한미간의 상호 안전보장을 위하여 삽입하도록 즉 우리측 초안을 미국측이 받아드리도록 요청할것임.

(2) 제 2 항에 있어서 미측은 한국전역에 걸쳐 항공 및 항해 보조시설의 설치를 명백히 허용하기를 요구하고 있고 또한 이들 보조시설은 한국에 기존하는 체제와 합치함에 있어서 일반적으로만 (generally)합치하여야 한다고 규정하기를 원하고 있고 또한 이러한 시설의 설치에관한 사전통고의 의무에 있어서는 가능한 경우에 (where practicable) 사전통고를 하도록 규정할것을 원하고 있음. 우리측 초안과 차이가있음으로 우리측 초안대로 수락할것을 주장한다.

29-3

0256

I 토지, 시설 사용문제

1. 토지, 시설의 사용권허여 문제는 한미 상호 방위조약 제 4 조에 의하여 미군의 주둔을 인정하고 있는 이상 미군의 주둔 목적과 그 공적 사명을 수행하는데 불가분의 관계에 있는것이다. 따라서 본 조항에서는 미국에대한 토지 시설사용권 허여에 관한 일반적 규정을두었고 구체적인 사용문제에 관하여는 합동위원회를 통하여 양국이 합의 결정하도록 하였다. 또한 현재 미군이 이미 사용하고 있는 토지 및 시설은 본 협정에 의하여 이미 사용된것으로 간주한다고 규정함으로써 본 협정 체결로인하여 토지 시설의 사용 현상에 급격한 변동을 가져오는 일이 없도록 하였다. 단지 현재 미군이 사용중인 토지 시설에관한 정확한 실태를 파악하기 위하여 합동위원회를 통하여 양국정부가 조사 결정하도록 규정하였다. (우리초안 1, 2, 3 항)

2. 토지 시설의 사용에 따르는 보상문제와이들의 유지비에 관한 책임은 미국측이 부담하도록 규정하였다. 기지 또는 현재까지의 제협정의 일반적인 경향이므로 별문제가 없을 없을것이나 단지 보상문제에 관하여는 민간인 재산에대하여 사용불능으로 인한 손실에대한 적절한 보상을 지불한다는 원칙을 규정하고, 세부사항은 합동위원회에서 검토하게 하였다. (4, 5항)

3. 토지 시설의 반환에 관하여는 주둔이 종결하는 경우 전부 반환하여야 함은 두말할 필요도 없는것이나 본 조항에서는 주둔중에 있어서도 불필요한 토지시설의 반환에 관하여 규정한것이다. 구체적인 토지시설의 사용에 관한 양국간의 약정을 일방 당사국의 요구가있는 경우에는 이를 수시로

39-4

0257

검토할수 있게 규정함으로써 사용중인 토지 시설의 반환
이나 또는 추가적인 제공을 용이하게 하려는데있다.
또한 주둔군에 대한 토지 시설의 제공은 영토의 할양이나
그 자체의 소유권의 이전과는 성질이 상이함으로 협정의 목적
수행에 있어서 불필요하게 된 부분은 반드시 그리고 즉시
반환하도록 하였으며 이를 위하여 양국정부가 토지 시설의
반환 필요성 여부를 항상 검토할것을 규정하였다.
그러나 미국측의 토지, 시설의 사용이 제공국인 우리정부의
일방적인 결정에 의하여 지장을 받지않도록 하기위하여
토지 시설에 대한 필요성 여부는 사용국인 미국측에서 계속
검토하도록 하고, 동시에 불필요한 사용을 가능한 한 제한하기
위하여 그러한 계속적 검토의 의무를 사용국측에 부과하고있다.
(6, 7 항)

4. 미국측의 사용을위하여 제공한 토지 시설이라 하드래도
미국측이 일시적으로 사용하지 않는 토지시설은 쌍방의 합의
하는바에 따라 본 협정의 목적에 배치되지 않는 범위내에서
우리측도 사용할수 있도록 하는 규정을 두었다. 미국측이
일시적인 불사용분에 대하여도 그 경제적인 가치등을 고려하여
우리측이 일시적으로 사용할수 있도록 함으로써 불필요한
유휴지가 발행하는 일이 없도록 하였다. 그리고 이와
동시에 본협정에 의하여 미국측에 제공된 토지시설 이외
군사 작전운련 등으로 미국측이 일정기간 동안만 일시
사용하는 토지 시설에 대하여도 합동위원회를 통하여 본
협정의 규정을 부분적으로 적용할수 있도록 규정하였다.
(8, 9 항)

37-5

0258

5. 미군이 사용하는 토지 및 시설에 있어서의 관리 및 기타 조치에 관하여는 토지 시설의 내외를 구분하여 그내에 있어서는 미국측이 설치. 운영, 경비, 통제등에 관한 제 조치를 취할수있게 규정하였다. 이는 미국측이 사용하는 토지 시설의 사용 허가에 본질적으로 수반되는 조치라고 인정되기 때문이다. 토지 시설의 주위에 있어서는 원칙적으로 한국측이 미국측의 요청에 의하여 적절한 조치를 취할수 있도록하였고, 양국간의 합의에 의하는 경우에는 미국측도 역시 필요한 조치를 취할수 있도록 하였다. 그러나 미국측에 부여된 이러한 권한이 한국내에서의 항해, 항공, 통신 또는 육상 교통을 불필요하게 방해하지 아니하도록 하는 제한을 가하고 미국측의 전파발사를 위한 주파수, 전력 등에관한 문제는 한미 쌍방의 합의에 의하여 결정하도록 규정하였다. 또한 미국측의 전기 권한 행사와 토지, 시설의 운영 한국의 공공안전을 침해하지 아니하도록 규정하였다. 그러나 미국측이 토지. 시설내에서 취할수있는 필요한 조치의 구체적인 내용에 관하여는 미일 협정의 합의의사록과 같이 별도 합의의사록에서 규정하였다. (10,11,12항 및 합의의사록 4항)

6. 사용한 토지 및 시설의 반환시에 있어서의 원상회복문제에 관하여는 원상보구라는 것이 실질적으로 불가능한 경우가 많으며 기술적으로 곤란한 사태가 허다함으로 우리 초안에서는 미군이 사용하던 토지 시설의 반환에 있어서는 미국측의 원상 회복 의무를 면제하였고, 이에대하여 한국측도 반환되는 토지 및 시설내에 대한 개선 또는 그안에 존재하는 건물, 축조물 또는 기타보급품에 대하여 미국측에 보상할 의무가 없음을 규정하였다.

0259

단지 미군이 사용한 사유재산의 반환시에 있어서 전기한 바와같이 원상회복 의무는 원칙적으로 없으나 미군의 사용 기간중 중대한 변개를 가함으로서 원 소유자에 의한 사용 가치가 극도로 감소된것에 대하여는 우리 정부의 요구에의하여 미굽정부가 원상회복 또는 이에 대신하는 보상을 행함에 있어서 동정적인 고려를하도록 규정하였다. (13. 14 항)

7. 토지 시설의 보상문제

현재 미국군대가 사용하고 있는 토지, 시설은 6.25 동란 발발의 긴급 사태하에서 1950년 7월 26일에 발해진 대통령 긴급명령인 "징발에 관한 특별조치령" 에 의하여 미국군대에 무상으로 제공되어 왔던것이다. 동 조치는 제 14 조에서 징발목적물 또는 피징용자에 대하여는 따로 대통령령이 정하는 바에 의하여 원상회복 또는 보상을 행한다고 규정하고 있으나 미군에 대하여 제공한 토지 시설의 사용붙음으로 인한 손실은 상당한 액수에 달하고 있으며 정부의 빈약한 재정 형편으로서 이 보상문제를 단독으로 해결한다는 것은 거의 불가능한 실정이므로 특히 경제적인 면에서 미군이 사용하는 토지 및 시설에 대한 보상문제의 해결은 가장 시급을 요하는 중요한 과제의 하나이며 이 보상금을 사용자인 미국측이 어느 정도 부담하도록 한다는것이 우리초안의 정신이다.

1. 미국측의 일반적인 태도

보상문제의 해결에 있어서 정부는 주둔군 지위협정의 조속한 체결을 촉구함으로서 이문제 해결을 시도하여 왔으며 보상문제에 관한 미국측의 일관된 태도는 보상문제의 해결은 한국정부의 단독적인 책임하에서 처리하도록 하라는 것이며 우리측의 보상요청에 대하여 시종 소극적이며 반대적 태도를 견지하여 왔다.

0260

2. 우리측의 보상요청 방법

양국간에 근본적인 견해차이를 시현하고 있는 보상 문제에 관하여 우리정부가 제기할수 있는 가능한 보상 요청 방법으로서는 아래와같이 구분하여 검토할수 있다.

(1) 시기적인 구분

(가) 6.25 동란이후 미군이 사용한 재산전반에 대한 보상요구

(나) 1954년 11월 17일 한미상호 방위조약의 효력발생 이후의 사용분에 대한 보상요구

(다) 행정협정 체결이후의 사용분에 대하여 보상요구

(2) 보상의 성질에 의한 구분

(가) 미군에 제공하기 위한 재산 취득에 소요된 금액에대한 보상요구 (이는 실제로 극히 소액에 지나지않음)

(나) 미군에게 제공한 재산의 사용 불능으로 인한 손실에대한 보상 (이는 상당한 액수로 책정될수도 있을 것임)

(3) 재산의 성질에 의한 구분

(가) 국.공 사유재산을 구분하지 않고 미군이 사용한 재산전반에 대한 보상요구

(나) 사유재산에 대하여서만 보상요구

(4) 재산의 위치상의 구분

(가) 소위 작전지대와 비작전지역을 구별하여 후자에 속하는 재산에 대하여만 보상요구

(나) 이를 구별하지 않고 일괄적으로 보상을요구

(5) 전기한 4가지 방법의 결합 또는 혼용

9-8 0261

3. 우리정부의 입장 (안)

가. 보상의 원칙

6.25 동란을 통하여 공산군의 불법적인 무력침략을 격퇴하는데 있어서 미국이 입은 정신적인 물질적인 피해와 부담을 고려하고 우리나라의 자유와 독립을 수호하기 위한 미군의 주한목적을 감안하여 다음과같은 보상범위 지침내에서 보상금을 요구한다.

나. 보상의 범위

위에서 열거한 제방법중에서 현실적이고 합리적이라고 생각되는 보상요구의 방법으로서 다음과같은 방법을 택할수 있을것임.

(1) 시기적 구분에 있어서는 휴전성립 이전의 전투기에 있어서 미군이 사용한 재산에대한 보상요구는 보상액산출의 근거가 희박하며 또한 한미간 상호 방위조약 체결이전에 대해서는 미군측이 마이어 협정을 들고 유엔군의 일원으로서 정치도의적인 견지에서 불합리한 점이 있으므로 이를 제외하고 상호방위조약 발효이후의 사용분에 대한 보상만을 요구한다.

(2) 보상의 성질에 의한 구분에 있어서는 미군에게 제공한 재산의 사용불능으로 인한 손실에대한 보상을 요구한다.

(3) 재산의성질에 따른 구분에 있어서는 국유재산에대하여는 보상요구를 포기하고 사유재산에 대하여서만 보상을 요구한다.

√ (4) 재산위치에 의한 구분에 있어서는 이를 우리측에서 먼저 제기할 필요는없다.

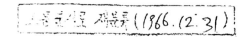

일반문서로 재분류(1966.12.31)

1966.12.31.에 예고문에 의거 일반문서로 재분류됨

0262

1962. 12. 14.
韓側이 提議.

Article (Facilities and Areas)

1. The Government of the Republic of Korea grants, under Article IV of the Mutual Defense Treaty between the Republic of Korea and the United States of America, to the United States the use of the facilities and areas in the Republic of Korea as provided for in this Agreement. Arrangements as to the specific facilities and areas shall be made by the two Governments through the Joint Committee.

2. Facilities and areas referred to in this Agreement include existing furnishings, equipment and fixtures necessary to the operation of such facilities and areas.

3. The facilities and areas of which the United States has the use at the time of entry into force of this Agreement, shall be regarded, for the purpose of this Agreement, as facilities and areas granted to the United States under this Agreement. For the purpose of this paragraph, all facilities and areas of which the United States has the use at the time

0263

of entry into force of this Agreement shall be surveyed and determined by the two Governments through the Joint Committee.

4. With regard to the private property used as facilities and areas by the United States armed forces under this Agreement, the United States shall make reasonable compensation through the Government of the Republic of Korea to the owners of such facilities and areas with a view to alleviating their losses. Detailed arrangements, including the amounts of compensation, shall be made between the two Governments through the Joint Committee.

5. The Governments of the United States bears without cost to the Republic of Korea all expenditures incident to the maintenance of the facilities and areas granted under this Agreement.

6. At the request of either Government, the Government of the Republic of Korea and the Government of the United States shall review such arrangements referred to in paragraph 1 and may agree that such

0264

facilities and areas shall be returned to the Republic of Korea or that additional facilities and areas may be provided.

7. The facilities and areas used by the United States shall be promptly returned to the Government of the Republic of Korea whenever they are no longer needed for the purpose of this Agreement, and the Government of the United States agrees to keep the needs for facilities and areas under continual observation with a view toward such return.

8. When facilities and areas are temporarily not being used by the United States, interim use by the authorities of the Republic of Korea or nationals may be arranged through the Joint Committee.

9. With respect to facilities and areas which are to be used by the United States for limited period of time, the Joint Committee shall specify in the agreements covering such facilities and areas the extent to which the provisions of this Agreement shall apply.

0265

10. Within the facilities and areas, the Government of the United States may take all the measures necessary for their establishment, operation, safeguarding and control. In order to provide access for the United States forces to the facilities and areas for their support, safeguarding and control, the Government of the Republic of Korea shall, at the request of the Government of the United States and upon consultation between the two Governments through the Joint Committee, take necessary measures within the scope of applicable laws and regulations over land, territorial waters and airspace adjacent to, or in the vicinities of the facilities and areas. The Government of the United States may also take necessary measures for such purposes upon consultation between the two Governments through the Joint Committee.

11. The Government of the United States agrees not to take the measures referred to in paragraph 1 in such a manner as to interfere unnecessarily with

0266

navigation, aviation, communication, or land travel to or from or within the territories of the Republic of Korea. All questions relating to frequencies, power and like matters used by apparatus employed by the Government of the United States designed to emit electric radiation shall be settled by arrangement between the appropriate authorities of the two Governments.

12. Operations in the facilities and areas in use by the Government of the United States shall be carried on with due regard to the public safety.

13. The Government of the United States is not obliged, when it returns facilities and areas to the Government of the Republic of Korea on the expiration of this Agreement or at an earlier date, to restore the facilities and areas to the conditions in which they were at the time they became available to the United States, or to compensate the Government of the Republic of Korea in lieu of such restoration.

0267

However, in case of private property extremely demolished by the use of the United States, the Government of the United States shall, upon the request of the Government of the Republic of Korea, pay due consideration to its restoration or compensation in lieu thereof.

14. The Government of the Republic of Korea is not obliged to make any compensation to the Government of the the United States for any improvements made in the facilities and areas or for the buildings, structures, supply or any other materials left thereon on the expiration of this Agreement or the earlier return of the facilities and areas.

0268

Agreed Minutes (Claims Article)

1. The amount to be paid to each claimant, under the provisions of paragraph 5(b) of this Article, except the cases being determined by adjudication, shall be communicated to the authorities of the United States before the payment is made.

In case any reply in favour of the decision is received from the U.S. side, or in default of a reply within one month of receipt of the communication envisaged above, the amount decided by the Korean Claims Authorities shall be regarded as agreed upon between the both Governments.

If, however, the authorities of the United States disagree to the amount decided by the Korean Claims Authorities and reply to this effect within the one-month period, the Korean Claims Authorities shall re-examine the case concerned. The amount decided as a result of the re-examination shall be final and conclusive. The Korean Claims Authorities shall notify the authorities of the United States of the result of re-examination as early as practicable.

The amount agreed upon between the both Governments or decided through the re-examination shall be paid to the claimant concerned without delay.

0269

2. The provisions of paragraph 5 of this Article will become effective after six months from the date of entry into force of this Agreement. Until such time the United States agrees to pay just and reasonable compensation in settlement of civil claims (other than contractual claims) arising out of acts or omissions of members of the United States armed forces done in the performance of official duty or out of any other act, omission or occurrence for which the United States armed forces are legally responsible. In making such payments United States authorities would exercise the authority provided under United States laws relating to Foreign Claims and regulations issued thereunder. In settling claims which are described as arising "..... out of any act, omission or occurrence for which the United States armed forces are legally responsible", United States authorities will take into consideration local law and practice.

0270

3. For the purpose of paragraph 5 of this Article, members of the Korean Augmentation to the United States Army (KATUSA) and members of the Korean Service Corps (KSC) shall be considered respectively as members and employees of the United States armed forces.

0271

COPY

EXCHANGE OF NOTES CONSTITUTING AN AGREEMENT BETWEEN THE REPUBLIC OF KOREA AND THE UNITED STATES OF AMERICA CONCERNING JURISDICTION OVER THE UNITED STATES FORCES IN KOREA

Entered into force July 12,1950

NOTE BY THE AMERICAN EMBASSY TO THE KOREAN MINISTRY OF FOREIGN AFFAIRS

American Embassy
Taejon, Korea
July 12, 1950

The American Embassy presents its compliments to the Ministry of Foreign Affairs of the Republic of Korea and has the honor to state that in the absence of a formal agreement defining and setting forth the respective rights, duties and jurisdictional limitations of the military forces of the United States(excepting the United States Military Advisory Group to Korea, which is covered by the agreement signed in Seoul on January 26, 1950) and the Government of the Republic of Korea, it is proposed that exclusive jurisdiction over members of the United States Military Establishment in Korea will be exercised by courtmartial of the United States of America.

It is further proposed that arrests of Korean nationals will be made by the United States forces only in the event Korean nationals are detected in the commission of offences against the United States forces or its members. In the event that arrests of Korean nationals ar made under the circumstances set forth above, such persons will be delivered to the civil authorities of the Republic of Korea as speedily as practicable.

The Ministry of Foreign Affairs and the Government of the Republicof Korea will understand that in view of prevailing conditions, such as the infiltrations of north Koreans into the territory of the Republic, United States forces cannot be submitted, or instructed to be submitted, to the custody of any but United States forces. Unless required, owing to the non-existence of local courts,

0272

courts of the United States forces will not try nationals of the Republic of Korea.

The American Embassy would be grateful if the Ministry of Foreign Affairs would confirm, in behalf of the Government of the Republicoof Korea, the above-stated requirements regarding the status of the military forces of the United States within Korea.

NOTE BY THE KOREAN MINISTRY OF FOREIGN AFFAIRS TO THE AMERICAN EMBASSY

REPUBLIC OF KOREA
MINISTRY OF FOREIGN AFFAIRS

Taejon, July 12,1950

The Ministry of Foreign Affairs of the Republic of Korea presents its compliments to the America Embassy and acknowledges the receipt of the Embassy's note of July 12, 1950, at Taejon.

The Minis try has the honour to inform the American Embassy that the Government of the Republic of Korea is glad to accept the propositions set forth in the Embassy's note of July 12, 1950,that:

(1) The United States court-martial may exercise exclusive jurisdiction over the members of the United States Military Establishment in Korea;

(2) In the event that arrests of Korean nationals by the United States forces are made necessary when the former are known to have committed offenses against the United States forces or its members, such persons will be delivered to the civil authorities of the Republic of Korea as speedily as practicable; and

(3) The Ministry of Foreign Affairs understands that in view of the prevailing conditions of warfare, the United States forces cannot be submitted to any but United States forces; and that courts of the United States forces will not try nationals of the Republic of Korea unless requested owing to the nonexistence of local courts.

0273

1962.12.14
美國側提案

DEFINITIONS ARTICLE

AGREED MINUTE

delete (美側 同意)

With regard to subparagraph (b), it is recognized that persons possessing certain skills, not readily available from United States or Korean sources, who are nationals of third states may be brought into Korea by the United States armed forces solely for employment by the United States armed forces. Such persons, and third state nationals who are employed by, serving with, or accompanying the United States armed forces in Korea when this agreement becomes effective, shall be considered as members of the civilian component.

Confidential
Confidential
Confidential
Confidential
Confidential
Confidential
Confidential
Confidential

0274

1962.12.14
美□側提案

DEFINITIONS ARTICLE

PROPOSED ADDITIONAL SENTENCE TO SUBPARAGRAPH (b)

For the purposes of the Agreement only, dual nationals, i.e. persons having both United States and Korean nationality, who are brought into the Republic of Korea by the United States shall be considered as United States nationals.

0275

1962.12.14
美國側提案

DEFINITIONS ARTICLE

AGREED MINUTE

With regard to Article 1(a), the expression "members of the United States armed forces" does not include personnel on active duty belonging to the United States land, sea or air armed services (for whom status has otherwise been provided) such as personnel for whom status is provided in the Military Advisory Group Agreement signed on January 26, 1950, and personnel of service attache offices in the Embassy of the United States of America.

Retain, "Agreed Minute".

0276

1962.12.14
美側提案 A

ARTICLE

1. (a) The United States is granted, under Article IV of the Mutual Defense Treaty, the use of facilities and areas in the Republic of Korea. Agreements as to specific facilities and areas shall be concluded by the two Governments through the Joint Committee provided for in Article of this Agreement. "Facilities and Areas" include existing furnishings, equipment and fixtures, wherever located, used in the operation of such facilities and areas.

(b) The facilities and areas of which the United States has the use at the effective date of this Agreement shall be considered as facilities and areas agreed upon between the two Governments in accordance with sub-paragraph (a) above.

2. At the request of either Government, the Governments of the United States and the Republic of Korea shall review such arrangements (agreement) and may agree that such facilities and areas or portions thereof shall be returned to the Republic of Korea or that additional facilities and areas may be provided.

3. The facilities and areas used by the United States shall be (promptly) returned to the Republic of Korea under such conditions as may be agreed through the Joint Committee whenever they are no longer needed for the purposes of this Agreement and the United States agrees to keep the needs for facilities and areas under continual observation with a view toward such return.

0277

4. (a) When facilities and areas are temporarily not being used and the Government of the Republic of Korea is so advised, the Government of the Republic of Korea may make, or permit Korean nationals to make, interim use of such facilities and areas provided that it is agreed between the two Governments through the Joint Committee that such use would not be harmful to the purposes for which the facilities and areas are normally used by the United States armed forces.

(b) With respect to facilities and areas which are to be used by United States armed forces for limited periods of time, the Joint Committee shall specify in the agreements covering such facilities and areas the extent to which the provisions of this Agreement shall apply.

0278

1962. 12. 14.
美國側提案 B

ARTICLE B

1. Within the facilities and areas, the United States may take all the measures necessary for their establishment, operation, safeguarding and control. In an emergency, measures necessary for their safeguarding and control may also be taken in the vicinity thereof. In order to provide access for the United States armed forces to the facilities and areas for their support, safeguarding and control, the Government of the Republic of Korea shall, at the request of the United States armed forces and upon consultation between the two Governments through the Joint Committee, take necessary measures within the scope of applicable laws and regulations over land, territorial waters and airspace adjacent to, or in the vicinities of the facilities and areas. The United States may also take necessary measures for such purposes upon consultation between the two Governments through the Joint Committee. (government of the)

agreed

2. (a) The United States agrees not to take the measures referred to in paragraph 1 in such a manner as to interfere unnecessarily with navigation, aviation, communication, or land travel to or from or within the territories of the Republic of Korea.

agreed

(b) All questions relating to telecommunications including radio frequencies for electromagnetic radiating devices, or like matters, shall continue to be resolved expeditiously in the utmost spirit of coordination and cooperation by arrangement between the designated military communications authorities of the two Governments. agreed on deletion

agreed

(c) The Government of the Republic of Korea shall, within the scope of applicable laws, regulations and agreements, take all reasonable measures to avoid or eliminate interference with electromagnetic radiation sensitive devices, telecommunications devices, or other apparatus required by the United States armed forces.

0279

3. Operations in the facilities and areas in use by the United States armed forces shall be carried on with due regard for the public safety.

0280

1962. 12. 14. C
美國側提案

ARTICLE C

1. The United States is not obliged, when it returns facilities and areas to the Republic of Korea on the expiration of this Agreement or at an earlier date, to restore the facilities and areas to the condition in which they were at the time they became available to the United States armed forces, or to compensate the Republic of Korea in lieu of such restoration.

2. All removable facilities erected or constructed by or on behalf of the United States at its expense and all equipment, materials and supplies brought into or procured in the Republic of Korea by or on behalf of the United States in connection with the construction, development, operation, maintenance, safeguarding and control of the facilities and areas will remain ~~the property~~ of the United ~~States Government~~ and may be removed from the Republic of Korea.

3. The foregoing provisions shall not apply to any construction which the Government of the United States may undertake under special arrangements with the Government of the Republic of Korea.

0281

1962.12.14 D.
美國側提案

ARTICLE

1. It is agreed that the United States will bear for the duration of the Agreement without cost to the Republic of Korea all expenditures incident to the maintenance of the United States armed forces in the Republic of Korea, except those to be borne by the Republic of Korea as provided in paragraph 2.

2. It is agreed that the Republic of Korea will furnish for the duration of this Agreement without cost to the United States and make compensation where appropriate to the owners and suppliers thereof all facilities and areas and rights of way, including facilities and areas jointly used such as those at airfields and ports as provided in Articles II and III. The Government of the Republic of Korea assures the use of such facilities and areas to the United States Government and will hold the United States Government as well as its agencies and employees harmless from any third party claims which may be advanced in connection with such use.

3. [Use of public utilities and services to be inserted later.]

0282

AREAS AND FACILITIES ARTICLE

PROPOSED ADDITIONAL PARAGRAPH TO

AREAS AND FACILITIES ARTICLE PERTAINING

TO RETURN OF FACILITIES AND AREAS

The Republic of Korea is not obligated to compensate the United States for improvements made in United States facilities and areas or for the buildings or structures remaining thereon upon the return of the facilities and areas.

0283

UTILITIES AND SERVICES

Proposed new third and fourth sentences, Paragraph 3 (a)

Article "D"

The use of utilities and services as provided herein shall not prejudice the right of the United States to operate military transportation, communication, power and such other utilities and services deemed necessary for the operations of the United States armed forces. This right shall not be exercised in a manner inconsistent with the operation by the Government of the Republic of Korea of its utilities and services.

~~0283~~
0284

The Republic of Korea will take such actions as deems may be necessary, with the cooperation of the United States where appropriate, to ensure the adequate security and protection of the United States Armed Forces, the members thereof, the civilian component, the persons present in the Republic of Korea pursuant to Article XVIII, their dependents and their property, and the installations, equipment, property, records and official information of the United States, and, consistent with Article XXII, to ensure punish the punishment of offenders under the applicable laws of the Republic of Korea.

0285

Article XVII

Re paragraph 1(a) and paragraph 2(a):

The scope of persons subject to the military laws of the United States shall be communicated, through the Joint Committee, to the Government of Japan by the Government of the United States.

Re paragraph 2(c):

Both Governments shall inform each other of the details of all the security offenses mentioned in this subparagraph and the provisions governing such offenses in the existing laws of their respective countries.

Re paragraph 3(a) (ii):

Where a member of the United States armed forces or the civilian component is charged with an offense, a certificate issued by or on behalf of his commanding officer stating that the alleged offense, if committed by him, arose out of an act or omission done in the performance of official duty, shall, in any judicial proceedings, be sufficient evidence of the fact unless the contrary is proved.

The above statement shall not be interpreted to prejudice in any way Article 318 of the Japanese Code of Criminal Procedure.

0286

Re paragraph 3(c):

1. Mutual procedures relating to waivers of the primary right to exercise jurisdiction shall be determined by the Joint Committee.

2. Trials of cases in which the Japanese authorities have waived the primary right to exercise jurisdcition, and trials of cases involving offenses described in paragraph 3(a) (ii) committed against the State or nationals of Japan shall be held promptly in Japan within a reasonable distance from the places where the offenses are alleged to have taken place unless other arrangements are mutually agreed upon. Representatives of the Japanese authorities may be present at such trials.

Re paragraph 4:

Dual nationals, Japanese and United States, who are subject to the military law of the United States and are brought to Japan by the United States shall not be considered as nationals of Japan, but shall be considered as United States nationals for the purposes of this paragraph.

Re paragraph 5:

1. In case the Japanese authorities have arrested an offender who is a member of the United States armed forces, the civilian component, or a dependent subject to the military law of the United States with respect to a case over which Japan has the

0287

primary right to exercise jurisdiction, the Japanese authorities will, unless they deem that there is adequate cause and necessity to retain such offender, release him to the custody of the United States military authorities provided that he shall, on request, be made available to the Japanese authorities, if such be the condition of his release. The United States authorities shall, on request, transfer his custody to the Japanese authorities at the time he is indicted by the latter.

2. The United States military authorities shall promptly notify the Japanese authorities of the arrest of any member of the United States armed forces, the civilian component or a dependent in any case in which Japan has the primary right to exercise jurisdiction.

Re paragraph 9:

1. The rights enumerated in items (a) through (e) of this paragraph are guaranteed to all persons on trial in Japanese courts by the provisions of the Japanese Constitution. In addition to these rights, a member of the United States armed forces, the civilian component or a dependent who is prosecuted under the jurisdiction of Japan shall have such other rights as are guaranteed under the laws of Japan to all persons on trial in Japanese courts. Such additional rights include the following which are guaranteed under the Japanese Constitution:

0288

(a) He shall not be arrested or detained without being at once informed of the charge against him or without the immediate privilege of counsel; nor shall he be detained without adequate cause; and upon demand of any person, such cause must be immediately shown in open court in his presence and the presence of his counsel;

(b) He shall enjoy the right to a public trial by an impartial tribunal;

(c) He shall not be compelled to testify against himself;

(d) He shall be permitted full opportunity to examine all witnesses;

(e) No cruel punishments shall be imposed upon him.

2. The United States authorities shall have the right upon request to have access at any time to members of the United States armed forces, the civilian component, or their dependents who are confined or detained under Japanese authority.

3. Nothing in the provisions of paragraph 9(g) concerning the presence of a representative of the United States Government at the trial of a member of the United States armed forces, the civilian component or a dependent prosecuted under the jurisdiction of Japan, shall be so construed as to prejudice the provisions of the Japanese Constitution with respect to public trials.

Re paragraphs 10(a) and 10(b):

1. The United States military authorities will normally make

0280

all arrests within facilities and areas in use by and guarded under the authority of the United States armed forces. This shall not preclude the Japanese authorities from making arrests within facilities and areas in cases where the competent authorities of the United States armed forces have given consent, or in cases of pursuit of a flagrant offender who has committed a serious crime.

Where persons whose arrest is desired by the Japanese authorities and who are not subject to the jurisdiction of the United States armed forces are within facilities and areas in use by the United States armed forces, the United States military authorities will undertake, upon request, to arrest such persons. All persons arrested by the United States military authorities, who are not subject to the jurisdiction of the United States armed forces, shall immediately be turned over to the Japanese authorities.

The United States military authorities may, under due process of law, arrest in the vicinity of a facility or area any person in the commission or attempted commission of an offense against the security of that facility or area. Any such person not subject to the jurisdiction of the United States armed forces shall immediately be turned over to the Japanese authorities.

0290

2. The Japanese authorities will normally not exercise the right of search, seizure, or inspection with respect to any persons or property within facilities and areas in use by and guarded under the authority of the United States armed forces or with respect to property of the United States armed forces wherever situated, except in cases where the competent authorities of the United States armed forces consent to such search, seizure, or inspection by the Japanese authorities of such persons or property.

Where search, seizure, or inspection with respect to persons or property within facilities and areas in use by the United States armed forces or with respect to property of the United States armed forces in Japan is desired by the Japanese authorities, the United States military authorities will undertake, upon request, to make such search, seizure, or inspection. In the event of a judgment concerning such property, except property owned or utilized by the United States Government or its instrumentalities, the United States will turn over such property to the Japanese authorities for disposition in accordance with the judgment.

0291

3. Except as may otherwise be mutually agreed, the conditions of employment and work, such as those relating to wages and supplementary payments, the conditions for the protection and welfare of employees, compensations, and the rights of employees, concerning labor relations shall conform with those laid down by the legislation of the Republic of Korea.

4. Employers shall insure the just and timely resolution of employee grievances.

0292

METHOD OF ACCOUNTING CURRENTLY USED BY USFK

1. The appropriate Technical Service has specifications prepared for the type of services or purchases desired and processes these specifications along with fund citations to the US Army Korea Procurement Agency.

2. The US Army Korea Procurement Agency analyzes the specifications, determines the type of action required, and then either advertises for bids from private Korean contractors or arranges for contract negotiations with Korean government agencies, as in the case of nationalized utility systems. Bids or negotiations are usually on the basis of unit price for the utility or service furnished. Contracts normally specify what is to be shown on billings so that a proper basis of making payments can be established.

3. Upon completion of successful bidding or negotiations the US Army Korea Procurement Agency awards the contract for the specified services or purchases. Normally service contracts run for one year and indicate that the contractor or Korean government agency will present a bill for the services every 30 days or at least once each quarter. A Contracting Officer Representative from the Technical Service concerned accomplishes inspection duties for the US armed forces and insures that the services rendered are of the quality and amount required by specifications. The appropriate Technical Service certifies to the correctness of the billing received and forwards the certified billing to the US Army Korean Procurement Agency.

4. The Army Procurement Agency processes the billing and prepares appropriate payment documents and processes these to the US Army Finance and Accounting Office.

5. US Army Finance and Accounting Office makes payment by check to the contractor or Korean agency involved.

0293

ARTICLE

1. The United States armed forces, the organizations provided for in Article __________, and the contractors provided for in Article __________ may employ ~~civilian~~ Korean personnel under this Agreement. (Such civilian personnel shall be nationals of the Republic of Korea.)

2. Local labor requirements of ~~the~~ United States armed forces and the organizations or contractors referred to in Paragraph 1 of this Article shall be satisfied with the assistance of the Korean authorities. The obligations for the withholding and payment of income tax and of social security contributions, and, except as may be provided for in this article, the conditions of employment and work, such as those relating to wages and supplementary payments, the conditions for the protection of workers, and the rights of workers concerning labor relations shall be those laid down by the legislation of the Republic of Korea.

3. Should the United States armed forces or the organizations provided for in Article ________ dismiss a worker and a court or competent authorities of the Republic of Korea decide to the effect that the contract of employment has not terminated, the following procedures shall apply:

(a) The United States armed forces or the said organizations shall be informed by the Government of the Republic of Korea of the decision of the court or such authorities;

0294

(b) Should the United States forces or the said organizations not desire to return the worker to duty, they shall so notify the Government of the Republic of Korea within ten days after being informed by the latter of the decision of the court or the authorities, and may temporarily withhold the worker from duty;

(c) Upon such notification, the Government of the Republic of Korea and the United States forces or the said organizations shall consult together without delay with a view to finding a practical solution of the case;

(d) Should such a solution not be reached within a period of thirty days from the date of commencement of the consultations under (c) above, the worker will not be entitled to return to duty. In such case, the Government of the United States shall pay to the Governmemt of the Republic the worker for a period of time to be agreed between the two Governments through the Joint Committee.

0295

ARTICLE

1. The United States armed forces, the organizations provided for in Article______, and the contractors provided for in Article______ may employ civilian personnel under this Agreement. Such civilian personnel shall be nationals of the Republic of Korea.

2. Local Labour requirements of the United States armed forces and the organizations or contractors referred to in Paragraph 1 shall be satisfied with the assistance of the Korean authorities. The obligations for the withholding and payment of income tax and social security contributions, and, unless otherwise agreed upon in this article, the conditions of employment and work, such as those relating wages and supplementary payments, the conditions for the protection of workers, and the rights of workers concerning labour relations shall be those laid down by the legislation, including decisions of the courts or the competent authorities, of the Republic of Korea.

3. Should the United States armed forces dismiss a worker and a decision of a court or the competent authorities of the Republic of Korea to the effect that the contract of employment has not terminated become final, the following procedures shall apply:

0296

(a) The United States armed forces shall be informed by the Government of the Republic of Korea of the decision of the court or such authorities;

(b) Should the United States armed forces not desire to return the worker to duty, they shall so notify the Government of the Republic of Korea within ten days after being informed by the latter of the decision of the court or the authorities, and may temporarily withhold the worker from duty;

(c) Upon such notification, the Government of the Republic of Korea and the United States armed forces shall consult together without delay with a view to finding a practical solution of the case;

(d) Should such a solution not be reached within a period of thirty days from the date of commencement of the consultations under (c) above, the worker will not be entitled to return to duty. In such case, the Government of the United States shall pay to the Government of the Republic of Korea an amount equal to the cost of employment of the worker for a period of time to be agreed between the two Governments through the Joint Committee.

0297

AGREED MINUTES

1. It is understood that the provisions of Article ______, Paragraph 3 shall only apply to discharges for security reasons including disturbing the maintenance of military discipline within the facilities and areas used by the United States armed forces.

2. It is understood that the Government of the Republic of Korea shall be reimbursed for costs incurred under relevant contracts between appropriate authorities of the Korean Government and the organizations provided for in Article____ in connection with the employment of workers to be provided for such organizations.

0298

기 안 용 지

자 체 통 제		기안처	미주과 이경훈	전화번호	근거서류접수일자

과 장	수석대표		보좌관		차 관	장 관
朴 12/15	(서명)		(서명)		대결	(서명) 15.

관계관 서 명	조약과장 (서명) 12-15 기획조정관 (서명)

기 안 년월일	1962.12.14.	시 행 년월일		보존 년한	감	정 서	기 장
분 류 기 호	외정무 416	전 체 통 제					

경 유 수 신 참 조	국가재건최고회의 의장 (참조 : 외무국방위원장) 내각 수반	발 신	장 관

제 목	주둔군 지위협정 체결을 위한 제9차 교섭회의 보고

1962.12.14. 하오 2시부터 동 4시까지 중앙청 외무부 장관실에서 개최된 표기문제에 관한 제9차 교섭회의에서 토의된 내용을 별첨과 같이 보고합니다.

유 첨 : 제 9차 교섭회의 보고서.......... 부. 끝

보통문서로 재분류 (1966. 12. 31.)

0299

18-1

승인양식 1-1-3 (1112-040-016-018) (190mm×260mm16절지)

1964 년 9월 30일 미주국 직권으로 III급비밀 로 재분류

의 무 부

외정무 1962. 12. 15

수 신 국가재건최고회의 의장

참 조 외무국방 위원장

제 목 주둔군 지위협정을 위한 제9차 교섭회의 보고

1962. 12. 14 하오 2시부터 4시까지 중앙청 외무부 장관실에서 개최된 표기문제에 관한 제9차 교섭회의에서 토의된 내용을 별첨과 같이 보고합니다.

유 첨: 제9차 교섭회의 보고서 .... 8부 끝

의 무 부 장 관 최 덕 신

0300

18-2

외 무 부

외정무 1962. 12. 15

수 신 내각수반

제 목 주둔군 지위협정 체결을 위한 제9차 교섭회의 보고

1962. 12. 14 하오 2시부터 동 4시까지 중앙청 외무부 장관실에서 개최된 표기문제에 관한 제9차 교섭회의에서 토의된 내용을 별첨과 여히 보고합니다.

유 첨: 제9차 교섭회의 보고서 .... 1부. 끝

외 무 부 장 관 최 덕 신

0301

18-8

제 9 차

한미간 주둔군지위 협정실무자 회의

보 고 서

1. 시 일 : 1962. 12. 14. 하오 2시부터 동 4시까지

2. 장 소 : 중앙청 외무부장관실

3. 참석자 : 한국측 :

진 필 식	(외무부정무국장, 수석대표)
이 경 호	(법무부 법무국장)
신 관 섭	(재무부 세관국장)
박 근	(외무부 미주과장)
오 원 용	(외무부 조약과장)
이 남 구	(국방부 군무과장)
지 성 구	(외무부 공보관)
이 경 훈	(외무부 2등서기관)
신 정 섭	(")
강 석 재	(외무부 3등서기관)
이 창 범	(")

미국측 : Lewis 영사(휴가중)를 제외한 교섭대표단전원

4. 토의사항 :

(1) 용어의 정의, 합동위원회, 통애통제, 선박 및 항공기의 출입 그리고 토지 및 시설문제를 순차적으로 토의함.

(2) 용어의 정의에관한 토의에 있어서 미국군대 구성원의 정의에 관하여 우리측은 미국측안에서 규정한 "except for those for whom status has otherwise been provided" 라는 구절을 삭제하고 그대신 합의의사록에서"행정협정에서 말하는 미국군대 구성원은 미국대사관 무관과 주한미군사 고문단 설치에관한 한미간 협정에 규정된자는 제외한다" 는 규정을 하자고 제의한데 대하여 (별첨 우리측 합의의사록 안참조)

0302

→

18-4

明年88-4(4)

0303

미국측은 동구절을 본문에 그대로두고 거기에대한 해석
합의 의사록안(별첨참조) 에서 이러한 "미국 대사관 무관과
군사고문단 설치 협정에 규정된자 등과같은 미국군대
소속 현역복무자를 포함하지 않는다" 는 내용의 규정을
하자고 제의하였음. 양측은 이문제를 다음회기에 다시 토의
키로 함.

(3) 용어의 정의에 있어서 "군속"에 관하여 우리측은 조문에는
미국국적을 소유하는 민간인에 한정시키고 제 3 국의 군속에
대하여는 주한미군의 근무에 지장이 없도록 하는것을 고려하는
범위내에서 예외적 규정을 따로두자고 주장한데 대하여
미국측은 처음 반대(의사)의사를 표명하다가 다시 (가) 만일
미국 국적의 소유자에 한정시키자는 한국측 제의를 수락할
시에는 원조문에 한.미 2중국적자는 미국인으로 간주한다는
요지의 조항을 원조문에 첨가하고 (나) 현재군속으로 채용
되고있는 제 3 국민에 대하여는 그들을 "군속"으로서 간주
한다는 요지를 합의 의사록에서 규정하자고 제의함으로서
우리측 주장에 어느정도 접근하여 왔음. 미측은 이에관한
첨가조항과 합의의사록 안을 제시하였기 양측은 이를 다음
회기에 다시 토의키로 함.

(4) 용어의 정의에 있어서 우리측은 "가족" 의 범주안에 "기타
친척" 도 포함시키는것에 동의하였음.

(5) 합동위원회에 관한 토의에 있어서 합동위원회의 기능에대한
예외적 규정인 " except where otherwise provided
for " 라는 구절에 대하여는 토지시설 조항 토의시 다시
토의키로 함.

(6) 합동위원회에 관하여 합동위원회에서 문제해결이 불가능할
시에 회부될 기관으로 "적절한계통"으로 하자는데 합의함.

0304

→

18-5

매문 88-4

0305

(7) 항해통제에 관한 토의에 있어서 우리측은 미국측 초안 1 및 2 항을 수락하고 통고의무에 관한 3 항에 대하여는 "정상적 상태하" 라는 단서 규정의 미국측 합의의사록 초안과 관련해서 설명하여 줄것을 요구하자 미국측은 이는 합의의사록에서 아주 엄격히 제한된것이라고 해명하였기 우리측은 검토해서 다음 회기에 다시 토의하자고 하였음.

(8) 선박 및 항공기의 출입 토의에 있어서 우리측은 미국측이 1 항에서 통신체제를 삭제한 이유가 무엇이냐고 묻자 미국측은 이를 토지 및 시설조항에서 규정할것이라고 하였기 다음 회기에 다시 토의키로 함.

(9) 선박 및 항공기의 출입에관한 2 항에서 우리측은 체제상 또는 내용상으로 보아 우리측안을 받아드릴것을 요구하자 미국측은 한국안과 미국안의 주요한 차의는 미국안은 항해 보조시설 설치를 허오받게 되어있는것이 명백히 규정된점이라고 지적하였고 이에대하여 우리측은 이 이외에도 설치할수 있는 장소로 우리안은 미국이 사용하는 토지 시설과 그부근으로 되어있는데 미국안은 전 한국과 그 영해로되어 있는점과 항해보조 시설은 다만 "일반적" 으로 한국의 그것과 합치되어야 한다는 규정과 또한 사전통고는 "가능한경우"에 한다고 하여 있는 규정들은 한국안과 미국안의 차의점이라고 지적하여 우리안을 수락할것을 주장하자 미측은 한국에서 현재까지 미국군대가 수행하고 있는 활동에 미측안이 더잘 부합 반영되고 있다고 설명하였음. 이문제는 다음회기에 다시 토의키로 함.

(10) 토지 및 시설에 관하여 양측은 각각 자국의 입장에 대한 설명을 한후 이에관한 조항을 교환하였음.

0306

→

18-6

비문 88-4

0307

5. 중요합의 사항

(1) 선박 및 항공기의 출입 문제에 관한 미국측 초안의 1, 2 항에 합의함.

6. 기타 사항

(1) 차기회의 일자 : 1963. 1. 7. 하오 2 시

(2) 차기회의 의제 : 차기회의시까지 양측 수석대표 간에 합의된 사항

7. 참고자료 : 미국측이 제의한 협정초안 (용어의 정의와 토지 및 시설) 별첨참조
및 용어의 정의에 관한 우리측 합의의사록 안

보통문서로 재분류(1966. 12. 31.)

1966.12.31.에 예고문에 의거 일반문서로 재분류됨

0308

18-7

미국문 88-4(4)

0309

were inserted in subparagraph 1(b) ~~an Agreed Minute~~ should be added which would define the status of persons not of U.S. nationality who might be employed by the U.S. armed forces. He indicated that some such arrangement had been found necessary in the case of other status of forces agreements. In the case of Japan, the solution had been an exchange of notes, which had been found necessary by the Joint Committee. Mr. Habib then tabled the draft of an Agreed Minute and an additional sentence to be added to subparagraph 1(b) if the Agreed Minute were adopted. With the Agreed Minute and the additional sentence, ~~xxxxxxxxxxxxxxxxxxxx~~ in addition to agreeing to the insertion of the phrase "of United States nationality", Mr. Habib noted, the U.S. side was ~~xxxxxxxxxx~~ acquiescing to the request of the Korean side but at the same time was providing a practical solution to ~~the practical nature of~~ the situation on a non-discriminatory basis. He pointed out that if these suggested changes were agreed upon, it would also be necessary to alter Paragraph 6 of the Entry and Exit Article by replacing the phrase "ordinarily resident in" with the phrase "nationals of". Mr. Chin stated that the Korean side would take the U.S. side's proposals under consideration for discussion at a subsequent meeting.

9. Pointing out that the only ~~xxxxxxxxxx~~ unresolved question with respect to subparagraph 1(c) was that concerning the phrase "other relatives", Mr. Chin stated that the Korean side had decided to agree to the U.S. draft of this subparagraph.

Joint Committee

10. Turning to the Joint Committee article, Mr. Habib stated that the U.S. side had compared the two drafts and believed the U.S. draft as tabled to be preferable. ~~as tabled.~~ Mr. Chin requested clarification of the phrase "except where otherwise provided".

11. Mr. Habib explained that the phrase "except where otherwise provided" [handwritten insertion, illegible] referred to another article, the draft of which would be tabled later in the meeting. He said that there are special arrangements and agreements regarding

17-78　　0312

communications which are very special and highly technical. Consultations regarding these agreements and arrangements were also xxxx of a very special nature. xxx Therefore, they should not come within the scope of the Joint Committee's labors. Mr. Chin stated the Korean side would reserve its views with regard to this phrase until the other relevant article was tabled.

12. Mr. Chin noted that except for the phrase just discussed, there was general agreement on the ~~xxx~~ U.S. draft of the article. The only other point at issue was the use of "appropriate" or "diplomatic" in paragraph 3. He said the Korean side had decided to agree to the use of the word "appropriate", with the understanding that "appropriate channels" means channels agreed upon by both sides in the Joint Committee, including diplomatic channels. Mr. Habib agreed to this understanding.

Navigation and Air Traffic Control

13. Taking up next the article dealing with navigational aids and air traffic control, Mr. Chin noted that the U.S. draft makes no mention of communication systems. Mr. Habib replied that this subject was covered in the U.S. draft of another article which would be tabled later in the meeting. He urged the Korean side to defer discussion of this point until the other article had been tabled.

14. Mr. Chin then commented that paragraph 2 of the Korean draft was more appropriate than the xxxxxxxxx corresponding paragraph in the U.S. draft. Captain Brownlie pointed out that the wording of the U.S. draft conforms more closely to the actual administrative and operational situation existing in Korea. He pointed out that the U.S. armed forces, which operate and maintain navigational aids in Korea, will require, from time to time, additional xxxx facilities of this nature. Mr. Habib pointed out that the SOFA should authorize the U.S armed forces to establish and maintain navigational aids, since they are already doing so and will need to establish additional aids in the future. ~~The U.S. draft~~ so authorizes explicitly but the Korean draft does so only implicitly ~~not~~. The U.S. draft, he added, was a little clearer in this respect.

15. Referring to the phrase "throughout the Republic of Korea and in the territorial waters thereof" [redacted] in paragraph 2 of the U.S. draft, Mr. Chin asked whether the U.S. draft meant that the locations of the aids to be established were to be selected unilaterally or in consultation with Korean authorities.

16. Captain Brownlie replied by first citing the locations of existing radio beacons and aipport control towers. He explained that modernization of facilities will require the introducation of more sophisticated equipment, the characteristic of which will require that it be located at sites not now occupied. In such cases, the selection of the new sites would be determined on the basis of bilateral discussion. He added that in case of hostilities, [some] facilities presently operated by civilians would have to be taken over by the ~~xxxxxxxxxxxxxxx~~ armed forces. Mr. Habib added that consultation between the U.S. armed forces and the ROK Government ~~xxxxx~~ obviously would be necessary with respect to the establishment of aids ~~xxx~~ in areas not within established facilities. He pointed out that the aids under discussion jointly serve the needs of the U.S. and Korean armed forces. He also reminded the negotiators that paragraph 2 of the U.S. draft requires notification, regardless of location and even where aids have been established within existing facilities.

17. Mr. Chin inquired whether the U.S. side was prepared to supplement the paragraph by providing for mutual consultation. When Mr. Habib requested clarification of the question, Mr. Chin pointed out that the Korean draft ~~provided for the establishment of aids~~ provided for the coordination of aids established "in the facilities and areas in use by the United States and in territorial waters adjacent thereto or in the vicinity thereof", whereas the U.S. draft provided for the authorization of their establishment "throughout the Republic of Korea and in the territorial waters thereof". He asked whether the ~~xxxxxx~~ language of the U.S. draft implied mutual consultation or unilateral action by the U.S. armed forces. Mr. Habib stated that he understood the question and that the U.S. side would respond to it ~~xxxxx~~ during subsequent ~~discussion of this~~ article.

0314

18. Mr. Chin pointed out that the U.S. draft stated that aids shall conform "generally" to the system in use. He asked if the word "generally" were necessary. Mr. Habib replied that this was a question of there being possible slight technical differences in certain types of new equipment from that the types already in use.

19. Mr. Chin then asked about the phrase "advance notification where practicable". Mr. Habib replied that under actual operating conditions, the situation may be such as to require action first and notification second. The only times when such a situation would exist would be during emergency conditions. Mr. Chin It was then agreed to continue discussion of this article at a subsequent meeting.

Access by Aircraft and Vessels

20. Mr. Chin suggested that two the article on access by aircraft and vessels be discussed on the basis of the U.S. draft since the drafts do not differ much in substance. Following assent by the U.S. side, Mr. Chin stated that the Korean side accepted paragraphs 1 and 2 of the U.S. draft.

21. Referring to paragraph 3, Mr. Chin requested clarification of the phrase "under normal conditions". Mr. Habib replied that appropriate notification would always be made, except in an emergency situation or when the nature of a vessel or aircraft is such that prior notification cannot be made because of security reasons. He said that this was a standard phrase and constituted not an exception but rather an abnormality. Mr. Chin stated that the Korean side would comment on this point during subsequent discussion of this article.

22. Mr. Habib stated that he would like to make one further comment regarding this article for the consideration of the Korean side. He referred to the second sentence in paragraph 1 calling for notification regarding cargo and passengers not accorded the exemptions of the SOFA. He stated that MAAG personnel and

19-18

0315

Embassy armed forces attached personnel would not be covered by this sentence, since ~~they~~ their status was otherwise provided for. However, any other personnel not entitled to the exemptions of the SOFA would be covered and their arrival would be notified to the Korean authorities.

Facilities and Areas

23. Colonel Solf then tabled four draft articles relating to facilities and areas, briefly summarizing the provisions of each. He pointed out that the U.S. side ~~ex~~ intended to add to the fourth article at a later date, a ~~xxxxxxxxxx~~ paragraph which ~~be the fourth article. The additional paragraph~~ would be related to the existing utilities agreement. ~~xxxxx~~

24. Colonel Lee then tabled a draft article on facilities and areas for the Korean side. In introducing this article, Col. Lee said that the ROK Government has cooperated in the past and will cooperate in the future in furnishing facilities and areas for use by the U.S. armed forces, for the purpose of facilitating the accomplishment of the mission of those forces. In view of the unusual situation existing in Korea, however, he continued, the Korean draft article provides for ~~xxxxxxxxxxxxxxx~~ the payment of compensation by the U.S. Government to the least unavoidable extent. It is intended, he went on, that compensation shall be paid only for the use of private property, with a view to alleviating the losses of the owners. The Korean side has given due consideration to the purpose of the presence of the U.S. armed forces in Korea. They have suffered tremendous losses in battle and the ROK Government has done its best to facilitate the achievement of their mission. In tabling this draft, he continued, the Korean side proposed article by article discussion in a spirit of honesty and mutual cooperation. Col. Lee indicated that the draft did not contain provisions regarding public utilities and services, which would be separately provided for.

1919 0316

25. It was agreed to reserve discussion of the draft articles on facilities and areas until the next meeting, thus permitting each side to study the drafts and understand the other side's position.

26. It was agreed to hold the next meeting on January 7, 1963, at 2:00 p.m., with the agenda to be decided upon by the two chairmen in consultation. The meeting closed with an exchange of cordial season's greetings.

27. Summary Points of Agreement:- The following portions of the text of the U.S. draft were agreed upon for inclusion in the final text of the Agreement:

Definitions Article -

Subparagraph 1(c)

Access by Aircraft and Vessels Article -

Paragraph 1

Paragraph 2

보통문서로 재분류 (1966. 12. 31.)

1966.12.31. 에 예고문에 의거 일반문서로 재분류됨

0317

19-20

JOINT SUMMARY RECORD OF THE 9 TH SESSION
STATUS FORCES NEGOTIATION

December 14, 1962

I. Time and Place : 2:00 to 4:00 p.m December 14, 1962 at the Capitol Building

II. Attendants:

ROK Side:

Mr. Chin, Pil Shik	Director Bureau of Political Affairs Ministry of Foreign Affairs
Mr. Yi, Kyung Ho	Director Bureau of Legal Affairs Ministry of Justice
Mr. Shin, Kwan Sup	Director Bureau of Costums Duty Ministry of Finance
Col. Lee, Nam Koo	Chief, Military Affairs Section Ministry of National Defense
Mr. Pak, Kun	Chief, America Section Ministry of Foreign Affairs
Mr. O, Won Yong	Chief, Treaty Section Ministry of Foreign Affairs
Mr. Chi, Sung Koo	Press Officer Ministry of Foreign Affairs
Mr. Shin, Chung Sup	2nd Secretary Ministry of Foreign Affairs
Mr. Lee, Kyung Hoon	2nd Secretary Ministry of Foreign Affairs
~~Mr. Lee, Chang Bum~~	~~3rd Secretary~~ Ministry of Foreign Affairs
Mr. Kang, Suk Jae	3rd Secretary Ministry of Foreign Affairs

US Side:

Mr. Philip C. Habib	Counselor of the Embassy for Political Affairs

미주과	양고재	담 당	과 장	국 장	특별보좌관	차 관	장 관

19-1

Brig. Gen J.D. Lawlor	Deputy Chief of Staff 8th Army
Mr. William J. Ford	First Secretary of the Embassy
Col. G.G. O'Connor	Deputy Chief of Staff 8th Army
Capt. R.M. Brownlie	Assistant Chief of Staff USN/K
Col. W.A. Solf	Staff Judge Advocate 8th Army
Mr. Benjamin A. Fleck (Rapporteur and Press Officer)	First Secretary of the Embassy
Mr. Robert A. Lewis	Second Secretary and Consul of the Embassy
Lt. Col. R.E. Miller	Staff Officer, JAG 8th Army
Lt. Col. W.A. Burt	J-5
Kenneth Campen	Interpreter

Definitions Article

1. The meeting began with consideration of the Definitions Article. Mr. Chin stated that the Korean side believed that the phrase "except for those for whom status has otherwise been provided" in subparagraph 1(a) was too vague. He proposed, therefore, that the phrase be deleted and that in its stead the negotiators approve and Agreed Minute which he thereupon tabled.

2. Mr. Habib replied that the U.S. side believed it desirable to hold to a minimum the number of Agreed Minutes to be attached to the Status of Forces Agreement. He suggested that, instead of adopting an Agreed Minute, the negotiators retain the phrase in the text and agree

0319

19-2

to let the written record show that this phrase is intended to apply to MAAG personnel and to personnel of the armed forces attache offices of the Embassy. Mr. Chin responded that the two sides were agreed on the substance of the point at issue. However, the Korean side believed that inasmuch as this phrase dealt with an exception to the application of the agreement, it should be spelled out in detail. It was the view of the Korean side that all exceptions should be clearly defined.

3. Mr. Habib then suggested that, as an alternative, the phrase be retained and an Agreed Minute be adopted in addition. Mr. Chin replied that the Agreed Minute which he had just tabled should be acceptable to the U.S. side since it clearly defined those military personnel who would be excluded from the provisions of the SOFA. He pointed out that these same personnel are also excluded from the provisions of the Mutual Defense Treaty.

4. Mr. Habib stated that the U.S. side would agree to the adoption of an Agreed Minute but believed that, in addition, the article itself should mention the fact that there were exceptions. He thereupon tabled the draft of an Agreed Minute. After perusing the U.S. draft, Mr. Chin stated that there was no substantial difference between the two drafts. Mr. Habib agreed. It was decided to study the two drafts for discussion at a subsequent meeting.

5. Turning to subparagraph 1(b), Mr. Chin noted that the only point of difference was whether or not to insert the phrase "of United States nationality" after

0320

19-3

the words "civilian persons". He asked whether the U.S. side had any further statement to make on this point.

6. Mr. Habib replied that the U.S. armed forces in Korea do employ persons of third country nationality. He said they are few in number and provide skills which are not readily available in Korea but which are necessary for the accomplishment of the mission of the U.S. forces. They are here solely for that purpose and have no other function, he added. Inasmuch as they are in Korea on the same terms as United States nationals, there is no reason or necessity for discriminating against them. He assured the Korean side that such persons are not hired when the requisite skills which they possess are found to be available in Korea. Therefore, the U.S. side does not believe the insertion of the phrase "of United States nationality" is either necessary or desirable.

7. Mr. Chin stated that the Korean side agreed that the number of third country nationals was relatively small. However, in the view of the Korean side, the SOFA was meant to apply solely to the U.S armed forces, and therefore the insertion of the phrase "of United States nationality" was both desirable and necessary. However, the Korean side had no intention of hindering the accomplishment of the mission of the U.S. armed forces. Perhaps, therefore, some other way might be found to cover third country nationals. He suggested the addition of another subparagraph which would state that third country nationals shall not be hindered from the performance of their duties.

0321

19-4

8. Mr. Habib replied that if third country nationals are in Korea solely for the purpose of facilitating the accomplishment of the mission of the U.S armed forces, they should receive the same treatment as other civilians who are in Korea for the same purpose. He then suggested that if the phrase "of United States nationality" were inserted in subparagraph 1(b), an Agreed Minute should be added which would define the status of persons not of U.S. nationality who might be employed by the U.S. armed forces. He indicated that some such arrangement had been found necessary in the case of other status of forces agreements. In the case of Japan, the solution had been an exchange of notes, which had been found necessary by the Joint Committee. Mr. Habib then tabled the draft of an Agreed Minute and an additional sentence to be added to subparagraph 1(b) if the Agreed Minute were adopted. With the Agreed Minute and the additional sentence, in addition to agreeding to the insertion of the phrase "of United States nationality", Mr. Habib noted, the U.S. side was acquiescing to the request of the Korean side but at the same time was providing a practical solution to the situation on a non-discriminatory basis. He pointed out that if these suggested changes were agreed upon, it would also be necessary to alter Paragraph 6 of the Entry and Exit Article by replacing the phrase "ordinarily resident in" with the phrase "nationals of" Mr. Chin stated that the Korean side would take the U.S. side's proposals under consideration for discussion at a subsequent meeting.

0322

19-5

9. Pointing out that the only unreasolved question with respect to subparagraph 1(c) was that concerning the phrase "other relatives", Mr. Chin stated that the Korean side had decided to agree to the U.S. draft of this subparagraph.

Joint Committee

10. Turning to the Joint Committee article, Mr. Habib stated that the U.S. side had compared the two drafts and believed the U.S. draft as tabled to be preferable. Mr. Chin requested clarification of the phrase "except where otherwise provided".

11. Mr. Habib explained that the phrase "except where otherwise provided" referred to another article, the draft of which would be tabled later in the meeting. He said that there are special arrangements and agreements regarding communications which are very special and highly technical. Consultations regarding these agreements and arrangements were also of a very special nature. Therefore, they should not come within the scope of the Joint Committee's labors. Mr. Chin stated the Korean side would reserve its views with regard to this phrase until the other relevant article was tabled.

12. Mr. Chin noted that except for the phrase just discussed, there was general agreement on the U.S. draft of the article. The only other point at issue was the use of "appropriate" or "diplomatic" in paragraph 3. He said the Korean side had decided to agree to the use of the word "appropriate", with the understanding that

0323

19-6

"appropriate channels" means channels agreed upon by both sides in the Joint Committee, including diplomatic channels. Mr. Habib agreed to this understanding.

Navigation and Air Traffic Control

13. Taking up next the Article dealing with navigational aids and air traffic control, Mr. Chin noted that the U.S. draft makes no mention of communication systems. Mr. Habib replied that this subject was covered in the U.S. draft of another article which would be tabled later in the meeting. He urged the Korean side to defer discussion of this point until the other article had been talbled.

14. Mr. Chin then commented that paragraph 2 of the Korean draft was more appropriate than the corresponding paragraph in the U.S. draft. Captain Brownlie pointed out that the wording of the U.S. draft conforms more closely to the actual administrative and operational situation existing in Korea. He pointed out that the U.S. armed forces, which operate and maintain navigational aids in Korea, will require, from time to time, additional facilities of this nature. Mr. Habib pointed out that the SOFA should authorize the US armed forces to establish maintain navigational aids, since they are already doing so and will need to establish and additional aids in the future. The U.S. draft so authorizes explicitly but the Korean draft does so only implicitly. The U.S. draft, he added, was a little clearer in this respect.

15. Referring to the phrase "throughout the Republic of Korea and in the territorial waters thereof" in paragraph 2 of the U.S. draft, Mr. Chin asked whether the U.S.

draft meant that the locations of the aids to be established were to be selected unilaterally or in consultation with Korean authorities.

16. Captain Brownlie replied by first citing the locations of existing radio beacons and airport control towers. He explained that modernization of facilities will require the introducation of more sophisticated equipment, the characteristics of which will require that it be located at stes not now occupied. In such cases, the selection of the new sites would be determined on the basis of bilateral discussion. He added that in case of hostilities, some facilities presently operated by civilians would have to be taken over by the armed forces. Mr. Habib added that consultation between the U.S. armed forces and the ROK Government obviously would be necessary with respect to the establishment of aids in areas not within established facilities. He pointed out that the aids under discussion jointly serve the needs of the U.S. and Korean armed forces. He also reminded the negotiators that paragraph 2 of the U.S. draft requires notification, regardless of location and even where aids have been established within existing facilities.

17. Mr. Chin inquired whether the U.S. side was prepared to supplement the paragraph by providing for mutual consultation. When Mr. Habib requested clarification of the question, Mr. Chin pointed out that the Korean draft provided for the coordination of aids established "in the facilities and areas in use by the United States and in territorial waters adjacent thereto or in the

vicinity thereof", whereas the U.S. draft provided for the authorization for their establishment "throughout the Republic of Korea and in the territorial waters thereof". He asked whether the language of the U.S. draft implied mutual consultation or unilateral action by the U.S. armed forces. Mr. Habib stated that he understood the question and that the U.S. side would respond to it during subsequent discussion of this article.

18. Mr. Chin pointed out that the U.S. draft stated that aids shall conform "generally" to the system in use. He asked if the word" Generally" were necessary. Mr. Habib replied that this was a question of there being possible slight technical differences in certain types of new equipment from the types already in use.

19. Mr. Chin then asked about the phrase "advance notification where practicable". Mr. Habib replied that under actual operating conditions, the situation may be such as to require action first and notification second. The only times when such a situation would exist would be during emergency conditions. It was then agreed to continue discussion of this article at a subsequent meeting.

<u>Access by Aircraft and Vessles</u>

20. Mr. Chin suggested that the article on access by aircraft and vessels be discussed on the basis of the U.S. draft since the two drafts do not differ much in substance. Following assent by the U.S. side, Mr. Chin stated that the Korean side accepted paragraph 1 and 2 of the U.S. draft.

0326

19-9

21. Referring to paragraph 3, Mr. Chin requested clarification of the phrase "under normal conditions". Mr. Habib replied that appropriate notification would always be made, except in an emergency situation or when the nature of a vessel or airdraft is such that prior notification cannot be made because of security reasons. He said that this was a standard phrase and constituted not an exception but rather an abnormality. Mr. Chin stated that the Korean side would comment on this point during subsequent discussion of this article.

22. Mr. Habib stated that he would like to make one further comment regarding this article for the consideration of the Korean side. He referred to the second sentecne in paragraph 1 calling for notification regarding cargo and passengers not accorded the exemptions of the SOFA. He stated that MAAG personnel and Embassy armed forces attache personnel would not be covered by this sentecne, since their status was otherwise provided for. However, any other personnel not entitled to the exemptions of the SOFA would be covered and their arrival would be notified to the Korean authorities.

Facilities and Areas

23. Colonel Solf then tabled four draft articles relating to facilities and areas, briefly summarizing the provisions of each. He pointed out that the U.S. side intended to add to the fourth article at a later date a paragraph which would be related to the existing utilities agreement.

0327

19-10

24. Colonel Lee then tabled a draft article on facilities and areas for the Korean side. In introducing this article, Col. Lee said that the ROK Government has cooperated in the past and will cooperate in the future in furnishing facilities and areas for use by the U.S. armed forces, for the purposes of facilitating the accomplishment of the mission of those forces. In view of the unusual situation existing in Korea, he continued, the Korean draft article provides for the payment of compensation by the U.S. Government to the least unavoidable extent. It is intended, he went on, that compensation shall be paid only for the use of private property, with a view to alleviating the losses of the owners. The Korean side has given due consideration to the purpose of the presence of the U.S. armed forces in Korea. They have suffered tremendous losses in battle and the ROK Government has done its best to facilitate the achievement of their mission. In tabling this draft, he continued, the Korean side proposed article by article discussion in a spirit of honesty and mutual cooperation. Col. Lee indicated that the draft did not contain provisions regarding public utilities and services, which would be separately provided for.

25. It was agreed to reserve discussion of the draft articles on facilities and areas until the next meeting, thus permitting each side to study the drafts and understand the other side's position.

0328

19-11

26. It was agreed to hold the next meeting on Jaunary 7, 1963, at 2:00 p.m., with the agenda to be decided upon by the two chairmen in consultation. The meeting closed with an exhcnage of cordial season's greetings.

27. Summary Points of Agreement:- The following portions of the text of the U.S. draft were agreed upon for inclusion in the final text of the Agreement:

Definitions Article-
Subparagraph 1(c)
Access by Aircraft and Vessels Article-
Paragraph 1
Paragraph 2

보통문서로 재분류(1966. 12. 31.)

1966.12.31에 예고문에

0320

19-12

협 조 전	응 신 기 일 1963. 1. 4.

문서번호 55 제 목 미국 BOA 업무한계 및 미8군 불하품 수입 신고액

수 신: 방교국장 발 신: 정무국장 년 월 일 1962.12.24. 제1의견

1. 본건은 방협 조약과에서 이송한 미대사관 B.O.A. 업무 한계교섭의뢰건과 미8군 불하품 수입 신고액에대한 조치건에 관한것임.

2. 미대사관 B.O.A. 업무한계교섭의뢰건중 제1및 2항은 미주과 소관사항으로 사료되오나, 제2항은 귀국 소관 사항에 관련된것임. 따라서 해당사항에관한 행정협정 조문안을 작성 제시하여 주시기바랍니다.

3. 미8군 불하품 수입신고액에 대한 조치건도 귀국 소관 사항에관련된것으로 생각되오니, 본건에대한 귀국의 의견과, 필요하다면 본건에 관련된 행정협정에 포함될 조문안을 작성 제시하여 주시기바라나이다.

별 첨 : 1. 미대사관과 B.O.A. 업무한계교섭의뢰

2. 미8군 불하품 수입신고액에 대한 조치. 끝

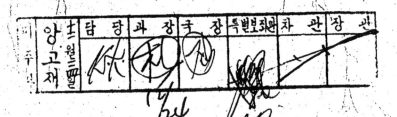

미주	양 고 재	담 당	과 장	국 장	특별보좌관	차 관	장 관

승인양식 1—34 11—13330—01 (195mm×265mm16절지)

0330

협 조 전	응 신 기 일 1963. 1. 4.
문서번호 3	제목 : 미8군 불하품 수입 신고액에대한 조치

수신: 통상국장 발신: 경무국장 년월일 1962. 12.24. 제 1 의 견

1. 최고회의로부터 미 8 군에서 민간인 앞으로 불하되는 각종군수물자에 대하여 우리정부로서는 기종발을 방안을 모사하여 오든 방침에 입각하여 현재 교섭중인 한미 행정협정에 반영도록 조치할것을 별첨 공한사본과 같이 지시하여 왔음.

2. 현재 진행중인 한미행정 협정교섭회의에서 본건과 관련된 한미간에 합의된 조항으로는 관세문제에 관한 조항중 "Except as such disposal may be authorized by the United States and Korean authorities in accordance with mutually agreed conditioneds, goods imported into the Republic of Korea free of duty shall not be disposed of in the Republic of Korea to persons not entitled to import such goods free of duty". 라는 항임.

3. 당국으로서는 현재 귀국에서 재한 미국 잉여재산 처분에관한 한미간 협정을 개정하려하고 있는것으로 알고있으며 이 잉여재산 처분에관한 협정은 전기 2. 의 행정협정 조문에서의 "....in accordance with mutually agreed conditions" 라는 부분에 해당되는 협정이 될것으로 생각되오니 이점 유의하시어 잉여 재산처분에 관한 협정개정에 별첨 최고회의 지시공한 내용을 반영시키도록 조치하시기를 바랍니다.

64-1

(195mm×265mm 16절지)

4. 당국의 참고를 위하여 현재 귀국에서 추진중에 있는 잉여재산 처분에관한 협정 개정에 관련된 수정코저 하는 내용과, 수정의 방향등을 알려주시기 바랍니다.

유첨 : 미8군 불하품 수입신고액에 대한 조치사본 1부, 끝

정 무 국 장 진 필 식

미주과	양고재	담 당	과 장	국 장	특별보좌관	차 관	장 관
			12/24				

44-2

0332

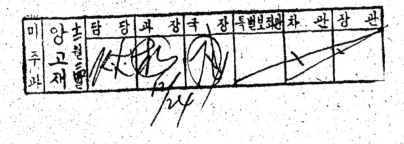

부 전 지

수 신 미주과장 1962 . 12.22.

제 목
요 약 공한 이송

설치고책이
별첨 재무부로 부터의 공한은 귀과의

소관 사항이라 사료되어 이를 이송하니 사수

하기 바랍니다.

유첨 1. 미대사관과 B.O.A. 업무한계
교섭 의뢰

2. 미 8군 불하품 수입 신고액에 대한
조치

관계부처

협 조 처

전화번호 주
부

발 신 조약과장 오 원 용

수인양식 1—24 (1112-040-032-023) (130mm×190mm 32절지)

0333

국 가 재 건 최 고 회 의

외국 제 616 호 1962. 12. 18.

수신 내각 수반

참조 외무부 장관

제목 미 8 군 불하품 수입 신고액에 대한 조치

미 8 군에서 58 년부터 62.10.31 까지 사이에 각종 군수물자를 대민 불하한 수입 신고액이 별첨과 같이 서울 세관대장에서 확인되였으니 미 측이로 부터 기증 받을 방안을 모사하여 오든 방침에 입각하여 추진중인 미 주든 군 지위 협정에 반영토록 조치할 것.

유첨 : 미 8 군 불하품 수입 신고액 집계표 1 부. 끝.

의장명에 의하여

총무처장 육 군준장 황 종 갑

0334

미 8군 불하품 수입신고의 집계표

품종 / 년도	병 참	공 병	병 기	통 신	계
1958	환 140,666,997	환 498,483,620	환 168,814,960	환 24,600,100	환 832,565,677
1959	〃 124,471,736	〃 282,343,525	〃 947,681,562	〃 23,847,582	〃 1,378,344,405
1960	〃 309,041,290	〃 901,513,855	〃 558,870,559	〃 40,236,260	〃 1,809,661,964
1961	〃 384,722,101	〃 1,030,865,659	〃 391,055,380	〃 112,172,583	〃 1,918,815,723
1962 10.30 현재	원 63,950,220	원 66,253,707	7 원 161,596,436	9,282,122원	원2 301,082,486
계	〃9 159,840,432.	〃9 337,574,372.	〃8 368,238,68	〃5 229,367,774.	〃1 895,021,263.

63-2

0335

1962년도 10. 31 현재 미8군 불하품수입 신고액

월별	공 병	병 참	병 기	통 신	계
1	환 24,961,000	환 8,744,500	환 20,357,197	환 738,000	환 54,800,697
2	51,964,229 〃	50,125,825 〃	11,758,000 〃		113,848,045 〃
3	104,640,133 〃	62,788,960 〃	291,789,000 〃		387,218,093 〃
4	72,023,400 〃	23,553,200 〃	3,042,400 〃	13,783,000 〃	112,402,000 〃
5	5,613,720 〃	73,962,630 〃	514,486,060 〃	860,400 〃	594,922,810 〃
6	7,815,723 원	12,113,751 원	1,974,145 원	원 944,370	22,847,989 원
7	4,566,725 〃	91,200 〃	9,226,270 〃	782,000 〃	14,666,195 〃
8	6,641,000 〃	696,130 〃	26,691,384 〃	81,020 〃	34,109,534 〃
9	15,854,140 〃	20,168,193 〃	40,748,302 〃	1,755,115 〃	78,525,750 〃
10	5,455,872 〃	8,963,435 〃	6,013,070 〃	4,181,477 〃	24,613,854 〃
계	원 66,253,707.3	원 63,950,220.5	원 161,596,436.7	원 9,282,122	원 301,082,486.2

43-3

0336

1961년도 미8군 불하품 수입 신고액

월별	공병	병참	병기	통신	계
1	36,120,654	19,732,020	11,543,000	33,377,100	100,772,774
2	84,870,000	106,143,620	75,000,000		266,013,620
3	119,389,142	18,714,400	28,883,500	1,864,890	168,851,932
4	27,486,600	78,664,789	52,310,400	2,949,300	161,411,089
5	31,946,838	9,631,900	4,220,000	3,397,300	49,196,038
6	23,082,400	101,324,100	81,849,456	1,485,000	207,740,956
7	60,600,820	12,574,332	88,565,940		161,741,092
8	148,349,540	1,206,300	8,221,884	4,891,380	162,669,104
9	147,874,325	10,099,600	36,688,600	18,836,613	213,499,138
10	104,802,780	9,068,700	2,170,000	38,333,000	154,374,480
11	101,010,010	12,027,900	1,143,000	4,268,000	118,448,910
12	145,332,550	5,534,440	459,600	2,770,000	154,096,590
계	1,030,865,659	384,722,101	391,055,380	112,172,583	1,918,815,723원

0337

1960년도 미8군 불하품수입 신고액					
월별	공 병	병 참	병 기	통 신	계
1	177,235,465	6,915,000	32,364,854		216,515,319
2	113,195,392	40,252,761	93,836,711	1,367,100	248,651,964
3	18,076,760	43,117,801	35,941,196	1,635,000	98,770,757
4	34,391,191	21,346,075	15,918,500		71,655,766
5	70,461,140	71,125,547	23,230,201	2,220,110	167,036,998
6	33,889,046	5,903,150	7,880,000		47,672,196
7	106,460,516	2,316,116	1,923,000	2,200,000	112,899,632
8	69,492,200	2,001,000	1,182,200	19,500,000	92,175,400
9	115,707,029	16,876,800	168,221,647	2,260,000	303,065,476
10	23,315,019	1,349,700	6,392,200		31,056,919
11	98,844,887	16,136,850	62,158,050	7,474,050	184,613,837
12	40,445,210	81,700,490	109,822,000	3,580,000	235,547,700
계	901,513,855	309,041,290	558,870,559	40,236,260	1,809,661,964환

0338

43-5

1959년도 미8군 불하품 수입 신고액

월별	공 병	병 참	병 기	통 신	계
1	22,781,700		69,800		22,851,500
2	36,425,200	5,702,000	6,437,000		48,564,200
3	28,823,400	21,699,200	6,294,800	93,000	56,910,400
4	59,999,000	12,002,600	6,623,800		78,625,400
5	42,083,000		5,229,800		47,312,800
6	49,904,000	3,131,000	3,273,000		56,308,000
7	11,932,700	20,214,224	2,355,800	251,000	34,753,724
8	3,660,900	336,000			3,996,900
9	2,625,200				2,625,200
10	1,175,800				1,175,800
11	1,056,500	24,893,702		12,360,782	38,310,984
12	21,876,125	36,493,010	917,397,562	11,142,800	986,909,497
계	282,343,535	124,471,736	947,681,562	23,847,582	1,378,344,405환

0339

63-6

1958년도 미8군 불하품 수입신고액					
월별	공 병	병 참	병 기	통 신	계
1	36,178,100	10,139,600	1,329,000	3,312,700	50,959,400
2	22,533,300	12,381,447	29,260,600	2,272,000	66,447,247
3	19,077,000	15,210,000	10,766,200	1,450,100	46,503,300
4	22,054,200	3,932,000	3,318,500	3,166,000	32,470,700
5	65,987,000	15,892,500	4,875,000	700,000	87,454,500
6	63,017,000	20,699,800	716,500	5,255,000	89,688,300
7	61,091,520	13,597,500	42,111,960	908,400	117,709,380
8	45,515,000	1,775,050	5,460,000		52,750,060
9	56,222,300		21,750,000	314,900	78,287,200
10	38,894,200	43,162,300	9,776,300	122,000	91,954,800
11	23,277,600	2,179,800	3,385,000		28,842,400
12	44,636,400	1,697,000	36,066,000	7,099,000	89,498,400
계	498,483,620	140,666,997	168,814,960	24,600,100	832,565,677

0340

40-7

0341

협 조 전	응 신 기 일

문서번호 경협 66　　　제목 미8군 분하품 수입 신고액에대한조치

수신: 정무국장　　발신: 통상국장　　년월일 62. 12. 27. 제1의견

1962. 12. 24. 자 귀 협조전 제 3 호에 대하여 당국의 의견을 다음과 같이 회보합니다.

1. 현재 당국에서는 상공부요청에 의하여 1959 년 10 월 1 일자로 체결된 "재한 미국잉여 재산처분에 관한 한.미협정" 을 별첨과같은 방향으로 수정코저 그교섭을 주한 미국대사관에 제의한바 있으나 (1962. 8. 18) 미국대사관에서는 본국정부로부터의 지시 (authorization)가 없다하여 아직 우리측 교섭제의에 응하지 않고 있읍니다.

2. "재한 미국잉여 재산처분에 관한 한.미협정" 의 내용은 미군당국이 소유하는 잉여재산은 한국내에서 매각처분 (disposed by sale) 하는경우를 특히 규정하고 있으며 별첨내용의 수정제의에 대하여도 미국측은 냉담하여 상금교섭에 들어가지 못하고 있으므로, 미8군이 민간인에게 분하하는 군수물자에 대하여 우리가 기증받을 방안을 모색하기 위하여는 "재한 미국잉여재산처분에 관한 한.미 협정" 보다 내용상으로 더 일반적이며 또 이미 교섭단계에 있는 한.미 행정협정에 기증여지를 반영시키도록추진하는것이 좋은것이며 그 1 방안으로는 귀 협조전에서 지적하신 관세문제에 관한 조항을

"Except ______________________________

____

____

shall not be disposed of in the Republic of Korea,

승인양식 1—34　　65-1　　(195mm×265mm 16절지)

1964 년 9 월 30 일, 미주과

협 조 전	응 신 기 일
문서번호	제 목

수 신: 발 신: 년 월 일 제1의견

- 2 -

by way of sale or gift, to persons not entitled to import such goods free of duty." 로 수정하는것도 생각 할수 있읍니다.

3. 귀국의 참고로 "재한 미국 잉여 재산처분에 관한 한.미협정" 의 수정방향을 별첨과 같 이 보내드립니다.

유첨 .. 재한미국 잉여재산 처분에 관한 한.미간의 협정의 수정안과 수정이유. 끝

통 상 국 장 대 심 명 원

196 . . 에 예고문에 의거 일반문서로 재분류됨

보통문서로 재분류 (1966.12.31.)

1964년 9월 30일 직권으로 예고문 ...

승인양식 1 — 34 11—13330—01 45-2 (195mm×265mm 16절지)

0342

별첨.

재한미국 잉여재산 처분에관한 한.미간의 협정의
수정안과 수정이유

원 안	수 정 안

1. 해석 및 양해각서 4 조

4. 대한민국에의 수입을 위한 판매에 제공되는 차량은 어느것이든지 고철로서만 매각되어 야하는것으로 양해한다.	주문전체를 삭제한다.

(이유)

현재 차량의 국내수요를 충족시킬국내 생산이 없으며 많은 종류의 부분품이 수입되고 있는 실정이며 운행차량의 대부분이 군용차량의 개조차인데 외국차량제작공장에서는 이미 그부속품의 생산을 중지하고 있어 유지용 부분품의 공급이 곤난한 실정이므로 대한민국에의 수입을 위한 판매에 제공되는 차량을 고철로서만 아니라 원형형태로도 매각될수 있게 하여 우리가 이용할수 있는 물자를 보다 구매하여 국내수요를 충족시킬수 있도록 하자는것임.

2. 협정본문제 4 조

.... 대한민국정부에 의하여 수입이 금지되거나 아니하거나에 불구하고 어떤품목이든지 대한민국으로부터의 반출을 위하여 제한 없이 매각될수 있다.	.... 대한민국정부에 의하여 수입이 금지되었을때에는 어떤품목이든지 대한민국으로부터의 반출을 위하여 제한없이 매각될수있다 .....

(이유)

국내고철 수요량은 증가하고 있으며 특히 대한중공업 공사의 고철수요는 그 대부분이 미국잉여 물자중의 고철에 의존하고 있는 실정인데 현행 협정은 수입금지품이거나 아니거나에 불구하고 미측은 여하한 제약없이 반출조건으로 잉여물자를 매도할수 있다고 규정하여 국내필요물자의 국외반출을 방지할수 없게되어 있으므로 수입금지품목이외는 전부 국외반출을 못하게하여 우리가 구매이용할수있도록 하자는것임.

0343

45-3

3. 매도되는 잉여물자의 가격조건을 합리적으로 책정하기 위한 한.미 잉여 물자 처리 위원회 (가칭)의 설치에 관하여 신설할것.

(이유)

현행 협정에 의하면 한국정부 또는 그지정기관이 잉여물자를 구매할경우에는 가격과 조건에 관하여 미국측과 합의할수 있는 기간이 60 일로 제한되어 60 일이 지나면 미국정부가 자의로 경쟁입찰에 부칠수 있게되어 있으므로 잉여물자의 매도가격은 대체적으로 고가이며 따라서 국내활용을 저해하는 요소가 되어있음. 즉 정부의 지정기관에 의한 협상구매의 경우 매도가격이 고가이기 때문에 당초정부가 의도하는 지정기관에 의한 구매가 이루어지지 않는예가 많고 일반공매의 경우에는 업자간에 부당한 경쟁을 유발하므로 가격인상을 초래하고 있는 현실임. 이와같은 사태방지를 위하여 한.미간에 조정역활을 담당하는 위원회 (상설)의 구성이 필요한것임. 끝

0344

45-4

협 조 전	응 신 기 일
문서번호 121	제 목 미국 BOA 업무한계 및 미 8군 불하품 수입신고

수 신: 정무국장 발 신: 방교국장 년 월 일 63. 1. 4 제1의견

1. 미국 BOA 의 업무한계에 관하여는 현재 교섭이 진행중인 한미간의 주둔군지위협정 우리측 초안 제 19 조 및 제 20 조 2 항에서 외환관리 및 금융기관의 유지 및 운영에 관한 규정을 두고 있으므로 이 문제에 관한 우리측 초안이 채택되는 경우에는 미국금융기관의 업무한계가 명백히 될것으로 생각됨.

2. 미 8군 불하품 신고에 관하여는 이 문제에 관한 행정협정의 일부로서 1959. 10. 1, 한미간에 체결된 미국잉여재산처분에 관한 협정의 테두리 안에서 이 문제를 해결토록 하여야 할 것임.

끝

방 교 국 장 최 운 상

승인양식 1 — 34 11—13330—01 (195mm×265mm16절지)

0345

외교문서 비밀해제: 주한미군지위협정(SOFA) 4
주한미군지위협정(SOFA) 서명 및 발효 4

초판인쇄 2024년 03월 15일
초판발행 2024년 03월 15일

지은이 한국학술정보(주)
펴낸이 채종준
펴낸곳 한국학술정보(주)
주 소 경기도 파주시 회동길 230(문발동)
전 화 031-908-3181(대표)
팩 스 031-908-3189
홈페이지 http://ebook.kstudy.com
E-mail 출판사업부 publish@kstudy.com
등 록 제일산-115호(2000. 6. 19)

ISBN 979-11-7217-015-8 94340
979-11-7217-011-0 94340 (set)